# Fifty Shades of Crimson

# Fifty Shades of Crimson

## Robert Fripp and King Crimson

PETE TOMSETT

*Guilford, Connecticut*

An imprint of Globe Pequot, the trade division of
The Rowman & Littlefield Publishing Group, Inc.
4501 Forbes Boulevard, Suite 200, Lanham, Maryland 20706
BackbeatBooks.com

Distributed by NATIONAL BOOK NETWORK



Unless otherwise noted, all images are from the author's personal collection.



British Library Cataloguing in Publication Information available

**Library of Congress Cataloging-in-Publication Data**

Names: Tomsett, Pete, author.
Title: Fifty shades of Crimson : Robert Fripp and King Crimson / Pete Tomsett.
Other titles: 50 shades of Crimson
Description: Lanham : Backbeat, 2021. | Includes bibliographical references and index.
Identifiers: LCCN 2021013593 (print) | LCCN 2021013594 (ebook) | ISBN 9781493051021 (paperback) | ISBN 9781493051038 (epub)
Subjects: LCSH: King Crimson (Musical group) | Fripp, Robert, 1946- | Progressive rock music--History and criticism.
Classification: LCC ML421.K52 T66 2021 (print) | LCC ML421.K52 (ebook) | DDC 782.42166092/2--dc23
LC record available at https://lccn.loc.gov/2021013593
LC ebook record available at https://lccn.loc.gov/2021013594

∞™ The paper used in this publication meets the minimum requirements of American National Standard for Information Sciences—Permanence of Paper for Printed Library Materials, ANSI/NISO Z39.48-1992.

# Acknowledgments and Thanks

This Tomsett is indebted to all those who helped in the series of events culminating in this book. My biggest thanks must go to my remarkable mother, Brigitte Tomsett, without whom nothing would have been possible. She just about knows the name Robert Fripp but would still prefer to listen to a bit of Volksmusik! Thanks to my brother, David C. Tomsett, for introducing my young ears to prog and psychedelia, and I am also extremely grateful to Carol Flannery, Barbara Claire, Jessica Kastner, Jessica Thwaite and all at Rowman & Littlefield/Backbeat.

Eternal gratitude to Robert himself, and my great thanks to the following for allowing me to do interviews of all shapes and sizes: Bill Bruford, Peter Giles, Gordon Haskell, Judy Dyble, Gini Wade, Ronan Chris Murphy and Robert S. P. Fripp. (Sadly, Gordon and Judy have since passed away.) Thanks for images, comments, contacts, passing chats, reading suggestions and general encouragement to Adrian Belew, Bill Bruford, Peter Giles, Gini Wade, Bev & May Strike, Bournemouth Library, John Henry, Tomoko Okamoto, Chris Arnold, Alison Beeton-Hilder, Peter Shearer, Chrissy Brand, Alex 'Bomber' Harris, Al Kirtley, Marius, Monika and Danny Olbert and Dave Simmons (Simmons Innovations).

Obviously, no one location was sufficient to contain the writing of this book, which was written in Wealdstone, Bournemouth, Salisbury, Littlehampton, Barcelona, Nice and assorted parts of Austria.

Tinkety-tonk and down with Nazis, viruses and dinosaurs.

# Contents

# Preface

It's no idle exaggeration to say that in 1969 five young Englishmen—Robert Fripp, Ian McDonald, Greg Lake, Michael Giles and Peter Sinfield—calling themselves King Crimson, altered the course of rock music. Their early live shows and their debut album, *In the Court of the Crimson King*, with its unforgettable Schizoid Man cover, shone a bright light on the road ahead for many other young musicians. While The Beatles, Cream, Jimi Hendrix and others had been opening doors to colourful and dramatic new possibilities, King Crimson boldly stepped through those doors, gathered up the various strands of what they found and made perfect sense of it all. In so doing they defined the developing progressive rock scene, mixing rock with folk, jazz and classical, and triggered its exponential rise. But despite achieving far more than they could ever have dreamt of, that line-up soon fell apart, and guitarist Fripp found himself as the only original playing member left, with lyricist, Sinfield, at his side. As a man with immense ambition and sense of purpose though, he was more than comfortable with being at the helm, and set about rebuilding the band, emerging as one of those rare people who have that special, indefinable ingredient in their make-up that makes them an innovator and leader.

With Fripp ultimately as the only constant, the line-up changes continued at an alarming pace, with no less than Elton John and Bryan Ferry being rejected along the way. But amidst the instability and a growing reputation of being difficult to work with, Fripp was not afraid to take each incarnation of the band to somewhere entirely new, putting out a string of acclaimed and influential albums. While the band's sound was frequently reinvented, the constant factor that infused all Crimson's music was the desire to go somewhere new and interesting, somewhere different to where the herd was going. For the first half of the seventies Crimson were regularly in the public eye and the album charts alongside the likes of Pink Floyd, Simon and Garfunkel and The Rolling Stones, and with Fripp also branching out into production and a ground-breaking collaboration with flamboyant sound shaper, Brian Eno, it seemed that there were no limits for the man. However, as one of the rock world's intellectuals, he was developing an intense dislike of the motives and practices of the music business, and of playing any kind of conventional rock star role, preferring to do things his way, whether others liked it or not. Having been so significant in changing a major part of what the mainstream was, from here on he would have a very uncomfortable relationship with it. This worked in its own chaotic way until 1974, when the guitarist shocked the music world by disbanding Crimson. On top of his cynicism about the music industry, Fripp had just come across the philosophical teachings known as The Fourth Way, which dramatically shook up his world view and instilled in him a belief that society was heading rapidly towards collapse. His response was to withdraw from the music business in order to prepare for whatever might emerge from this collapse.

That could quite easily have been the end of the story, although if it had been, Fripp and Crimson had already earned their places in music history. Fortunately, it was far from the end, though from here on Fripp's involvement in music would be much more on his own terms. His first tentative toes back in the water involved performing guitar duties for David Bowie and Peter Gabriel, playing on several successful albums and singles. Having moved to New York and becoming immersed in the vibrant music culture there, he then released a series of innovative solo albums. He still craved something more though, and in the early eighties did the one thing that no one was expecting, and reformed King Crimson. For the post-punk world this was a very different Crimson, fronted by exuberant American Adrian Belew, the first time another guitarist had been allowed in the band. Three more acclaimed albums followed, but again, just as things had seemed stable on the surface, Fripp called another halt to the band.

While the music again took a back seat, Fripp's marriage to pop star, presenter and actress Toyah Willcox gave the media a new angle of interest on him. Not able to completely leave music alone however, he set up his own unique guitar courses, drawing on elements of The Fourth Way, and as he began to miss being in a band, he started taking his students out to play gigs and formed a band with Toyah. Having become something of a crusader for the rights of artists, and feeling that he was owed a large amount of unpaid royalties, the early nineties also found Fripp starting a lengthy legal dispute. Despite the distractions and hitting middle-age, he again did the unexpected, setting up his own ethical record company, reconvening Crimson again and creating a new form of instrumental music. Crimson and many others who had grown out of the prog era had not only survived the attempt of punk to sweep them away and being dismissed as dinosaurs but were being re-habilitated and acknowledged all over again as the geniuses they were. Moving into the early noughties, the pace hardly slackened. However, a deep unhappiness was brewing inside the Fripp mind once more and Crimson fizzled out for a third time. Worse still, by 2011 he felt he had to call time on his professional music career in order to focus on his legal disputes. As predictably unpredictable as ever, in 2013 he pulled one last rabbit out of the hat, announcing a new seven-headed beast Crimson that mixed new members with old. Older fans couldn't believe their luck and a whole new generation had the chance to see what all the fuss was about. As new life was breathed into old material, those unexpected extra years took us to Crimson's fiftieth anniversary and beyond, and towards a far more satisfying conclusion than had seemed likely for a long time.

It's tempting to describe this as something of a schizoid book, as while the histories of Fripp and King Crimson are deeply intertwined, they are far from being one and the same thing. Fripp has always maintained that Crimson has never been 'The Robert Fripp Band', and this is largely true beyond the fact that he has the final say on everything. Similarly, Fripp's career has been so much more than just his work with Crimson. The many hugely talented individuals who have passed through the ranks of the band are also far more than just incidental to the plot, and several from the early line-ups went on to great, if not greater, success in their lives after Crimson. Most high profile of these were: Greg Lake with ELP; Ian McDonald with Foreigner; Bill Bruford with UK and Earthworks; and John Wetton with UK and Asia. Original lyricist, Peter Sinfield, moved on to write for ELP and, rather unexpectedly, for several mainstream artists. Also passing through the revolving door of early Crimson were Mel Collins, later with Camel, Boz Burrell, later of Bad Company, and Gordon Haskell, who struck gold in his solo career with a big Christmas hit in 2001. Ever present from 1981 into the noughties, Adrian Belew could be described as being by far the most significant member of the band for those years, other than Fripp himself.

Some words of warning to the unwary reader. This is, for the most part, not a tale of sex, drugs and rock 'n' roll. While sex does, of course, rear its head along the way, and some Crims did indulge in illegal substances, this is above all a story of boundary-pushing music and of striving for originality. It's rock music, Jim, but not as we know it! The man at the centre of the story has been as contradictory and frustrating as he's been inspiring and inventive. Fripp couldn't seem to live with his own band for too long, yet he couldn't live without it. Countless musicians wanted to work with him, but few could survive doing so for long. He has spent his life forging ahead in his chosen field, yet at heart has remained rather old-fashioned, and while he would for the most part shun publicity, his music and life would frequently attract it.

My introduction to this musical territory came through having an older, long-haired, Afghan Coat–wearing brother. This meant that, despite being preoccupied with Thunderbirds and Subbutteo, I was exposed to the likes of Hendrix, Floyd, Caravan and the Mahavishnu Orchestra at an early age. I was then drawn into the complexities of the Crimson universe as a teenager just beginning to discover the pleasures of the more serious end of rock music. I first knowingly heard Fripp on Bowie's *Heroes*, the second album I ever bought, and shortly after, a friend played me Fripp and Eno's *No Pussyfooting*. That wasn't exactly commercial pop for teenagers, but as we were already developing a taste for the unconventional, this had a strange appeal. Then, one evening in a loft bedroom on the Pinner Road, another friend played me *In the Court of the Crimson King*, and life would never be the same again, as I fell in love with the album's epic qualities, which seemed to me exactly how music should be. I knew nothing of hiatuses or revolving-door line-ups, and I failed to grasp that I wasn't supposed to like prog, new-wave and Steely Dan at the same time. Having been too young to see the early incarnations of Crimson, I was the perfect age to catch the second wave of Fripp and Crimson activity. Within a few years I'd seen a Frippertronics gig, the short-lived The League of Gentlemen and a Fripp band which briefly performed as Discipline, before deciding they were, in fact, the new King Crimson. Becoming a musician of sorts myself, I wanted to be another Fripp, buying a bundle of effects boxes to clumsily and unsuccessfully try to imitate the man. Since those days, when music was a vast, undiscovered country for me to explore, I've been to countless Fripp and Crimson gigs of all shapes and sizes, and quite a few by ex-Crims, and collected a vast array of vinyl, cassettes and CDs, some from unlikely places. Not many eighteen-year-olds return from the Costa Blanca clutching a *Starless & Bible Black* LP, for example. In my thirties I found myself casually picking up Belew's *Young Lions* in an L.A. Airport café, buying *Thrak* at Niagara Falls, and spotting a second-hand cassette of *The Lady or the Tiger?* in a Sydney record shop, while waiting for a bus.

Though I'm not by default a lover of all things prog, all these years later my love for this music hasn't faded. In fact, if anything, it's grown—as has my respect for the abilities of all concerned—partly as a reaction to finding little new that's worthy of occupying my ears, but also because I still get so much out of it. With this book I not only want to fill in the gaps for existing fans who already know parts of this tale, but also to help spread the word much wider. This collection of unbelievably talented people has created a catalogue of music that deserves never to be forgotten. I want to tell people about the extraordinary mind that conceived *Red* and *Fracture*. I want people to discover for themselves the beauty and power of *Starless*; the neglected classic, *Lizard*; the deeply felt emotions expressed through Fripp's soundscapes; and the quirky experimentation of *The Zero of the Signified*. It troubles me that when people hear Bowie's *Heroes*, most don't know that it's Fripp's guitar sound that gives the track its character. I could go on! It's not all Fripp, though. It's important that people understand that the lesser-sung talent of the original Crimson was Ian McDonald, and that Crimson in the eighties and beyond would have been nothing without Adrian Belew. It's important to also say that, despite my passion, I haven't thrown away my critical faculties and haven't shied away from saying so if something really doesn't make the grade. Not to acknowledge this would be foolish and blinkered and would devalue what I have to say about just how good the good is. Of course, this is all subjective and there will be people who vehemently disagree with my opinions, even on *Earthbound*. Being an outsider to the Crimson fold, I also don't gloss over the many, many interpersonal difficulties that have plagued Crimson over the years, and I certainly don't fall for the re-spinning of the past that has been indulged in here and there. As someone who doesn't believe in 'good fairies', I have parted company with my hero in some ways over the decades. While this doesn't affect my opinions of his music, I look for much more down to earth explanations for where the music comes from.

Moore, making a particular impression on him. A small but fateful event then happened in the eleven-year-old's life, when on Christmas Eve he was bought his first guitar by his mother at the end of a day out together in Bournemouth. She'd already bought all his presents but was persuaded to part with an extra six Guineas (six pounds and six shillings) for a special extra one from Minns music shop in Westbourne. It was just an acoustic at this stage, and one that he'd struggle to play as the strings were set too high, but it was a guitar nonetheless. Sixty years on, when Patricia Fripp posted an old photo on social media of her brother with that new guitar on Boxing Day 1957, posing with one leg in the air, it prompted Bob of 2017 to comment that 'this is likely the most physically demonstrative day of my guitarist life!' [2]

In 1958, Bob took up guitar and violin lessons at the School of Music in nearby Corfe Mullen. These lessons eventually led to his first public performance, in April 1959, in a show put on by the school's junior orchestra, the twelve-year-old's contributions being to play second violin with the orchestra, and a solo-guitar piece. A couple of similar local shows followed later that year, confirming that playing second fiddle was never going to be his thing, and that the guitar should be his main focus. As he was clearly showing potential, Bob's teacher at the music school, Kathleen Gartell, recommended that he go for more specialist lessons with Don Strike, a guitar teacher who ran another music shop in Westbourne. After he'd bought a more easily playable acoustic guitar and given the first one away to a cousin, for the next couple of years Bob's parents happily indulged this childish desire, his mother dutifully driving him down to Westbourne, while his father footed the bill. Despite being well into middle-age, in several ways Strike would be quite an influence on Bob, and he considers him to have been his first proper guitar teacher, as it was through these lessons that his confidence in his own ability really began to grow. Strike also helped to further broaden his musical taste, getting him listening to bands from the Trad Jazz revival sweeping the U.K. at the time, and to Belgian jazz guitar legend Django Rhinehart. Another pupil of Strike's, a young Gregory Lake, later described their teacher as 'a very kind man' who took 'extraordinary pride in his students'. When it came to the lessons, though, 'he would stand no messing around'. Strike would set them pieces to learn before each lesson, and as Bob and Gregory became friends, the pair would practice these together at each other's houses. Some of the techniques they were taught, including cross-picking, which derived from Strike having been a professional banjo player in his youth, were to prove useful to Bob, Gregory and others later in their careers. In 1960, Bob graduated to an electric guitar, with a small amp to plug it into, this time purchased from Strike's shop. It was no cheapie on this occasion but a stylish Hofner President with 'f holes' cut into the body. [3]

By the age of fifteen, having battled what he has described as the disadvantages of being left-handed (but learning as a right-hander), tone-deaf and having no sense of rhythm, after some prompting from Strike, Bob set about forming his first band. That band, The Ravens, was formed in the summer of 1961 with drummer Graham Wale and rhythm guitarist/vocalist Tino Licinio. Three years older and with Italian looks that would draw in the ladies, Licinio also came with the bonus of a loft-bedroom at his parents' house where they could practice. They still needed to find someone to play bass, and Bob hit on the idea of persuading his friend and classmate Gordon Haskell to give it a try. Born just a few days before Bob at the same nursing home, Haskell first met him on the Wimborne Grammar sports field, and they would subsequently play rugby and a squash-like game called fives at school. By this point Haskell was round at the Fripps' most days after school, describing himself and Bob as being part of a 'gang of four . . . inseparable from the age of twelve'. He was a reluctant candidate for their band, having only minimal experience on piano and acoustic guitar, however, Bob's persuasion worked, and they took a trip together down to Don Strike's. Being from a poorer background, Haskell had to pick out the cheapest bass he could find, and even then, still had to buy it on hire purchase. Bob then set about teaching him the basics, unwittingly placing his friend at the beginning of a long and winding road to success. [4]

According to Fripp, The Ravens' debut gig came that July in a field next to the youth club in the village of West Moors. Haskell, however, believes that their actual first public performance was even less glamorous, playing outside a block of public toilets on Bournemouth beach. They had permission from the authorities but hadn't thought through the practicalities, and as they played, Wale's drum kit slowly sank into the wet sand. The tone was raised somewhat a few weeks later when they played in the hall adjoining Wimborne Minster, and the following year was spent playing whenever they got the chance—at village halls, night clubs and youth clubs around the eastern side of Dorset, warranting the occasional mention in the local paper, the *Bournemouth Evening Echo*. Their sets consisted of such rock 'n' roll staples as Buddy Holly's *Rave On* and the much-covered *Red Sails in the Sunset*, but as they gained confidence, they would also slip in a Licinio-written instrumental. For Haskell, although 'Lonnie Donnegan was the king', it was British band The Shadows who were the epitome of cool, and as he made progress on his instrument, he modelled his playing on their bassist, Jet Harris. Importantly, while none of them were particularly well off, to Haskell, 'life was fun'. As well as the excitement of being in a band, he recalls, 'We went fishing [and] we had the beaches of Bournemouth, all relatively cost free'. For him, at least, the fun went further, mingling with some of the better-off families in the area, who he found would 'still let you go out with their daughter, who'd love to take you into the woods'. As far as the music was concerned, Fripp was happily playing rock 'n' roll, and even by this stage was 'very good', according to Haskell, but it was classical music that was increasingly working its way into his listening and making a lasting impression. As exams then got in the way, the music had to take a back seat, with Fripp passing seven 'O' Levels. [4]

The cultural shift that had begun in the late fifties in Britain was still going on around Fripp and his friends at an unstoppable pace. This was epitomised musically by the early Beatles singles such as *Love Me Do* and *She Loves You*, and their debut album, *Please, Please*

*Me*, which took British pop music to a whole new level. In 1963 Fripp went on holiday with his sister to Jersey and took his guitar along with him for some intense practising. The bug had now firmly bitten him, and he returned home, desperate to commit himself to music. An unexpected obstacle then materialised however: the fear of disappointing his parents. Although his mother later played down how strongly she'd reacted, according to Fripp she just burst into tears when he boldly announced to her and his father that he wanted to turn professional. After this, he didn't dare bring the subject up again and continued to study for the career they preferred for him. He wasn't about to give up music, though, and shortly after he joined up with local singer and accordionist Douglas Ward. As part of Ward's trio, they would play a Saturday night residency at the upmarket Chewton Glen Hotel, a few miles along the coast from Bournemouth. While this would ultimately be incidental in music terms for Fripp, it was his first paid music work and gave him valuable experience of playing in front of a different kind of audience. Ward also proved to be a valuable contact to have a few years later.

The following spring, the remnants of The Ravens evolved into The League of Gentlemen, named after a 1960 British crime-caper film. The new band still included Fripp, Haskell and Licinio but had a new drummer, Stan Levy, and local Roy Orbison wannabee, Reg Matthews, on vocals. Feeling the need to move up a notch for their rehearsal space, the band converted the garage at the back of the Matthews' family home for the purpose. The local gigs and occasional local press coverage continued as before, press photos showing the five-piece as smart-suited, mostly bespectacled and rather respectable-looking young men. Sets now included covers of Four Seasons songs, as well as Orbison, with Licinio developing his skills at working out vocal harmonies. The frontman was, in fact, taking it more seriously than the others and insisted on them practicing twice a week, 'which was a bore', from Haskell's point of view, as he'd become more interested in playing the youth clubs simply 'because of the girls!' Musically, the band soon became considered amongst the best in the area, and at one point they were introduced to an American producer, Kim Fowley, who had just relocated to England. He tried to get them to learn James Brown's recently released *I Feel Good*, but the style just wasn't right for them, and Fowley soon lost interest. The Ravens also hung out together socially, going to gigs in Bournemouth. One highlight was seeing highly regarded local singer, keyboardist and general showman Zoot Money, who would go on to moderate success and quite a few TV and film appearances. Another year passed in this vein before Fripp decided that he had to give up the band so he could focus heavily on his studies. Haskell was none too concerned, as he still lacked confidence in himself as a musician and had already made his own decision to move on and join the Metropolitan Police. He'd also become distracted by trying to trace and contact his birth father, having only recently discovered his true identity, finding that he was Greek-American, rather than just plain English. He would ultimately look back on his time in teenage bands with Fripp as a good experience, but tellingly noted that his guitarist friend was either unwilling or unable to play like his contemporaries, something which had been a mild point of friction to the others. [4]

As rock music (as opposed to rock 'n' roll) was being born, with guitarists discovering the joys of distortion, and even American folk hero Bob Dylan plugging in, Fripp was often buried in books and essays. Balancing studying economics and political history at Bournemouth College with working for his dad, he would still try to find a little time to persevere with the music side-line. In the autumn of 1965, after an audition and an anxious wait by the phone, he landed himself paid work with the Majestic Dance Orchestra, the grandly named five-piece house band of the Majestic Hotel in the East Cliff area of Bournemouth. His feelings as to where he was aiming to go in the long run were now somewhat confused and contradictory, and things were hanging in the balance between career paths. Playing foxtrots and waltzes three or four nights a week was perhaps not especially fulfilling for him in terms of creativity, but for now the music was for the sake of income (around £10 to £12 a week), this income was to fund his place at college, and going to college was for the sake of becoming an estate agent. At the same time, getting this gig was a step on the path towards professional musicianship, and also showed that Fripp had already reached a level of competency that enabled him to tackle the standards of the era and to hold his own alongside a group of more seasoned musicians. The slot had become available after the previous guitarist had moved on, deciding to try his luck in London after having got into hot water with the band leader for disobeying his orders not to get involved with the young ladies at the dances. That previous guitarist was Andrew Somers, another pupil of Strike's who, after adjusting his name to Andy Summers and a stint in Zoot Money's band, would go on to global fame and fortune with The Police. Work for musicians at The Majestic was surprisingly varied. While they would often play for wedding parties and bar mitzvahs, at other times they could find themselves providing backing for cabaret shows. For Fripp, this included shows by comedians Bob Monkhouse and Norman Vaughan, both of whom would go on to become household names as presenters of the ITV game show *The Golden Shot*. While filling Somers's shoes as a musician, Fripp would be far less likely to fall foul of the rule regarding the ladies. Despite being like most young men who did much of their thinking with their private parts, he had to admit that the girls at The Majestic tended not to have too much interest in him. There was a great interweaving of friends and aspiring musicians in the area, pretty much everyone crossing paths with everyone else, and Fripp and Somers already knew each other through the local music and social scenes. Those scenes would spawn several other major artists, including Al Stewart, later famed for *Year of the Cat* and *On the Border*. Though originally from Glasgow, Stewart also grew up in Wimborne, buying his first guitar from Somers and having guitar lessons from Fripp after meeting him on a local bus. Fripp would later say that Stewart only became successful 'by ignoring everything I tried to teach him'. Another well-regarded local musician,

Al Kirtley, who knew Fripp from local dance venues and meeting him at Strike's shop, had noticed this younger man's developing abilities. 'I remember being very impressed by his guitar figures and solos. We all knew each other in Bournemouth in those days and I remember him as being a nice bloke'. [5] [6]

While much of Dorset may have been something of a rural backwater—Fripp's hometown even losing its much-loved steam train connections in the infamous Beeching cuts—the heady mix of culture and politics unfolding in Britain was spreading far beyond the major cities. The fledgling rock music world was changing fast, with strands of it evolving through 1966 and 1967 into psychedelia, as musicians on both sides of the Atlantic pushed boundaries like never before, drawing on wider influences and experimenting with structures and sounds, not to mention drugs. The year 1967 would be significant for Fripp, too. He had taken his 'A' levels in January and passed them, securing himself a place at university to study estate management, placing him at a fork in the road where he could still have chosen the family-pleasing career over music. However, he could no longer hold back and, despite fears of further parental disapproval, on his twenty-first birthday he made the momentous decision to plunge himself fully into being a professional musician. It was interesting timing, coming just four days after the release of Jimi Hendrix's debut album, *Are You Experienced*, his single *Purple Haze* also having reached No. 3 in the U.K. a few weeks earlier. It also came days before The Beatles' *Sergeant Pepper* came out, lodging itself at No. 1 for months. While Hendrix was creating a whole new vocabulary for rock guitarists, The Beatles' album represented a turning point in terms of how rock albums were constructed and perceived, gaining much wider respect as a format. This was the first so-called concept album and, as rock biographer Mick Wall put it, 'the album that transformed the world from black and white to colour'. Notably, both albums also moved things on in terms of the use of effects and studio manipulation. It wasn't only The Beatles and Hendrix setting the world on psychedelic fire though, with Pink Floyd's debut, *Piper at the Gates of Dawn*, coming that summer, as well as the Velvet Underground's songs of sex and drugs, horrifying self-respecting post-war parents. The world had changed and Fripp wanted to be part of it! [7]

The guitarist's route from his life-changing decision to the creation of one of the most influential bands of the era still had a few good twists and turns to take however, and it didn't start well. He first got together with local singer and bassist Howard Pettridge and a drummer in a semi-pro band called Cremation. After fixing up a couple of local gigs though, he cancelled them, feeling that they just weren't good enough and that he'd have been embarrassed if anyone he knew had seen them play. Then on 28th August 1967 he attended an audition in the function room of the Beacon Royal Hotel that overlooked Bournemouth seafront, with drummer Michael Giles and his bassist brother, Peter. The brothers were looking for a keyboard-playing vocalist but, having drawn a blank, had concluded that they may as well audition the non-singing guitarist who'd got in touch. It was a good move, as they liked his mix of competence, confidence and humour, and asked him to join them. It also helped that Fripp already had a few gigs lined up in London, with Doug Ward, which they could also be part of. A little older than Fripp, the Giles brothers' introduction to music had been through their father, a skilled violinist who used to take them to see the Bournemouth Symphony Orchestra. Michael's first instrument, however, was a humble washboard, which he played in a local skiffle group—a British phenomenon where kids used improvised instruments. He moved on to proper drums a few years later, and soon formed his first rock 'n' roll band, Peter going along to watch their rehearsals. After witnessing their frontman struggling to sing and play bass at the same time, after a few sessions Peter was asked if he wanted to give the bass a go, and, having already begun to dabble on guitar, 'took to it like a duck to water'. They started gigging, and the month's trial he was supposedly on was quietly forgotten. [8]

to do something new with their music and I wanted to deliver it with care and subtlety as well as passion'. Away from the music, though, Lake's unflinching self-confidence meant that, according to Fripp, he viewed the residency as a chance to 'line-up the birds for the coming week'. What Fripp learned from seeing his friend in action with the women there, was that the act of pulling involved being 'pushy and insincere'. Putting this into practice at Change Is, he got to know a local seventeen-year-old model. He returned home with more than just a memory, finding out later that he'd caught an STI. She also told him that he looked better with his clothes off, though he believes this was almost certainly due to his iffy dress sense and not his body! Back in London, Fripp and Lake moved into a one-room flat in London's Leinster Square in Bayswater, putting a cardboard partition down the middle to try to accommodate each other's personal lives. Neither was especially domesticated, and Lake remembers that their kitchen fast degenerated into a particularly disgusting state and was best avoided. Things seemed to be looking up when a waitress Fripp had also met at Change Is, came down to stay with him for a few days. However, taking the precaution of visiting a sexual health clinic with Lake shortly after, Fripp discovered she'd given him a second STI, gonorrhoea. [2] [3] [4]

Word was spreading about the extraordinary music emerging from beneath Calatychos, and as Crimson developed their early repertoire, these rehearsals began to attract attention with other musicians, such as The Moody Blues and their producer, dropping in to watch. To take full advantage of the opportunities beginning to open up to them, the band needed proper management. There were a couple of false starts, with the agencies Marquee Martin and Chrysalis, but the band had the courage of their convictions to ditch them when things didn't feel right. They struck gold, though, when Fripp asked the founders of the brand-new E. G. Management along to a basement session, after which a deal with them was sealed. E. G. took its name from the initials of its founder's surnames, David Enthoven and John Gaydon, who had first met as pupils at Harrow School, the famous

Public (i.e., private) School in North-West London. As a teenager, Gaydon had had a stint as guitarist in A Band of Angels, with Enthoven roadieing for them, but their futures lay elsewhere in the music industry, both moving on to work for the Noel Gay Artists Agency, whose clients had included a quirky band called Giles, Giles and Fripp. Having decided to go into management, to fund their venture take on managing, they re-mortgaged the house that had been bought for them by Enthoven's mother. While that was something of a gamble, in the short term it meant they had plenty of cash to splash on promoting their promising new artists. As confident men in their mid-twenties, E and G both looked and behaved as much like rock stars as the people they were managing, with long hair, leather jackets, riding motorbikes and taking drugs. With perhaps even more self-confidence than their artists, they have been described as possessing a 'raffish charm', which helped to get them through their business dealings. Fripp would later describe E. G. in their early years as an exceptional company that was 'artist led', with a spirit of 'realistic idealism'. Eno biographer David Sheppard (Eno later also managed by E. G.), has called their style, 'astute hippy entrepreneurship'. The relationship between band and management was largely based on trust rather than being defined on paper which—naïve though it seems in retrospect—was something that would initially work for both parties. [5]

King Crimson's first gig billed as King Crimson, and which Fripp considers their first gig, was a small affair on 9 April 1969 at The Speakeasy Club in Central London. Following in the footsteps of Hendrix, Floyd and Deep Purple, the event was, in effect, the launch of the band, and was as much a press reception as a gig. The venue was a popular stepping-stone for new bands, as despite paying peanuts, it was frequented by music journalists, agents, other musicians and even the occasional record company bigwig. Many were there to down as many free drinks as they could rather than paying any attention to the music, but it was still a place where a band might get noticed by someone significant. One young musician present that night, Yes guitarist Pete

Banks, was there for the music, and is said to have been so engrossed by the band that he forgot to drink his pint. Two days later, Crimson's second outing was at The Lyceum in The Strand, supporting Tyrannosaurus Rex, this time in front of a more substantial and more interested audience. In attendance was Yes's young drummer Bill Bruford, who missed his last train and ended up with a long walk home. Beginning to ditch some of their covers as their stock of self-written material grew, what Crimson's early audiences were being so blown away by was music that seamlessly straddled rock, folk, jazz and classical, all tinged with a mix of doom and reflectiveness. Most significantly, it was all being done with a high degree of inventiveness and without slipping into the blues clichés that far too many others relied on. They still had space in their sets for some covers, one being a jazzy arrangement of English folk singer Donovan's *Get Thy Bearings*, which fitted well with their other material, another being an improv based on Holst's orchestral melodrama, *Mars: The Bringer of War*. Crimson's take on the latter was an ambitious blending of classical with rock, something that was becoming a trend, but Crimson doing it in a very different way to other bands. Procul Harem's *A Whiter Shade of Pale*, for example, had successfully squeezed a pastiche of Bach's *Orchestral Suite No. 3* into a rock format, while Cream had pastiched the distinctive *Mars* rhythm for sections of *White Room*. Ravel's *Bolero* had become a popular piece to borrow from too, such as on (Jeff) *Beck's Bolero* and H. P. Lovecraft's *The White Ship*. Crimson's approach to *Mars* was to start much closer to the original but then divert into an improv that could go almost anywhere, only held together by the rhythm. On one level it was a sophisticated thing to try, but at the same time was quite raw and naïve. Whether their audiences found it stirring or challenging, it was the kind of experimentation that rock fans were prepared to give a chance to, understanding that bands like this saw themselves as serious artists in the vein of the classical composers. The *Mars* improv was also a manifestation of Crimson's growing onstage confidence, being comfortable taking diversions away from the written parts of tracks, exciting and dangerous diversions Giles describes as playing 'without a safety net'. [5] [2]

Courtesy of E. G.'s efforts and the buzz the band was generating, after just six gigs Crimson were invited to record a session for the BBC Radio One show, *Top Gear* (no connection with the later motoring show), which showcased 'underground' bands, and was presented by a youthful John Peel. At that time, except for pirate radio, the BBC was all there was in Britain, so this was a useful stepping-stone. The session was recorded and broadcast in early May 1969 and featured early versions of self-penned tracks *21st Century Schizoid Man* and *The Court of the Crimson King*. It was the first taste the wider British public had of the band, and with a listenership that was hungry for the latest new music, the show was the ideal platform to grow their reputation. Soon after, they landed a three-month Sunday-night residency at the Marquee Club in Soho, in the heart of London. It was a venue where the music was extremely loud; it was often too hot and had small dressing rooms that stank of booze and cigarettes. At the same time, it was considered cool and prestigious, and a residency there was a sign that a band was potentially heading for the big time. Amongst the many who saw Crimson there was a now-world-renowned Jimi Hendrix, who has been quoted as saying, 'This is the best band in the world!' The Voodoo Chile was taking an enforced break from gigging himself, as he was nursing an arm injury.

During their first few gigs, Fripp had played standing up, as is the convention for rock guitarists. He'd felt very uncomfortable, though, and ended up protesting to the others that 'this is hopeless, I just can't play this way'. As he'd been taught to play sitting down, playing seated onstage seemed more natural, so he gave it a try, and despite disparaging comments from the others, has continued that way ever since. With him not being inclined to perform the exaggerated antics that other guitarists indulge in, this would become one of his trademark quirks. Another change came when Sinfield decided he wasn't so keen on the roadieing side of things, and instead began to develop his role as lighting man. Innovative as it was for the time, Fripp has described what he came up with as being made of 'plywood and bacofoil, with coloured light bulbs and a strobe light'. [6] [2]

By May, Fripp and Lake's personal lives were still suffering the consequences from the Newcastle trip. Fripp's seventeen-year-old model acquaintance came down to stay, but only with the ulterior motive of tracking down another musician she'd met before Fripp. Discovering that this other man was married, she cut one of her wrists in Fripp and Lake's bathroom, but survived, and went on to meet her man. The experiences didn't deter Fripp from his attempts with the ladies, though, and as the band's success grew, he found he was pretty much expected to 'carelessly and frequently rut'. To try to live up to this, he developed the strategy of 'taking on a persona', finding that 'Robert Fripp of King Crimson could proposition with a confidence that Bob Fripp, young thinker of Wimborne, couldn't'. Getting their minds back on the music, Crimson played a second gig at The Speakeasy. A young David Bowie, just weeks before *Space Oddity* propelled him to stardom, was amongst those invited that night (by his agent, not the band), on his first night out with future wife, Angie Barnett. He has been quoted as saying, 'We were sitting in the corner feeling pretty bored and I turned to Angie and said, "Can you jive?"' She said yes, so they got up and had a dance. Sadly, history doesn't record whether this was during Crimson's set, an impromptu jam with Donovan afterwards or to records being played by a DJ in-between. Angie's interviews over the years have since revealed that they went on to spend their first night together after the gig. [4] [7]

Things were already moving pretty fast for Crimson, but the pace was about to increase, as amongst those whose attention had been drawn to their stunning new sound were several record companies. At first, E. G. negotiated with Threshold, a new company set up by The Moody Blues and their producer, Tony Clarke, with a distribution deal with Decca behind them. As a consequence, in June, Crimson went into Morgan Studios in North-West London—also being used then by

Free and Led Zeppelin—to begin to record their first album. Clarke was the natural choice as producer for the project, and for four days they worked together, committing several tracks to tape. Gig commitments meant that the sessions had to come to a temporary halt, however, the band were already concerned that things were not going the way they'd envisaged. Clarke's experience suggested he should have had the right sort of approach to work with Crimson. However, they felt that there was a sizeable gap between what they wanted and what Giles felt was Clarke's attempt to transform them into 'another Moody Blues . . . with lots of strumming guitars'. [8]

Despite this uncertainty, Crimson were about to get an extraordinary break. with E. G. managing to get them on the bill as one of several support bands for a massive Rolling Stones free concert in London's Hyde Park on 5 July. The event had been planned for some time but was given extra poignancy by the death of Stones' founder member, Brian Jones. Having been sacked from the band a month earlier, he'd been found dead in his swimming pool two days before the gig, shocking the music world. Crimson were first onstage, on a very crowded bill that also included Family and Alexis Korner's New Church, and had to trim their set to just forty minutes, ending with their managers turning on some air raid sirens to add to the drama at the end of *Mars*! While they had three months of gigging under their belts, this was a step onto a truly big stage, with estimates of the crowd for that heady summer's day of five hundred thousand or more, the largest audience Crimson would ever play to! Suddenly finding themselves playing outdoors in front of a sea of faces stretching off into the distance, Crimson handled the event with remarkable self-belief and maturity. Being essentially a vast hippy-fest, and taking place during a heat wave, this was one of those occasions when going onstage early was a good thing, with the crowd growing through the day, and many inevitably getting the worse for wear as the day progressed. In a literal sense it was a big stage, too, and being physically further apart than they were used to, they had to rely much more on signals and intuition for particular points in the tracks, the only minor hitch coming when a large poster of Brian Jones fell on Lake while he was performing. Understandably, given the circumstances, The Stones' performance that day was relatively poor; however, over the years the concert has attained near-mythical status. Most mentions of it naturally focus on Jagger and co, but the day gave incredible exposure to Crimson to a highly receptive audience, and the gig effectively broke them in the U.K. Fripp and McDonald's diaries recorded that day in interestingly contrasting ways. While Fripp gushed about it being a 'mammoth success of importance which will take time to appreciate', McDonald casually noted that he went there by bus, that there were half a million people, that Crimson were good and The Stones were not. [9]

Most people seeing Crimson at this point knew nothing of the trials and tribulations of GGF that had gone before. To them, this band seemed to have appeared ready-made, overnight. McDonald and Sinfield's arrival had already taken them a long way from their hapless meanderings to transforming them into a serious outfit, but it was Lake's arrival that had been the final piece of the jigsaw. This was not just due to his input and the rock sensibilities he brought with him, but also for the effect his presence had on the ideas put forward by the others. Lake's stately voice, with a hint of Justin Hayward, was proving to be the ideal means of turning Sinfield's poetic lines into powerful song lyrics. Such was his confidence, in fact, the clarity and tone that you might think that the boy from the Poole prefab was actually from a far more well-to-do background than he was. The knock-on effect was to further inspire the others, who could now see what could result from the ideas they put forward. Giles had also finally been given a platform on which he could explore his true potential. It's the transformation of Fripp, however, that seems the most marked, although he still had a way to go. Already talented on his instrument and massively motivated, it took working alongside McDonald and Lake to begin to reshape him. He was no longer the grinning man on the *Cheerful Insanity* cover, with bags of ability but no discernible style or direction. Instead, he was fast turning into the serious rock guitarist he wanted to be. He was being transformed in his appearance too, now with more fashionable clothes and longer, frizzier hair.

After coming back down to earth with a more routine gig at the Marquee the night after Hyde Park, just two days later Crimson were back recording with Tony Clarke, giving the relationship another chance to work. This time they were in Wessex Studio, a converted church hall in Highbury, North London. However, the change of location didn't remove the gulf between band and producer, and the band still felt that Clarke just didn't grasp what they wanted to do. As a result, the five made the staggeringly bold decision to stand by their principles and call a halt to working with Clarke on 16 July. Those principles could have proved costly, as this also put an end to the deal with Threshold. This upstart band was rejecting a deal with a major record company! In an equally bold move, Crimson took the decision to simply carry on, recording at Wessex without an external producer. Their management was fully behind them; Enthoven even agreed to personally cover the costs while looking for a new deal. To get that deal, E. G. were rapidly on the case, approaching Island Records, a company set up in Jamaica by Brit Chris Blackwell. Blackwell had, at first, concentrated on ska, but in the late sixties, on moving back to the U.K. he wanted a slice of the new rock scenes. E. G. had, in fact, been tentatively negotiating with them earlier; however, Island's A&R people had been unconvinced by Crimson. But that was *before* Hyde Park, and—witnessing the reaction they got from the crowd there had changed their minds. Within days, Island snapped them up, although the signing process had to be handled by A&R man Guy Stevens, as Blackwell himself is said to have never actually liked Crimson's music! Enthoven and Gaydon knew what a coup they'd pulled off and marked the completion of the deal by going out to buy expensive, new, matching motorbikes. A distribution deal with Atlantic Records would also follow later in the year, to cover the North American market.

Less than two weeks after the collapse of the Threshold sessions, Crimson were in Wessex Studios, the sessions now paid for by Island, and with Island's approval, taking on the production role themselves. Although Fripp, Giles and Lake already had studio experience, and McDonald had a good understanding of arrangements (not to mention all-round technical musical knowledge), it was still something of a leap of faith on the record company's part to permit this, none of them having any production experience. The passing years have spawned differing claims as to who took overall charge out of Lake, Giles and McDonald, though logic would suggest that it was a mixture of the skills of all three, with Fripp and Sinfield not shying away from putting their oars in. While the mood wasn't all sweetness and light, the personal chemistry, mixed with tolerable amounts of creative tension, meant that they drew out the best in each other. This was not just in performing what they had already written, but with other ideas materialising as they went along. Remarkably, between blocks of studio sessions, they were still gigging across southern England and at the Marquee, their crammed transit van by this point having to be supplemented by a VW Beetle borrowed from E. G. While there would be no Woodstock appearance for Crimson, that August they slotted in a dash down to the Jazz and Blues Festival at Plumpton Race Course, near Brighton. The bill included luminaries like Pink Floyd, The Nice and The Who on the main stage. however, Crimson found themselves relegated to a minor stage following an obscure band that rejoiced in the name Fat Mattress. Fripp suspects that this treatment was due to the involvement of one of the management companies they'd rejected, who were taking their chance to get a bit of revenge. As a variation that day, they gave the Crimson improv treatment to Eric Coates's 1930s British light-music classic, *By the Sleepy Lagoon* (a.k.a., the *Desert Island Discs* theme), taking it to extremes of noise and near silence, before shifting into their more regular *Mars* improv. In addition to the ongoing gigging, it was remarkable that Fripp was effectively homeless during the album's recording. Lake had moved his new Danish girlfriend into their flat, which made Fripp feel he had to leave. That didn't stop Yes bassist Chris Squire from subsequently moving in to take his place. 'At the end of a long day's recording I would set out to find a bed wherever I could', Fripp would later recall. It was an alarmingly uncertain way to carry on, but some days he fell on his feet, such as when he ended up at an expensive Chelsea apartment with a wealthy lady friend of Lake's. By mid-August, though, Crimson had completed the recording process all over again, and most importantly, were all extremely happy with the results. [4]

The band had been lined up for the Isle of Wight Festival, but decided instead to take up the chance to record a second BBC session. The broadcast of that session in early September and ongoing gigging helped to keep building their profile in the intervening weeks until their debut album, *In the Court of the Crimson King*, was released on 10 October 1969. Arguably one of the most accomplished debut albums ever released, it was the culmination of the extraordinary year these soon-to-be-famous five were having. Pretentiously subtitled *An Observation by King Crimson*, at Fripp's suggestion, it consists of five songs that deservedly catapulted the band to international fame. Their months of intense effort paid off as the public went out and bought it in huge numbers, helping it to race rapidly up the U.K. chart to rub shoulders with the likes of The Beatles *Abbey Road* and *Led Zeppelin II*, peaking at number five. Notions of what to expect from rock bands had already been well and truly shaken up, but Crimson were still breaking new ground, and while *Court* received a good reception in many quarters, it wasn't universally loved. As Fripp later put it, the album 'drew as much hostility as acclamation', its intensity and visions of doom being just too much for some. Some very useful high-profile praise came, however, from Who guitarist, Pete Townsend, who called the album 'an uncanny masterpiece'. Whether by luck or judgment, the five had achieved some remarkable balances. *Court* managed to be of its time while adventurously forging ahead, sounding as if it was painstakingly pieced together but not laboured, exuding maturity and clarity of vision that was truly remarkable for a bunch of twenty-somethings making their first album together. It was commercial, in terms to be listenable to a broad rock audience but was utterly uncompromising. As the material that fans had heard evolving through that year had shown, the innocence and humour of GGF had been quietly consigned to history. Here instead was drama and beauty blended in a way no one had before. Although the band would not have been thinking in such terms, the tracks worked as lasting pieces of music, being strong musically and with lyrics that were not locked into a particular time period. While the Vietnam War lies behind a lot of Sinfield's words (a conflict that had already lasted five years, the Soviet-backed north fighting the U.S.–backed south), it's never mentioned by name, so the songs haven't dated with the passing decades. As well as the international issues of that period reflected in the material, the album came out at an interesting time politically and culturally in Britain. Labour's pipe-smoking Harold Wilson was in 10 Downing Street, flamboyant talents like George Best and Peter Osgood graced the nation's football pitches, the iconic Michael Caine film *The Italian Job* had come out a few weeks earlier, and a radical new comedy show, *Monty Python's Flying Circus*, had just hit the nation's TV screens. [2] [6]

It's hard to imagine a better way for any rock band to open its debut album than with *21st Century Schizoid Man*, a startlingly original seven-and-a-half-minute adventure, loosely describable as heavy but with a hefty dose of jazz blended in. Briefly throwing listeners off the scent, it starts with thirty seconds of organ pipe noises that McDonald intended to sound sinister but ended up just sounding a bit strange, the track proper then opening with a guitar/sax riff that musicians worldwide would have given their right arms to have created. With the likes of Hendrix, Clapton and Page being widely worshipped as guitar-wielding gods, this was a smart move, instantly getting the rock audience on their side. What really sets the track apart, though, are Lake's vocals, which unlike his live performances, were distorted to chilling effect, as he delivered Sinfield's blend of social comment and bizarre imagery. The first verse sets the tone, warning of sinister genetic experiments to come in the wrong hands, and you don't have to dig too deep to find Vietnam, with a reference to napalm, the liquid used in flame throwers, that was one of the new horrors unleashed in the conflict. Although that year had seen major protests in the U.S. and Europe against the war, there is nothing overtly political here, and this is nothing as obvious as a protest song, being more a grim extrapolation of the future. When introducing the song on tour in the U.S. later in the year, Fripp would dedicate it to U.S. Vice-President Spiro Agnew, a proponent of the war. Fripp tended to shoot from the hip with his stage pronouncements, and humorous jibes could and did sneak out. Sinfield's *Schizoid Man* was, in fact, a premonition of society's tortured state of mind in years to come, rather than a specific person, and the title was simply a great line that encapsulated his more generalised fears for humankind. After two verses, the rock gives way to something jazzier, as they embark on a lengthy guitar-and-sax-lead-instrumental section, named *Mirrors*. Within this is a stop-start section played by all four musicians in unison that involves such complexity of timings at such a high speed that you cannot help but be stunned by the imagination and ability on display. Having evolved out of all recognition from a McDonald and Sinfield idea from their Infinity days, the writing of the track is credited to all five personnel. More specifically, while the words came from Sinfield, the riff was Lake's baby, tweaked by McDonald, while the middle sections were based around ideas from Fripp and Giles. It's all too easy to neglect a drummer's contributions, but Giles's imaginative and skilful performance on the album is as significant as the others. In particular, on *Schizoid Man*, he was pivotal in making the arrangement work, with the numerous switches of time signature. In fact, with the release of the album, he was catapulted from being unknown to being considered amongst the world's best.

After this opening aural assault, in stark contrast *I Talk to the Wind* peers reflectively into the middle distance. As survivor from the GGF and friends period, This sits somewhere between the innocence of GGF and the melodramas now materialising. According to McDonald, this was musically inspired by The Moody Blues, but since the early versions, the band had stripped back the layers of instruments and refined its textures to draw out the track's gentle beauty. This allowed more emphasis on the vocals, Lake singing two lines of harmonies, something that would be a rarity on Crimson songs; it also gave McDonald space to show his versatility on the flute. While the tone is very different from *Schizoid Man*, Sinfield is still expressing despair at the world around him, its sentiment being that the calm, sane, rational man in the midst of the chaos finds that no one is listening to a word he says. By coincidence, a song called *I Talk to the Trees*, sung by Clint Eastwood, featured in that year's film version of *Paint Your Wagon*. That actually dates back to the stage musical version from 1951, however, being a love song in a western, there's only a passing similarity in the lyrics and sentiment to Sinfield's song. As McDonald's flute solo fades away, a kettle drum roll from Giles announces the monumental *Epitaph*. Perhaps the epitome of early Crimson, the song is certainly the epitome of doom and gloom (although Zager and Evans's *In the Year 2525* would give it a run for its money) and the cause of the term 'doom-rock' being bandied about for a time. The words and elements of the music seem to be transporting us back into medieval or ancient times, but this is a thin veil for commenting on contemporary life. As both a personal epitaph for the narrator and a continuing gloomy perspective on the human race, it's clear that all hope is lost. Its intro features an understated, brooding guitar line from Fripp; however, this is a mellotron-driven drama, and the instrument's first appearance on the album. All hanging on a simple set of chords, with a minor-to-major switch thrown in, the complexity and intensity comes from the layering of instruments, mostly courtesy of McDonald. While there is again a hint of The Moody Blues, the track is imbued with such originality that whatever its initial inspiration, Crimson made it very much their own. For example, where you'd expect to find the second chorus, they divert to a middle section, titled *March for No Reason*, with the feel of a medieval funeral procession. This, in turn, serves to emphasise the power and passion of the final verse and fadeout, the track reaching a near-orchestral feel, as wave after wave of sorrowful melody washes over us, and kettle drums thunder away menacingly in the background. The fadeout itself was given the sub-section name, *Tomorrow and Tomorrow*, taken from Shakespeare's early-seventeenth-century play, *Macbeth*, from a speech about the relentless and ultimately meaningless passing of days that only leads to death.

The opening of side two shifts back down the gears, with the gentle dreamscape of *Moonchild*. Unlike the rest of the album, this materialised during the studio sessions, being developed to its finished form of more than twelve minutes after *Drop In* and *Get Thy Bearings* were rejected and space needed to be constructively filled. It also has the album's only positive, or at least non-negative, lyrics. In the third of 1969's Apollo missions, Neil Armstrong and the crew of Apollo 11 were the first to land and walk on the moon, an event which gripped the world, and which happened while Crimson were in the studio. Bowie's *Space Oddity* single also came out during that time, getting a lot of air-play and being used during the BBC's coverage of Apollo 11's return. All in all, the moon as a subject was unavoidable. Sinfield touched on it in his own oblique way, dipping into astrology rather than science, the name *Moonchild* being associated with the star-sign Cancer. This is the closest the album gets to hippiedom, although we need to hear this in context to the gloom being expressed all around it. The lunar module carried the modern hopes and dreams of the human race, and symbolised technological progress. In contrast, Sinfield's *Moonchild* encapsulates the innocent, naïve hopes of the so-called flower children of the era. While Armstrong was making his 'giant leap for mankind' statement, *Moonchild* was wandering in a timeless, mystical garden, her existence being in a dreamlike bubble of nature, beauty, love and gentleness, removed from the world's harsh realities. Over an arpeggio chord sequence, loosely resembling *Lucy in the Sky with Diamonds* switched to 4/4 time, Fripp conjures up a magical mandolin-like guitar, blending with soft touches of McDonald's mellotron and Giles's imaginative, restrained percussion. While the main body of the song is barely two-and-a-half-minutes long, instead of ending, a mist of sound hangs in the air, evolving into a lengthy vibe, guitar and percussion improvisation by McDonald, Fripp and Giles, with Lake watching from behind the recording desk. Given two sub-section titles—*The Dream* and *The Illusion*—this is a mix of what we'd now term ambient and avant-garde jazz and, as you might expect, it's impossible to tell where one ends and the other begins. Winning the prize for the strangest use of a King Crimson song in a movie, the song part of *Moonchild* appeared in the 1998 comedy *Buffalo 66,* with eighteen-year-old Christina Ricci dancing in a dark, deserted bowling alley. [10]

The album closes with a second epic mellotron drama, *The Court of the Crimson King*, the song whose lyrics spawned the band name. Penned by McDonald and Sinfield, its origins date back to a set of lyrics Sinfield had written prior to his meeting McDonald. McDonald told Sinfield that he loved the words but that his music was terrible, and instead came up with his own, giving birth to a historic piece! Its distinctive structure would be mimicked by others for many years to come, as for nine minutes we are escorted through majestically delivered verses and instrumental breaks, each flowing back into the original melody, an imperious combination of mellotron and voices. Sinfield provides a bottomless pit of metaphors and interpretations to dive into, although you can safely just let the medieval fantasy imagery wash over you. Of the easier aspects to interpret, as the Crimson King was Sinfield's term for the devil, the inference is that *The Court* is his realm, hell, or—given the wider context—that they, or we, are living in some kind of hell on earth. Also, amidst the stream of lavish scenes filled with assorted characters and largely obscure analogies is a thinly veiled reference to China's behind-the-scenes manipulation in relation to Vietnam. For the rest, though, the truth is that, like many lyricists, Sinfield simply loved playing with images and ambiguity. Individual lines may have meant something when first written down, but finished sets of lyrics, especially after the vocalist has got hold of them, are often just collections of lines that sound good together and seem to mean something, whether they do or not. The track exudes a tone of great portent, except when McDonald slips in a bit of light-heartedness at the end as a playful bit of organ appears—subtitled *Dance of the Puppets*—cueing in a full-blown reprise of the main melody. The organ bridge passage has itself been lovingly parodied over the years, the most prominent being by Genesis in 1980, as the link between *Duke's Travels* and *Duke's End*. None of the tracks on *Court* were particularly appropriate to be released as singles, but this didn't stop Island from trying, unceremoniously splitting the title track across the A and B sides. It would go on to creep into the lower reaches of the American chart, the only time a Crimson single would ever do so. Luckily, another major shift in the rock world was going on in the wake of *Sergeant Pepper*. It was now acceptable for the more serious bands to simply be 'album bands'. No longer were they obliged to try to conjure up three-minute pop ditties for the singles charts; they could focus instead on longer epics and concepts.

Completing the package, the album's cover is nothing short of an artistic masterpiece. It's designer, Barry Godber, wasn't a professional artist but a computer programmer friend of Sinfield's who had been to see some of Crimson's rehearsals and had contributed some arty pieces of stage decoration for them to use. The front is filled with a painting of a grotesque face—the schizoid man—crying out in fear, as a modern day take on Munch's *The Scream*. The calmer inside cover of the original gatefold design, features a moon-faced being—the Crimson King himself—amidst red, floating spots. It effortlessly achieved everything you would want from a cover, in that it is eye-catching, unforgettable and perfectly suits the material. Decades later, it would still appear in lists of favourite album covers, and without doubt was part of the reason for the album's success. The tragedy was that this would be Godber's only cover, as he died from a heart-attack just four months after the album's release. On the cover and on the record's labels, the sub-section names given to the instrumental passages in the longer tracks were slipped into the listings. While they added extra angles to the imagery, they were actually there to increase the apparent number of tracks to twelve, then considered a standard number for an album. This was so that they would be paid royalties for twelve tracks instead of five, as at the time the payments system didn't take into account the length of a track. Three of the five tracks are credited as being written by all five band members, it being considered churlish to separate credits when a track was the result of a combination of ideas. However, the core writing team was undeniably McDonald and Sinfield, who are specifically credited for the other two tracks. Adding to the ambiguity as to whether or not Sinfield was actually part of the band, he is credited, as if a band member, not with any instrument, but with words and illumination. In subsequent years, glossing over the issue but not wanting his friend's role to be diminished, McDonald described Sinfield as being the band's 'all round cheerleader and visionary'. [2]

In addition to the strength of the material, changing approaches to studio recording, were also a significant factor in creating the album's sound. Multi-track recording was still in its infancy, but the Wessex Studio gave Crimson the luxury of eight tracks to play with, something that had only recently become available in the U.K. Even so, the layers of mellotrons, woodwind and backing vocals they wanted to use, meant that much bouncing down of tracks had to be done to cram it all into the space available. Not everything ran 100 percent smoothly, however. In the months between the mastering and the album's release, it was found that there had been a technical glitch in the process. This had caused some loss of treble and some unwanted distortion in places. However, other than those on the inside, nobody noticed, and this certainly didn't hinder the album's success. With the original multi-track tapes then going missing for years, tapes from further along in the process had to be used to make later editions, involving a minor loss of quality. Fortunately, the original tapes were located in 2003 and these were used to produce the faultless, digitally remastered, fortieth anniversary edition.

It's often not clear whether something is genuinely significant in its own time or a five-minute wonder. You can only really begin to judge perhaps a decade or more later. But to many people *Court* felt like a giant leap for musician kind, and time did indeed decree it to be a monument in music history. You can loosely trace paths to how it came into being—after all, nothing happens in a vacuum—and, consciously or not, everybody brings influences with them into a band. But *Court* was so significant because it moved things on. You can still taste psychedelia in the mixture, but Crimson ignored the templates of how to do rock music, in particular steering clear of the growing clichés of rock and blues, and the standard themes of rock lyrics, and for the most part also steered clear of the more hippie-trippy path others were taking. This caused them to push in more imaginative directions and, in doing so, their debut became the template itself for a large swathe of rock for the coming years. In a 1997 interview, Michael Giles summed up their approach back in 1969, by saying, 'We didn't want to be like any of the other bands. We wanted to find out what we were like. What we could create'. The more colourful end of late-sixties and early-seventies rock music is closely associated with drug culture, especially cannabis and LSD. Because of this there is often a nudge, nudge, wink, wink–type assumption that such imaginative music as Crimson's, which arrived on the coattails of psychedelia, must have been drug induced. There was, and perhaps still is, an assumption that rock bands just do that sort of thing as a matter of course. However, while most of the band were smokers, over the years band members have made a point of saying that their writing—at this point, at least—was in no way assisted by illegal drug use. In fact, it has been suggested that the original Crimson's rapid success was helped by their absence of drug use, as they could stay focussed while many around them were off with the fairies. But while the band remained relatively clear-headed, it's a safe bet that this principle wasn't being observed by the Afghan coat and flared jeans brigade in their audiences, and certainly wasn't by their management. [11]

In the coming years, the term progressive, or prog, rock would increasingly be used for Crimson and other bands in similar territory. Its origins lie somewhere between Caravan using it on their 1968 debut album's cover, and rock critic Lester Bangs using it to describe a broad range of emerging styles in the late sixties. It could be loosely characterised as mixing rock with classical, jazz, folk and other influences, with epic or fantasy themes, often with long, multi-sectioned tracks. In *Progressive Rock Reconsidered*, Kevin Holm-Hudson summarised it as 'self-consciously complex rock', while music journalist Paul Morley observed that it 'tended to downplay the explicit blues style', though 'the blues is not ignored altogether'. To him, 'the music drifted further away from even the vaguest abstract of what rock and roll is all about', which comes across as a criticism, but was, in fact, what many loved about the genre. In the end, genre labels serve little purpose other than being a convenient shorthand or, from a more cynical viewpoint, to try to define a passing bandwagon to which artists can try to attach themselves. The members of early Crimson have never cared much for the label, and it has irked Fripp ever since that Crimson were casually lumped in with the more indulgent prog bands that followed, even though they were not guilty of the excesses for which prog would become known. However, as the term came into common use, and early Crimson became the touchstone for a lot of music that followed, good or bad, the label is unavoidable. Rather than questioning Crimson's role in it, Bill Bruford, who in 1969 was merely a wannabee Crim, has offered his own explanation of the social/cultural factors that caused prog rock to come into being. Quite simply, he characterised it as music made by 'nice middle-class boys like me' from South-East England, many of whom were involved with the Church in their formative years. His view from the inside was that prog was essentially the expression of a 'bohemian middle-class intelligencia'. Of course, some didn't fit the description, but overall Bruford has a point! It's interesting that McDonald, a key figure in stimulating the rise of prog, has said that although he came to accept the album as being part of that genre, he never specifically felt himself to be part of the prog scene as such. He was simply 'introducing different influences into basic rock music', citing the example of *I Talk to the Wind*, describing it as 'a very simple, folky song' that 'just happened to be done in a context that one might call progressive'. Objective discussions of prog were severely hindered for twenty years or so after punk appeared in 1976, with bands like Crimson finding themselves dismissed as dinosaurs and the 'prog' label used as a term of abuse. Thankfully, perspectives have changed somewhat in more recent years! [12] [13] [14]

While it's simplest to just accept King Crimson as prog rock, what is more open to debate is whether *Court* itself was the beginning of the genre. Several of the bands that we'd immediately associate with it, such as Genesis, Yes, Camel and Pink Floyd, only made what you could call prog albums after *Court*. Of the stronger candidates from before, The Beatles' *Sergeant Pepper* is often the big one thrown into the discussion. But while the Fab Four's shift from pop to the weirder stuff opened the door to new influences and methods, it could perhaps be regarded more as psychedelic-tinged pop. Moving closer to prog, Cream's *Wheels of Fire* from 1968 is a psychedelic blues record, with many progish elements. In similar territory, Hendrix's *Electric Ladyland*, also from 1968, can lay claim to being the inspiration for many things. One of its longer tracks, *1983*, certainly fits the prog definition, including its doom-laden lyrics about leaving the planet's war-torn surface to live under the sea. Often neglected in these discussions is Soft Machine's *Volume Two*, released three weeks before *Court*. Never a big seller, it has been quietly influential in several spheres, its approach being more from a jazz starting point. Its only un-prog aspect is that any hint of pomposity is deliberately undermined by Robert Wyatt's humorous anti-lyrics. The strongest candidates are perhaps The Moody Blues, who, from 1967, began to develop their folk/rock sound into something much grander, with *Days of Future Past* and *In Search of the Lost Chord*. Wherever we each choose to draw our line, all things considered, *Court* wasn't strictly the first, but one of a number of albums moving in a similar direction that came out in that period. What is much safer to say is that *Court*, more than any other album, crystallised the ideas that were being expressed by the bands who crossed paths at places like The Marquee and The Speakeasy. And because it became so high profile, it was one of the main triggers for the genre taking off. Of course, those rare, highly influential bands like Crimson that seem to appear out of nowhere, just do what they do and have no interest in being pigeon-holed. They are leaders and pioneers, and if others choose to follow, that's up to them.

In the heady whirl that took the band over in the days just after *Court*'s release, they still had a handful of gigs to complete around London. What lodged most vividly in McDonald's memory though, in this new world of acclaim and recognition, was how his girlfriend, Charlotte, had to desperately search for Lake one night when the band were about to go onstage. She eventually found him 'bonking in the changing room', calling him 'a great big ego—a penis on legs'. Courtesy of their distribution deal with Atlantic and signing up with North American management agency, Premier Talent, the tail end of this year of unimaginable progress found the band on a twenty-one-gig tour of America, playing as an opening act for the likes of Joe Cocker and The Band. It was the first time they had set foot in the country, as well as the first time the band had gigged anywhere outside of England. Flying into New York, they transferred to what Lake described as 'an old two-propeller plane of the type that Buddy Holly and Otis Redding had crashed in'. They survived, though, and performed a low-key warm-up gig to stoned students who, thanks to a misprint, were expecting a soul band, in a college cafeteria in Rainfield, Vermont. The tour then got going in earnest, taking them round the cities of Boston, Chicago, Detroit, New York, Los Angeles and San Francisco, as well as a festival in Palm Beach, Florida. It all nearly came to a premature halt early on in Chicago. With *Court* about to be released in the U.S., the band's visit to the city had started in a relaxed and productive way. McDonald had been out sightseeing and had picked up a new guitar for $40, while Fripp—as de facto band leader—had been on the phone to the U.K. music press about the tour, and was very upbeat, telling them that they had been writing new material in their hotel rooms and that a second album would be recorded in February. However, the roadies then wedged their hired van under a low roof outside their hotel, causing lots of damage, and after the first of Crimson's two scheduled nights at the Kinetic Playground, gangsters set fire to the venue as punishment for missed 'insurance' payments. One of the other bands on the bill, Iron Butterfly, lost much of their equipment; however, Crimson got away relatively lightly, only losing a mellotron, which had taken a bad soaking as the fire brigade put out the blaze. The following night's show, where Crimson had been due to support The Who, had to be cancelled, the damage to the venue being so bad that it would take three years for them to reopen. While the band and their roadies were kept busy drying out their equipment with hair dryers for a couple of days, a replacement mellotron was flown out ASAP from England. [8] [3]

Playing at the three-day Palm Beach Festival at the end of November made all the arduous zigzagging across America worthwhile, as while *Court* would only get into the lower reaches of the U.S. Top Thirty, the event helped break them on that side of the Atlantic. Held at the International Raceway, the festival was graced by some of the biggest names in rock, such as The Rolling Stones, Janis Joplin and Jefferson Airplane, with artists and their crews being flown in and out by helicopter. Crimson had been scheduled to play on each day, but long overruns from others on the final day meant that they were squeezed out and only got to play twice. Timings were the least of the organiser's worries though, as amongst other things, they had seriously miscalculated the finances of the event. With the crowd only being around one-tenth that of Hyde Park, and many of those attending having found ways to get in free, they had a financial disaster unfolding before them. On top of that, the weather deteriorated badly, and in plummeting temperatures fans struggled to keep warm, commandeering anything they could find to make fires. What had been billed as The First Annual Palm Beach Festival was therefore also the last. In the midst of the organised chaos, Crimson roadie Richard Vickers was having the time of his life. The U.S. tour was one big adventure for him, but the coup de grace came on the final day at Palm Beach. Heavy rain had turned the site into a mud bath, and he found himself giving a young woman a piggy-back ride to the stage area so she could avoid the mud. It was only when she invited him backstage to watch the Stones and have a drink that he realised it was Janis Joplin! Just after the festival, *Billboard Magazine* published an extraordinary review of Crimson's New York gig the previous month, characterising their sound as 'cosmic jazz' and 'a symphonic explosion that made listening compulsory, if not hazardous'. Lake was described as 'a hoody choirboy' as he delivered Sinfield's 'foreboding poetry' and 'pseudo-religious exaltation'. It couldn't have been more appropriate had they written it themselves! [15]

But as the tour was approaching its end, all was not well, and the drug-free approach went up in smoke for some, cannabis and speed being used depending on what they felt was needed as the strain got to them. Here were five young men, each with growing self-belief and their own ambitions, and while the band had, up to then, been something of a democracy, three of the members each felt that they should be in the driving seat, seriously disagreeing about their future direction. Notably, while Fripp had been steered down this line of music by McDonald, Lake and Sinfield, as the man who had his hands most firmly on the steering wheel, he was the one now pushing for more of the same, while the others were looking to be more diverse. Personality clashes were also becoming a factor, Sinfield later describing Fripp as 'eccentric, moody, hard to handle' and 'a special sort of awkward'. McDonald was also becoming openly critical about Fripp's playing, at one point telling him his style wasn't right for the band. Added to this, the multi-instrumentalist was badly missing his home and his girlfriend while away, and it all came to a head as they were driving up the Californian coast from L.A. to San Francisco, when he told Fripp that he was going to leave the band after the tour. Fripp was horrified and offered to leave himself if McDonald would stay, but his offer was declined. Giles had been missing home too, and the rigours of overseas touring were already becoming such a strain that he suggested Crimson should just be a studio band. The rise of the band had been so fast, it made everything feel to him as if it was 'running out of control'. Hearing of McDonald's decision, he decided that he should jump ship alongside him. With these bombshells having been dropped, and the band in a somewhat depressed mood, the final gigs, at the Fillmore West in San Francisco in mid-December, were the last of this line-up. Thanks to the quick thinking and remarkable foresight of Vickers, when he saw that recording equipment was available, those shows were recorded for posterity. [16] [2]

With half the playing members of the band gone, a devastated Fripp returned to England. He considered the U.S. tour to have been a great success, and with good cause, yet somehow was returning home with his band disintegrating. That wasn't the end of the bad news for him, as when the remaining three reconvened, Lake also announced that he was leaving. Fatefully, towards the end of the U.S. tour, Crimson had been on the same bill as The Nice, whose line-up included Keith Emerson, a virtuoso and showman perhaps describable as the Hendrix of keyboards. Impressed by Emerson, and aware that his own band was falling apart, Lake had made plans to leave and form a new band with the Nice man, after chatting with him at their hotel following the gig. Had they all just taken a few weeks to unwind and get some perspective on their situation, they may perhaps have made different decisions. They didn't, though, and this latest blow left just Fripp and Sinfield carrying the band name and staring into the abyss.

Premature though the split was, King Crimson Mk I made an undeniably vast impact and left a sizeable legacy. We hear all too often that such and such a band or artist changed the course of music history, when the reality just doesn't come close to the claim. But here, for this incarnation of the band, the claim is entirely true. As well as the legacy of the music itself, the audiences watching their gigs contained a great many young musicians who'd go away deeply inspired by what they had heard. As well as those already mentioned, a nineteen-year-old Peter Gabriel was moved to take up the flute after seeing McDonald play, and would put the cover of *Court* on the wall of the Genesis rehearsal room to remind them of what they were aspiring to match. It was an album that they all listened to endlessly, according to Genesis's bassist, Mike Rutherford, and it even prompted them to buy their own mellotron. Steve Hackett, who would become Genesis's guitarist a couple of years later, was another to be greatly influenced by those 1969 gigs, along with his brother John, who would give up the guitar to take up the flute. Violinist and soon-to-be founder member of Curved Air, Darryl Way, would be motivated by hearing Crimson's approach to crossing classical with rock, while members of Yes realised they had to raise their game, with Bill Bruford even setting his sights on one day joining this band. Other young drummers, such as Canadian Neil Peart, later of Rush, would also be specifically inspired by the talents of Giles behind his kit. Finally, while it would be unwise to draw too direct a connection, a floundering Pink Floyd, who were about to release the disappointing *Ummagumma*, got their act together and shifted to a markedly more prog style after *Court*. In its relatively fleeting existence to this point, Crimson had set new standards and shone a bright light on new possibilities and directions that many would follow.

3

# Cirkus

## *1970 to Mid-1972*

In years to come, Fripp would ask the sort of question that fans would have been asking in 1970: 'How could anyone leave a group of that originality and power?' More than that, how could anyone leave a band that had just released such a successful debut album? When the split was made public, McDonald explained that he felt he was being pushed too much to do more of the same doom-laden rock when he wanted the freedom to do something different. In retrospect, he would put his decision down more to youthful impetuousness than musical differences. Either way, although he would ultimately find commercial success elsewhere, there were times when he regretted leaving Crimson. However, in leaving and prompting others to follow him through the exit door, as well as the impact on Fripp, he left the lingering question of what would have happened had the original line-up stayed together. Lake would have no such regrets. For him, the answer to Fripp's question was simply that he saw better prospects and a better fit with Emerson than with a disintegrating Crimson. Heart-breaking though it was to the sizeable following Crimson had already built up, McDonald, Lake and Giles did leave, plunging Fripp into what seemed like a hopeless situation. Still, he didn't need to think twice about continuing since, from his perspective, quitting was just not an option given the status of the band name that he found himself in possession of. Importantly, Sinfield opted to stay with him, a decision that shouldn't be underestimated. Fripp was not a lyric writer, and regardless of his confidence as a musician, without Sinfield's contributions he would have stood little chance. Even so, the next two and a half years would be rather tortuous. [1]

As there was no band as such, their first task was to cancel the tour dates they had planned and instead focus on rebuilding. At the same time, however, the pair were coming under pressure from Island for the follow-up album that Fripp had been promising and had to dive straight into working on that. Such a state of turmoil is no way to record what people would these days call 'that difficult second album', but fortunately there were a few works in progress left over from the original band to use. Otherwise, by default Fripp had become the music writer. It would be a steep learning curve for him, as he only had a handful of GGF tracks to his name as regards being the sole music writer, but it was something he was prepared to whole-heartedly throw himself into. Crimson was now his vehicle, and the immense sense of purpose that had got him this far was undiminished. The pressure was relieved a little when Michael Giles agreed to stay around to complete the recording. His brother Peter was also temporarily enlisted on bass. Having spent the last year as a computer operator in Putney, he'd actually become oblivious to the band and its fortunes, feeling that 'it was absolutely nothing to me and my new life outside music'. As one of the few who hadn't been at Hyde Park or The Marquee, he'd been rather surprised to find just how successful they'd been and that his brother and McDonald had subsequently decided to leave. Fripp still urgently needed to find a vocalist, and a then-unknown Londoner by the name of Elton John was booked by E. G. to do a session. However, on hearing Elton's first album, *Empty Sky*, also released in 1969, Fripp cancelled the arrangement, though it's said that Elton was still paid his session fee. The future Rocket Man was probably glad not to have gone down any kind of Crimson route, as his second album would soon become a massive hit on both sides of the Atlantic, along with the single, *Your Song*. E. G.'s John Gaydon then auditioned, only to be rejected as well.

Ultimately, Lake was persuaded to do the vocals as a guest, as he had time before his new band got together, being given some of Crimson's P.A. equipment as payment. This meant that there would a large degree of continuity, after all, with four of the original five involved. Two newcomers were then recruited as guest musicians for the album. Sax-and-flute player Mel Collins was enlisted to partially fill McDonald's shoes, already being well acquainted with Crimson from seeing them several times at The Marquee. Although he grew up in Surrey, Collins was literally born on tour, on the Isle of Man, while his musician parents were playing there. After briefly pursuing a career as a professional photographer after leaving school, eighteen-year-old Collins realised that music was to be his thing, getting experience through setting up his own bands and answering ads in the *Melody Maker*. He was glad to receive Fripp's call at this point, as his current band, Circus, were themselves on the verge of breaking up. Also new to the fold was blonde-haired, West Country pianist Keith Tippett, another Marquee regular whose band had supported Circus. His free jazz style would add an entirely new ingredient to the Crimson sound. [2]

Not standing on ceremony, Fripp's cobbled-together line-up headed to the Calatychos basement to rehearse, before moving on to Wessex Studio in January 1970. With pressure from the record company to keep up their profile, a very untypical song, *Cat Food*, was hurried out as a single from these sessions. The song had been co-written with McDonald before his departure, but instead of mellotrons and medieval imagery, this time we get Tippett's jangling, jazzy piano and Sinfield's lyrics of cynical humour about consumerism. The single led to what would be Crimson's only appearance on the BBC's flagship programme, *Top of the Pops*, on 25 March, although the record still failed to make the charts. This was to be the only stage appearance of any kind for the Giles, Giles, Fripp, Lake and Tippett temporary line-up (Collins not yet featuring) and, as with most acts on the show, they were miming to the pre-recorded track. It was here that the returning Giles brother first noticed a change in Fripp. 'My brother was exactly as he'd always been', he observed, 'but I was very surprised to see Robert and Greg obsessively preening themselves before going on stage. I had never seen Robert like this before'. Other than this he felt that Fripp behaved as he always had with him, in that 'there was a mutual respect tempered with the odd pissing about'. Partial footage of the appearance resurfaced decades later, unfortunately featuring the band being introduced by the now-disgraced (and deceased) presenter Jimmy Saville. Footage also survives of a similar performance on a German pop chart show. The song was released with a partly improvised and not particularly good instrumental B-side called *Groon*. For this one track only, King Crimson consisted of Giles, Giles and Fripp. [2]

As the studio sessions continued into April, with a band made up of people halfway in and halfway out, Fripp and Sinfield paid a social call on McDonald. They were there ostensibly to play him their album-in-progress, but they also wanted him to know that the door was still open to him if he wanted to change his mind about leaving. McDonald, however, read their visit as an attempt to squeeze a last few ideas out of him, and he was having none of it. The second album, *In the Wake of Poseidon*, was duly completed and rushed out in May, just seven months after *Court*. The feel is superficially similar, some tracks sounding like parallels of tracks from the first album, and fans who didn't know what had been happening could have been forgiven for thinking little had changed. The reasons for this are simple. Given the time pressures, the absence of a stable line-up and having to do what was his first album in full charge, Fripp simply took the template of *Court* as his starting point and made the best of existing ideas and a few hastily gathered new ones. While this is, by default, a Fripp-dominated record, with he and Sinfield co-producing, the ghost of Crimson Mk I is working through him. It's particularly hard to avoid the feeling that McDonald is present throughout much of it, with several tracks having been in development before his departure, and the Fripp-written material carrying on in the vein of the McDonald's. Still, the end-result is more than just the echo or pastiche of *Court* it's sometimes dismissed as. While there *are* weaknesses, there is a lot of substance, and the record is best regarded as a snapshot of Fripp transforming himself into a full-fledged music writer.

Without an ounce of irony, considering the band's situation, the album opens with *Peace—A Beginning*. Written by Fripp and Sinfield, this is a minute of Lake's unaccompanied voice gently emerging from a wash of reverb, the words reflecting Sinfield's ongoing reaction to Vietnam. The mood changes abruptly with *Pictures of a City*, a track written on tour in the U.S., and which the band had been performing live as *A Man, A City*. Its bluesy sax-and-guitar intro has the feel of a 1950s American gangster movie theme, though Sinfield's lyrics describe a harsh, modern metropolis. A fast-playing middle section, which parodies the middle of *Schizoid Man*, leaves little doubt as to the parallels with the first album. However, the track lacks the perfect textures of its predecessor, and the verses sound wooden. Lake wasn't able to complete the whole album before leaving, and Fripp had to hurriedly find someone else to record the vocals for one song, *Cadence and Cascade*. This was another idea that had been in development before the split, and Lake had got as far as doing a demo version. In order to complete the album version though, Fripp again called on his friend Gordon Haskell, having been impressed by his vocals on his solo album. Haskell's solo career had stalled after *Sail in my Boat* and having seen the original Crimson live at The Marquee, he was impressed enough to help his friend out, even though his musical tastes had gone in a different direction. While his voice was markedly different to Lake's, being richer and silkier but without the dramatic power, it doesn't seem out of place here. As the album's parallel to *I Talk to the Wind*, the track also gave an opportunity for Collins to demonstrate his own virtuosity on the flute.

Fripp had taken over mellotron duties and, on the title track, showed what he had learned about the instrument from being around McDonald. The track has been rather neglected over the years, never being performed live and sometimes dismissed as merely a parody of

*Epitaph.* While there are obvious similarities, Fripp managed to squeeze out something original and find a lot of emotion. With naïve, almost hymn-like melodies, which are particularly powerful in the instrumental middle and the fadeout, it gave fans a bit more of the doom-rock they were craving. The mix of religious, medieval and ancient imagery of the lyrics also supplies another bottomless pit of interpretation to delve into. Sinfield's words this time connected to the album's relatively understated cover, a 1967 painting by Tammo De Jongh, known as *The Twelve Archetypes.* Inspired by the New Age philosophical writings of Richard Gardner, the archetypes stem from the twelve combinations of what were in medieval times seen as the four elements of earth, air, fire and water. These were believed to create characters that, between them, cover the full spectrum of human nature, such as the fool, the warrior, the joker, the enchantress and Mother Nature. The track title itself adds a further layer of meaning, Poseidon being the ancient Greek god of the sea and the forces of nature. The title is not part of the lyrics however, the link being through a reference to Plato, the great philosopher of ancient Greece, whose writing formed the basis of Western philosophy. There is the ever-lurking danger of over-indulging the rock lyricist again, looking for meanings that may not be there, but Sinfield's evocative words about smiling madmen, kneeling children and Jesus, strike chords at some level without the need for in-depth analysis.

The short instrumental, *Peace—A Theme,* which opens side two, is a rare piece of solo acoustic guitar from Fripp, instrumentally echoing the opening of side one and partly recycling his GGF demo, *Passages of Time.* This is followed by a longer edit of the quirky *Cat Food,* a little out of place amongst the epics but breaking the pattern of parallels to the first album. The bulk of side two is taken up with a pastiche of Holst's *Mars: The Bringer of War.* Although the original Crimson had regularly played an improv based on this, Holst's estate objected to Fripp's plan to use the piece on the album, thereby scuppering the intended juxtaposition of war and peace in the track titles and forcing him to hastily come up with something similar to fill the space. The resulting multi-sectioned piece was given four titles: *The Devil's Triangle*, *Merday Morn*, *Hand of Scerion* and *Garden of Worm*—once again bumping up the number of tracks they would be paid royalties for—with *Merday* credited as a Fripp/McDonald co-write, acknowledging the evolution of the track. For simplicity, the whole thing is generally just referred to as *The Devil's Triangle* (an alternative name for The Bermuda Triangle). The first few minutes are recognisably Holst-like, but different, and eerie enough for a section to be used in a 1971 episode of the BBC's Time Lord drama, *Doctor Who*. After about seven minutes, the inspiration runs thin though, and the strain Fripp was under shows through. There was still vinyl to fill, prompting the band to valiantly throw in the kitchen sink. Even so, it meanders for several minutes to an unsatisfactory conclusion. *Peace—An Ending* comes to the rescue, tying together the earlier loose ends by combining Lake's vocal and Fripp's acoustic guitar, and the album, which had opened softly with *Peace*, closes abruptly on the word *war*.

Although Crimson's *Poseidon* adventure provoked a variety of reactions, the undeniable parallels to *Court* were an open goal for critics. What seems remarkable in retrospect is that, although it would be condemned to live forever in *Court*'s immense shadow, this baptism of fire for Fripp the writer went to No. 4 in the U.K., a place higher than its esteemed predecessor. This was almost certainly due to the expectations built up after the first album, and as far as the U.K. was concerned, would be the highest a Crimson album would ever get. As a whole, however, *Poseidon* lacks the complete and confident feel of *Court*, suffering from the loss of the collective musical brains of Crimson Mk I. That said, producing something that was good quality by most people's standards in so short a time was remarkable and said a lot about Fripp. With the album out, and everyone who was going to leave having now left, the long, drawn-out demise of Crimson Mk I was finally complete. By this time, the rock world had another seismic event occupying its thoughts and overshadowing everything else: the split of The Beatles and the release of their final studio album.

While the Giles brothers had been busy recording with Fripp, McDonald had been constructively occupying himself by developing ideas for a breakaway project under the name McDonald and Giles. Once *Poseidon* was done and dusted, the brothers were able to join him for recording sessions, which McDonald has rather pointedly described as being enjoyable for being free from conflict. He avoided referring to conflict with anyone in particular, instead talking about 'how much conflict there is around the world and between colleagues'. The fact that he felt the need to mention conflict at all is telling, and as everyone except Sinfield had deserted Fripp, it wasn't hard to work out who he was referring to. The brothers also found the sessions with McDonald enjoyable, and were happy to be working together. Peter Giles later recalled, 'There was humour in our playing which sometimes erupted. Michael and I always had a good time when we were playing together'. As ex-members of a band that was a hot property, Island were at first happy to indulge McDonald and Giles, and they spent the better part of three months recording. Because of this, an even wider range of McDonald's multi-instrumentalist, composing and arranging abilities were allowed to be explored. The record company's patience and generosity of paying for studio time had its limits, and they ultimately had to push the musicians for a finished product, though McDonald was still far from happy with the feel of several tracks. [3] [4]

While Fripp had struggled to fill his album, the breakaway team had no such trouble, although much of what they ended up using were ideas from during or before their Crimson year. The eleven-minute opener, *Suite in C*, which McDonald started writing towards the end of the U.S. tour, was the first track he'd written using his own lyrics. Leaning a little towards the lighter feel of GGF and allowing his Beatles influence to show through more, McDonald was turning his back on the grandiose sound he'd been integral in creating and, in fact, the whole album seems to be a reaction against doing more of the same. Lyrically, the track is simply a light-hearted tale of McDonald fancying a girl on a tube train, that girl being Charlotte Bates, who had since become his girlfriend. It is replete with references to archetypal London suburbia, suggesting that he had been missing home as well as Charlotte while on tour. Steve Winwood of Traffic was recording in a neighbouring studio at the time and was roped in to add piano and organ solos to a largely improvised section. McDonald and Giles had met him at a New Year's party shortly after the Crimson break-up, and then got together for a relaxed jam, along with Traffic's flautist, Chris Woods. The four had discussed the possibility of recording together, but the idea fell by the wayside, Winwood having too many other commitments. As a result, the *Suite in C* passage would be their only collaboration. The rest of side one continued to plough a Beatle-esque furrow to varying degrees, next up being *Flight of the Ibis*, a curiosity for Crimson fans, being McDonald's take on the idea that became *Cadence and Cascade*. As a work-in-progress from earlier sessions, both sides felt they had a right to claim the idea, and the tracks have taken on their own identities. With lyrics supplied by a poet and music journalist friend of McDonald's, B. P. Fallon, sentiment-wise we are in *All You Need Is Love* territory, while the reference to an ibis in the title derives from the bird having been regarded as a symbol of rebirth in ancient civilisations. Even more McCartney in tone, and entirely performed by McDonald, *Is She Waiting* is a sombre, reflective love song he had penned for Charlotte during his Crimson year. It is a prime example of something that probably wouldn't have been allowed on another doom-laden Crimson album. The one Michael Giles–written track is *Tomorrow's People*. Developed from lyrics he'd written in his GGF days, this is Giles's angle on the 'children are our future' theme, with him being a parent by this point. The drummer also doubles as vocalist, his voice given the Lennon-style echo treatment. In a bizarre twist, a distinctive percussion section of the track was sampled by rappers, The Beastie Boys, for their 1998 single, *Body Movin'*!

Although Sinfield had elected to stay with Fripp in the split, some of his lyrics found their way onto this album, in sections of *Birdman*, which filled side two. Comprising of six parts, elements of which had been worked on by Crimson late in 1969 and aired live as part of a track called *Trees*, it charts the story of an inventor's attempts to fly, mixing fantasy with reality, using elements of an ancient story and mixing them with something more modern. Sinfield doesn't identify the era in which the story is set, although a mention of Walthamstow connects it with pioneering English aviator A. V. Roe and his attempts to fly a plane on Walthamstow Marshes in 1909. Roe's plane for those attempts was a flimsy *Magnificent Men in their Flying Machines*–type triplane he constructed in a workshop in nearby railway arches. But while the early verses paint him as an old-fashioned English eccentric, Roe went on to create the company that built Lancaster bombers for the RAF for World War II. The style of the music is also rooted in English-eccentric territory for the first three sections, and again inspired by The Beatles, but this time with a bit of early Floydian trip thrown in. It's only in the later parts that we get more of what we would have been expecting musically from a Crimson off-shoot, and the lyrics shift too, describing a modern-day Icarus attempting to fly, with wings made of feathers. The fourth part, *Birdman Flies*, appropriately enough, is where things really take off, with a long build-up around a repeated sequence played by a mix of pianos and flutes. However, the final two linked sections, *Wings in the Sunset* and *Birdman—The Reflection*, are the standout pieces of the album. The former consists of a few lines of verse to complete the story—Birdman coming back down to earth after his successful flight—while the latter continues with the same melody, building into a five-minute-long, Crimson-esque ending. But though you are waiting for the moment the mellotrons burst in, they never do, as McDonald made a point of not using any, instead opting for organ, voices and real orchestration. The orchestration proved to be a challenge, as the studio wasn't big enough for all the musicians to fit in together, and they had to be recorded in sections. Still, it was a suitably triumphant way to end the album, evoking our hero's return from his flying experience and reflecting on his new perspective on the world. The track structure McDonald used here, which involved repeating the same sequence many times, adding in layers of harmonies, fills and instrument doubling, was relatively unusual in rock music, especially for a proficient writer and musician, where the temptation would be to add in other sections. Others would take this layered repetition method and develop it in their own ways in the coming years, the most notable example being Brian Eno, on such early solo tracks as *Here Come the Warmjets* and *On Some Faraway Beach.*

The pink-tinged, gloriously hippie-style cover shows the duo walking through woods with their respective partners—McDonald with Charlotte, and Giles with Mary Land. By the time *McDonald and Giles* was released in January 1971, the wind had well and truly gone out of their sails though, with Island having been reluctant to put it out. It's not clear what the pair's expectations had been, but the enjoyably different road they had taken turned out to be a cul-de-sac, and careerwise they had shot themselves in the foot. There was no ill feeling, but McDonald and Giles went their separate ways, McDonald heading for America while Giles found session work. Without the Crimson name on the cover and no ongoing band to promote it, sales were low, and while much loved by those who bought it, the album soon slipped into forgotten-treasure territory. They had succeeded in creating an album of a different kind, which is what they had set out to do, but the uncomfortable reality for McDonald in particular was that he had gone from obscurity to being the talent at the heart of an acclaimed band and back to obscurity again in the space of just two years. The album was eventually re-mixed and tweaked by McDonald for a CD release in the noughties, enabling it to be discovered by a wider audience. One of his more unusual tweaks was to diplomatically replace the word *pussy* in *Suite in C* with *kitten.*

While fans scrutinised the evidence and pondered the second Crimson album that might have been, had the original band stayed together, there was another strand leading off from Crimson; that of Lake's new project with Keith Emerson. They began to get ideas together in the spring of 1970 and to look for a drummer to complete their intended setup. One serious contender was Mitch Mitchell, who until recently had been playing with Hendrix. They got him to come to an audition but were so alarmed by the heavies that seemed to come as part of the package, they had to reject him. Instead, they recruited another showman, Carl Palmer, enticing him away from another prog band, Atomic Rooster. The trio's decision to use their surnames in alphabetical order—Emerson, Lake and Palmer—created a band name that would soon lodge itself in music history, Lake's role being to cover bass, vocals and guitar. After a low-key debut gig in Plymouth in August 1970, their second came a few days later at that year's legendary Isle of Wight Festival. With crowd estimates of up to six hundred thousand—making it the largest-ever music event in the U.K.—they were on a truly staggering bill alongside The Doors, Miles Davis, Joni Mitchell and Jimi Hendrix, the latter playing what would turn out to be his last gig. Appearing on the fourth day of the five-day event, after his Hyde Park and Palm Beach experiences, Lake at least would not have been fazed by the vast scale of the crowd, and right from the start ELP let people know what they were going to be about, which was a no-holds-barred blending of classical and rock. The bulk of their set that day, in fact, consisted of just one piece—a massively ambitious thirty-five-minute arrangement of *Pictures at an Exhibition*, written in 1874 by Russian composer Mussorgsky. Opening with its familiar stately theme, as well as adapting it for their rock instrumentation, ELP added entire movements of their own and their own lyrics to the closing movement, *The Great Gate of Kiev*. As the trio settled down to more normal scale, gigging around the U.K. and Europe, they were able to begin to take stock, and having all taken a huge leap of faith in ditching their previous bands to work together, the initial signs were that it was very much working out for them. Tragically, in those weeks following the festival, Hendrix died at the age of twenty-seven. While rubbing shoulders with him at the festival, ELP didn't get to properly meet him, although through ELP's contact with Mitchell there had been discussions about arranging a jam together. Over the years this has been blurred with the fact that Emerson and Lake had auditioned Mitchell, leading to the erroneous story that Hendrix was considering linking up with ELP (who would perhaps have become HELP!). The story was left to stew for many years but, eventually, Lake confirmed that there never was any possibility of Hendrix joining them.

For Crimson, things were still very fluid line-up wise, in the wake of *Poseidon*. Peter Giles was at one point offered a six-month slot as bassist for a tour of America and France, and duly arranged time off from his job to enable this. Crimson and E. G. then decided it would have to be for twelve months, which was too much for him; he returned instead to his computer work. Tour plans were then put on hold in any case, as Fripp decided he had to throw himself into getting material together for a third album and sorting out a permanent line-up. Collins, Haskell and Tippett were all asked to step up to being members rather than guests. Collins accepted straight away, while Haskell hesitated, now having serious misgivings about the style of music the band was favouring. Knowing that Fripp was under a lot of pressure, he ultimately gave in. His role was expanded to being vocalist and bassist, his technical ability for the latter being higher than Lake's had been initially, with a decade's worth of experience on the instrument and having been given lessons by Duck Dunn of Booker T and the MG's along the way. Tippett turned down Fripp's offer, being too much of a pioneer himself to be subsumed into Fripp's entity. He agreed to continue as a guest, and ironically would last longer with the band than several supposedly permanent members. For a drummer, Fripp followed up a recommendation from Lake to try Andy McCulloch, then with Manfred Mann, who had previously played alongside Lake in Shy Limbs. McCulloch accepted the offer and brought with him a dynamic and fluid style that is barely distinguishable to the casual listener from that of Giles. The core line-up was supplemented by two other guests borrowed from Tippett's band: Mark Charig on cornet and Nick Evans on trombone, with Robin Miller called up from the BBC Symphony Orchestra, on oboe and cor anglais. When you add in the appearance of a guest vocalist, the album would be put together by a personnel of ten. But while Fripp was now the only playing member left from the original band, there would again be a fair degree of continuity from the previous album.

With Fripp having more time to develop material and to properly move on, it was this album, *Lizard*, that was a more considered follow-up to *Court*. Recorded in August and September 1970, the doors were thrown wide open to influences, the result being an even more exaggerated melding of rock, jazz and classical, this time with some electronics thrown in. It's a mixture that ended up in unique territory but without disowning its ancestry. Either feeling that he just wanted to pursue his art, or that Crimson had such a reputation that people would follow him whatever he did, Fripp also felt able to more decisively put his own stamp on it and, consciously or not, veered away from the relative accessibility and commerciality of *Court*. He was now a man on a mission, though exactly what that mission was, even *he* would have struggled to pin down. Pursuing that mission would override most other considerations, even if it meant there would be casualties. But while you could justifiably describe much of the album as indulgence, Fripp, as both guitarist and band leader, largely resisted any temptation to indulge in guitar solos. In fact, what's notable about his role on *Lizard* is that, although he had broadened it out even further to playing guitar, mellotron, electric keyboards and 'devices', in places his playing presence is minimal, as he stepped back to being composer, arranger and co-producer, letting the numerous other musicians take the strain. There was another significant dynamic going on too. While Fripp was becoming an increasingly dominant figure, Sinfield was determined not to be just a side man, and something of a power struggle was developing between the pair. All the tracks are credited as Fripp and Sinfield collaborations, and the lyricist very much had his say on everything. However, Fripp was beginning to find he was struggling to cater for the kind of lyrics he was being given to work with, which, in places, had taken a distinct turn to the surreal. It wasn't just the lyrics, though, and Fripp later pinpointed the beginning of his problems with Sinfield to a phone call between them a few weeks before the *Lizard* sessions. 'I sensed a change in Peter's attitude towards me', he later recorded in his diary, 'and our relationship subsequently deteriorated'. While acknowledging his skills as a lyricist and with organising cover art, over the coming eighteen months his biggest difficulty would be with Sinfield increasingly pushing for 'role equivalence', or being 'co-owner' of Crimson, 'without a practical musical background or experience'. Fripp concluded that 'Peter's ambitions were unrealistic, perhaps misplaced'. [4]

The album opens with *Cirkus*, a unique piece of jumbled beauty, drama and odd lyrics that were rooted in Sinfield's family connections with circus acts and a childhood visit to the Magic Circle. The changed spelling alerts us that this isn't about an afternoon of fun for the kids but something darker, perhaps a metaphor for the chaos of life, if not of the whole of humanity. Harp-like ripplings of electric pianos lure us in, along with romantic opening lines, but we're put straight by the first appearance of a dramatic mellotron riff. The song then moves through several verses of Sinfield's most surreal lyrics to date, Haskell coping remarkably with lines that don't rhyme or scan. Collins comes into his own on sax in the gentler instrumental passages, having more creative involvement on this album, and the whole thing is rounded off by a sequence where Charig's cornet brilliantly takes chances with the key and gets away with it. With some echoes of *Cat Food*, *Indoor Games* is a romp through sexual adventures in middle-class suburbia, rather than about Ludo or chess. Jaunty saxes and touches of VCS3 synthesiser give it a playful feel, the track ending with Haskell inadvertently dissolving into laughter as he reached for a big bluesy *yeaaahh*—but couldn't go through with it. They could simply have done another take, but Fripp chose to leave the laughter in, as it fitted the slightly crazed feel of the song. According to Haskell, rather than illustrating what fun they were all having, it was in exasperation at what he was being asked to sing! The VCS3, which Fripp and Sinfield were toying with here and there on side one, was a new piece of electronic wizardry that only a few musicians were daring to try. The analogue Voltage Controlled Studio 3 was tricky to master, especially as it didn't come with a built-in keyboard, though one could be added. It was intended more as a device for producing noises or for processing other instruments rather than as a melodic instrument. In a sense it was strange to find cutting-edge electronics in the mix with the medieval feel and jazz elements elsewhere. However, that was the nature of this album and Fripp's approach. Fripp himself didn't stick with the instrument for long though.

The descending guitar chords and pulsing electronics of the intro to *Happy Family* seem to have us back in the *Cirkus* tent, but what follows, despite promising ingredients, is the weak point of the album. Suffering from being too jumbled and disjointed, and with a hideous mess in the middle, it's also spoilt by Haskell's voice being plastered in effects and being too low in the mix, while Tippett's rambling electric piano is too prominent. The family concerned are The Beatles, who were by this time no longer happy, having split up. With John, Paul, George and Ringo renamed Jonah, Judas, Silas and Rufus, while Sinfield supposedly didn't intend to poke fun at the former Fab Four, it doesn't exactly come across as a resounding tribute, with a thinly veiled reference to Lennon's marriage to Yoko Ono, which is often cited as a cause of the band's break-up. The bizarre imagery is then all packed away for the gentle romance of *Lady of the Dancing Water*, based around voice, acoustic guitar, electric piano and flute. Its feel is medieval however its roots lay in late sixties hippiedom and Sinfield's travels in the Balearics (more of which would appear later), also perhaps echoing Crosby, Stills and Nash's similarly inspired *Lady of the Islands*.

The glory of this album is the twenty-three-minute title track, which filled the whole of the original side two. Side-long epics were becoming a trend in prog/psychedelia, and Fripp indulged here for the one and only time in his Crimson career. The opening section, *Prince Rupert Awakes*, features Jon Anderson of Yes as guest vocalist, having accepted an invitation from Fripp, via Lake. His vocal range, being an octave above most other male vocalists, gives the song a more ethereal quality than it might otherwise have had, delivering it in a way that was well outside Haskell's range. Anderson was intrigued by Fripp's work but there was never any intention of his joining. There had, however briefly, been a chance for Fripp to join Yes, after their guitarist, Pete Banks, had left. They were yet to make any real breakthrough, though, and Fripp felt he was better off with his own band. Although Fripp was developing fast as a writer, the basic melodies for this and *Lizard*'s other sections still leant towards the simplistic and naïve. Here though, Fripp throws in the extra dimension of deliberate discords with the otherwise-medieval feel. For the purveyors of doom-rock, the chorus is surprisingly uplifting, even featuring handclaps in places, and for once, the medieval imagery of Sinfield's words is not a metaphor for modern life but actually a medieval tale, of sorts. Nevertheless, they are amongst his most impenetrable lyrics, scattered with clues as to what it might be about. The most obvious interpretation is that they refer to the seventeenth-century German, Prince Rupert of the Rhine, who was a nephew of England's King Charles I, and took up arms in numerous causes, most significantly being a Royalist General in the English Civil War in the 1640s. The lyrics are otherwise littered with obscure references few are going to get (including the rest of the band) that once again just blur into enjoyable imagery. These include a mention of Polonius, a character from Shakespeare's *Hamlet* known for his bad judgment, and, more obliquely, a reference to the conflict between Parliament (mostly populated by landed gentry at the time) and forces backing the king. Most obscure of all though is the use of the word *Piepowder*, the name of a court in medieval England that settled trade disputes. A sideways reference to Prince Rupert's teardrops, however, gives away the game Sinfield was playing. These are not the actual tears of the figure in the song, but a type of glass bead introduced to England by Rupert and named in his honour. Slipping this in tells us that the song is merely clever wordplay, and if you were to somehow unravel all the clues, there would be nothing to find in the middle. It may be a clue as to Sinfield's initial inspiration that the epic Civil War film, *Cromwell*, hit the cinemas of Britain shortly before Crimson went into the studio, with future James Bond Timothy Dalton playing Prince Rupert. Sinfield has been happy to let his songs become shrouded in interpretations and ambiguity over the years, the *Promenade the Puzzle* section of his website featuring a fog of references to tarot cards, alchemy and more, which serve to deepen the mysteries rather than clarify them.

The track then passes seamlessly into a beautiful instrumental passage called *Bolero—The Peacock's Tale*, where Fripp's presence in terms of playing is minimal, Miller, Evans and Charig instead coming to the fore. Fripp is still firmly in control however, as composer and arranger, as he experiments with mixing classical with free jazz. There is a moment of jarring incongruity when the piece takes its jazzy diversion, but once you accept that Fripp is doing this deliberately, it works within its own parameters. Ultimately, once the guests have all done their thing, it swings back round to a heart-meltingly passionate reprise of the original melody, complete with touches of mellotron. As the last cymbal crash of *Bolero* dies away, we reach the third section, *The Battle of Glass Tears*, a long-neglected piece of drama destined not to be played live by Crimson until 2017. Here, a climbing cor anglais line from Miller snakes its way into the air, pastiching the opening bassoon of Stravinsky's *Rites of Spring*, a work that prompted a riot at its 1913 premiere. Haskell's final vocal section then describes what seems to be a romantic country scene but is merely the deceptively calm setting for fearful soldiers preparing to march into a bloody battle at dawn. With his final words, a note of cor anglais lingers. You can feel that something dramatic is about to happen, and it does in no uncertain terms, as drums and bass burst in and mellotrons take over the melody before switching again to something jazzier. The section's title is, if you go with the Prince Rupert story, a reference to the Civil War Battle of Naseby in 1645, where the Prince fought for Charles I against Cromwell's New Model Army. It was a devastating defeat for the Royalists, however the Prince lived to tell the tale, going on to a role in the Admiralty and, on his death, being given the honour of a burial in the crypt of Westminster Abbey. The last sub-section of *Battle* is *Prince Rupert's Lament*, where a funereal rhythm of bass and distant drums evokes a post-battle scene. Over this, Fripp delivers a guitar solo resembling distant bagpipes, with his first use of the fuzz/sustain sound that was to become one of his trademarks. The album is rounded off with *Big Top*—which had been the working title for the album—a suitably warped reprise of a section of *Cirkus*, speeding up and slowing down, creating the effect of being transported drunkenly through a fairground. When it came to the later re-mastering, the speed changes were ditched in favour of the track more soberly shifting from channel to channel.

Continuing the series of memorable album covers, *Lizard*'s is a remarkable piece of artwork, painted by Gini Barris, a nineteen-year-old just out of art school. Working as a housekeeper for another E. G. artist, Julie Felix, on hearing that Sinfield was looking for someone to design a cover, she contacted him about an idea she had of using medieval-style miniature pictures. They met up to discuss it more fully and, with Sinfield liking the idea, Barris recalls, 'He just gave me the words and total freedom to interpret them as I wished'. The man she met that evening had become one of the world's highest-profile rock lyricists over the previous year or so, but Barris took this in her stride, saying, 'I liked him. He was just an ordinary bloke to me'. The basis of her design is the band name in large, illuminated writing, with a variety of contorted peacocks squeezed into the outlines of the initial letters, with a series of drawings in and around the letters, some interpreting scenes from the songs, others with Barris just letting her imagination have free rein. Most literal is the collection of archetypal circus characters in the large 'C', while the curves of the 'S' contain depictions of *Indoor Games*. Most pointedly, the characters around the 'I' of Crimson represent The Beatles in *Happy Family*, with the head of Yoko Ono appearing genie-like from a pot held by Lennon. As the sun sets over them, a yellow submarine and the Loch Ness Monster can also be spotted in the background. Playing on a reference to Rupert and bears in *Prince Rupert Awakes*, Barris sneaks the children's book character Rupert Bear into the 'N' of Crimson. Sinfield was simply having a subtle joke with his words here, leaving people searching for a non-existent historical meaning. Barris wasn't in on the joke; she simply had the same line of thought. In that picture, Rupert is flying a plane behind a trio of musicians, two of which depict Jimi Hendrix and Ginger Baker, Barris's favourite musicians of the time. The third is her flautist boyfriend, Dave Wade, who came up with the beige marble design used on the inside cover. While Barris's design is a contender for best prog album cover of all time, she was never actually a prog fan, never saw Crimson live and didn't like the album! 'I have always been a funk and soul girl' she admits, 'so it was just a job [but] a very nice one'. Although there was some discussion of her doing a cover for Led Zeppelin, as she knew John Paul Jones, Barris would only do one other cover, for Julie Felix. After moving to the country and having a family, she went on to be a book illustrator and teacher of lithography and printmaking, later becoming a funk-and-soul DJ. With Gini being short for Virginia, on marrying boyfriend Wade, she became Virginia Wade, the namesake of a top British tennis player of the seventies, something she says that people can't help but comment on. [5]

The album was released that December, meaning there had been three Crimson albums in just fourteen months, the band getting through no less than fourteen members and guests in the process. After the chart success of *Court* and *Poseidon*, though, sales were lower, and *Lizard* only reached twenty-six in the U.K., making no real impression across the pond. With nothing that could realistically be considered as a single, that route to promoting the album was out, and events to follow would scupper any promo-tour. To this day, *Lizard* divides opinion amongst fans, and this extremely worthy, if flawed, album also left most of its participants with a bad aftertaste, some of the ill feeling lasting a great many years. With half the band leaving again, Crimson now had the kind of revolving door of membership that would plague many bands of this era. Most artists would normally defend their work regardless of what critics throw at them, but in his diary in 1999 Fripp described the album as being 'unlistenable'! This was going too far, though, and his opinion had softened by the time of its re-mastering, with his finally being able to disentangle the music from the mess of personal conflicts. However, Fripp's coming of age as a writer had ended up leaving several of his colleagues hating him, and he didn't even have the consolation of being able to enjoy the results at the time. [6]

The worst conflict was with Haskell, which came to a head as the band were rehearsing for a post-album tour. The vocalist clashed with Fripp over how to perform a particular track live and abruptly found himself heading for the exit door. Haskell has been very critical over the years, describing Crimson's music as 'satanic nonsense that was creeping up from the sewer', and his lifelong association with the band as 'a prison sentence', wishing his name could be removed from the cover so that he wouldn't be asked about it. As well as having problems with Sinfield's lyrics—as expressed by his laughter at the end of *Indoor Games*—he found Fripp's methods tortuous and boring. For some passages in particular, once the basic track was laid down the other instruments were then over-dubbed one at a time in short sections. This was not only painfully slow to do, it went totally against the grain for the jazz musicians involved. On top of this, he would subsequently embark on legal action over the share of royalties he felt he had been promised but not paid. In the longer term he believed that his involvement caused damage to his reputation in the circles he would have preferred to be moving in, and that it took him five years to rebuild it. His solo fortunes seemed to revive briefly in 1972, recording the album, *It Is and It Isn't*, for the mighty Atlantic Records. After getting some airplay and a good reception, things soured again, and Haskell ended up asking Atlantic to drop him. Others were none too happy with Fripp over the recording of *Lizard* either, and even the mild-mannered Collins later expressing what was becoming obvious to the world outside at that time—that Fripp isn't the easiest person to work with! McCulloch didn't enjoy the experience either. Haskell has described what he saw as Fripp's 'bullying attitude' towards him, and the drummer also left, going on to more sustained success with Greenslade and session work with original Genesis guitarist Anthony Phillips, before quitting music for the yachting industry. All in all, *Lizard* was an unhealthy experience, although history has shown us that many a beautiful palace has been built by a tyrant. The demise of the short-lived *Lizard* band would, in a sense, draw a final line under Crimson Mk I. This was not in terms of personnel, as most had already gone, but in terms of style, as this would be the end of the mellotron epics and medieval imagery that had lingered for two albums beyond *Court*. [7]

Although they still needed each other, relations between Fripp and Sinfield were also now seriously strained. Fripp was unhappy with the direction Sinfield's lyrics were taking, while Sinfield had been getting angered by Fripp's growing distraction with other projects during the recording-and-mixing process, such as Tippett's Centipede and Van Der Graaf Generator's *H to He* album, the lyricist being left to sort out finishing the album himself. When *Lizard* came to be remastered almost four decades later by Steve Wilson, he found that the sixteen channels of the original tapes had been confusingly filled. As the engineers had struggled to fit in more parts than there were channels, one instrument would be crammed into the space on a channel between parts of another instrument, and unused alternative takes of some parts were not erased. The problem was that no notes had been kept to guide anyone revisiting the mixing at a later date, presumably on the assumption that no one ever would. The biggest of Fripp's distractions back in 1970 was the unusual concept that was Keith Tippett's Centipede, who put together a double album called *Septober Energy*. As well as Tippett, its fifty strong line-up (fifty people having a hundred legs—hence a centipede) included Crimson guests, Evans and Charig, former Crim, McDonald, and a Crim-to-be, Boz Burrell. There were two other big names from the jazz-fusion world, Elton Dean and Robert Wyatt. It had been intended that Fripp would double as producer and guitarist—his first non-Crimson producing—but only the former happened, as he became occupied with the production side of things. Even with such a magnificent roll call of names, this was to be another fascinating album condemned to obscurity.

While Crimson were repeatedly falling apart, things were running more smoothly in the ELP camp, and having also been snapped up by Island Records, October 1970 brought the release of their eponymous first album. Courtesy of their combined reputations and I. O. W. appearance, this reached the heights of No. 4 in the U.K., and No. 18 in the U.S. With an album under their belts, they headed across the Atlantic the following spring for their first attempt to break America. Their second album, *Tarkus*, was released in June 1971, becoming what would be their only U.K. No. 1, and quite a surprising one in retrospect, the twenty-minute title track of poly-rhythmic keyboards with a couple of Lake-written vocal passages being quite a challenging listen. Massive achievement though it was, having knocked the Rolling Stones off the No. 1 spot, it was itself replaced a week later by Simon and Garfunkel. By confidently and competently doing their own thing, ELP were riding a wave of prog popularity, and Lake's new band had totally usurped Fripp in terms of sales. By this point, it wasn't all sweetness and light in ELP either. With three big characters involved, internal band relations could get heated, though this was only about the music, never getting personal, or so the party line went. Held back until after *Tarkus*, a live version of their arrangement of *Pictures at an Exhibition* was put out the following year. Live rock albums were not held in the same regard as studio albums, and it was put out as a budget release, but with its mix of genius, outrageous ambition and indulgence, it has become regarded as a classic work of the band, encompassing all that was good and bad about the trio in their early years. It certainly says a lot about rock audiences in this period that a classical-based prog piece over thirty minutes in length was met by rapturous applause at sizeable venues, with audiences still growing as word spread about ELP.

As Fripp approached working on a fourth Crimson album, yet again his band was in shreds. Although Sinfield still stayed aboard, Collins went off in despair to try to reform Circus, only changing his mind when Fripp found a new drummer in the shape of Ian Wallace. Wallace was a Lancastrian who had most recently been playing with Neil Innes's post-Bonzos band, The World, his style inspired by the legendary jazz drummers Tony Williams and Elvin Jones. Notably, he was a housemate of McCulloch's, and would therefore have been forewarned as to what he was getting into! Auditioning for a vocalist brought about another item of note for posterity. This time, Fripp and Sinfield turned down Geordie art school graduate Bryan Ferry, who would go on to form Roxy Music. But while they felt Ferry was not right for Crimson, Fripp and Sinfield liked him enough to recommend him to E. G. When later asked about the audition, Ferry said that Fripp was a 'wonderful character', 'a very good musician' and 'a bit mad'! In the end, Crimson chose twenty-five-year-old Boz Burrell from Lincolnshire, who Fripp had met, via Tippett. Boz (real name, Raymond) was a vocalist who had played a bit of rhythm guitar and had appeared on a handful of singles in the late sixties with The Sidewinders and The Boz People. His musical leanings were more towards jazz and blues, but in tone he was much closer to Lake's voice than Haskell had been—a distinct advantage if he was going to tackle the back catalogue live. After holding auditions for a bassist, twenty-nine-year-old Dorset man Rick Kemp was invited to join. But after just a couple of weeks of rehearsals he decided that this band was just not for him. His interest lay far more in folk and he joined Steeleye Span instead. Fripp couldn't face starting auditions again, and when he saw Boz have an impromptu go on a bass someone had left in the studio, he decided that he should be bassist, too. The fact that he didn't play the instrument wasn't seen as an obstacle, Fripp decreeing that he and Wallace would teach him the basics on the job. [8]

With Fripp finally having a band to take on the road again after a fifteen-month gap, in March 1971 Crimson were back rehearsing in the

Fulham Palace Road basement. Whether truly ready or not, the following month they set off touring, beginning with a few warm-up nights in Frankfurt, West Germany, which were Crimson's first-ever gigs on mainland Europe. Fripp then took a couple of days out to contribute to his friend Peter Hammill's *Fool's Mate* album, before Crimson's U.K. tour began in earnest. Remarkably, other than four London area gigs in October 1969, these were Crimson's first U.K. gigs since the release of *Court*. Not only would they be performed by almost entirely different personnel, but the band now had a much jazzier, bluesy feel than the crowds would have been expecting. As well as a few new ideas, their sets incorporated an eclectic mix of earlier tracks, such as *Cirkus* and *Cadence and Cascade*, alongside the still-essential *Schizoid Man*, though with acres of space given over to soloing from Fripp and Collins. The covers of *Mars* and *Get Thy Bearings* also remained, with a revived *Groon* also in the set as a loose framework for improv. Fripp knew that some older tracks were just not going to work with this line-up, and most of the doom-rock was simply jettisoned. It was still a tricky balancing act for Boz, channelling both Lake and Haskell while finding his own voice in this new context. The Fripp that the crowds would see onstage had evolved since the 1969 band, now much more in command than before, and with an enhanced stage presence, doubling on mellotron in places, posing with his guitar still strapped on. In a break between legs of the tour that summer, relations between Fripp and Sinfield soured further. When writing-and-rehearsal sessions recommenced, they did so amidst what Fripp describes as 'growing hostility' from Sinfield, who at times took to deliberately cut himself off from communications with Fripp. Maintaining his campaign for an equal standing in the band, the lyricist was now pushing in a different musical direction to Fripp, after his recently acquired love of Spanish landscapes and the jazz of Miles Davis made him want a far more laid-back feel. This, added to the less-than-disciplined approach of the other musicians, made for a tricky balancing act for Fripp while trying to maintain some kind of control. [9]

The album that Crimson Mk II produced, *Islands*, sticks out like a sore thumb in the Crimson cannon, being unlike anything before or since, and to many, it's the least-satisfying Crimson studio album. With another hurried turnaround, it was recorded in gruelling evening-and-night sessions from late September to early October 1971 and released in early December. Perhaps as a result of the rush, the package as a whole feels disjointed, and even the cover for the U.K. and European release—a photo of the Trifid Nebula, from the stock of an astronomical observatory—just doesn't link with the music except as a rather clunky extension of the islands analogy within the album's themes. A plainer, Sinfield-designed cover was initially used for North America, but this was subsequently changed to the nebula design, with Sinfield's moved to the inside. Fripp was again the sole music writer, with Sinfield once again supplying the words, his lyrics veering away from the looming danger of vanishing into a black hole of unfathomability, to more accessible songs of love, sex and infidelity. With the core band again supplemented by several guests, Fripp again pulls back somewhat from performance on some tracks and sits again in the writer/producer/arranger chair. The band was now in effect owned by him, with the others paid a wage and therefore his employees. As a result, the days of Crimson democracy were over. From here on some would feel that Crimson was 'The Robert Fripp Band', which Fripp would always assert was not the case, but on *Islands* it came closest to being just that. Despite this, the music was still the result of everyone's input, and Fripp was bending to the leanings of the others, even if he was trying to assert a much greater degree of control.

Whatever the flaws of *Islands*, and there are many, the linked opening pair of tracks are wonderful adventures. *Formentera Lady* is cloaked in references to Homer's ancient Greek tale *Odyssey*, and to James Joyce's early-twentieth-century novel *Ulysses*, which loosely parallels *Odyssey*. When you lift the literary cloak, you find a celebration of the hedonism of the era, its inspiration essentially a young man finding sexual freedom while travelling in the Balearics. The island of

Formentera is the sparsely populated, lesser-known neighbour of Ibiza, which received the overspill from its neighbour in the hippie-led tourist boom that began in the late sixties. In those days it was largely undiscovered and seemed exotic and was also far enough from the Spanish mainland to keep under the radar of Franco's dictatorship, becoming a haven for the psychedelic crowd and poets such as Sinfield. Stars like Bob Dylan even paid a visit, but it was the 1969 film, *More*, with its Pink Floyd soundtrack, that put the island on the map. Perversely, despite the anti-capitalist notions of the invaders, it was their spending that rescued Formentera from economic oblivion. For Sinfield, it would be the start of a long relationship with the island, which in years to come would be his home, and in 2009 a street in the resort of Es Pujols was named Carrer De King Crimson! The track is fairly minimalist at first, lazily drifting along amidst a tinkling of bells and swirls of flute, both adding a suitably disorganised, hippie feel. A subtle quirk is that there are two basses, with Boz's simple bass line complemented by string bass from guest Harry Miller, another musician borrowed from Tippett's band. In fact, the album opens with growling bass from him, something that could have been a turn-off for those hoping for something at least moderately accessible. Fripp's playing presence is also minimal, only coming in midway with some unobtrusive acoustic guitar. Sinfield sets the scene of whitewashed buildings, lizards and dancing young visitors, in amongst which our poet is pondering the nature of humankind. Thoughts of sex are not far away, with mentions of Circe, an ancient term for a nymph, and barely veiled sexual requests to the lady of the title. After the second chorus, the track slips gently into a long, languid end section. While all underpinned by just one chord, there is a luscious melding of a scat vocal from Boz; a wordless soprano vocal from another guest, Pauline Lucas; and sax soloing from Collins. Ultimately a melody emerges, played on cellos and violins, heralding what is to appear in the following track.

As *Formentera Lady* reaches its conclusion, Wallace's ride cymbal switches to a faster rhythm, cueing in *The Sailor's Tale*, another title from a literary source, this time one of Chaucer's *Canterbury Tales*. Over Boz's repeating bass line, layers of Fripp's fuzz/sustain guitar intertwine with Collins's sax, developing the melody from the end of *Formentera Lady*, only now in a jazzed-up 3/4 time. If you were listening to this without knowing it was a 1971 recording, you might think this was simply a piece of archetypal Frippery. At this point, though, it wasn't archetypal at all but the emergence of something entirely new and highly significant. After some sax-and-guitar soloing, the track switches to a straight 4/4, over which Fripp performs a remarkable, frenzied, jagged, chord-based, heavy-funk solo of a kind he had never performed before. As this reaches its peak, they shift back to 3/4 and an epic ending hits us, with multi-layered mellotrons from Fripp and with Wallace in full flow. The recording was a little raw and the sound textures a bit off in places, while the guitar ends up slightly out of tune and sounding like an insane electric banjo, but it was magnificent, and time would show that this was in a sense the birth of a new Fripp. While determinedly his own man, Fripp was also being driven by what was going on in the developing jazz-fusion world from the likes of Miles Davis and the Mahavishnu Orchestra, the latter having recently released their first album, *Inner Mounting Flame*. This first result, *Sailor's Tale*, was bold, exciting and imaginative, something of which only Fripp was capable. In what would turn out to be a fog of disagreements, discord and people pulling in different directions, he was finding a new identity, and arguably only now beginning to develop his true guitarist self. Closing side one, *The Letters* is a recycling of Fripp's GGF demo, *Drop In*, which had already been reinterpreted by the 1969 line-up. It was too good an idea to lose, but Fripp's lyrics had gone, and instead, in the vein of a TV costume-drama, Sinfield tells the tale of a woman writing to her lover's wife, revealing their affair. It ends with the wife writing back to say she is about to take her own life, and with the implication that she has also killed her husband. The track encapsulates the different musical tendencies being accommodated within this Crimson, switching between delicate sections and raucous blues, in deliberately stark contrast, though not necessarily to good effect.

*Ladies of the Road* is so surprising for a Crimson song that you could accuse it of being un-crimson, if measured against the unspoken blues avoiding principles of the original band. Sex was clearly still on the lyricist's mind—in this case, groupies—in a track that shifts between sleazy, raucous blues and soft Beatle-esque vocal harmonies. With lines about unzipping and eating meat, little is left to the imagination, and in places it's a bit too close to teenage sniggering about sexual conquests. The track features one of Collins's raunchiest sax solos, which *Rolling Stone Magazine*'s Lester Bangs described as 'beautifully obscene', and despite the sentiments being expressed, Fripp singled the song out for particular praise shortly before the album's release, calling it 'quite magnificent'. *Prelude—Song of the Gulls* is unique for a Crimson track, in that it features no band members, instead being performed by oboist Robin Miller, and an uncredited ensemble of classical session musicians. Having successfully composed a bolero, here Fripp tried his hand at a more purely classical piece. With its roots in his *Tremolo Study in A Major* GGF demo, in the end it's more of a starchy period drama in waltz time, than something that touches our emotions. [10]

A prelude in classical music is normally the first movement of a suite, but in this case, it precedes the nine-minute title track. With its music constructed around simple but strong vocal melodies and poetic lyrics, Sinfield returns to his Balearics theme. But while *Formentera Lady* explored sexuality, *Islands* wallows in the calm and glorious isolation of this paradise. The lyrics draw analogies between the island slowly giving in to the elements and Sinfield giving in to love; it also observes that the seemingly separate and isolated islands are, in fact, connected beneath the surface of the sea. Fripp, again, largely stays in the director's chair, leaving the accompaniment mostly to Tippett's piano, but for once this doesn't quite feel right, Tippett having to restrain his more playful tendencies. In fact, the band were just not playing to their strengths here. Jazz musicians were not the right choice for something that needed a more delicate emotional touch, and there are moments when the track feels confused about what it wants to be. Midway it starts to build, but while Fripp's mellotron puts in an appearance, he resists going down the predictable epic-ending route, keeping it all fairly restrained, with a Charig cornet solo taking the limelight. Sadly, while the track has beauty and atmosphere, Fripp's approach renders it overly long, to the point of being boring, which is a rarity for anything bearing the stamp of Fripp/Crimson. As Lester Bangs put it, talking about the album as a whole, it 'ultimately ends up closer to the most tenderly anaesthetising musak'. The track also serves to emphasise the oddity that so much of this guitarist-led album has little or no guitar on it. Fripp's desire to experiment was valid and laudable but he was trying too hard to prove himself in broader terms, not wanting to be just another rock guitarist, and the internal battles and inherent contradictions within his band only further confused his mission. Boz carries off the vocals well, but while he may have initially wondered how he'd gone from nowhere to fronting a major rock band, by this point he'd have been forgiven for wondering how he'd ended up singing songs like *Islands*. With the vinyl era's equivalent of a hidden CD track, the album ends with a minute or so of tuning up of the session musicians on *Prelude*. We also hear Fripp giving instructions, briefly lifting the veil on some of what went on behind the scenes. [10]

Surprisingly, in retrospect, the album got a reasonable amount of praise in the music press on its release, although there was also some longing for more in the vein of Crimson Mk I. What is also surprising is that Fripp said of the recording of *Islands* that it was 'certainly the most enjoyable thing I've ever been involved with in the studio'. Frankly, *anything* would have been an improvement on the recording of *Lizard*, so he was perhaps feeling a sense of relief as well as indulging in a bit of spin. The workload was punishing in this period, and the band barely had a break before they were off on tour around the U.K. again, and then across the Atlantic. In terms of gig numbers, the latter was more than twice the size of the original band's U.S. tour, and with more headlining, Crimson now being a much bigger name. However, while they were there a sadly familiar story began to unfold. Firstly, long-building tensions with Sinfield led Fripp to finally dispense with his services in December 1971. He felt forced to act, saying, 'One of us has got to go and I'm not leaving', and the result of all Sinfield's angry pushing for a bigger say meant he now didn't have any say at all. While it wasn't quite on the Lennon-McCartney breakup scale, it was an acrimonious end to a major partnership, and the bitterness and resentment would linger for a long time. This was a significant moment in both their careers, Fripp breaking his last connection with the original line-up, and Sinfield having to find a way of plying his trade without the vehicle of Crimson. Fripp would later acknowledge that, without Sinfield, Crimson would never have happened, but where the band was now was no longer appropriate for the lyricist. As he returned to England, Sinfield's departure coincided with the release of *Islands*, but checking its progress in the chart did nothing to cheer him up. The wiggle room Crimson earned from the legacy of *Court* had by now vanished and, commercially speaking, *Islands* fared the worst of the Crimson albums to date, only briefly troubling the lower reaches of the U.K. chart early in 1972. As with all Crimson releases, it would have its avid fans, but *Islands* would not tend to be listed amongst many fans' favourites. The reality was that those who loved the more adventurous and colourful rock of this period had a great many other places to go for music that didn't require them to have to work so hard. [11] [12]

Worse was to come. If Fripp had thought that demonstrating his power by sacking Sinfield would put an end to the internal band conflict, he was very much mistaken. It only set up the contradictory situation that while he was trying to be more dictatorial, he actually ended up feeling outnumbered in his own band. Wallace observed years later that the evolving line-up had unintentionally pulled the band's direction away from where Fripp really wanted to go, and although Fripp was open to many influences, the very different directions the parties were pulling were proving almost impossible to accommodate within one band. Whether he was putting on a brave face or not, Fripp gave an interview to the music paper *Sounds* in November 1971 and was seemingly happy about the band and its new album. Encapsulating Fripp's confused feelings, they discussed the fact that on tour the band had performed *Court* in a mocking blues cliché style. *Sounds* reported that McDonald 'was understandably upset when he heard what they had done with his song', which may have been journalistic licence, but as the song was part of the anything-but-blues repertoire that made the original band what it was, McDonald would not have been the only person who would have been weeping at this turn of events. Fripp's response to being told this was to say that they were considering doing 'an album of Crimson songs the way they shouldn't be done', including a reggae *Schizoid Man*, but mercifully this was just a throwaway line. As well as musical differences, the big personality differences between the intensely intellectual Fripp and the other three, who were inclined to just relax and enjoy themselves, was creating a feeling of distance between them. As their differences subsequently grew too great, Boz, Wallace and Collins all resigned, but confusingly all then agreed to do the remaining leg of the U.S. tour! Through doing this, they began to change their minds about leaving, but found it was too late. Fripp was already looking elsewhere. [9] [13]

After two months at home, in February 1972 Crimson headed back out to the U.S. for that remaining tour, on bills sandwiched between the godfather of British blues, Alexis Korner, and bluesy proggers Humble Pie, who had already established a big following across the States. American sound engineer Hunter McDonald was hired to fill Sinfield's shoes at the mixing desk, while for lighting they had to settle for using whatever happened to be at each venue. Being surrounded by blues musicians each night suited Collins, Wallace and Boz down to the ground, and they would take whatever chances they could to get together with Korner and Humble Pie's Steve Marriott, to jam in local hotel bars before and after each gig. After the final gig, in Birmingham,

Alabama, Fripp simply returned home, while the others stayed in America, partying for weeks with the other musicians they'd met on tour and forming a band with Alexis Korner and Peter Thorup. Fripp subsequently asked Collins to stay on in Crimson, but even *he* could no longer face working with him. In a 1997 interview with Chris Groom, Collins made it clear that he felt at the time that 'it was either leave or be destroyed'. Taking this into account, and Boz later letting on that he thought the lyrics he'd been singing with Crimson were 'gobshite', it's hard to see where Crimson Mk II could have gone next. Fripp, meanwhile, was living his own version of *Groundhog Day*, recording an album, then losing most of the band and being back to square one. This time, though, he was left completely alone. [14] [15]

In March 1972, after a couple of months of feeling low and pondering his future, Sinfield linked up with Roxy Music as producer for their first album. Roxy were under the same management as Crimson and were big fans of the band, although they were playing arty, glam-tinged pop rather than prog. They had initially wanted Fripp to produce the album, but the timing wasn't right, so they instead approached Sinfield. Their line-up included Brian Eno who, in addition to being known for his flamboyant dress sense, was more of a sound manipulator and experimenter than any kind of conventional musician. Sinfield found him annoying at first but later began to feel that they were two of a kind as regards their roles within their bands. The album would sell well and help set Roxy on the road to success, though Sinfield found the job a struggle, and suffered much criticism for his production efforts. Roxy had never been in a studio before, and for all their ideas, they were all still learning their trade, something that was in stark contrast to the well-honed skills in Crimson to which Sinfield was accustomed. From his point of view, he simply made the best of what he was given to work with, the process all being crammed into just ten days. As the album was due for release, Roxy and Sinfield went back into the studio to record a single, *Virginia Plain*, which was put out shortly after and tagged on to later editions of the album. Aided by glittering TV appearances, this is the song that began to cement Roxy's place in the public's consciousness, peaking at No. 4 in the U.K.

As if things hadn't been challenging enough for Fripp, what Island Records did next was inexplicable. In 1972, driven by the urge to get a live Crimson album out, they decided to release a budget-priced album of tracks from the final U.S. tour of the *Islands* line-up. The problem was that the tracks were taken from cassette tape recordings, and while cassettes were about to become indispensable for home hi-fi use, their quality was significantly lower than reel-to-reel tape. Because of this, the five-track *Earthbound* album was of noticeably poor sound quality, to the extent that Atlantic Records refused to release it in North America. Its leaning towards lengthy improvisations and the inclusion of a long drum solo plastered in effects meant that there wasn't room to include much in the way of fan pleasers either, other than *Schizoid Man*. To round off the disastrous decision making, it came in a dreary, mostly plain, black cover. As with every Crimson release, it has its fans, but Fripp himself even attempted to get the album deleted at one point. The crime has since been put right several times over, through digitally cleaned-up archive releases of this line-up, but to this day *Earthbound* is widely seen as the worst album put out under the King Crimson name. This, however, didn't stop Genesis drummer Phil Collins from citing that Wallace was his favourite drummer that year!

Crimson Mk II existed for about the same time as the original band but has struggled for credibility over the years compared to other line-ups. It's telling that, despite his praise for *Islands* at the time, by the noughties, Fripp could only bring himself to say that 'the jury is still out on this Crimson'. Wounds would ultimately be healed, except between Burrell and Fripp, and tracks from this phase, that would be neglected for decades, would eventually be recalled and revitalised, acknowledging that, while this wasn't a particularly happy time for the band, there was still a good legacy of material. In fact, it's a terrible shame that Crimson's music of this period is so tainted by bad relations. Earlier members were by now scattered to the four winds and generally happier to be out of it. Notably, though, after the commercial flop of his album with Giles, McDonald largely sat out this period beyond having the satisfaction of playing sax on T-Rex's No. 1 single, *Get It On*. Perhaps Lake was the only one truly smiling from ear to ear, with ELP going unstoppably from strength to strength. Ultimately, Fripp would look back on this as a time that he just had to get through, not that he had any idea what was on the other side! In the meantime, he was again bandless and somewhat slightly dazed, now without even Sinfield as an ally. He still didn't want to call it a day with Crimson, if possible, as he knew the band name still had a towering global reputation, even if his personal image was getting rather tarnished by the turmoil that seemed to follow him around. [9]

# 4

# No Pussyfooting

## *Mid-1972 to 1974*

Over the next couple of years prog-rock would hit its commercial peak, in amongst a colourful mix of glam, heavy rock and jazz-fusion. It's a time that's often looked back on with a fair amount of disdain and ridicule, due to the indulgence and excess of some, and the dubious fashions of many more. But given the calibre of music produced by Crimson and the likes of Pink Floyd, Mike Oldfield, Bowie and Herbie Hancock, a few dodgy stage outfits and overlong solos can be forgiven. At the beginning of this phase, Fripp was back home in England and having to start from scratch once again, with a world-renowned band in name but no actual band. From the outside this seemed like a sizeable negative, and there were fleeting moments when Fripp considered abandoning Crimson. In the end, he took this as a chance to reset, and he did so in no uncertain terms, and after the nightmarish instability of the previous two years, the next two would be relatively stable in Crimson terms. With a startling change of direction, almost on a par with that of GGF to Crimson Mk I, Crimson Mk III would mark an end to Fripp being dragged to places he didn't want to go. Increasingly abandoning conventional track structures and chords—not that early Crimson had been a slave to convention—this was the beginning of the rest of Fripp's music life, setting a course that would underpin much of the rest of his career. Sales would still be good enough to keep the record company happy, but more importantly, the material produced would be widely regarded as matching, if not surpassing, that of the original band. It would also give Fripp a more lasting sense of personal satisfaction. Of course, things wouldn't run smoothly for long in the Fripp world, and having put in the hard work, he would throw it all away in an extraordinary fashion. Away from Crimson, ELP would continue to ride their incredible wave of success, Boz would find a happier home in a successful new band, and Sinfield would embark briefly on a solo career.

The reviews of *Earthbound* had barely subsided in the music press when, in July 1972, Fripp was able to announce a surprising new line-up. The process for forming Crimson Mk III involved a mix of chance meetings, recommendations and negotiations, followed by a series of casual jams of sub-groups to see how people worked together. But this was more than simply finding another batch of willing musicians. A line was being firmly drawn under the past, and you could say that this was; the start of an entirely new band that just happened to have the same name. Another significant change was that Crimson had so far been a vehicle for people to go from obscurity to the big stage. Fripp was now finding that he could attract people away from other successful bands. He started by turning once more to his Dorset connections, tempting an old Bournemouth College friend, John Wetton, away from the band Family. The twenty-three-year-old, originally from Derbyshire, had come close to joining during the *Islands* line-up, when he and Fripp had stumbled across each other back in Dorset. With the others in the band at the time saying that they wanted to stick with Boz, Wetton didn't want to step into the middle of a band he could see were heading for turmoil. In the intervening time, Family's records had been selling well, and they had made several TV appearances around Europe, including the cringingly titled German pop show, *Hits A Go Go*. Wetton had bigger ambitions though, and with Fripp offering him the chance to be vocalist, and bassist and to be involved in the writing, the time was right to say yes. Having also been a vocalist in his teenage band years, Wetton was ready and willing for the traditional dual Crimson role.

Edinburgh-born percussionist Jamie Muir became the first non-Englishman to join, bringing with him influences of American jazz drummers, a passion for improvisation and experimentation, and an unmissable Dali-esque moustache. He would add an extraordinary array of sounds, mixing conventional percussion with almost anything else he could get a noise from. Fripp's interest in him was a sign of the radical changes coming. Having learnt several instruments in his youth, including piano and trombone, Muir settled on being a percussionist. He moved to London in the mid-sixties to play a short residency run by Lindsay Kemp, the man who would later famously teach mime to Bowie. He decided to stay in London, forming the Music Improvisation Company, a five-piece outfit that mixed sax, guitar and avant-garde electronics with his own brand of percussion; the group putting out a couple of highly experimental albums. Muir had been one of the hordes who had seen Crimson Mk I in Hyde Park in 1969, and as his interest in rock grew, he formed a band called Sunship in 1971, with young guitarist Allan Holdsworth playing what Muir describes as 'art-music'. They would never make it as far as studio recording, however. In the summer of 1972, during a Sunship rehearsal, Muir received a call from Fripp, who had been pointed in his direction by a music journalist. The call was to ask him to join Crimson, and much to the displeasure of the rest of Sunship, he eagerly accepted, relishing the prospect of being involved in the more intelligent end of rock music.

But while Fripp was excited by Muir's ideas, he needed a second drummer to play the straight man, relatively speaking. The drummer he got was by far the biggest surprise of the new line-up—Bill Bruford, who had been tempted away from Yes. Born in Kent, Bruford started on drums at the age of thirteen. While everyone around him was seemingly hypnotised by The Beatles and The Stones, he would spend the next few years absorbing jazz, particularly American drummers Max Roach and Art Blakey. After briefly experiencing the world of conventional work, having a hand in building a stretch of the Sevenoaks By-Pass, he turned pro as a musician at the age of eighteen. By the mid-sixties Bruford had gained more of a taste for those who were blending jazz with rock, such as John McLaughlin and Jack Bruce. They played what he called 'a terrific kind of high-octane crossbreed', and he learnt from them that there was no need for a distinction between the genres. It was considered a surprise for him to switch bands, as Yes had only recently released *Close to the Edge*, their third U.K. Top Ten album in succession, and had had a hit single on both sides of the Atlantic with *Roundabout*. The twenty-three-year-old was therefore jumping ship from a band he'd co-founded, just as they were achieving what they had set out to achieve! Bruford later joked, 'Much more of this and I would have turned into a rock star'. His reasoning was that, much as he loved it, *Close to the Edge* had taken three months of agonising and indecisive night sessions to record, and he just couldn't go through anything like that again. He'd also grown tired of band arguments and over-indulgence in alcohol, having suggested the album title because it reflected the state the band were in during its recording. Leaving Yes proved expensive in the short term for him, parting with equipment, cash and a share of album royalties to compensate the others for gigs that had to be rearranged. In the long term, however, it was worth it, not only to join Crimson but as he also avoided being involved with *Tales from Topographic Oceans*. When he'd seen Crimson in 1969, he'd thought, 'These people knew something I didn't, and whatever it was, I wanted to know it too'. In the meantime, he'd viewed the band from the outside as 'a darker and more mysterious organisation', and had, in effect, been stalking them, going to their gigs, buying their albums and even bending Fripp's ear whenever the opportunity arose. This was especially the case when Crimson had supported Yes in the U.S. in 1971. To him, Crimson was the ultimate gig to aspire to, and he could see the possibilities for developing himself by playing alongside the older Muir, their relationship regarded almost as that of teacher and pupil.

He found he'd got the job after Fripp dropped in for a seemingly casual jam, which turned out to have been an audition. [1]

In a line-up of surprises, the final one was Fripp's signing up of twenty-three-year-old violinist David Cross, who he had overheard rehearsing with an unsigned band called Waves. The son of a piano-and-organ-playing father, Plymouth-born Cross had started with music even earlier than Fripp, buying a second-hand violin for £1 at the age of nine. After studying the classics and becoming his school's rugby captain, he went down a more formal musical education route, studying music (and drama) at college and becoming the leader of his college's orchestra. His band experience to date had only been with a variety of obscure folk-rock groups, so joining Crimson would be a dramatic step into the limelight for him. While a violin would be a new weapon in the Crimson armoury, there was a growing trend of rock bands having a violinist in their line-ups, such as Darryl Way in Curved Air, Eddie Jobson in Roxy Music and Jerry Goodman in the Mahavishnu Orchestra. Fripp's explanation for this change for Crimson was that he'd simply had enough of saxophones. Cross's role would be to add extra colour, not only on violin but also doubling on keyboards, in some ways acting as a counterpoint to what Muir would be throwing into the mix.

The new line-up would also need someone to supply lyrics, and Wetton knew just the man to ask: Richard Palmer-James. Palmer-James was yet another Dorset man, one who had been a guitarist in local bands alongside Wetton in his youth. By 1969 he was playing in a prog band called Daddy, who shortly after changed their name to Supertramp. As no one else could be bothered, he knocked out some words and found himself becoming the band's lyricist by default. Supertramp's debut album was released in the summer of 1970 to that familiar tale of good reviews but poor sales. Palmer-James decided that he'd already had enough of disagreements with his bandmates, and by the end of the year had left to begin a new life in Munich, a city he'd liked the look of while on tour. He committed to take the lyric-writing more seriously, studying how others approached the task, and now, courtesy of his friendship with Wetton, would have the chance to put what he'd learnt into practice for a major band. His role in Crimson would be very different to Sinfield's, only supplying lyrics from a distance when requested, and with none of Sinfield's other duties. The brief he was given by Fripp was simple: 'anything but love songs'. [2]

While musicians were still queuing up to join Fripp, Viv Albertine, who would later become known as the guitarist in an all-female punk band, The Slits, was less than charmed by her encounter with him in 1972. Her boyfriend, pianist Jan Hart, was a friend of Fripp's, and took her to meet him while they were all in Bournemouth for a weekend. At eighteen, she was excited to be meeting a famous musician who was on a record in her collection, but she didn't get the welcome she was expecting. Instead, on walking into the room that Fripp and his friends were in, she recalls that he just looked at her while commenting to Jan, 'You shouldn't have broken up with Sue. She was great. Much better'. For the rest of their time in his company, Albertine believes that Fripp didn't so much as look at her, let alone speak to her. [3]

While constructing another all-new Crimson, Fripp was also unknowingly at the beginning of a new partnership, this one with Roxy Music's Brian Eno. That relationship was to prove long and fruitful, and as influential on him as his early Crimson years. In one of those casual-but-pivotal moments in music history, the pair first met across a mixing desk in the summer of 1972, Fripp producing an album for Robert Wyatt's Matching Mole, that Eno was guesting on VCS3 for one track. Considering where their partnership would lead, it's notable that Fripp and Eno's first collaboration, on *Gloria Gloom*, produced long, almost ambient opening-and-closing sections, book-ending a track with mock-inane party conversations and light-hearted left-wing musings from Wyatt. Although the pair had common ground in terms of pushing boundaries and ignoring conventions, they were, in other ways, quite different. In contrast to Fripp's guitar virtuosity and growing abilities as a writer, Eno considered himself an experimenter, going as far as describing himself as a 'non-musician'. Although this was always something of an exaggeration, to a large extent his role in Roxy was not as a musician in any conventional sense, but to add treatments to the other's sounds and voices. While this is a commonplace part of production now, it was a rare, mysterious art at the time. The Suffolk-born twenty-four-year-old was also something of an extrovert, appearing onstage with Roxy dressed in outrageous glam style, with glittery clothes, lots of make-up and, at times, even feathers; Fripp, by contrast, was more sombre and restrained, both in appearance and manner. None of this would matter, though.

Coincidentally, Eno had lived for a while in a shared flat in the road parallel to where Crimson had been formed; he had since bought his own spacious flat just down the road, in Maida Vale, a place. Eno biographer David Sheppard described as his 'domicile-cum-recording studio-cum-love nest'. Being impressed by Fripp's approach as a producer, Eno invited him over and introduced him to a tape-repetition system he'd been trying out. Since his days as an art student in Ipswich, Eno had become an avid collector of recording equipment to aid his experiments, and the particular system he wanted to show Fripp consisted of two reel-to-reel machines together, with tape running from the right reel of one machine to the left reel of the other. By doing this, the tape would pass over the record head of the first machine and then the play head of the second, resulting in the sound being repeated as if in a loop. New sounds could be continually added, the delay between repetitions being variable though changing the distance between the two machines. It wasn't an entirely new idea, having been used by the likes of Terry Riley since the early sixties and, to light-hearted ends in 1970, by Pink Floyd on *Alan's Psychedelic Breakfast*, however, Eno could see there was great potential for further experimentation. Fripp was sceptical after their first dabblings, but Eno persisted and convinced him to give it a further try. As Crimson Mk III were beginning rehearsals, that September Fripp took his guitar and some effects pedals round to Eno's flat to give it another try. Eno's persistence proved justified, as, using Fripp's directly input guitar as the only sound source, the pair recorded a genuinely ground-breaking piece that mixed layers of repeated sounds and sequences with overdubbed solo guitar. While their earlier efforts had been interesting at best, this time they knew they had put down something special. As significant as the recording was, though, Eno had unwittingly bypassed the usual level of expectation Fripp had for the musicians he worked with, getting him to take seriously working with a non-musician. Fripp had already been ploughing unconventional furrows, but Eno was now drawing him into a new world of possibilities. [4]

The track, which they would later name *The Heavenly Music Corporation*, seamlessly melds raw experimentation with technical ability. It starts in minimalist fashion, with three minutes of dronings of fuzzed/sustained notes, before Fripp's overdubbed solo guitar makes its entrance, in the style and sound we'd only heard before on *Prince Rupert's Lament*. Through the rest of its twenty-one minutes, the backing runs through sequences of layered wailings and dronings, created by Eno from notes and phrases from Fripp's guitar. These provide the backdrops for more solo guitar, which slips between grandeur, drama and questioning tones. It eventually passes into an end section of eerie, machine-like swooping sounds, which slowly vanish into the distance. It was daring and imaginative, and a radical departure from what either of the pair had done before. On its own, though, it wasn't enough to release, and with both having band commitments to get back to, its fate would be left hanging. Over time, the casualness of its creation would get a little exaggerated, and listening to Fripp in subsequent interviews, you'd get the impression that he just stepped into Eno's flat and they knocked it out while downing a bottle of wine, with Fripp not having a clue what Eno was doing. Startlingly original though the piece was, its roots can be traced back to experimental musicians such as Cornelius Cardew, Terry Riley and La Monte Young. Riley's *Poppy Nogood and the Phantom Band*, released in 1971, while bypassing most of the population, had been a huge inspiration to those who lived on the musical fringes, with its twenty-plus minutes of tape manipulation and echo experiments. Eno himself had been part of the recording of another seminal piece, by Cardew, also in 1971. As a teenager, Eno had met Cardew when he was teaching at a South London art college, becoming one of his small troupe of devotees and later being involved with a loose collection of personnel known as The Scratch Orchestra, who would record some of Cardew's works. As a result, Eno was one of the many voices on *Paragraph Seven*, part of a larger work called *The Great Learning*, inspired by sixth-century B. C. Chinese philosopher Confucius. Cardew's method was to give out simple instructions to the participants, such as short pieces of text to sing, and how frequently to repeat them. Everything else was left open, including pitch. Much of the 'composition' was therefore left to chance and to how the participants reacted to each other. Cardew's imaginative approaches had made a deep and lasting impact on Eno and he was now, in effect, passing on these influences to his new guitarist friend.

Through the circles of the weird and wonderful Fripp was now mixing with, he was introduced to the occult, and the nebulous concept of wicca, by a pagan white witch, Willi Elmlark, who is said to have exorcised one of Bowie's homes! Fripp was so taken by these ideas that he recorded a spoken word album with Elmlark, creating a backdrop of music alongside percussionist, Frank Perry, and using a tape loop sequence from Eno. While the album, *The Cosmic Children,* would never be released and the tapes subsequently lost, Fripp's interest in non-mainstream belief systems would bubble away in his mind as he returned to his main business.

With just five weeks of writing-and-rehearsal sessions under their belts, the genuinely exciting new Crimson Mk III went on the road in October 1972, warming up in Frankfurt before touring England. Predictably jettisoning much of the old repertoire, except of course for *Schizoid Man* and, rather unexpectedly, *Peace—A Theme*, audiences once again found an almost entirely different band, with different instrumentation, playing radically different music, much of it improvised. According to Muir, improv would be a major part of this Crimson's approach to composing, starting with loose jams and playing until something useable began to evolve, when Fripp would impose more of a structure. It was a formula that seemed to pay dividends from the outset. However, it wasn't so much the new ideas that were the early talking point, but Muir onstage. Steve Peacock of *Sounds* described him as 'the wild one' with 'fur wings on his boiler suit', at times leaving his percussion 'to writhe around the stage' or 'run screaming through the audience'. Cross has said that he 'nearly died' when he saw the percussionist's onstage antics for the first time, which at their most extreme included swinging chains around his head and spitting blood. This was not quite what the others had been expecting, as he hadn't done that in rehearsals. As for Muir, he has said that he was just as surprised himself, getting so caught up in the excitement of the performance that he would go further than he'd intended. While it was a coincidence that Fripp had begun working with Eno and Muir at around the same time, the gentle influence of Eno probably helped to open Fripp up to Muir's ideas even more than he otherwise might have been. Now the serious work was under way, Bruford felt he'd made the right move, even though he would find himself facing criticism from both Fripp and Muir. He chose to use this positively to shake up his thinking. In fact, he revelled in where it was making him go, later saying, 'For me, the excitement in music lay partly in making people's heads turn, slightly unsure of what they'd just heard; in doing it differently the following night (in which I managed to annoy a lot of bass players); in imagining possible futures for drumming. In short, to contribute'. [5] [6] [7]

Giving some rare insight into touring conditions, Bruford found Crimson's to be a small but noticeable step up from Yes—not that he'd had to slum it too much with them. 'In the early days with Yes, there were rough hotels, but I think I only shared a room on a couple of nights with Tony Kaye, who was perfectly pleasant. The rest of the time I had my own room, thank the Lord'. According to the drummer, some unwritten rules of etiquette quickly evolved, especially in Crimson: 'The only inviolable rule on the road is that you don't come into my room and I don't go into yours unless invited. The space is sacrosanct. After living in each other's pockets all day, the travelling performer tends to need time out. That carried over to breakfast, which I liked to take alone, as did Robert. We never shared breakfast, just acknowledged each other across the buffet'. As well as the inherent risks that came with racing up and down the country on Britain's early motorways, Bruford found there were other pressures that came with these more intense levels of band activity. 'We whiled away three hundred miles in a van with nothing but a book and some gossip, immediately hitting the next hotel room with a phone for two hours of steady phoner previews, interviews and, if there was time, family, before the soundcheck'. It was the way it had to be, and they just rolled with it. [7]

With the difficulties of the previous line-up forgotten, and only a few shocks from Muir to worry about, Fripp took his new band into Command Studios in Central London in January 1973. A few weeks later, the result was *Larks' Tongues in Aspic*, a six-track concoction produced by the band, worlds away from anything that Fripp had been a party to before. The album is a blues-free, rock convention-free, horizon-broadening artistic adventure. It would still fall under the description of 'prog', but a *different* prog, one that bore little relation to Crimson Mk I, and none at all to Mk II. On *Larks'*, the more recognisably rock elements were surrounded by all manner of atmospheric diversions, sound experiments and the sort of time signatures you would usually find in jazz. In contrast to the previous two albums, Fripp was now very much present throughout, in terms of playing, although the rest of the band were given free rein to express themselves and contribute. As well as the mix of personnel and the new approach, another factor looming like a mountain in the background, prompting, inspiring and challenging Fripp to get his guitarist act together, was the growing stature of jazz-fusion band the Mahavishnu Orchestra, led by one of Fripp's own heroes, John McLaughlin. Probably the closest in sound of any other band to this phase of Crimson, they were making their own huge impact. In an interview that Fripp himself conducted with McLaughlin in the eighties, he claimed he would deliberately avoid listening to the Mahavishnu Orchestra through the seventies, to avoid imitating them. Whether or not this was completely true, their albums would be lined up, side-by-side, in many a long-haired young man's record collection. Bruford, however, didn't avoid the Mahavishnu Orchestra's albums, loving the explosive drumming of Billy Cobham.

Fripp's reading list in the last year had included the theories of Joseph Schillinger, a Russian composer-turned-music professor, who would later teach in New York. His ideas, from decades earlier, aimed to shake things up in terms of methods of composition, freeing the composer from the shackles of tradition by introducing simple maths into the process in relation to scales, melodies, harmonies and rhythm. On the surface, this sounds as if it could be very dry and produce mechanical-sounding results. However, its effect was to broaden the possibilities available in the right hands. Schillinger died in 1943 at the age of forty-eight, although his work continued to be promoted by his widow and was subsequently developed by Vincent Persichetti and Nicolas Slonimsky. Fripp was far from being the first to incorporate such thinking, with such diverse composers as Debussy, Gershwin, John Barry, and closer to the rock world, even John McLaughlin using elements of it. The most immediate and obvious incorporation by Fripp was to use sequences changing key at regular intervals using a particular number of semi-tones, creating an impact very different from the well-worn rock or blues changes. In the coming years, with this type of thinking becoming a significant element in his writing, he would also come up with riffs that seemed to evolve as much out of maths as music, but in his skilled hands would result in something with extraordinary power or emotion.

Fripp always liked to play down the bandleader tag, describing himself as more of a facilitator. But while others in the band always had significant input, as it could only exist with Fripp's say so, with his being the others' employer and having the final say on everything, this was always splitting hairs at best. There were, however, some interesting insights from the others in the band into how things worked at this time. If there had been any doubt about who was in charge, Muir was unequivocal on the subject in an interview in the nineties, saying, 'Fripp was definitely the boss, there's no question about it, and that was fine. He seemed to me to be a very good band leader'. Bruford found that while Fripp set the mission that the band was on, what the mission actually was was never stated. The rest were somehow just supposed to know, or as he put it, Fripp was 'in possession of some arcane or possibly occult knowledge to which the rest of us weren't privileged'. Of course, Fripp didn't entirely know either, but he had a strong instinct about what fitted and what didn't, when he heard it. However, while *Larks'* was put together under the firm guidance of this new Fripp, it undeniably bears the stamp of all participants. [6] [1]

The album opens uncompromisingly with the thirteen-minute *Part One* of the title track, a multi-sectioned mix of improv and structure, credited to all five members. With a disdain for commerciality that would have alarmed their record company, it takes almost three minutes before anything even vaguely like a rock track appears. Those opening minutes are filled with a jumble of glockenspiels, kalimbas and percussion, the influence of Muir apparent from the outset. The more structured sections—and the first signs of Schillinger—feature tense, pulsing layers of violin from Cross, with guitar from Fripp oozing around them like a metallic serpent, the whole thing periodically exploding into a sort of misshapen heavy rock. With no vocals on the track, Wetton makes his impact with his bass, in places playing it through a wah pedal, creating a sound that blends perfectly with the violin and guitar, and is especially stunning in the end sequence. The mix of arty dabblings with heavy rock, classical and even a short, serene Japanese section, was quite a feat. With much multi-tracking of Muir, Cross and Fripp in the studio, it was tricky to re-create live, although this didn't deter them from opening their sets with a shortened version. The track and album title, suggested by Muir, derived from a dish eaten in medieval Europe (bird's tongues preserved in a sort of jelly), has been assumed by many to be a play on Vaughan-Williams's *Lark Ascending*. With violin phrases that could be interpreted as echoing phrases in the Vaughan-Williams piece, and even some bird song in one section, it seems a reasonable assumption. Nevertheless, the band has always maintained that this was just a coincidence.

The subject of the mellow *Book of Saturday* is a troubled young romance described through a series of analogies. Both percussionists take a break here, and we are introduced to the rich tones of Wetton's voice and the first Crimson lyrics of Palmer-James. Generally fitting his words around the band's ideas, Palmer-James's style would prove much more down-to-earth and contemporary than that of his predecessor. Cross solos sweetly in the middle, while Fripp fills the spaces with backwards guitar. The most emotional impact comes from the third track, *Exiles*, which is to a large extent Cross's baby, contributing the main theme and playing flute, piano and mellotron, as well as violin. It starts with a collection of eerie noises created by Muir, brooding signs of life then emerging from this primordial soup, in the form of a sequence recycled from Fripp's 1969 idea, *Mantra*. Cross's gentle melodies are then given space to develop and flow before being echoed in the verses by Wetton. The subject of the lyrics is left deliberately vague but there are clues that it's written from the point of view of an Eastern European dissident finding himself succumbing to the indulgencies available in his adopted Western home. However, just like taking the outer layer off a Russian doll, inside are Palmer-James's feelings about living away from his own home country, and the track carries off the feat of having a suitably Crimson-epic feel, but with a more personal perspective. A solo by Fripp rounds it off, using a fuzz/sustain sound modified by a wah pedal—some of the feel of *Heavenly Music Corporation* now feeding into Crimson.

Opening side two, *Easy Money* swaggers in with Wetton's wordless vocal over Fripp's two-chord power riff and a clanging bell. Lyrically, it's not an entirely serious song. Describing the sleazier side of the rock world they were inhabiting, with Wetton sometimes using alternative lyrics live, referring to drugs and sex with under-aged girls. The joy of the track however, is the myriad of percussion and playful sound effects, such as the sound of unzipping, added by Muir, taking his cues from the lyrics. Slowly appearing out of wind, congas and whirring noises, created by Muir twirling hosepipes around his head, *The Talking Drum* is seven minutes of build-up around a repeated bass line and no chords. The band gradually move up through the levels, with Cross's violin taking the lead while Fripp's guitar murmurs away in the background. Ultimately, a guitar phrase bursts out and Wetton switches in the overdrive and wah on his bass. Then, with nowhere left to go, it's brought to a halt by ear-piercing screeches. Jointly created through improv, it's a perfect example of how a track can form around minimal written components. Because of its potential for being different with every performance, it would be a band favourite for live shows. Although not featuring on the track, the title derives from a drum used in West Africa that mimics vocal sounds.

The album closes with *Part Two* of the title track, a seven-minute instrumental that would become an integral part of Crimson live sets. While Cross's violin is again the lead instrument for much of the track, this is solely a Fripp composition. There are hints of Stravinsky in places, and also perhaps Vaughan-Williams again, but what really makes this track stand out are the highly original sequences in 5/4. With a riff played on guitar and violin, these climb and climb through angular, Schillinger-inspired, key changes, which alternate with changes on Wetton's bass, creating a magical mix of warmth and tension. This type of sequence was to be a powerful new tool in the guitarist's expanding armoury and would make several appearances in the coming years. Whereas *Sailor's Tale* had been a raw early sign of the emerging new Fripp, here he began to nail down what Fripp the guitarist and writer was about, finally having something he'd written entirely himself that ranked alongside *Schizoid Man*. He was later prompted to start legal action against the makers of the film *Emmanuelle*, famous for its sex scenes, when part of the track was used in it. (The matter was settled out of court.) Ironically, Radio Four journalist Andrew Collins included the track in his 2006 list of 'the top-ten worst tracks to have sex to'!

The release of the album in the spring of 1973 provoked a predictably wide range of reactions for something so radical. Of the more negative reviews, the *Melody Maker*'s Richard Williams thought its 'ultimate failure' was due to its 'acceptance of compromise'. *Rolling Stone*'s Alan Neister at least had the presence of mind to defer judgment. Even though he found 'it doesn't even make good background music for washing the dishes', he knew that challenging records like this 'sometimes offer the most rewards and lasting pleasure in the long run'. At the other end of the scale, *Let It Rock*'s Chris Salewicz saw it as 'a near perfect miracle piece of vinyl', while the NME's Ian McDonald understood that Crimson 'plays to explore, not to pass the time'. McDonald also used an abundance of interesting and appropriate adjectives for Fripp, seeing him as a 'civilised hippie', 'truly eccentric' and 'daft and sex crazed'. It hadn't exactly been a make-or-break situation for Fripp, but the album helped to restore the faith, even if it left some a bit baffled, and it ultimately peaked at No. 20 in the U.K. The design for the cover features a tantric symbol made up of an interlocking sun and moon with faces. Produced by Tantra Designs, while it had a hippy feel, it very much suited this post-hippie era album. [8] [9] [10] [11] [12]

Two things happened in the weeks between finishing the recording and its release. Firstly came Bruford's wedding, with members of Yes and Crimson amongst the guests. Other than the marriage itself, the event was notable for Jamie Muir introducing Jon Anderson to the work of a yogi, Paramhansa Yoganada, he had become interested in, which is said to have inspired Anderson to write the concept album, *Tales from Topographic Oceans*. Secondly, Crimson Mk III had its first casualty, though for once not because of poor relations with Fripp.

Muir had already grown to hate touring, feeling that he wasn't being heard adequately in the mix because his assortment of items was not all miked up. Despite being part of only around forty gigs, the band's roadies for their part had already grown tired of the amount of kit they had to assemble and then pack away for him each time. The final straw came when Muir accidentally injured himself during a gig in February. He had to drop out of the next couple of shows, then realised that he couldn't face the prospect of the months of touring that loomed ahead and decided to jump ship. As he'd been developing an interest in Buddhism, he instead headed for a Tibetan monastery in Scotland, where he stayed for several years. It was a blink-and-you'll-miss-it episode in the grand scheme of Crimson, but Muir's influence is all over *Larks'*, taking it to places it otherwise would not have gone. As a free spirit valiantly channelled by Fripp for a few months, perhaps it simply had to be just a brief partnership. Muir himself has said, 'I think I was a wee bit too much for him', but that 'it was a very admirable creative decision to actually work with someone like me'. Bruford had mixed feelings about Muir's departure. 'You know when you're in the company of powerful people' he would later comment when asked about Muir, seeing him as a visionary and a strong personality. But although he learnt a lot from him, he felt Muir had been unkind to him about his abilities, and so wasn't too sad to see him go. The pair never said goodbye and never crossed paths again. Muir would only dabble in music intermittently in the following years, eventually selling his equipment and focussing on being a painter. Crimson would, of course, continue, but even by this point it wasn't all sweetness and light amongst the remaining four. [13] [14]

The tour schedule for 1973 was full on, including a total of five months in North America, split by a few weeks of summer back in Blighty. These tours, while high on excitement, came with their own quirks and vagaries. For example, even bands of Crimson's standing had to use scheduled flights for the longer distances, with their equipment all having to be crammed into the hold as extremely expensive excess baggage. Despite this, Bruford recounts that it was made quite a relaxed process for the musicians: 'In the 1970s U.S. air travel was exceedingly cheap, and this was pre-metal detectors. So, we could get up and leave the hotel late, no more than an hour before the flight, receiving a boarding pass acquired by the road manager who had gone ahead with passports and checked us in. [We could] walk straight on to the plane; no identification, no security, no delay in the smooth flow from hotel lobby to airplane seat'. There was a downside to it all being so casual as Bruford found that 'an itinerary was seldom seen' and, to an extent, their managers 'just made up the travel arrangements as they went along'. [7]

Between legs of the North American tour, Cross, Wetton and Bruford all took much-needed holidays. Fripp, however, decided to use the time for writing new material in solitude, taking a guitar, amp and notebook down to his home in Holt, a stone's throw from Wimborne. This change of situation worked well, and he emerged three weeks later with around half an album's worth of ideas, including the mind-boggling intricacies of what would become *Fracture*. He viewed sacrificing his chance of a proper break as preferable to spending more time than necessary writing with the band, as he knew what was coming! Musically, this line-up might well have been more fulfilling, but when it came to internal relations it was the same old story. When Fripp came to look back on this phase decades later, he described this Crimson as being 'inherently unstable', and 'not a comfortable place to be'. When the band got together for rehearsals in Kingston in South-West London, the sessions 'set new standards of horror', according to Fripp. Bruford more specifically described a 'simmering hostility' between Fripp and Wetton, which seems remarkable so soon after Fripp had given Wetton such a big opportunity. Fortunately, touring helped to relieve the bad feeling, and that relief was just a few weeks away. An innovative plan was also forming in Fripp's mind as to how to use the forthcoming tour to further minimising the time the band would have to spend in close proximity in the studio. [15] [1]

In a later break from touring, Fripp returned to working with Eno in that August. While this would be a relaxing diversion for him, for Eno there was a sudden urgency, as he'd just angrily left Roxy Music. Despite Roxy's success, Eno's personal popularity with fans and the media had become increasingly bruising to Ferry's ego, to the extent that he had been talking to teenage prodigy Eddie Jobson about taking Eno's place. With relations having broken down between them, and Ferry said to be unwilling to wield the axe, Eno took matters into his own hands and announced at a press conference that he was leaving. In debt, band-less and without any coherent plans, Eno needed some new career options, and fast. Fortunately, his record company kept the faith and offered to back him in starting a solo career, however. Pursuing the experimental ideas he had begun to explore with Fripp, while not too promising commercially, seemed like a good place to start. They booked themselves into Command Studios, where Fripp had just completed *Larks'*, partly for the better facilities a proper studio offered, but also because Eno's flat was currently out of bounds to him after a bust-up with his girlfriend. After knocking around a few ideas, the pair completed a second, long instrumental piece, with Fripp again soloing over a backdrop of layered repetition. The repetition this time was constructed from jangling guitars, a bubbling-and-squawking VCS3 and a piano phrase reminiscent of Tchaikovsky's *1812*. Finding a picture at the studio of naked women giving Nazi salutes, they named the new piece *Swastika Girls*.

This new track became side two to *The Heavenly Music Corporation*, with the two pieces released in November 1973 as the album *No Pussyfooting*, the name deriving from a note Fripp had left for himself on his pedalboard. It very nearly didn't see the light of day, as presented with two long tracks with no vocals, no drums, no bass and no discernible rhythm in any conventional sense, Island were reluctant to release it. Although Fripp and Eno were both saleable artists, the company felt that this unusual offering would confuse fans about their artists' directions and harm sales of subsequent Crimson and Eno albums. Their respective standings gave them a more privileged position than other experimenters. Island yielded, putting it out in the U.K. at a discount price, presenting it as a novelty item rather than a piece of avant-garde artistry. Getting a release in North America was even trickier and would take a couple of years more to achieve. Journalists didn't know what to make of an album of distorted guitars, but which didn't sound like rock, and it got poor reviews. It was even said to be disliked by Fripp's bandmates but, surprisingly in retrospect, it did chart briefly. For much of the record-buying public, though, even a public that was lapping up *Tubular Bells* with its two side-long tracks, *No Pussyfooting* was a step too far. It did get a little airplay, most notably from Radio One DJ John Peel, who, using a tape copy, accidentally broadcast the whole thing backwards. No one is thought to have noticed except for a Mr. B. Eno of Maida Vale who phoned the Beeb to inform them of their error! A re-release in the noughties commemorated this by including backwards versions as bonus tracks. Despite the moderate sales, for several reasons *No Pussyfooting* was almost as important as *Court* for Fripp, as it opened the door to a different area of music and was a precursor to a whole swathe of his later output. The significance for Eno was even more immense, the album later seen as proto-ambient because of what followed for him. Even allowing for the Riley, Cardew and Young roots, it was a genuinely innovative album, and because this relatively mainstream pair of musicians had put out something so experimental, it shone a light down an unlikely avant-garde avenue and gave a boost to those who inhabited such avenues as a matter of course. Sales have continued to trickle along over the years since and, though it still divides opinion, it maintains its status as a reference point for new generations of fans of more left-field music. While it may not have made anyone rich, *No Pussyfooting* was quite possibly the cheapest album ever made prior to the home-computer era. With *Heavenly Music Corporation* costing just the few pounds Eno had to spend on reel-to-reel tape, the only significant costs were for the four days' studio time needed to record and mix *Swastika Girls*.

Matching the ground-breaking music, they pulled out all the stops for the cover, which cleverly echoes the repetition in the music. The front shows the two musicians playing cards in a room with mirror walls, the photo taken from an angle that creates numerous repetitions of the image tailing off into the distance. Notably, it was the first time since GGF that Fripp had allowed himself to appear on one of his album sleeves. Based on an idea of Eno's that mimicked a sixties art installation by Lucas Samaras, this was created by rising star of fashion photography Willie Christie. To create the scene, Christie asked a builder who was working on his house at the time to assemble a three-walled mirror room for him at a Maida Vale photography studio. Eno then filled it with assorted items, including a fireplace and a clear plastic mannequin; Christie's wife, however, supplied the most apt object, a guitar-shaped mirror. The back cover was the same as the front but without the musicians, echoing an aspect of the music that once the system is set up, the performers can leave, and it just carries on by itself. On the original cover, the title was put in brackets, suggesting it was merely a provisional one, though some later editions would drop these. Bridging the two strands of Fripp's work, *Heavenly Music Corporation* would serve as Crimson's entrance music on tour during this period.

Also that November, between legs of the latest Crimson European tour, Fripp again made time to work with Eno, contributing guitar to three tracks of his first solo album. Eno was on his own steep learning curve, having to reinvent himself as more of an actual musician, vocalist and writer, with the added bit of motivation to get it right that Roxy's first album without him, *Stranded*, had just been released and would soon hit No. 1 in the U.K. With a limited budget he was in the cheapest studio in town, in a converted theatre in Clapham High Street, but on the other hand he had the goodwill and assistance of many musician friends, including some from Roxy, which proved absolutely vital for him. The album was named *Here Come the Warmjets* (a reference to urination) and was released in January 1974, distinct from Roxy but still in art/glam rock territory. Of the tracks that Fripp is part of, *Baby's on Fire* is the stand-out, Eno singing two verses of cynicism and bitchiness over a mechanistic rhythm of hi-hats, bleeping electronics and two basses, one of which was played by Wetton. Fripp steals the show, however, letting rip with a wild, heavy, fast-echoed solo, punctuated by dramatic pauses just long enough for feedback to build before he plunged back in. The track was later given a boost by being singled out as a personal favourite by Bowie and would feature in the soundtrack to the 1998 film *Velvet Goldmine*. Fripp and Eno co-wrote the more humorous *Blank Frank*, with Fripp adding a machine gun-like, Bo Diddley–esque guitar solo over the tracks. Fripp's third contribution was on the less memorable *Driving Me Backwards*. Thankfully, the reviews were good, and initial sales saw it get into the lower regions of the U.K. top thirty. Eno's solo career could easily have taken an instant nose-dive, but was, instead, up and running. According to David Sheppard, the sessions also provided Fripp with a new girlfriend, Mandy, one of Eno's many women friends, who had taken a liking to him while at the sudios.

Having seen how Roxy Music had made an album with fairly basic music skills, Sinfield gave in to his urges to have a go himself. Fortunately, he hadn't burnt his bridges with his former bandmates and could call on a long list of Crims and others to help him with the recording. This took place through the winter of 1972–1973, with Collins and Lake in particular helping shape the project. With Sinfield covering most of the vocals, some guitar and synth, and much of the writing, his album, *Still*, was released on ELP's new Manticore label, but passed by all but the most diehard Crimson fans, falling into curiosity territory. Sinfield had, in essence, been trying to demonstrate that he was capable of creating something on a par with Fripp, but for the most part he fell short, slipping all too easily into a mix of hippie-trippiness and being strangely middle-of-the-road. The best-known track is *The Song of the Sea Goat*, which incorporated some Vivaldi melodies, with Collins, Wetton, Wallace and Tippett forming the backing group. With its meaning buried beneath a mountain of poetic allusions, it's quite possibly about Sinfield himself and how he's moving on to something new post-Crimson. With Collins as part of Sinfield's band, it was performed on the BBC's *Old Grey Whistle Test,* a much-loved TV showcase for 'serious' rock music. Also shrouded in cryptic Sinfieldisms is *Envelopes of Yesterday*, the clues poking out from mists here suggesting that this is a more bitter variation on his feelings about parting company with Fripp. While grumbling that he was treated as if he needed him to survive, again he professes to want to put it all behind him and to have thrown away the letters that were in those envelopes. As a follow-up of sorts to *Cat Food*, the bluesy *Wholefood Boogie* shows a different side to Sinfield. Featuring Lake, Wetton and Collins, here Sinfield preaches the virtues of whole food over the overly processed products filling our supermarket shelves. More appealing to his general Crimson audience, *The Piper* is a taste of light, hippie folk, Collins and his flute in effect playing the title role. The fake Welsh accent Sinfield adopts here (and, to a lesser extent, elsewhere) works within the context of this song, though is bizarre considering that he isn't even partly Welsh. The high point is Sinfield's reviving of *Under the Sky*, which he wrote with McDonald in their GGF period, this version being even more pleasantly dreamy than the Dyble-sung original. The title track, which closes the album, splits the vocals between Sinfield's lost-in-poetic-thought verses and epic choruses from Lake, and for better or worse we get the epitome of Sinfield's more hippie-style lyrics here, such as wondering about being a tree. It's a largely forgotten episode between Sinfield leaving Crimson and taking up an offer to write for ELP, but for a while he gave the solo career a serious go. As well as the album and the TV appearances, he toured Europe with a backing band that included Collins, supporting Italian prog band PFM. Sinfield also wrote lyrics for PFM, full name Premiata Forneria Marconi, which translates as Award-Winning Marconi Bakery. Seeing which way the wind was blowing, the solo career was abandoned. and he focussed on his strength of lyric writing.

In the summer of 1972, ELP brought out their third studio album, *Trilogy*. Crimson's sales may have been on a downslope, but the public's appetite for Lake and Co. was undiminished, the album reaching No. 2 in the U.K., and No. 5 in the U.S. A highlight is their version of contemporary composer Aaron Copland's *Hoedown*, a fast-paced organ-and-synth workout showing off Emerson's virtuosity. The ELP juggernaut rolled on into 1973 with some heavy-duty touring, the band investing in a disused cinema to use as a rehearsal space. The latter was done not only for convenience, but so they could develop new material in a live-performance setting. It was a sign of the excess that ELP would become known for, but if your albums consistently hit the top five and your tours sell out, you can get away with that sort of thing. Indulgence or not, their strategy kept the ideas flowing, resulting in their fourth studio album, *Brain Salad Surgery*, released that November. It again reached No. 2 in the U.K., and peaked at No. 11 in the U.S., ultimately gaining the band their first gold disc in the U.K., and their fourth in the U.S. The three showmen continued with their unique formula, opening with their take on the Blake/Parry anthem *Jerusalem*, featuring Emerson playing the first polyphonic synth, the Moog Apollo. The first Sinfield lyrics for his new employers appeared in *Benny the Bouncer*, a light-hearted affair about a doorman at a dance hall who comes to a sticky end and finds himself working the door for St. Peter in heaven. At almost thirty minutes long, *Karn Evil 9*, which also incorporates Sinfield's lyrics, was ELP's longest studio track, the title simply being a play on the word carnival. The trio then headed back out on the road for their biggest world tour to date, which continued well into 1974. There was still no sign of their commercial bubble bursting; however, ELP then needed to take a long break from one another, all agreeing to put the band on hold.

Following the break-up of Crimson Mk II and his stint with Snape, Boz Burrell was looking for a new band again in 1973. Falling on his feet, courtesy of the instrument he'd been persuaded to take up by Fripp, he passed an audition to be bassist for the newly formed Bad Company. Formed by the ex-Free duo of Paul Rodgers (vocals/keyboards) and Simon Kirke (drums), with Mick Ralphs (guitar) from

Mott the Hoople, and named after a 1972 western, this was to be a hard-edged, blues-loving rock band. The omens were good, with the band being the first to get signed up by Led Zeppelin's label, Swan Song, and. when Led Zep were unable to use a mobile studio slot they'd booked that November, the band dived straight in, completing an album in just two weeks, joined on some tracks by Mel Collins on sax. They began gigging in England in March 1974, moving on to America shortly after, just as their eponymously titled debut album was released, racing up to No. 3 in the U.K., and No. 1 in the U.S. Their approach has been described as stripped-down, and this was reflected in the album's mostly black cover, with just *Bad Co.* in big, bold type, diagonally across the middle. Stylistically, there was no link to Crimson, not even Boz's edition. Bad Company were rock 'n' roll plain and simple, flirting with rock clichés with a heavily American slant, but doing it knowingly and doing it well. Their debut single that summer, *Can't Get Enough*, got to No. 1 in the U.S., and No. 5 in the U.K., earning Boz and friends their first prestigious *Top of the Pops* appearance. There would be plenty more to follow.

The sixth King Crimson studio album, *Starless and Bible Black*, was released in March 1974, Wetton lifting the title from Dylan Thomas's 1950s play *Under Milk Wood*, a film version of which had recently been released. Put together by the quartet of Fripp, Wetton, Bruford and Cross, the most unusual thing about this album is that a large portion of it wasn't recorded in a studio at all. Notes accompanying the 1997 archive release, *The Night Watch*, a recording of their November 1973 gig in Amsterdam, highlighted that six of the eight tracks on *S&BB* were wholly or partly recorded live, four of them that night. Although they neglected to mention this on the cover, it was never a secret, as anyone not too stoned to take it in would have heard Fripp announce in Amsterdam that the gig was being recorded for use on the next album. The band took the concert tapes and, where necessary, overdubbed extra instruments or re-recorded any parts that weren't deemed good enough, also removing all crowd noise. The only downside, unforeseen back in 1974, was that when they came to use the concert tapes more than twenty years later for the archive release, it wasn't always possible to distinguish which parts were from the concert and which were overdubs. Worse still, some live parts had been recorded over. Also not immediately obvious on *S&BB* is that four of the tracks are live improvisations, improvs being an established feature of Crimson gigs, and the results are often highly imaginative. The band had one vital rule onstage for these, according to Wetton, that that 'if one person went out on a limb, the rest would follow', so they would sound as if they were working together. While Fripp's motive in using these for the album was to minimise studio time and the potential for band conflict, he inadvertently blurred the distinction between live and studio. Fripp would express interesting views on Crimson studio albums in general in the coming years, particularly that, to him, they were not a 'final statement' on the material but merely 'provisional . . . however definitive [they] may seem in retrospect'. The mix on *S&BB*, while not obvious to most listeners, was therefore an intriguing concoction of provisional statements of differing natures. Fripp's supposed motives just didn't wash with Bruford, though, and he has been scathing about the disguised use of live improvs here, referring to a 'spectacular shortage of material' and tracks 'born of desperation'. He even went so far as describing it as 'subterfuge', wondering if it was related to lower royalties being paid for live recordings. [16] [6] [1]

The changes between *Larks'* and *S&BB* highlighted the double-edged sword of Crimson's instability. The constant turnover of personnel meant that no line-up had yet had the chance to develop from one album to the next. On the other hand, it did mean that things kept moving on, and the dynamics between the band members shifted each time. While the personnel had only changed by one person this time, the collapsing of relations between Fripp and Wetton—not helped by Wetton's use of cocaine—had pushed Fripp into more isolated writing, and the more arty, abstract, Muir dimension had gone. Feeling more tightly constructed, despite all the improv, *S&BB* is also up a notch or two in heaviness, Wetton becoming increasingly assertive, if not aggressive, with his bass, pumping up the volume and overdrive. Cross's response to this was to use a lot more distortion and wah on his violin, and at times it can be hard to distinguish it from Fripp's guitar. With Wetton also now getting more involved in the writing, Cross was beginning to be squeezed out, with no writing credits on *S&BB*, other than where they were shared for the live improvs. The end-result of this new mix of dynamics and creative tensions was that they explored, as Fripp put it, 'places where other musicians of that rock generation mainly avoided'. They 'looked into the darker spaces of the psyche and reported back what they found', which is, after all, what people would want King Crimson to do. Fripp also came up with the perfect sound bite for the quartet, saying that 'this band could be disturbingly powerful . . . and powerfully disturbing'. [15]

The opening two tracks of side one were the only entirely studio-recorded tracks on the album. In stark contrast to the opening of the previous album, *The Great Deceiver* is loud, tightly constructed and charges in at breakneck speed with a glorious violin/guitar riff. Mixing Palmer-James's words with a couple of lines from Fripp—the first time Fripp had written lyrics for a Crimson song—*The Great Deceiver* in question is the devil, the phrase coming from sixteenth century philosopher René Descartes in his *Discourse on Method*. Descartes's work included his famous 'I think therefore I am' line, where in trying to find a baseline of absolute certainty from which to build, he wonders if everything that he thinks he sees is actually an elaborate hoax being played on him by the great deceiver. The rest is relatively cryptic for Palmer-James, with American references—dipper-ride, Cadillacs, Dixieland—creeping in. Easing off the pace, *Lament* is one of the tracks Fripp wrote the music for in his Dorset solitude. Here we find a rock guitarist looking back to his heyday when he wowed sell-out crowds and the songs just flowed. Although the track was performed at Amsterdam, a studio version was deemed necessary, and is much stronger. The first of the live improvs, *We'll Let You Know*, from a gig in Glasgow, is perhaps the most successful of the improvs used on the album, almost sounding written. Fripp sets the ball rolling with some guitar harmonics that hang in the air. The others initially go along with the atmospheric feel, until Wetton takes things by the scruff of the neck with some punchy bass, setting Fripp off in a playful funky blues direction, which the rest then respond to. As with all the improvs used, this would end up as a hybrid of stage and studio, as they took the opportunity to tweak the mix and trim off unwanted parts at the beginning or end, to give it a more polished feel. It says a lot about this Crimson's collective standard of musicianship, imagination and mutual understanding, that tracks like this were good enough to stand in for written studio material. [17]

Palmer-James's lyrics for *The Night Watch* were inspired by the seventeenth-century Rembrandt painting of that name, depicting a company of Dutch militiamen. This very un-rock 'n' roll subject matter was turned into something very Crimson, as the lyricist affectionately mixed history with his own imaginings of the men's circumstances, the Netherlands then in a war of independence against Spain. The recording is partly from the Amsterdam gig, although much had to be re-recorded after Cross's mellotron broke down and scrambled the recording of other instruments. There's some mild irony that this particular track went wrong at that particular gig, Amsterdam's nearby Rijksmuseum being the home of *The Night Watch* painting. The finished article was, in the end, far better for being re-recorded, as some of the instrumentation was changed and Cross was able to play more parts. Wetton's warm rendering of the words is interwoven with archetypal guitar lines from Fripp and an understated solo. There's also an instrumental section where Cross's keyboards take the track in a mock-Japanese direction, which works beautifully despite being at odds with the Dutch Old Master theme. It ends reflecting on how the painting preserves a passing moment, and the statements the men were making about themselves, the painting being commissioned by The Watch's Captain Cocq. A band photo-shoot subsequently blended the Dutch Old Master theme with their hippie, glam look, with the four gathered round a mock-up of a candlelit feast. Three of the band kept that look on stage too, however, Bruford was now favouring the comfort and more youthful look of dungarees!

*Trio* is another live improv, this time from Amsterdam, where Bruford decided he would stay silent throughout, indicating this to the others by holding his drumsticks across his chest. This left Fripp (mellotron flute), Wetton (bass) and Cross (violin) working through a delicate idea, with a hint of *Stairway to Heaven* about it, which magically appeared between them on the night. Bruford was generously credited as a co-writer alongside the other three; hence, he receives royalties for keeping quiet! The track is also interesting for revealing, once again, how different things can appear from the perspective of the performers to that of the listener. According to Cross, by the time they reached Amsterdam they were all very tired, and he remembers they had just hit a particularly low point in the gig. A core professionalism kept them going to the extent that, rather than forlornly going through the motions, the audience were still given an inspired performance. Another improv-based track, *The Mincer*, taken from an earlier show in Zurich, finishes side one. This was given an extra dimension by Wetton overdubbing a few lines of vocals and harmonies in the studio on a rhythmic section. The piece goes from darkness to a lively, almost jazzy feel in the space of just four minutes, ending abruptly as the tape ran out on the live recording.

Side two ended up being entirely instrumental, consisting of just two long tracks, although this wasn't the original intention. The first of the pair, and the album's title track, is the second live improv from Amsterdam. The band had been knocking around a Wetton song idea that would have borne the name *Starless and Bible Black*, but this ended up being rejected, and a live piece was instead drafted to fill the space and acquired the title. The improvs used on the album are quite varied in tone and format, however, partly because of the instrumentation and the inevitability of discords, these nightly adventures could feel quite dark, and this is very much the case with *S&BB*. Its inclusion tips the album's balance too far towards improvs rather than written material, but it is nevertheless an interesting nine minutes, with Cross switching between various keyboard sounds and violin, while Fripp's guitar seethes and howls. *Fracture*, which closes the album, is the last of the pieces Fripp came up with in his Dorset solitude. Another of the tracks recorded at Amsterdam—albeit with some parts replaced in the studio—this is the love child of heavy rock and geometry, with Schillinger and Persichetti as godparents—Fripp also citing the influential Austrian composer, Schönberg—and is eleven minutes of compositional triumph. While there is maths behind the notation, it is, by turns, playful, intense and brooding, stalking you in the dark, waiting to pounce, its complex arrangement of riffs and angular key changes feeling like an evolution from ideas explored on *Larks'*. After about seven minutes it teases you by seemingly winding down to an ending, then hitting you with such an explosive end sequence that you are left breathless, Bruford throwing in his trick of shifting into 4/4 during a 5/4 riff, to great effect. Fripp considers *Fracture* the hardest of his own compositions to play and using the live-recording method for such a complex piece meant there were a couple of moments where they strayed off script, and it has that slightly rough-edged feel you get from a live recording. A song the band had been playing live for several months, *Dr Diamond*, failed to make the cut, despite the shortage of written material. With the fastest singing Wetton ever had to tackle, and Mahavishnu-esque leanings in the music, it went through much tweaking over time but still failed to make the grade. Although, on the surface, this is about an Underground train driver, it was another Palmer-James analogy for the devil, and perhaps one too many for this album. Live recordings of it would eventually see the light of day, and in 1997 Palmer-James himself recorded a version with Wetton.

*S&BB*'s front cover is relatively plain, with the title and band name in stencilled writing over a smudge of watercolour on an otherwise-white background. The intrigue was saved for the back, where in amongst the track names and credits is a small box containing a seemingly random section of text from a book. Designed by artist Tom Phillips, the text is painted over except for one word from each line, leaving the enigmatic phrase, 'this night wounds time'. Whether it affected album sales or not is hard to say, but *S&BB* came out during a period of economic and political gloom in Britain. It was a time of high inflation, industrial disputes and the three-day working week, a restriction imposed on businesses by the Conservative Government of Ted Heath, desperate to save fuel and avoid blackouts after a huge increase in the price of oil. Arty new albums were perhaps an indulgence some decided they would have to forgo for the time being, and even with the help of a BBC radio broadcast of the Amsterdam gig, it only reached No. 28 in the U.K. The album was, again, largely well received, with several tracks that could be considered (say it quietly . . .) commercial, even if, as a whole, it still leant towards the uncompromising. Deeply powerful though it is, its material would be rather unfairly overlooked, partly because of the improvised nature of much of it, but more because of what had come just before and what was yet to come. [18]

Always in demand elsewhere, Wetton temporarily joined up with Bryan Ferry in the spring of 1974, for the recording of the Roxy frontman's hit solo album, *Another Time, Another Place*, and hit single, *The In Crowd*. Though just a sideman here, this gave Wetton a window into the kind of commercial success he desired but wasn't getting in Crimson. He could easily have jumped ship and found plenty of other willing partners; however, he decided against doing so, despite the rising tension with Fripp. Several months more Crimson touring then followed, to showcase the parts of *S&BB* that they could, while pushing on as ever with new ideas and, notably, a resurrection of the original *Starless and Bible Black* song idea, getting an opportunity to perform it in its entirety on French TV.

Just as it looked like the Crimson story might finally be running smoothly, events were about to blow things apart. Firstly, towards the end of the tour, Wetton had started pushing for Cross to be fired. The others eventually agreed, and at the end of the U.S. tour, he was shown the door, reducing the band to a trio. The reason given by Fripp was that the band's increasingly heavy direction was less suited to a violin, and it had clearly become much harder for Cross, a much milder personality than the forceful trio around him, especially in the nightly battle with what Bruford describes as 'the muscularity of the rhythm section'. Cross had found himself being pushed increasingly into being more of a keyboardist, and this had made him feel less of a proper part of the band. Crimson could be a cruel testing ground for a young musician, and, in retrospect, he was treated quite unfairly. He was also perhaps a victim of faddism, the era of the rock violin now rapidly fading away. Still only twenty-five, Cross was jettisoned back into obscurity after only two years. He would soon be able to take consolation in the fact that events would make all that irrelevant, as for Wetton and Bruford there was a massive shock in store. [1]

In July 1974, the day before the remaining Crimson trio were about to go into the studio, Fripp started reading the book *Is There Life on Earth?* by philosopher and scientist John G. Bennett, from an organisation called The International Academy for Continuous Education (IACE). What Fripp read had such an immediate and immense impact on him that it would mark a major turning point in his life. As he later put it, 'The top of my head blew off! It simply became apparent to me . . . that I would have to leave [the band] even though the following day we were to begin recording *Red*'. Bennett regularly wrote and lectured about a philosophy that had become known as The Fourth Way, based on the teachings of the Russian George Gurdjieff, earlier in the twentieth century. At the core of the philosophy is the premise that people live their lives in a state of waking sleep, but by following a path to self-development, a far greater level of consciousness is possible. The philosophy also puts emphasis on the environment, seeing the human race as custodians of the biosphere, and it was Bennett's focus on this that blew Fripp's mind. Bennett believed that environmental, economic and social collapse was rapidly approaching for the human race and was being brought about by what he called the 'dinosaur civilisation' that twentieth century society had become. To Bennett, the dinosaurs were the big companies and major industrial nations with great power but little intelligence in terms of looking after their long-term survival. What he suggested was that society needed to reorganise into new kinds of communities, focussing on sustainability and greater understanding of nature. From an individual point of view, this meant needing to become far more self-sufficient. This viewpoint had been reinforced by the publication of E. F. Schumacher's much-acclaimed *Small is Beautiful*, with its message that the economies of the Western world were unsustainable. The backdrop for all this was the energy crisis of the early seventies, where a massive oil price hike had caused turmoil and the economies of the industrial nations all stalled. With environmental concerns beginning to be taken more seriously across the world, as well as the debate about the heavy reliance on oil, this was a huge wake-up call for the West, and made forecasts of disastrous scenarios, as prophesied by the likes of Bennett and Schumacher, seem all too feasible. [19]

With Bennett's ideas stirring vigorously in Fripp's mind, Crimson went into Olympia Studios in London through July and August to record studio album number seven, the core band supplemented by a host of guests to add the extra colour. Fripp was already a changed man but chose not to mention his sudden enlightenment to the rest of the band. The others noticed a definite change in his approach, though, with his being noticeably more accepting of their offerings than usual, almost to the point of indifference, but they couldn't understand why. Fripp later described feeling that he had lost his ego, and for several months simply didn't feel justified in having an opinion. In contrast, Wetton later told Will Romano, 'Bill Bruford and myself knew exactly where it was going. We took the front seat and pushed for that very up-front, in-your-face guitar'. Nevertheless, nobody foresaw what was coming, when with the album barely complete, Fripp announced to an astonished world on the 24th September that Crimson had 'ceased to exist'. A few days later he gave an interview to the *Melody Maker*, where he explained why he had done the unthinkable. He didn't cite Bennett by name, referring only to 'one contemporary philosopher', but he had clearly taken his ideas to heart, and breaking up the band was just the first stage of applying this new thinking to his own life. Viewing the world from this new perspective, Fripp believed that the big players running the music industry were amongst the dinosaurs, and even major bands like his were in danger of being too unwieldy for the new world. In another interview, in *Rolling Stone* in December 1974, Fripp detailed how he was convinced that society would soon start collapsing 'on a colossal scale' in the manner of the Minoans (regarded as the earliest European civilisation), on what is modern-day Crete, around 1450 B. C. The crunch time was forecast to come in the 1990s, which would be 'a decade of considerable panic'. He added that 'the depression era of the thirties will look like a Sunday outing compared to this apocalypse'. Such was his sense of urgency that he believed that 'the transition between old and new has already begun. The old world is, in fact, dead and what we're seeing now is, if you like, the death throes'. To survive in this new world he felt he had to learn to be self-sufficient, and as regards his life as a musician, instead of having a band and ever-growing crew, he was going to transform himself into what he described as a 'small, independent, mobile and intelligent unit'. [20] [19]

In the *Melody Maker* interview, Fripp gave three other reasons for the break-up of Crimson. The first was to do with his personal education, saying that 'the education of King Crimson has taken me to this particular point, but it can no longer educate me in the manner I need to be educated'. This on the surface seems fair enough, as any artist can feel the need to move on to something different, but it would be fair to ask: since when was being in a rock band about education? He also highlighted how the time commitment necessary to be in a major band took its toll on the rest of his life. In recent years, he'd only managed to grab the occasional day to himself between rehearsing, writing, touring and recording, and he now found this too much. In fact, that one day before the *Red* sessions was his 'one full day off in the country' that year. Perhaps looking for the sheen of a more conventional reason for the break-up, he also threw in the good, old-fashioned reason of musical differences, saying that he was now feeling that 'perhaps it was too much of a compromise'. He described Wetton as 'a rocker', while Bruford had a 'detailed and meticulous approach', suggesting that they were pulling in different directions. Fripp went on to say that he felt the trio were together because there wasn't anyone else 'of the same quality and proficiency outside'. While the way he expressed it sounded rather contradictory, he was once again acutely feeling the differences between them and lost sight of their common ground. There were holes in Fripp's logic that you could ride a coach and horse through, but one way or another, Crimson was just not where he wanted to be anymore, and it was over. [19]

In the wake of this unbelievable turn of events, at the end of October the new album was released. Entitled *Red*, it was of staggeringly high quality. Ironically, given Fripp's state of mind, it exudes a far clearer sense of purpose than anything since *Court*, events having accidentally created an environment that enabled such a creation! The largely black front cover was the first to include photos of the band, showing the side-lit faces of Fripp, Wetton and Bruford. The back cover photo, of a volume meter on a mixing desk with the needle pushed into the red, gives us a clue to the otherwise-ambiguous meaning of the album title. On a simple level, it's telling us the music inside is loud and heavy, but also perhaps that the music is pushing the limits, or even that the band's members were feeling pushed into overload. It's the album's personnel listing that is the most fascinating aspect, however, as amongst those being thanked as guests are David Cross (through being on a live improv), returning guests Robin Miller and Mark Charig, but also two returning ex-Crims, Mel Collins and founder member Ian McDonald. Richard Palmer-James was not listed, despite supplying some of the lyrics.

*Red* is also the title of the first track of the five on the album, and is six minutes of unique, heavy instrumental. Here it feels as if Fripp has reached some kind of perfection, attaining a goal he has been reaching for over the last two years after working his way through *Larks' Tongues* and *Fracture.* Combining another collection of riffs to end all riffs, whatever else had been going on in Fripp's mind, musically the ideas were flowing. The opening arpeggio sequence climbs through a scale that no one else would have even thought of using, and on an album that would prove to be highly influential throughout, this opening alone would be echoed many times. As comedian and Crimson fan Stewart Lee pointed out in the *Sunday Times* in the nineties, Radiohead's *Just* 'lifts the guitar part of *Red* wholesale', while the colourful post-punk sophisticates Magazine pastiched it for *Shot by Both Sides*, as well as pastiching a distinctive bass part for *Permafrost.* Influence works in all directions, and elements of the track can themselves be loosely traced to the Mahavishnu Orchestra's *Meeting of the Spirits* and *Visions is a Naked Sword*, even if the influence was subliminal. Throughout the track, Crimson flit casually between time signatures and their now-familiar angular key changes, the core trio being so tight by this stage that they make the most complex sequences sound as if they're one entity moving together. The distinctive middle section that Fripp came up with here is simultaneously a thing of beauty and menace. For this, he drafted in a session musician to play a biting low-cello part, the classical instrument perfectly at home with the swirl of distorted guitars around it. [21]

*Fallen Angel*, another term for the devil, this time deriving from Milton's seventeenth-century poem *Paradise Lost*, shows more American influence filtering through, as Palmer-James's lyrics tackle the subject of New York gang violence. Miller adds touches of oboe in the verses, while Charig's cornet adds colour in the instrumental passages in amongst the weighty multi-tracking of guitars. The American themes continue with *One More Red Nightmare*, on this occasion the words coming from the pen of Wetton—a sign of his growing role and confidence—telling the tale of someone experiencing their worst waking-nightmare in a plane. Musically, its lineage is traceable to *Fracture*, especially the intro of Fripp-style heavy riffing and crunching Bruford percussion. After a couple of verses, a shift of time signature ushers in a McDonald sax solo that he is especially proud of before the final verse reveals that our hero has simply been having a bad dream while dozing during a Greyhound bus ride. Always on the lookout for something new to try, Bruford had found that he could get an interesting sound from a broken crash cymbal that he'd rescued from a bin at the studio. This features a lot on *Red Nightmare* and would become part of his kit until it was too damaged to use.

*Providence*—yes, the one in Rhode Island—which opens side two, is a live improv from the last American tour, named after the town in which it was performed. It was far from being a last resort but was used in the absence of any other new studio material being available. Cross's violin leads the way for the opening minutes in what is another imaginative variation on their dark explorations, Wetton using detuning and feedback, his bass becoming the lead instrument in places. The towering, gleaming treasure of this album—and some would say of the whole of Crimson—is the twelve-minute *Starless*, waiting patiently to be discovered at the end of side two. Written by Cross, Fripp, Wetton, Bruford and Palmer-James, but performed by Fripp, Wetton, Bruford, McDonald and Collins, this is what ultimately evolved out of the Wetton idea abandoned during the *S&BB* sessions, now with new lyrics and several new sections added. With the obvious title already spoken for, they opted for a shortened one for the much-amended version, which goes from inspirational beauty and delicacy, through jazz-fusion-style complexity, to nothing short of tear-inducing levels of power and emotion. Evoking a feeling of Crimson past, the long intro begins with sleek mellotron strings, followed by a beautiful melody, written and originally played on violin by Cross, but now played by Fripp in a spine-tingling-yet-understated fashion. The lyrics consist of just twelve lines but somehow seem to occupy a much greater space, describing feelings of bleakness and depression, Wetton mixing and matching lines from alternative versions with some of his own. As he sings what would be his final Crimson words, the music shifts and we enter the lengthy multi-sectioned middle. The basis of this is a bass line described as 'demonic' by journalist Nick Deriso, not written by Wetton but by Bruford, the drummer looking to contribute more to the writing, or as he put it, 'life past the cymbals'. He attributes his wanting to do this, to the influence of Yes frontman Jon Anderson, although not necessarily for positive reasons. 'He liked to distinguish between two types of musician: those who write the music and those who don't. Implicit here is the outmoded idea that the composer is in some way superior to the performer, with the performer as his or her mouthpiece'. For several minutes, the section switches between the unusual time signature of 13/4 and the more straightforward 4/4, with Fripp's guitar janglings climbing and building in intensity through each repetition, interspersed with train-like screeches and playful percussion from Bruford. Ultimately, it explodes into a fast-paced, heavy-jazz section, in an even more disconcerting mix of time signatures. But what all this is leading up to is the return, in the most breath-taking fashion, of the opening melodies, only this time a passionate, full-on reiteration with mellotron and sax. Many tracks use the device of returning to an opening melody after a long diversion, but this is one of those moments where the music feels like it's saying something unutterably powerful and touching your emotions without any need for words. If this was to be the final track of the final King Crimson album, there was no better way to go out. [16] [1] [7]

The album would ultimately be regarded by many as one of the best, if not *the* best, ever put out under the Crimson name. *Red*'s initial sales and impact were surprisingly moderate in retrospect however, the album only reaching the U.K. Top Fifty for a single week, while hardly registering in the U.S. With no touring to stir up interest, it would take a while for the world to begin to appreciate how stunning an achievement it was. Remarkably, it would also take Fripp quite a while to fully appreciate this himself, although Wetton and Bruford would suffer no such confusion. Some reviewers grasped what the album was about more than others, *The Belfast Telegraph*, for example, describing it as 'aggressive and loud enough to strip the wallpaper off your living room wall'. Others queried the lack of solos or found it ponderous in parts, in essence, criticising it for not being something it didn't set out to be. Powerful, intelligent and original, its status would grow immensely over the years, and while it may not have caused the instant explosion of a genre, it did begin to carve out new territory of weighty, yet thoughtful, more metallic prog, influencing a generation or more of musicians from the new wave era through to the nineties. Once enough time had passed for him to put the break-up behind him, McDonald would perfectly sum up the album as 'the best of the next wave of Crimson', also feeling that Fripp had 'found his voice . . . guitar-wise'. Back in 1974, with his remaining commitments over, Fripp took himself off to meet Bennett in person, attending a lecture at the IACE's U.K. headquarters at Sherborne House in Gloucestershire. This would be the only time they would meet, as Bennett was already well into his seventies and in poor health; he died just a few weeks later. His influence on Fripp would last a long time, though. [22] [20]

With hindsight, it's all too easy to see Fripp's breaking up of Crimson as an extreme over-reaction. However, he was a highly intelligent man, still only twenty-eight, who had spent his early adult years enveloped by the trappings of a major touring and recording band. The Fourth Way can perhaps be seen as filling a spiritual void in his existence and offering a more coherent approach for him to making sense of the world around him. To grossly oversimplify, you could say that this was Fripp's equivalent of the dabblings in Eastern religions of Western musicians such as The Beatles, Donovan, John McLaughlin and Carlos Santana. In some ways he (and the philosophy) wasn't so wrong, as decades on we generally take social and environmental doom-and-gloom very seriously—it's just that we see it as more of a slow-motion car crash. With distinct echoes of Bennett, in 2019 acclaimed veteran naturalist Sir David Attenborough warned of the collapse of society through the impacts of Climate Change. It's also inescapable that degrees of social collapse and world recessions do happen. Bennett's (and therefore Fripp's) timescales were all wrong, though, and he didn't seem to foresee that even his dinosaurs would act to mitigate, or arguably to just postpone collapse. And laudable though the sentiments are, expecting wholesale social change to some kind of *Small is Beautiful* style sustainability was hopelessly unrealistic and not necessarily desirable, as Fripp would learn in the coming years. All in all, his interpretation of what he was hearing was hasty and poorly thought through. Even the Minoan comparison was dodgy, as they are thought to have been devastated by a tidal wave caused by the eruption of nearby Thira, rather than any kind of economic collapse. For Fourth Way reasons at least, Fripp simply didn't need to break up the band. However, this is how things appeared to him at the time, and he acted as he thought necessary. In terms of needing a break from the rigors of his Crimson existence, that's an entirely different and more understandable matter. That version of Crimson was perhaps doomed to fall apart anyway, as despite the maturing of that remaining trio, other tensions were later revealed. Some of these related to payments, or the lack thereof, from their record company, but despite Fripp's more passive acceptance of others' offerings, there were also said to be negative feelings in rehearsals, once again showing how different things appear inside a band compared to a fan's perspective.

The ending of the band had serious consequences for the others who would have been part of the ongoing line-up. For McDonald, it was a bitter blow, having just committed himself to rejoining, Fripp having asked him to be part of the next American tour. McDonald had eagerly said yes, only to now find the band scrapped because someone had told Fripp the end of the world was nigh. Wetton, Bruford and McDonald suggested a few weeks of Crimson touring in Europe instead, either as one last hurrah or in the hope that Fripp would perhaps snap out of his current frame of mind. He was not for turning, though, dismissing the idea as impractical. McDonald suspected that Fripp had already decided he was going to break up the band when he asked him to re-join, as payback for him having caused the destruction of the original line-up. It's impossible to say whether there had been any desire for revenge lurking in Fripp's mind, but it seems likely that he only made up his mind on that fateful day before the *Red* sessions, keeping quiet about it for the duration of the recording. In the intervening years, while McDonald had been pottering around in the wilderness, Fripp had grown immensely in terms of being a writer and guitarist, so the chemistry and balance between the two would have been much changed had they continued. Events left that as another of the great Crimson what-ifs though.

Neither Bruford nor Wetton would be short of work, Wetton walking straight into a role with Roxy Music. Bruford, however, had given up a great deal to join Fripp, only to find himself left high and dry in terms of finding something of equal standing. Despite the trauma, the drummer has become quite sanguine over the years about the break-up and who was at fault. 'I think the assigning of blame is neither helpful, possible or necessary. Certainly, Robert was the only man who could start or stop the group, but I'm sure the several understandings between all three of us were sufficiently muddled as to precipitate cataclysmic change of some sort. Personally, I could have continued but, in retrospect, I was glad to be able to escape for some fresh air'. He had no shortage of offers of session or short-term work, and happily accepted some of these to keep the income flowing. Artistically, however, this was most unsatisfactory for such a creatively ambitious man. One of those jobs, and one which almost certainly seems funnier looking back, was filling in for two months of touring with hippie band Gong. A vacancy had appeared when the band's drummer was refused entry to parts of Europe after being caught in possession of certain substances. Although this was during what many believe was Gong's best period, on the inside Bruford found chaos, largely stemming from internal band relations, which disrupted the focus on the music. The tour was rounded off in Norway in December 1974, in a tour bus that was totally inadequate for Scandinavian winter conditions, and inevitably led to them getting stranded when it broke down. Nevertheless, the mid-seventies saw Bruford's personal reputation grow exponentially, his name bandied around by prog lovers with the kind of awe that was rarely used for the guy sitting at the back knocking out the beat, alongside the drumming elite such as Cobham and Palmer. Being just a jobbing drummer wasn't what he had in mind after the heights of Yes and Crimson though, and despite the acclaim, Bruford felt lost and lacking in purpose. [7]

By the end of 1974 it looked like it was all over for Crimson. In its five-and-a-half years of existence it had often been a troubled entity, albeit one that produced seven largely remarkable albums. It had gone through twenty-three personnel (including guests and lyricists), which is messy by anyone's standards, but whatever else was going on, in the last two years Fripp had settled into using many of the sounds and styles that we would come to think of as typically him. While the combination of working with Eno and the influence of McLaughlin undoubtedly shaped him in this period, he was indisputably his own man, and without his own ideas and remarkable strength of character, none of this would have happened.

Though never stated, Fripp probably came to regret having gone so public with his reasons for breaking up the band, especially the doom-and-gloom prophecy. It would take a while, but as time passed, he could see how others were seeing the world and pursuing their own livelihoods despite being aware of such pressing issues. In fact, by 1979 Fripp would be giving interviews that sought to shift the reasoning for the break-up to music based reasons, though he only made himself seem confused and contradictory, as well as simply being wrong. On the one hand he asserted that, 'Crimson has stopped evolving both in a commercial and musical sense', with 'a lack of strength in the music'. While on the other hand he explains, 'I never let Crimson fall into the success trap. I have always instinctively tried to avoid this success'—a clear case of facing both ways at once, and not having thought things through! But while there's no avoiding the dubious reasoning, going down this route opened him up to new perspectives and to possibilities in music and life in general, ultimately making him a more rounded human being than he would otherwise have been. It also compelled the others, now cut adrift, to explore their options and find different routes. The fog created by the Fourth Way factor made it harder to see, but this was an extraordinary period for Crimson. It wasn't so immediate, but as with Mk I, the influence of Crimson Mk III would also reverberate through the rock world for decades to come. All fans could do for now, though, was wait for the dust to settle and see what Fripp would actually rule in and out under his new way of thinking. [23]

# 5

# Disengage

## *1975 to 1977*

After the six extraordinary years he'd just been through, and still being only twenty-eight, was Fripp really ending the professional music career he'd worked so hard to achieve? By virtue of having no plans beyond a possible small tour with Eno and attending a lengthy Fourth Way course, the answer is could well have been yes! His interviews had explained much but there were still a lot of questions as to how this withdrawal would work in practice. He was clearly pulling back from the mainstream of the music business, as regards being part of an ongoing band, but he had specifically left the door open to production, session work, teaching guitar and even small-scale tours. He had enough money saved to live off for three years, but did he think the activities he'd still permit himself would earn him enough to live off after that? More importantly, would that be creatively satisfying enough for him? The truth is, that however certain he felt about his reasons for doing what he was doing, he didn't really have much of an idea where it was leading, but fortunately, what could have turned into a retirement would simply be a hiatus, and 1976 would be the only calendar year where there wasn't an album released with a significant Fripp contribution. However, having a reputation he could trade on for years to come, Fripp had earned the space to get away with behaving like this, and his pulling back from the music business at what was arguably the height of his individual powers would only end up creating another layer of intrigue around the man. And while no one could have forecast it, the next few years would turn out to be just as fascinating for Fripp as those that had got him to this point. But while he was withdrawing, others from the long list of ex-Crims were not about to leave the mainstream if they could help it, joining or forming bands, or being session men on high-profile singles and albums. And while this would be an era of massive shake-ups in the rock/pop world, supposedly shoving the old guard aside, you could scratch the surface of many successful records of this phase and find a Crimson connection. It could also be argued that one ex-Crim inadvertently set another prog band's drummer on the path to mega-stardom.

The body of the Crimson King was still warm when, in May 1975 Island put out a live album of tracks recorded towards the end of the last American tour of the Bruford-Cross-Fripp-Wetton line-up. Called *USA*, it was a welcome dose of the band to fill the void, not to mention actually being listenable compared to *Earthbound*, underlining what a remarkable live outfit Crimson Mk III were. The gig tapes they chose to use, from New Jersey's Asbury Park Casino, were said to need a few studio overdubs because of glitches, so with the parts in need of repair being violin and keyboards, through Wetton's Roxy Music contacts, they called on Eddie Jobson to help out. Six tracks made it on to the original vinyl release, opening with the now-obligatory *Larks' Tongues: Part Two*, and *Lament*, with Wetton's bass pushed up to grungy, dominant levels on the latter. In a strong version of *Exile*s, the live arrangement needed Fripp and Cross to juggle instruments throughout, each playing their mellotron while the other was engaged in playing his more customary instrument, one swap even coming in the middle of a section. A single vinyl album was a small vessel to squeeze live Crimson into, though, and the inclusion of a lengthy heavy funk improv, *Asbury Park*, in some ways seemed an indulgence, although it did have the virtue of capturing a vital aspect of the live Crimson experience. It also inadvertently captured aspects of what was wonderful and what was going wrong in this line-up. As a piece plucked out of thin air, it demonstrated their collective confidence and originality; however, for questionable reasons, Cross's playing was mixed out for the album, and all that was left of his participation was some barely audible mellotron picked up by other mikes. With Cross being ousted shortly after the tour, his being overdubbed or mixed out of four of the six tracks leaves an uncomfortable feeling. The album closes with *Schizoid Man*, with a decent performance, other than Wetton discovering that attempting to distort vocals live could lead to ugly results. An expanded and remixed re-release in the noughties corrected the imbalances by including two extra written pieces, *Fracture* and *Starless*, plus the full *Asbury Park*, with Cross's part restored. That remixed edition was created by engineer Ronan Murphy using a studio setup in his own living room while living in Seattle. Although much of his work for Crimson would be using digital recordings, at such times when he found himself handling old master tapes, he recalls that 'the combination of being objectively aware of the value of these old recordings and being a fan, made me nervous as hell for sure!' The album's predominantly blue cover shows a woman's hand holding a U.S. Army–style dog-tag with the words 'King Crimson USA' imprinted on it. This connected the album being from a U.S. tour and some lingering references to Vietnam in the material, with the suggestion that all that was left to identify the band by was its identity tag. On the back, there were no sleeve notes as such, just the three letters, 'R.I.P.'! Crimson was dead and gone as far as Fripp was concerned, a sentiment you could also draw from the fact that Wetton was the only one who made any effort to promote *USA*, doing the rounds of the music press. [1] [2]

Fripp had booked himself on to a course with the IACE, but for the few months before that started, he was happy to be part of a few small projects. Whether it was because he was about to disappear or despite this, in this limbo phase he would record some music that would rank amongst his best. Firstly, he returned the 'overdub assistance' favour to Jobson, performing on the Ferry/Jobson–written *As the World Turns*, which finds Ferry in crooning mode. This would appear as the B-side to Ferry's 1977 hit *This is Tomorrow*, a song featuring Wetton on bass. May 1975 also brought an unlikely echo of Fripp's years as a backing musician for cabaret artists when he was invited to play on a single for comedian Charlie Drake. Drake had been a singer before turning to comedy, becoming a regular on British TV in the sixties and seventies. He'd had a few hits in his early years, the best-loved being *My Boomerang Won't Come Back* in 1961, but at the age of fifty he felt the urge to be back in the charts. A new song, *You Never Know*, was written for him by Peter Gabriel and his lyricist friend Martin Hall, who then called up a few friends to record it. Alongside Fripp and Gabriel, the unlikely backing group also included Phil Collins, Keith Tippett, bassist Percy Jones and former Fairport Convention vocalist Sandy Denny. Other than Drake's squeaky voice, it isn't as strange a concoction as the mix of personnel might lead you to expect, the track being in the vein of the *Willow Farm* section of the Genesis epic *Supper's Ready*. Unfortunately, it fell between the two stools of comedy and 'serious' music, and when it was released that November, it failed to produce the hit that Drake had desired. [2]

While Fripp was taking time out to ponder his future, that January Eno had come horribly close to not having a future at all. Struck by a taxi while crossing the Harrow Road near his London home, he ended up in hospital with a nasty head injury. Over the following months he made a good recovery, accidentally coming up with the idea for what he would later call ambient music while at home recuperating and planning the mini tour that Fripp had referred to the previous October, to showcase their experiments. The pair had first talked about taking this sort of show on the road after doing *No Pussyfooting*, and with Fripp now at a loose end for the summer, the opportunity presented itself to make it a reality. Not overly ambitious, the tour amounted to just seven gigs from late May to early June 1975, around Spain, France and England; however, these were, in effect, the first, tentative outings for Fripp's small, mobile, intelligent unit. Described on some of their publicity material as a superstar show, fans who came along expecting some kind of Crimson/Roxy blend were in for a shock, as what they found was Eno playing prepared backing on tape or manipulating Fripp's live guitar to create backing, with Fripp soloing over the top. Their setup onstage was unusual too, with the emphasis being on a backdrop of projected images rather than on the musicians. Few would bat an eyelid at arty experimentation like this now, but at the time this was unusual, especially for such established artists. As for the musicians themselves, Eno looked rather like an art teacher, sporting a beret and long hair, while Fripp took on a slightly more sober appearance, with neatly trimmed hair and beard. Although each gig was loosely planned a few hours beforehand, there were no rehearsals as such, the emphasis being on improvisation. The length of the shows was left open too, depending on how they felt. It all got off to a shaky start in Madrid, when after only a few minutes the pair left the stage, leaving the backing tape running, much to the bewilderment of the audience. The rest of the overseas gigs were reasonably successful, except for St. Etienne, where they were booed off after technical problems added to the confusion. Returning to England, they performed at the Assembly Hall in Tunbridge Wells, and rounded things off at the London Palladium, surviving the pre-gig scare of a broken-down VCS3. Even by this stage, reviews tended to focus more on the fact that a few fans with false expectations had walked out, rather than on the music, and this light-yet-difficult tour had markedly different impacts on the two men. Fripp would successfully take an adapted format on the road again a few years later, while Eno would conclude that he was primarily a studio musician and would rarely play live again.

Having struck a rich vein of ideas and personal chemistry, whatever the highs and lows of their tour, the Fripp-and-Eno partnership offstage was alive and well. Within a few weeks of arriving home, Eno was in Island's Basing Street Studios in West London, working on his third solo album, and with Fripp still around for a few more weeks, he invited him to play on parts of it. Providing backdrops for Fripp had drawn Eno much more towards instrumentals and sound textures rather than the relatively conventional songs of his first two albums. Adopting this approach for his solo work, his new album, *Another Green World*, would have a much more laid-back feel, oozing with atmosphere and including some pieces that would be further stepping-stones on the path to his ambient albums. Having initially hit a wall of unproductiveness, he began to use Oblique Strategies, a set of cards he'd developed with artist friend Peter Schmidt, which suggest less obvious things to try in such situations, freeing an artist from their self-imposed restrictions. This worked well for him and the ideas began to flow, the album being finished with ideas to spare. Another Eno idiosyncrasy that proved successful was his use of unmusician-like ways of expressing what he wanted from other musicians. For example, on *St. Elmo's Fire* he asked Fripp to play in the manner of the jagged line of electricity produced by a device known as a Wimshurst Machine in London's Science Museum. Eno was developing a habit of getting the best out of Fripp, and what his methods brought out of him this time was a gorgeously flowing, uplifting solo using his fuzz/sustain/wah sound. In his sleeve notes, Eno went to town with descriptions for the instruments used, Fripp's guitar on this track listed appropriately as 'Wimshurst Guitar'. There were similar results on *I'll Come Running*, Fripp's part listed this time as 'restrained lead guitar'. This achingly romantic song also became the B-side to Eno's gimmicky cover of *The Lion Sleeps Tonight*, put out as a single before the album. On *Golden Hours*, with its theme of doubt and uncertainly, Fripp's guitar interlude is described simply as a 'Wimborne Guitar' after his hometown. The learning process between the two had been a two-way street, and on several other tracks Eno plays his own basic Fripp-like guitar, using similar sounds. The album went on sale in September 1975, selling too poorly to chart but getting a warm reception. That reception, and Island's different approach to artists compared to the more mainstream companies, saved Eno's solo career, and with its mix of lush, tropical sounds and textures, it lodged itself in the hearts of many people, becoming highly influential to a generation of musicians. It also laid the foundations for Eno becoming regarded as an experimental music guru in the coming years. As Eno biographer David Sheppard put it, the album was 'neither an affirmation of the old order nor a harbinger of the new. *Another Green World* was a globe unto itself'. For Fripp, his work with Eno was the antithesis to the increasingly weighty music he'd been doing with Crimson, Eno now only flirting with rock music as such. There was still another release in the pipeline, but Fripp's contributions here would be his last recorded guitar work for quite some time, work that over the years would rank amongst his best loved. [3] [4]

The outside world could have been forgiven for not noticing that Fripp had withdrawn from the music biz, when a new Fripp-and-Eno album, *Evening Star*, was also released a few weeks later. As a follow-up to *No Pussyfooting*, this was assembled from a mix of the Revox-based tracks they had put together a year earlier, and material from the pair's tour. The front cover, a minimalist painting of a tropical island by Peter Schmidt, and a back cover showing the duo relaxing, conveyed a laidback-to-almost horizontal contentedness, both freed from the pressures of their touring rock bands, and perfectly matching the pieces within. The opening track, *Wind on Water*, partly a live recording from Paris, gently washes in with layers of rippling melodic sound, in a style Fripp would return to much more in the coming years. This, as does the rest of the album, lends itself to use in soundtracks, and would crop up in episodes of *The Hitchhiker's Guide to the Galaxy* radio series and in the 1983 remake of the film *Breathless*. After five-and-a-half minutes this melts away and the title track emerges. For this, some simple, looped guitar chords and harmonics provide the backdrop for a fuzzed/sustained guitar solo that beautifully weaves its way in and out, spanning the tonal ranges from some kind of electric cello to a mellow set of bagpipes, creating the archetypal Fripp solo of this period. The pretty janglings of *Evensong* then fade in and out all too soon, illustrating the beauty of the tape-delay system in creating sequences outside of conventional, or even identifiable, time signatures. *Wind on Wind* is a few minutes of Eno-only synthesised ambience that had been used as backing on their tour, Eno releasing a much longer version shortly after as *Discreet Music*. Side two is entirely filled by the twenty-eight minutes of *An Index of Metals*, which despite the chemistry textbook title, drifts its way through several sections of what could be the soundtrack to an eerie space film. Fripp resists the temptation to add any solos, even though he had done so live, and perhaps because of this, the track never quite scales the heights of *The Heavenly Music Corporation*. The pair didn't consider the album's level of sales to be too important, as it was so far outside the mainstream, but their names at least guaranteed a moderate return for the record company, and it would also prove gently but persistently influential in the coming years.

Then, after a few days roughing it as a member of the audience at the Reading Music Festival, that September Fripp's withdrawal became a reality, as he checked himself into the IACE at Sherborne House to learn more about the philosophy that had so blown him away. Despite the death of Bennett, the work of the IACE continued under the leadership of his wife, Elizabeth, who Fripp would come to regard as a second mother. This was no casual commitment for the guitarist, being a rigorous ten-month residential course, and was certainly no holiday camp for middle-class intellectuals. His life during this time, along with around a hundred others, was filled with exercise, physical outdoor work, classes, meditation and lectures on such things as cosmology and psychology. Living arrangements were basic, bordering on monastic, Fripp sharing a dorm with five other men, and days would start at 6.00 a.m., unless they were on the rota for the breakfast service shift, which would require them to be up at 4.30 a.m. He has described the experience as physically painful and spiritually terrifying, and that 'life in general was very hard', with around a fifth of the students giving up well before the end. 'It was one of the most uncomfortable physical experiences of my life', he would later recall from the comfort of a warm pub during a *Melody Maker* interview. 'It was always horribly cold'. This hair-shirt existence would, however, give him a new sense of purpose and a new perspective, helping him to be rid of the 'feeling of uselessness that had haunted him for years', as it had 'stripped away the affectations of the fame he'd had as a rock star'. Fripp found that he wasn't entirely removed from music while there. He'd made a point of not taking a guitar with him, but others had brought theirs, and concerts were held monthly which he would sometimes participate in. Also, as contact with the outside world was not forbidden, a few friends would visit from time to time too, including Peter Gabriel and his family. [5]

Although the concepts of personal development and self-awareness at the core of the Fourth Way are hardly controversial to twenty-first-century eyes, and Bennett's environmental concerns are now accepted as mainstream, there were inevitably connotations of the organisation being a type of religious cult. Gurdjieff, however, drew an important distinction with religion, in that they didn't encourage blind acceptance. He believed that there is no faith as such but that 'a man must satisfy himself of the truth of what he is told and, until he is satisfied, he must do nothing'. There are other aspects that are more problematic to the more sceptical observer, the worst being Moon Symbolism, a Gurdjieff theory that during their lives people gain a type of matter which, upon their deaths, is somehow transferred to the moon. In addition, while Gurdjieff didn't believe that people were born with souls—he believed that a person could develop one by following his teachings. As part of their personal-development programme, students were taught about exercises known as Gurdjieff's Movements or Sacred Dances, which were performed in groups. With parallels to yoga and Tai Chi, these were not regarded simply as exercises: each movement was seen as being embedded with knowledge that had been passed down through time by successive sets of pupils, each posture holding some kind of cosmic truth. Russian composer and Gurdjieff pupil Thomas De Hartmann co-wrote some piano music with Gurdjieff to accompany the movements, some of which were captured in the 1979 film *Meetings with Remarkable Men* starring Terence Stamp and

Warren Mitchell (of Alf Garnett fame), based on a book by Gurdjieff. One aspect of the teachings that was to have a long-term impact on Fripp was the emphasis on the role of hazard and chaos in a person's life. In plainer language, letting chance and events make your choices for you, the thinking being that, in opening yourself to this, while there is a risk of failure, you allow in possibilities of progress that may not otherwise have occurred. [6]

Whatever Fripp's newfound philosophies, Wetton was still happy to battle it out in the big, bad rock world, though for the next three years he would have to make the best of being 'just' a bassist. Being friends with Roxy Music, Wetton was the obvious choice when they needed someone to step in for the promo tour for their *Country Life* album, a bit of casual work that resulted in his being on much of the highly regarded live album *Viva*. Long before that was out, he'd already moved on, joining prog-leaning hard rockers Uriah Heep. Some felt that Wetton was out of place in such company and only there for the money. While he was happy to admit he did need to keep working, he had also wanted to just get back to playing more straightforward rock again. This would turn into another success story for him, as over the spring of 1975 they recorded *Return to Fantasy*, the band's first album to break into the U.K. Top Ten. Wetton stayed with the band for the follow-up, *High and Mighty*, but then got another call from Bryan Ferry, asking him to be part of his band for his solo career. As a result, along with Mel Collins on saxes, Wetton found himself in the U.K. singles chart on Ferry's cover of *Let's Stick Together*, which peaked at No. 5. Boz Burrell also preferred life at the sleazy heart of seventies rock, Bad Company again hitting No. 1 in the U.S. with *Straight Shooter* in 1975. As the album cover of dice-on-a-craps-table tells us, this is hard-drinking, hard-gambling, bluesy rock, and is what many consider to be the band at its peak, spawning the hit single *Feel Like Making Love*. Along with the commercial success, offstage the band also found themselves enjoying some of the infamous wild partying of their label mates Led Zeppelin.

*Fripp's childhood home, Leigh Road, Wimborne.*

*Don Strike (later Fripp's guitar teacher), c. 1930.*
Courtesy of the Strike family

*Don Strike's in Westbourne Arcade, where Fripp and Lake took guitar lessons.*

*93 Brondesbury Road, Kilburn, where GGF lived and King Crimson was formed.*

*Bruford with hybrid kit c. 1981.*

*Fripp arriving at a London record shop, July 1985.*

*Fripp signs autographs, London, July 1985.*

*St Mary's Church, Witchampton, where Fripp and Toyah were married, May 1986.*

*Red Lion House, Cranborne, bought by Fripp in 1986 for his Guitar Craft students.*

*Bruford poses for an ad with his Simmons kit, c. 1995.*

*Reddish House, Broad Chalke, where Fripp and Toyah lived, 1987 to 1999.*

*The Arundells room where Fripp and Toyah dined with former Prime Minister, Ted Heath in 2000.*

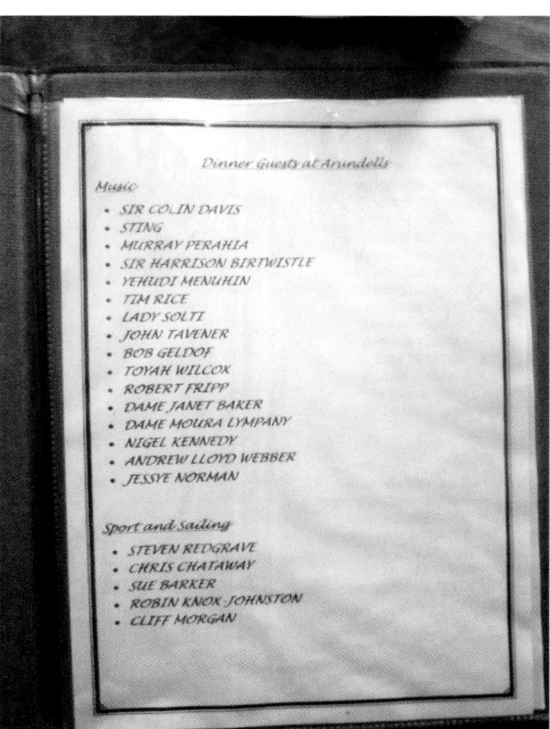

Dinner Guests at Arundells

Music

- SIR COLIN DAVIS
- STING
- MURRAY PERAHIA
- SIR HARRISON BIRTWISTLE
- YEHUDI MENUHIN
- TIM RICE
- LADY SOLTI
- JOHN TAVENER
- BOB GELDOF
- TOYAH WILCOX
- ROBERT FRIPP
- DAME JANET BAKER
- DAME MOURA LYMPANY
- NIGEL KENNEDY
- ANDREW LLOYD WEBBER
- JESSYE NORMAN

Sport and Sailing

- STEVEN REDGRAVE
- CHRIS CHATAWAY
- SUE BARKER
- ROBIN KNOX-JOHNSTON
- CLIFF MORGAN

*Ted Heath's birthday guest list, including Fripp and Toyah, 2000.*

ELP were still on their rather lengthy break from each other, but as a by-product, this year of unexpected, Crimson-related events was rounded off by singles chart success for Lake with *I Believe in Father Christmas*. Although it's something most people would describe as a Christmas song, complete with sleigh bell–mimicking tambourines, Lake initially denied that it was specifically a Christmas record. But with that proving futile, others leapt to its defence, characterising it as an 'atheist Christmas song'. In fact, it's a subtle and clever song, and an antidote to the otherwise-vacuous standard seasonal fare. Once you get beyond its warm, family-gathered-round-the-log-fire feel, its Sinfield-penned lyrics are about the disappointment of what a heavily commercialised Christmas actually delivers, rather than what the romantic notion promises, and that we bring this on ourselves. While its message is lost on most casual listeners, its effect on Lake's bank balance would more than compensate. Lake's prog tendencies show through with the incorporation of a rousing Prokofiev melody from his *Lieutenant Kije Suite*, included at Emerson's suggestion. The U.K. public loved it and it reached No. 2. Beelzebub had a devil put aside for Lake, though, his record being kept off the No. 1 slot by Queen's massive prog hit, *Bohemian Rhapsody*. Lake has put out a couple of reworkings of the song since, and it has worked its way into being one of those songs played endlessly in shops and on greatest hits stations every December.

Late in 1975 Bruford briefly linked up with his friend Phil Collins, who was working on an album for his jazz-fusion side project Brand X. They ended up talking about how Genesis could continue post-Gabriel, as they had so far failed to find a suitable replacement. In the interim, Collins had stepped in to cover the vocals and was doing it well, but with a big tour coming up they had to find a permanent solution, either finding a vocalist or a second drummer. Bruford leapt at the chance, volunteering himself to cover the live drumming role, freeing up Collins to be the frontman. The idea got the approval of Banks, Rutherford and Hackett, and Bruford joined them for a tour of Europe and North America, in the process completing a prog hat-trick, being part of Yes,

Crimson and Genesis. This was a Genesis-in-transition, though, not only with Collins reinventing himself but their live shows getting a major revamp. There was also growing disquiet from Hackett, and he too would soon head for the exit door. Meanwhile, with such a capable second drummer on board they began to develop what would become a staple of Genesis gigs: having two drummers in the longer instrumental passages and even indulging in drum duets. It seemed to be a partnership that worked for both parties, Bruford playing with a high-profile band, while Genesis found that having Bruford involved added to their credibility and brought in a wider audience. There was a downside, though, the drummer later confessing to having 'behaved badly'. Instead of being a polite and positive guest, he found himself sniping and criticising. As he had no creative input, he didn't feel any emotional involvement with the music, and treated it as simply a job. Even this he found difficult as time went by, as his inclination was to have a degree of variation in live performances, while his colleagues wanted a tight re-creation of Collins's performances on the records, needing specific drum fills as cues. Once the tour was over, with the music press reporting that Bruford was rehearsing with another band, Genesis decided instead to enlist the more amenable Chester Thompson. Nevertheless, Bruford had been the catalyst for the Collins-fronted version of Genesis and, by extension, for the Collins solo career that would happen a few years down the line. Bruford had, to an extent, ended up back where he'd started, but working alongside Collins had planted the seed of an idea in him for how he could progress. [7]

Elsewhere, the rich tapestry of Haskell's career continued, including try-outs with big names, a tour of Japan and singles with short-lived bands. In 1975 he was working on a potential album of songs by the duo of Pete Sills and Mike Allison, who would shortly have a big hit with Olivia Newton-John. That album would never materialise, however, Haskell had made an important impression. 'Bruce Welch of The Shadows produced it and liked my bass playing', he remembers. As a result, four of the songs featuring Haskell's bass parts found their way onto

Cliff Richard's highly successful 1976 album, *I'm Nearly Famous*, also produced by Welch. Now in his early thirties, the Batchelor Boy was being reinvented as more of a rock star, and as a spinoff, Haskell was invited to be part of his band for a U.K. tour. He was happy to accept the offer, even if it wasn't his type of music, and the tour certainly left him with far happier memories than had Crimson. Even here, he came away feeling short-changed, saying he was told by one of the managers, 'If you do this tour for half wages, I'll see you get the next world tour', which, of course, didn't happen. Haskell's roller-coaster ride rolled on, and soon after, through contacts of his actress wife, Sally, he was invited to stay at the home of Hollywood star Susan George. Ostensibly there to make contact with record companies in California, he made the best of things, enjoying three weeks of lounging by her pool and mingling with assorted stars. Unfortunately, he also managed to crash his host's expensive sports car! [8] [9]

With his IACE course completed, in 1976 Fripp began to test the waters of the music world again. Adopting a Fourth Way–style approach, at first his strategy was to wait and see what presented itself, but when something did, to deliberately keep himself in the shadow of others. Not only did he need to reconcile this with his much-changed world view and grave misgivings about the music business but he also had to adjust to a rapidly changing musical landscape. Although barely two years had passed, the pop/rock music context he was re-emerging into was undergoing nothing short of a revolution, if not three simultaneous revolutions: punk, synthesisers and disco. With glam and prog rapidly falling out of fashion, 1976 was the year that punk exploded on the U.K. music scene, before evolving rapidly into the broader and more record-company-friendly New-Wave. Born out of the despair of British youth in the mid-seventies, who were facing rising unemployment and inner-city decay, if the punk movement had any coherent aims beyond a little anarchy and being provocative for its own sake, some of its proponents professed to wanting to sweep away the flabby indulgence and excesses of prog. There was a new musical democracy emerging, based on a DIY philosophy, which took some of its cues from what had been emerging in New York over the previous couple of years. It didn't matter if you couldn't play or sing, it was much more about ideas and attitude. These were exciting times, if a little frightening to those outside-looking-in, as it challenged the establishment in ways that previous generations would never have dared. The Sex Pistols, The Stranglers and The Clash led the way, or rode the wave the best, and things would never be the same again. Of course, Eno had long been pioneering music for non-musicians, so the philosophy wasn't entirely new, but now it was about to become mainstream and involve a lot more fuzz boxes. As well as the three-chord wonders that were blazing a new trail, the increasing availability of affordable synthesisers was also broadening this democracy. Pink Floyd, Genesis and others had been incorporating synths into their music for a few years already, but now the likes of Kraftwerk and Jean Michel Jarre were making them their main instrument and finding chart success. Soon, many more would be acquiring the technology and trying to follow in their footsteps. The biggest revolution, in commercial terms at least, was disco. Having exploded across the Atlantic from its roots in New York, it was also fast becoming a dominant feature in the U.K., epitomised by The Bee Gees, Donna Summer and Earth, Wind and Fire. The question was, was there still room for a discontented, reinvented prog-guitar hero in this new world? Most of the older bands were not, in the end, swept away by punk or anything else, and The Enid were only just getting started, but at the time these were developments that artists and record companies ignored at their peril. In the meantime, Island put out *The Young Person's Guide to King Crimson*, a double LP which seemed to draw an even thicker line of finality under the Crimson era. To their credit, instead of opting for a standard 'best of . . .' selection, they asked Fripp to choose the tracks, and because of this some unexpected things made it in, such as *Cadence and Cascade*, *Groon* and a home-demo version of *I Talk to the Wind* featuring Judy Dyble from the pre-Crimson days.

Fripp's first tentative steps back into the fray came towards the end of 1976 at the behest of Peter Gabriel and his producer Bob Ezrin. Gabriel had parted company with Genesis at around the same time that Fripp was disbanding Crimson. But as the split had been amicable, for the early sessions for his debut solo effort, Gabriel had tried working with some of his former Genesis colleagues. This didn't feel right to him, though, and he took himself off to Toronto to start again. There he teamed up with Ezrin, who suggested drafting in Fripp, alongside American guitarist Steve Hunter, who'd made his name playing with Alice Cooper. As being a session guitarist fell within the activities Fripp was allowing himself, he accepted the offer, although that acceptance came with the proviso that if he didn't like it after a few days, he had the option to leave. The sessions went well from Gabriel's perspective, but Fripp's contributions were not really what his friend had envisaged. In fact, they ended up being disappointingly minimal, with Hunter being the album's main guitarist and another ex-Alice Cooper guitarist, Dick Wagner, adding a couple of other solos later. The album was released early in 1977, climbing into the U.K. top ten after a few weeks. The first (Frippless) single from it, *Solsbury Hill*, was a moderate hit, followed by a minor hit with Fripp on *Modern Love*. Despite the more commercial leanings, Gabriel hadn't thrown integrity out of the window, with plenty of his characteristic playfulness and bewildering imagination on display. Yet despite contributing to a successful and rewarding project, as it was for everyone else, Fripp came away having hated the experience. He'd felt that being there wasn't appropriate for him, but he had stayed for the sake of the others, or as he bizarrely put it, 'I didn't want my friends to be ravaged'. It's ambiguous whether he meant that the others would have been exploited by the music business or metaphorically ravaged by Ezrin. Describing the album's production as 'vulgar', he appeared to blame the producer personally for his feeling unable to express himself. He went on to suggest that Gabriel had felt the same, which may be something of an exaggeration when you look at the evidence of the album, although that would be the only Gabriel album Ezrin would produce. The explanation for these extreme reactions lies in another statement Fripp later made, saying 'Robert Fripp was not present'. The Fourth Way philosophy had swallowed him whole, and he had still been recovering and rebalancing himself after the rigours of his Sherborne experience. On the positive side, as well as being Fripp's first hesitant steps back, it was in the *Gabriel I* sessions that he first met American Tony Levin, who was to figure strongly in his future. While Levin mainly plied his trade as a bassist, he was a man of many talents, also playing tuba and leading a barbershop quartet on the light-hearted *Excuse Me*, a track on which Fripp merrily strums away at a banjo. [5]

Feeling very uncertain about where he was going in relation to his music career, Fripp initially returned to London. Working with Gabriel had left a lot of contradictory feelings revolving in his head, and while he was railing against the music business and preparing for society to collapse, he'd even been considering being ordained as a minister. However, he couldn't escape the fact that Gabriel and others were simply getting on with things. The ex-Genesis frontman had his own huge misgivings about the music business, hating what he felt it was trying to turn him into, but Fripp had now seen at first-hand how he did not need to reject the rock world wholesale or be small and mobile. Instead, he was reinventing himself in the face of the new (musical) world order, with no little experimentation and without selling too much of his soul. The discomfort Fripp had come back with from the recording sessions was perhaps from being forced to ask questions of himself and about the new thinking about which he had been so strident. Meanwhile, he had volunteered to take on the immense task of archiving the work of Bennett and editing tapes of his lectures, so, putting the bigger decisions on hold, for a while he just threw himself into that.

Gabriel hadn't given up on Fripp, though, and invited him back over to North America to be part of his tour band. While this smacked of being part of a dinosaur-scale touring band, falling foul of his principles, Fripp was tempted and flew back across the Atlantic. The tour began in March 1977 but, reflecting his contradictory feelings about being involved and so that audiences didn't know it was him, Fripp performed under the name Dusty Rhodes, and in one case had himself announced as Ned Strangler. In the earliest gigs of the tour, he even played just offstage, something that he'd made a condition of his joining the tour! He explained later that he used the different names as he felt he was a different person post-IACE and was 'tired of the associations made with the name Robert Fripp'. He'd also wanted to use the alias on the credits to *Gabriel I*, but Ezrin had refused to allow it. With this awkward arrangement, he completed the U.S. tour and some European dates that followed but declined to re-join for further touring later in the year. While this behaviour seems almost humorous, and just part of the eccentricity that we were learning to expect, Bruford has suggested this was one of the more extreme manifestations of a deep flaw in the man. His own experience with Fripp was that he tended to 'maintain a safe distance on the edge of things'. When he had to work with people, Fripp, Bruford believed, was often in 'uncomfortable attendance' because of the 'added difficulty of a relationship with human beings'. Nevertheless, Gabriel's persistence with Fripp was slowly working and, as a spinoff from his time in North America, Fripp decided that New York should become his new base, finding himself a loft apartment in the Hell's Kitchen district of Manhattan. He'd toured America a few times by this point, but something clicked last time round, and he saw the possibilities the city offered. It was an interesting decision in that, if you're fearing the imminent disintegration of society, parts of New York in the seventies were the sort of places that might well confirm such fears. In fact, President Carter that year had called for 'the moral equivalent of war' from the U.S. population, to avert a 'national catastrophe' from the effects on society of the energy crisis. Nevertheless, as well as the cultural possibilities, Fripp found that, as with his original move to London, the change of location greatly improved his love life, as in The Big Apple there was a much better ratio of women to men, especially for lively men in their thirties. [5] [7] [10]

Almost parallel to Fripp, McDonald had also moved back to New York. Other than the brief *Red* episode and a little production and session work, he had been absent from the music scene for around five years and had grown frustrated with his life in England. This change of scenery turned out to be a smart move as, in May 1976, he almost immediately formed the basis of a band with Mick Jones, a thirty-one-year-old British guitarist, also now living in New York. After auditioning dozens of potential vocalists, they chose Louis Grammatico, at the time playing in an obscure band and working on construction sites to pay the bills. He would soon shorten his name to Lou Gramm for band purposes. With three further recruits to complete the line-up, the new band was born. At first calling themselves Trigger, they learned that there was already a band using the name; they switched to Foreigner, three of them being from the U.K. and, therefore, foreigners. Any Crimson fans tracking McDonald's career were in for some surprises. Firstly, he was to be as much a guitarist as a sax-and-keyboards man. Secondly, while he would be involved in arrangements, he would only play a minor role in the writing, and thirdly, the band's sound was full-on commercial, American rock. McDonald has said that Foreigner were specifically 'designed as a hit-record-making venture', and they were duly snapped up by Atlantic Records and in the studio by November. Their eponymous debut, released in March 1977, was staggeringly successful, and their radio-friendly sound also spawned the top ten singles *Feels Like the First Time* and *Cold as Ice* in the U.S. and U.K. While no one begrudged McDonald his new success, opinion on the band was split. For those who liked their music a bit more off the beaten track, this was just too far into rock cliché territory and incongruous for one of the key figures of early prog. However, McDonald didn't see himself that way and didn't feel any compulsion to stay within the confines of any genre. In fact, feeling that he'd been deliberately messed about by Fripp over re-joining Crimson had given him the perfect motivation to do something completely different and to succeed without him. As well as the commercial success, life was exciting. McDonald was enjoying touring with a band that were packing out big venues, without the hassle of having to deal with Fripp. There would be one thing that would niggle with him for years about his time with Foreigner though which was that people didn't grasp his level of contributions to the music, and he would find himself having to still explain this decades later! [11]

Having moved to a loft apartment in the Bowery district of New York, Fripp returned to experimenting with the tape-repetition system, seeing if this was something he could use for live performances on his own. Whereas Eno had created backdrops for him to solo over, the idea he was now trialling behind closed doors was to develop his own pieces from scratch. His new girlfriend, poet Joanna Walton, on seeing him working on this suggested the term Frippertronics for this setup, which he duly adopted. Critics have had a go at Fripp over the years for using the term, missing the important distinction that, out of deference to Eno, he defined Frippertronics specifically as being the interaction of himself and the relevant equipment, not claiming to have come up with the system himself. His experimenting would mostly take place in his own apartment, with occasional sessions in local studios. But it would be a while before he'd take the idea any further, as other projects would present themselves to him in the meantime.

A few weeks later, in July 1977, the first of those other projects appeared, and would be a vital one in channelling Fripp back towards fuller involvement in music. Bowie was in Berlin working on a new album, accompanied by Eno and producer Tony Visconti, having already been living in the city for months soaking in its atmosphere and the music of German electronic music pioneers like Kraftwerk, La Düsseldorf and Cluster, along with the edgier feel of new wave that was in the air. Following on from *Low*, which had been steeped in bleakness, half-instrumental and just what his record company hadn't wanted, they were recording in Hansa Studios. The studio building had been used by Gestapo officers during the war and was so close to the infamous wall that divided the city that the armed guards in the watchtowers, in Soviet-controlled East Berlin, were able to peer in using binoculars.

After all the basic tracks had been recorded, Eno and Bowie felt that some needed the addition of a solo guitar. Fripp crossed their minds, so they phoned him up and asked him if he'd come over. Although he expressed doubts as to his abilities, being so out of practice, he accepted what fate was presenting to him and, flying in from New York a couple of days later, a jet-lagged Fripp threw himself into the role, despite being eager to go out and experience West Berlin's decadent nightlife while there. Bowie and his crew were blown away by the guitarist's approach, completing his contributions in just forty-eight hours, plus keeping the others amused between takes with what Visconti described as his 'very dry west country humour'. [12]

On the six-minute track that would become *Heroes* (which, at that point, still lacked lyrics), Fripp put down three takes of guitar processed via Eno's synth in a suitcase, the AKS Synthi. Situated between markings on the floor that showed where he'd get the optimum feedback, what Fripp played was mostly just a series of two- or three-note phrases. However, the combination of these, using the evocative sounds Eno's knob twiddling had created, gave the track a whole new dimension. While Fripp and Eno had combined to create these new ingredients to use, it took Visconti's vision and skilful (pre-digital) cutting and pasting to construct the wonder of the finished article. Visconti also inadvertently inspired some of the lyrics, Bowie seeing his producer kissing backing vocalist Antonia Mass in the shadow of the Berlin Wall. Bowie also credited Fripp's 'plaintive guitar cry' as being the trigger for him to turn an otherwise-moderate idea into its ultimate form. The album was still far from finished by the time Fripp departed—the Berlin nightlife would have to wait for another visit—but he had given them plenty to work with, and he appears on four other tracks. The less-heralded *Joe the Lion* also has a complex tangle of guitar parts, opening with Fripp's edgy lead guitar played over a seething backdrop of distortion and feedback, while Carlos Alomar holds the whole thing together with layers of rhythm and melody. Here Bowie's punkiest vocal on the album tells of the illusion of excitement that heavy drinking conjures up in otherwise-mundane lives. For the mock menace of *Beauty and the Beast* and the angst-ridden *Blackout*, the Fripp/Eno combination produced further, heavily filtered, synth-like lead guitar parts, on which Visconti could again work his magic. Fripp's only appearance on the largely instrumental side two was on *V2 Schneider*, where he plays big, crashing chords in amongst Bowie's jaunty saxes and vocodered voices. In a perverse bit of Bowie humour, the track title dubiously melds a name check of Kraftwerk's Florian Schneider with the infamous Nazi flying bombs of World War II. [13]

RCA were far from overjoyed with the finished product but nevertheless surpassed themselves in marketing it, coming up with the legendary slogan, 'There's old wave, there's new wave and there's David Bowie'. A few weeks before its release in September 1977, while the world was coming to terms with the death of Elvis Presley, an edited version of *Heroes* was put out as a single, with versions sung in French and German also made for the European market. Considering the status the song has attained over subsequent years, turning up in films, ads and trailers, not to mention being played endlessly at sporting events, you could be forgiven for thinking that someone miscounted its sales at the time. It peaked at only No. 24 in the U.K., not helped by Bowie miming to a weak, Frippless recreation of the song on *Top of the Pops*, and failed to chart at all in the U.S. The album itself, also called *Heroes*, would peak at No. 3 in the U.K., lingering in the chart for around six months. As with *Low*, it was considered a relative commercial failure at the time, but grew to be extraordinarily influential, being one of the key albums that triggered the rise of the New Romantics a couple of years later. In retrospect, the album's personnel list suggests some kind of supergroup that you might assume had spent weeks mingling their talents. In reality, vital aspects of the album came simply from a fleeting crossing of paths at the right time and in the right place. Bowie was producing consistently high-quality music throughout this period, but without that call to Fripp, this would have been a very different beast. Towards the end of 1977, Bowie suggested that Eno and Fripp join his tour band to perform *Heroes* live. Fripp declined, subsequently saying that he felt Bowie wouldn't have been able to give him enough 'creative space', and that he felt he was 'worth too much to be a backing guitar player'. Eno simply no longer wanted to play live. [14] [5]

ELP reconvened after three years apart and headed back to the studio, though not always at the same time as each other. They had all been working on solo projects but had reluctantly concluded that their prospects were still vastly better together. Of the four sides of the double album, *Works: Volume One*, which these sessions produced, only one was performed by the whole band, the rest being shared out amongst them for their solo efforts. The unusual format was presented positively but reflected their divisions, if anyone chose to read between the lines. They were largely going against the grain of the music revolutions, and for a while it seemed as if this wasn't doing them any harm, as the album climbed up to No. 9 in the U.K. They also scored some unexpected singles chart success in the summer of 1977, with their upbeat synth-rock take on Aaron Copland's *Fanfare for the Common Man*. Drastically edited down from the nine-minute album version, it slowly climbed to No. 2 in the U.K, only Hot Chocolate's *So You Win Again* keeping it off No. 1. Its progress was much helped by a hurriedly made but memorable promo film aired on *Top of the Pops*, featuring the trio playing in a freezing cold and otherwise-empty Montreal Olympic Stadium, where they'd been rehearsing in a room underneath. *Fanfare* managed to sound original and distinctive, even amongst all the new music being created around it, but at the same time fitted in nicely as a bit of accessible pop, with Emerson's bright synth brass linking it with the surge in electronic music. To this day, ELP's track lays claim to being in the top handful of best-selling instrumental singles ever. The idea had evolved from Emerson playing around with bluesy variations on Copland's original, with Lake and Palmer suggesting the pulsing rock rhythm. Tweaking the timing of the melody to fit this, their now-world-famous version was born. Even then it might never have seen the light of day, as the music publishers initially refused to allow them permission to use it. ELP decided to bypass them by going straight to the seventy-six-year-old composer himself, who gave it a listen, very much approved and gave ELP the go-ahead. The most memorable of Lake's solo tracks is *C'est La Vie*, a beautiful song sung over an acoustic guitar, with an accordion solo and Sinfield's lyrics lending it an air of wandering wistfully around autumnal Parisian boulevards. In similar vein, *Closer to Believing* is a passionate Lake/Sinfield song, with ambiguity as to who or what the singer is closer to believing in, be it himself, his lover or God. The band then took their show back on the road across North America, the early shows incorporating a seventy-piece orchestra. The antithesis of Fripp's small, mobile, intelligent unit, for those who still wanted prog-rock excess, they needed to look no further than ELP and the fleet of articulated lorries required to transport their stacks of equipment around. The orchestra was soon ditched, though, as the massive cost of hiring and transporting them was in serious danger of bankrupting the band, who were funding them out of their own money. When asked his opinion of ELP around this time, Fripp described them as 'part of the rock industry's dinosaur structure'. That didn't stop him from going to see them live three times in New York, although his motive was more to try to rekindle his friendship with Lake, something Lake was less bothered about. [15]

Back in New York City in August 1977, the next call for Fripp came from American singer/songwriter Daryl Hall. Hall and Fripp had first met back in 1974, when despite being in very different musical territory, they got on so well that they decided they should work together at some point. After his success as one-half of soulful Philadelphia duo Hall and Oates, Hall was feeling frustrated with the direction in which his record company were pushing him, and had started work on a solo album, trying out some different ideas. He decided it was time to get Fripp involved and invited him to the studio to see what might happen. For Fripp, the time he'd spent in Berlin with Bowie had been a turning point, and he had no doubts about saying yes. In any case, Hall was working so close to where he lived, it would have been churlish not to have given it a try. He'd barely stepped through the door when Hall put him in charge of production, and although the songs would be mostly written by Hall, Fripp would take the chance to inject some of his own new ideas into the mix. Of the ten tracks recorded for the album, *Babs and Babs* stands out from the pack, with quirky lyrics about an internal debate between two sides of a persona, accompanied by a compelling riff and some early use of Frippertronics. Had things gone according to plan, this would have been the outside world's first encounter with Frippertronics, at first jarring with the flow of the song, but then starting to make more sense before fading away. After the final verse, the Frippertronics return, creating a grandiose and unconventional ending, segueing into *Urban Landscape*, a few minutes of eerie Frippertronics on their own. This ambience crashes into the abrasive *NYCNY*, the only track listed as a Hall/Fripp co-write. The punky influences all around them had been seeping through the walls of their studio, as Fripp hit on some harsh chords and Hall followed suit with his vocals, though the result was quite raw. At the other end of the spectrum, *The Farther Away I Am* is a beautiful, minimalist Hall song, washed over by gentle Frippertronics. It was an interesting way for the pair to combine their talents and is a line they should perhaps have explored further. Ultimately, though, Hall and Fripp didn't mesh as tightly as they had expected to, and much of the rest of the album is surprisingly conventional, and the incongruity of the alliance is more apparent. However, this only makes what happened next seem all the stranger. The pair were happy with the finished project, entitled *Sacred Songs*, and publicly gushed with praise for each other, Hall saying he'd never found it so easy to make music as with Fripp, while Fripp was bowled over by Hall's versatility. The album was scheduled for release in 1978 but Hall's record company, RCA, became so alarmed at the change of direction from their man, and how uncommercial it seemed, that it was shelved. Angered by the attitude of the record company 'dinosaurs', Fripp took to giving out cassettes of the album to music journalists to try to force the issue. His strategy failed but the company's action elevated the suppressed music to near-mythical status, and with pressure slowly building from fans, the album was eventually put out in 1980. Sales were moderate but there was certainly no noticeable damage to the rise of Hall and Oates. [16]

Fripp's work with Bowie, Gabriel and Hall, as well as other offers now coming in, made him conclude that he hadn't actually retired after all. He'd seen the world through new eyes, courtesy of Bennett, but things had had time to settle into place now, and he could balance his new perspective with the musician Fripp that was still alive and well within him. The hiatus was therefore over, and he now looked to move forwards, drawing up ambitious plans for a trilogy of linked albums. These were intended to be the now-held-up album with Daryl Hall, his own first solo album, and a second Gabriel solo album that he had just accepted an invitation to work on. To get things moving with his own music, Fripp got together with Wetton and former Mahavishnu Orchestra drummer Narada Michael Walden to record some demos, the latter struggling to carve out a solo career at the time. Wetton would have been hoping that this might just lead to a new Crimson, but that wasn't in Fripp's mind.

During 1976, Mel Collins briefly reunited with Boz again in sessions for Bad Company's lesser-acclaimed *Burnin' Sky* album. After too much rock 'n' roll lifestyle and with the rise of punk, their bubble was bursting, and ideas were drying up. Collins then accepted an invitation to tour with Camel, to promote their *Moonmadness* album. Camel was a well-established band, producing their own largely instrumental brand of prog, with nods to Genesis, Floyd and Crimson, but without the same commercial success. The original line-up was beginning to fall apart as Collins linked up with them, and with direction changes in the air, they were about to become another band with a revolving-door membership. After the tour, guitarist Andy Latimer and keyboardist Pete Bardens were assembling a new line-up and asked Collins to formally join. With a sense of deja-vu, Collins declined but agreed to be available for recording and touring. With the addition of the vocal-and-bass talents of Richard Sinclair, formerly of Caravan and Hatfield and the North, and some touches of Eno on one track, they produced one of Camel's most accomplished albums, *Raindances*. Released in September 1977, it spent two months in the U.K. chart, peaking at No. 20, successfully moving the band's sound on without abandoning its roots. Collins tended not to be a writer as such but was credited as a co-writer on *One of These Days I'll Get an Early Night*, a strong track on a strong album, created out of an atmospheric jazzy jam. The band's love of Crimson was apparent on the opening song, *Metrognome*, which unashamedly pastiched *The Court of the Crimson King*, but with the twist of having lyrics that aimed to be reassuring in the face of gloom. With Collins being half-in and half-out of Camel, he had plenty of space for session work, which, at the high-profile end, included being part of the Rolling Stones' *Some Girls* sessions, featuring on an extended version of the single *Miss You*. Lower in profile, he was part of Phil Manzanera's large cast for his *Listen Now* album, particularly on the title track, credited as a one-man big band. Collins stayed with Camel for the next tour and the follow-up studio album *Breathless* in 1978; however, internal relations were deteriorating fast and the record ended up capturing the sound of a band losing its way. Bardens saw the writing on the wall and left, and the subsequent tour ended with gigs being cancelled and Sinclair leaving due to 'the pressure of touring'. What Collins had hoped would be a happier home than Crimson turned out to have its own problems. He maintained good relations with Latimer, keeping the door open for future work together. [17]

With his misgivings from *Gabriel I* long gone, Fripp would be producer as well as guitarist for Gabriel's follow-up and would stamp his character all over it. Going into the studio in the autumn of 1977, Fripp's prompting of Gabriel to go for a less-lavish sound ensured that any lingering echoes of Genesis were banished. There would be a smaller band too, with Levin still on bass but with former Bowie and Springsteen piano man Roy Bittan added. The production approach Fripp was favouring now was to try to capture much more of a live, realistic sound. What Eric Tamm describes as 'his zeal for sonic sobriety and acoustical honesty', in this case rendered the sound rather crunchy, and neither Gabriel nor Fripp was particularly happy with the end-result, although the fact that some indifferent material made it through didn't help. Everything fell together perfectly, however, at the end of side one for the sleek, seductive *White Shadow*, with Gabriel's cryptic lyrics and understated vocal, and one of Fripp's life-affirming solos. On the largely disappointing second side lurks *Exposure*, co-written by Gabriel and Fripp. This is a slowed-down, heavy funk, with minimal lyrics played over a backdrop of Frippertronics, and due to the delay to *Sacred Songs* was unintentionally the first appearance of Frippertronics on vinyl. The only one of Fripp's trilogy of projects to come out on schedule, *Gabriel II* was released the following year, and as with its predecessor, reached the U.K. top ten. Around this time Gabriel's former colleagues in Genesis were looking for a guitarist to replace Hackett, who had decided to go his own special way. Fripp was initially on their shopping list but it was never going to be something he'd consider, which was probably just as well for all parties. Genesis filled the vacancy internally again, with bassist and part-time guitarist Mike Rutherford expanding his role. [18]

Despite the mixed experiences of his spell with Genesis, Bruford had been impressed by how Phil Collins treated Genesis like a day job and Brand X just for the enjoyment of the music. His trick was to stay realistic about the potential of the latter, in terms of audience and sales. Having had experience with three major rock bands, Bruford had a heartfelt desire to get back to the kind of music that was the original reason for his becoming a drummer, so while still trying to find a day-job band, he set his sights on his own Brand X equivalent. The first task was to try to assemble a group of compatible musicians, and crossing the Atlantic to make personal contact, he enlisted American bassist Jeff Berlin. Closer to home he found Allan Holdsworth, a guitarist from Yorkshire with his own unique prog/fusion style. Since Sunship, he'd got an impressive array of credits under his belt, including Soft

Machine, Tony Williams and Gong, all fairly short-lived, though. Completing the line-up was keyboardist Dave Stewart, formerly of Egg and Hatfield and the North, with whom Bruford had crossed paths with during his temp jobs. In August 1977 they created *Feels Good to Me*, an album of intense jazz-fusion, appropriately enough with Brand X's keyboardist, Robin Lumley, brought in as producer, and their guitarist, John Goodsall, guesting on the title track. It was to be released under the name Bruford, technically as a 'solo' album, but this would be held up for a year. Nevertheless, the recording represented Bruford properly moving on after the shock of Crimson vanishing. As the drummer later observed, 'Change may be unwelcome in the moment but, in my experience, it has always led to something equally valid. In my case, a sharper focus on the possibilities of making my own albums'. The drummer had already shown his ability to contribute to the music writing of his bands but was now devoting his time to learning about jazz harmony and melody, to enable him to write more. He is self-effacing about his motives for this, suggesting that 'both arrogance and vanity will perk up at the idea of controlling the audio collaboration from the start by composing something'. Beyond that there was also an element of panic and guilt at times. 'I started writing seriously ten minutes after I'd called a bunch of musicians to come over and have a play. What were they going to play? I had to find something in a hurry!' On the day job side of things, it was, however, proving a lot harder. He and Wetton thought they had formed a band with potential with Bruford's former Yes colleague Rick Wakeman, getting as far as a photo shoot on a film set. When Wakeman's record company got wind of this, however, they stepped in to block the idea. Crimson castoffs were, it seemed, not acceptable for their man. Bruford and Wetton then forlornly contacted Fripp again to attempt to persuade him to reform Crimson, but this was a non-starter for the guitarist as he had other ideas. [19]

While there was no Crimson reunion on the cards, the wider Crimson family had not only survived the revolution that was supposed to have swept their kind aside, but things were actually looking extremely healthy. McDonald, Collins, Burrell, Lake and Wetton were all enjoying success—some much more lucratively than others—and fans would soon be able to enjoy the more decisive return of Fripp himself. Having first peeked at the music business through a few back and side doors to see how he felt, he was now ready to use the front door. The media were still fascinated by him, and thanks to his collaborations of the last few years, he was now on the radar of an even wider fan base. The big question that remained was, just how would he balance the person he'd become with his needs as a musician and the inevitable music industry dealings he would have to negotiate?

6

# The Last Great New York Heartthrob

## *1978 to 1980*

While Fripp was happily back in the swing of things, in terms of working on other people's albums, it was still far from clear what shape his own music would take, especially as it was now outside the framework of King Crimson. He had emerged from his hiatus a markedly different man, not just in his world view and personal philosophy but also in his approach to music and even how he looked and dressed. Having set up camp in New York, the city was getting under his skin and was changing him further. It was a frantic, exciting and chaotic place to be, with creative possibilities presenting themselves to him at every turn. In fact, through a combination of having an open approach to ideas and potential collaborations, and being in such a thriving place of culture, almost anything could have resulted from his being there, and not just limited to music. His drive and invention were back to the levels that had taken him through the roller-coaster ride of Crimson, and while nothing could entirely match that time in terms of his influence on the wider music world, these few years after his return would be almost as productive and innovative, while remaining highly relevant. It would be a different kind of relevance and influence, though, the position he was now carving out for himself being as much as a crusader against the music industry as well as a musician. Back in England, Bruford was a happier man too, with his side project up and running, and he would soon find himself swept along as part of an exciting, new venture alongside Wetton, still a man with big ambitions he was determined to fulfil. As for McDonald and Lake however, they would find their respective good times were coming to an end.

Early in 1978, sessions began at New York's Hit Factory Studio for Fripp's debut solo album, a project that would start positively but would turn into a frustrating experience. His personnel list over the coming months would consist of a very enthusiastic Daryl Hall as vocalist; Tony Levin from Gabriel's band on bass; and Barry Andrews, formerly of new wave band XTC, on organ. Jerry Marotta, also borrowed from Gabriel's band, would be his main drummer, supplemented by sessions from Narada Michael Walden and Phil Collins, the latter with a bit of time to spare ahead of a Genesis U.S. tour. Gabriel himself and Eno would also contribute. At the same time, Fripp decided to venture into the outside world with Frippertronics, its first public outing coming on 5 February. He'd initially planned a private gig for a few friends in Joanna Walton's apartment, but as the day approached, they realised the plan was impractical, not to mention how much of a nuisance it would be for his neighbours, and hastily switched the event to a small Soho arts centre called The Kitchen. This was a place that specialised in experimental music and avant-garde arts in general, with the likes of composer Philip Glass casually hanging out there, and Talking Heads playing some of their early gigs there. Somehow word got around the city and an unexpectedly large crowd started to gather. Remembering the difficulties of his tour with Eno, Fripp decided to open affairs by lowering expectations, telling the audience that he 'reserved the right to be boring and unintelligent'. All went well concerning equipment and performance, and few, if any, felt that he was either boring or unintelligent. In fact, by the middle of the night there were still so many people trying to get in that, after an interval, he performed a second set. While tea and biscuits were handed out, that interval itself was turned into a performance, of sorts. Teetering on the boundary between deep and meaningful and absurd, it was filled with 'silent physical performances' inspired by Oblique Strategy cards, while a taped piece by Walton was played. Fripp would later describe this trial run for Frippertronics as 'one of the best days of my life', and its success inspired the idea of a full tour. [1] [2]

One of the big attractions of living in New York was the presence of a great many other musicians, either looking for their big break or, like Fripp, more established. It was an incredible cocktail of people crossing paths in the way it had been in London in the sixties, and Fripp was thriving on the sheer energy of the place. He could socialise with or just casually run into the likes of Talking Heads, The Ramones, Devo or Blondie, and there was an endless string of gigs to attend. A favourite meeting place was CBGB, a small, sleazy downtown club, just a few minutes' walk from where Fripp was living. This was the place for bands to get experience and get seen, particularly American punk bands, who were a lot more arty and less angry than their U.K. equivalents. It was through going to gigs in the city that Fripp struck up a friendship with members of Blondie. After seeing them play one evening, he made a point of meeting them afterwards to tell them how much he liked them. This was Blondie shortly before hitting the big time, already with admirers including Bowie and Iggy, in the process of evolving from their raw and arty early years into a slick pop band. In the coming months Fripp would make occasional guest appearances onstage with them, prompting some unusual things to make it into their set, such as a short rendition of Crimson's *Sailor's Tale* segueing into a cover of Iggy Pop's *Sister Midnight.* That summer Fripp also briefly joined the band at New York's Record Plant studio, adding a solo to *Fade Away and Radiate*, which would appear on *Parallel Lines*, the album that would launch them into the stratosphere. With the company he was keeping, it would have been all too easy to slip into some kind of rock-star lifestyle, but Fripp made a point of keeping himself grounded. It wasn't exactly the hairshirt existence of Sherborne House but he would do his own shopping, wash his own clothes and stick to the subway and buses, which also helped stretch out the savings.

The friendship with Blondie could even have led to Fripp starring in a film. Guitarist Chris Stein and vocalist Debbie Harry, who also had desires to start an acting career drew up plans for a remake of Jean Luc Godard's sixties sci-fi film *Alphaville*. Unperturbed by Fripp's lack of acting experience, they offered him the part of Lemmy Caution, a secret agent and love interest of Harry's character, Natacha von Braun. Plans got beyond it just being a fantasy, with Harry and Stein acquiring the rights to the script, appointing a director and screen-testing potential actors. However, they struggled to find financial backing and the idea eventually fell by the wayside. Harry has speculated that Fripp's premature mentioning of the plans in a *Melody Maker* interview possibly put the mockers on it. In any case, Blondie's mega-success was about to push all other plans to the back burner.

While Fripp's acting potential would stay hidden, he was making regular appearances on a New York cable TV show called *TV Party*. Stein and Harry were again involved, both in front of and behind the cameras, and there were regular guest appearances by the likes of Nile Rodgers from Chic, Mick Jones from Foreigner, and David Byrne from Talking Heads. In its chaotic way the show broke new ground, described by its main host, Glenn O'Brien, as 'anti-format . . . punk TV' that 'thrived on disaster'. Passing almost unnoticed in amongst all this, in August 1978 Fripp offered his services to local band, Television, who had been significant in getting the punk scene going in the city, being the first of this new type of band to play at CBGB, inspiring many others to follow suit. They had just broken up, however, just weeks after the release of their charm-the-pants-off-you second album, *Adventure*. Inexplicably poor reviews and the increasingly problematic drug use of one of their members led to frontman Tom Verlaine deciding to go solo. Having been impressed by seeing them play live, when Fripp subsequently met members of the band, he suggested that they should get back together—with him also on board. It was perhaps just a knee-jerk reaction from Fripp, being thoroughly bowled over by the new music he was hearing in the city and wanting to be part of it, but Television declined his offer. [3]

By September 1978 Fripp had collected his thoughts on his formal return to action and encapsulated them in a document he called 'The Drive to 1981'. In a style more like a political manifesto than something you would expect from a rock musician, he described his plans as 'a campaign on three levels: firstly, in the marketplace but not governed by the marketplace. Secondly, as a means of presenting a number of ideas which are close to my heart; and thirdly, as a personal discipline'. He'd realised that dealing with the big, bad music business was necessary if he wanted any kind of livelihood from his efforts, and The Drive was his way of rationalising this for himself and explaining to the wider world how he would balance creative integrity with returning to being involved in a business he despised. In a subsequent interview, Fripp added that his music was 'to help finance a number of interests and ventures outside the music business', which probably referred to ongoing production of tapes of Bennett's work and other Fourth Way activities. According to Eric Tamm, the end of the three-year plan was timed to coincide with an event of astronomical and astrological significance—an alignment of planets—when 'Fripp evidently believed that mankind was in for an awakening of apocalyptic import'. That September, Fripp also thought that he had completed his solo album, and a white-label version was circulated with the dubious, provisional title of *The Last Great New York Heartthrob*. With Hall appearing on seven tracks, on hearing it his management started pushing for it to be billed as a Robert Fripp and Daryl Hall album. That debate soon became redundant when a huge, dinosaur-shaped spanner was thrown into the works by Hall's record company, RCA. They objected to their star singing on so much of it, thoroughly alarmed by what this left-field music might do for his Hall and Oates reputation, and refused Fripp permission to release it. This initially left Fripp 'thoroughly demoralised and depressed', feeling that his 'life was completely knocked askew'. He managed to negotiate a compromise that allowed him to use Hall's vocals for two songs, his manipulated voice also appearing on a third. This still left Fripp having to re-think or re-record the rest. A plan to record a cover of Donna Summer's disco hit, *I Feel Love*, with Debbie Harry doing the vocals, was also scuppered when Blondie's record company, Chrysalis, refused to allow their new superstar to appear on the album. [4] [5]

Being open to all sorts of offers, Fripp would continue to have unlikely collaborations, the most incongruous being with The Roches, an acoustic guitar-and-vocal harmony group of three sisters from New Jersey. Two of the sisters had already recorded together and had backed Paul Simon. Now, with their third sister involved, in the autumn of 1978 they had been signed up by Warner Bros. and were about to record their first album as a trio. Having come across this quirky English guitarist, they decided to ask him to produce it for them. Although he was hastily re-working his own album, Fripp was happy to do so, and even called up members of Gabriel's band to help. It was no takeover, though, the end product being very much the sisters' mix of witty folk and country. Fripp branded his production method here as Audio Verité as, even more so than on *Gabriel II*, he was trying to capture a live feel. It was almost an anti-production method, with minimal reverb, equalisation or artificial panning, Fripp seeing it as a more honest approach. Whether it was more honest or simply an alternative approach, in adopting it, he was at odds with Eno's studio-as-instrument viewpoint, and with the lush production of much prog and rock. The eponymous album that resulted has more of the feel of a cabaret act than a rock or folk band, and only *Hammond Song* really stands out, with big harmonies from the sisters and some soloing from Fripp making it a much bigger production than the rest. Fripp's involvement helped to give it a much wider audience than it would otherwise have gained, with his even appearing live with the sisters at local venues to help promote it.

Back in the U.K., Bruford and Wetton were working together on demos for a potential solo album for the latter and discussing having another serious go at forming a band. They came up with the idea of allowing each other to pick one other musician to join them. Bruford's choice was Allan Holdsworth, the guitarist from his solo project; Wetton chose the youthful keyboardist and violinist Eddie Jobson. Something of a child prodigy, Jobson's big break had come when he joined Curved Air at just eighteen, before moving on to his high-profile stint with Roxy. That had since come to an end, and both he and Holdsworth were happy to accept their offers. Naming themselves UK—all being Brits—a new band was born. With much promise and with no record company objections, they got straight down to writing and recording. Although this had started as a Wetton-Bruford initiative, the core writing team that emerged was Wetton and Jobson. What also rapidly emerged, according to Bruford, were rumbling difficulties with his pick, Holdsworth. Despite his much-acclaimed talent, Bruford found him to be 'more or less permanently unhappy'. This largely stemmed from him being very self-critical but also from his sense of guilt at the looming prospect of mainstream success, the very thing the others were craving. The setup worked, however, and their eponymous debut album came out in the spring of 1978 to a good reception and even better sales. Doing what others would do in the nineties, they didn't throw prog out the window but instead blended it with newer influences, especially electronic music. Other than Wetton's rich vocal tones and Bruford's distinctive drumming style, the album had none of the feel of *Larks'*-era Crimson. Instead, it had more in the way of pop sensibility, mostly due to Jobson's synths, which brought a brightness to the mixture. Nevertheless, with two ex-Crims involved it was something that starved Crimson fans could get their teeth into. The opener, *In the Dead of Night*, was essentially a sampler of all you could expect from this setup, being a thirteen-minute, multi-sectioned track, with unusual time signatures and several instrumental passages. It was also melodic, upbeat and had enough hooks to engage a wider audience than Crimson had. There was another special ingredient the band had up their sleeves. After a couple of verses, a beautifully fluid jazz-fusion-style solo from Holdsworth appeared from a backdrop of Jobson's synths. *Thirty Years, Nevermore* and *Time to Kill* are a similar mix of ingredients, the variations coming in the form of *Alaska*, a Jobson-only synth piece, and the jazzier *Mental Medication*, which featured some rare Bruford lyrics. [6]

Capitalising on this new vein of success, UK set off on a massive tour, focussing particularly on America. It was a tough schedule but, thanks to record company backing and media clamour for this 'supergroup', it was a very lucrative time. After all the frustrations and dead ends, Wetton and Bruford had hit on an original new sound, with integrity and commercial appeal. The Crimson-esque tendency for line-ups to fall apart was alive and well, however. Wetton and Jobson reaching a point where they could no longer work with Holdsworth, and he was ousted. Other than being fed up with what they felt was his general complaining, coming more from a jazz angle, he baulked at being asked to reproduce the same thing note for note, night after night. Bruford sided with the guitarist and found himself leaving too. Wetton and Jobson were, in any case, planning to push in an even more commercial direction, and this was somewhere Bruford didn't want to go. The last year had been an intense period for him, not only being in UK and fitting in his own side project when he could, but his wife had also given birth to their first child. He therefore took the philosophical view that while the band had helped them all to understand better what sort of musicians they were, leaving was actually something of a relief. In the fullness of time, this line-up of UK, for all its success, seems almost incidental. However, it was very much the making of Jobson, and allowed Wetton to re-emerge as a frontman. Wetton and Jobson continued without a guitarist, filling Bruford's shoes with ex-Zappa drummer Terry Bozzio, releasing one additional studio album before their own differences grew too great and the prevailing climate seemed too much against them. Just prior to the release of UK's first album, Bruford's solo album, *Feels Good to Me*, had also finally been slipped out, and with his and Holdsworth's involvement in UK now over, they returned to the side project. This time, Bruford decided it would be a band under the name Bruford, rather than considering it as a solo effort, although this was a subtle distinction as he'd still be in charge. Their first album would be *One of a Kind*, in 1979, the title enabling the joke of having tracks called *One of a Kind, Parts One* and *Two*. The standout tracks, however, are the synth-heavy, 7/4 time *Hell's Bells* and *Fainting in Coils*, the latter opening with Bruford speaking lines from Lewis Carroll's surreal fantasy, *Alice in Wonderland*. After the mainstream success of UK, the drummer was back to playing the small-scale venues of the university circuit, but he was happy to live with this and the inevitable lower sales as the side project would repay in other ways, earning him a great deal of respect in the fusion arena.

Elsewhere, it was a mixed bag for ex-Crims. What had seemed like the dawn of a new era for ELP in 1977 turned out to be just an Indian summer, as their personal differences remained, and their brand was now desperately out of favour. *Works: Volume Two* came out in 1978 to little fanfare, after which the trio decided to break up. Finding that they still owed their record company one more album, ELP went off to the Bahamas and recorded *Love Beach*. Released towards the end of 1978, this is an album that even some die-hard fans find hard to love. ELP awkwardly trying to jump on assorted bandwagons, especially soft rock. Even the cover was a source of ridicule, showing the trio beneath palm trees, with shirts unbuttoned and chest hair on display—more Bee Gees than ELP! Reactions to the album were irrelevant to the band, though, as after its release they went their separate ways. McDonald's commercial success with Foreigner continued, with him also becoming co-producer on their 1978 album, *Double Vision*. He would stay on board for only one more album though, *Head Games*, as unlike the democracy of early Crimson, in Foreigner a clear hierarchy had evolved. Jones and Gramm wanted to have control of a smaller band, and the record company backed their view, which meant that McDonald and keyboardist Greenwood were squeezed out. Too good a drummer and too big a personality to languish in low-key session musicianship for long, Ian Wallace was auditioned by Bob Dylan, and got the job. Appearing on his much rockier 1978 album, *Street Legal*, Wallace was also kept on Dylan's tour band for the following year. While the music was serious, offstage it was no-holds-barred-indulgence in alcohol, drugs and women. 'It was a hedonistic time', he later told Dmitry Epstein. 'Bob hadn't quite found religion . . . we partied hard . . . plus we had our own plane in the States'. [7]

Riding out Britain's Winter of Discontent on the other side of the Atlantic, by January 1979 Fripp had re-finished his solo album. He'd had no shortage of alternative vocalists to call on, with Peter Hammill flying over from England, and Terre Roche also stepping into the breach with dramatic results. Prior to its release, Fripp embarked on his first major tour in five years, not to showcase the album but to perform improvised Frippertronics pieces. This first Frippertronics tour, which he characterised as 'music for restaurants', lasted from April to August, taking him around much of North America and Europe. Many of the venues were rather unconventional—enabled by his small, mobile setup—such as record company offices, record shops, hotels and a pizza restaurant, although there would be the occasional, relatively conventional theatre. Fans who came quickly accepted this as Fripp being Fripp, and that what they were seeing was part of his new normal. It's worth remembering, however, that here was a man who had played on stages across the world, before massive crowds baying for his music, now presenting himself on his own, in tiny venues, for little or no payment, with minimal equipment and no pre-written material. On top of this he was also playing a new line of music that might be challenging even to some of his existing fan base. This was something that took a staggering amount of self-belief, as well as being thick-skinned enough not to be disheartened if anyone criticised what he was doing or chose to walk away. As well as creating new pieces live, he would often play back one of the pieces he'd recorded that day to solo over, as he had on the Eno tour. The politics of the music business was as much on Fripp's mind as the music itself, and he would find that playing in these venues gave him a perspective on Polygram's operations that no one else in the organisation had. Fripp has commented that, although it was the hardest tour he had done up to that point, it was the most rewarding. In fact, he has described it as 'the only tour I remember without regrets'. His observations and thoughts on the future of the music industry would subsequently be detailed in articles in *Musician, Player & Listener Magazine* and *Sound International* over the next three years. [5]

Eno was by this time also living, working and sleeping with as many women as possible in New York, initially sleeping on Fripp's sofa while looking for an apartment. Getting involved in the local music scene—his relationship with Bowie having now cooled somewhat—one of his jobs was producing the third Talking Heads album, and in the latter stages of the recording, he invited Fripp in for a session. The intention was for him to play on *Life During Wartime*, but although a take was recorded, it was discarded from the final mix. Instead, he added an extra guitar to *I Zimbra*, the irrepressibly joyous faux-African concoction that would open the *Fear of Music* album. This was co-written by Heads frontman, David Byrne, with Eno using a 1920s Dadaist nonsense poem by Hugo Ball as a means of getting round Byrne's writer's block. Fripp and Eno then found some studio time to try out ideas for a third album together under the provisional title, *Music for Healing*. They wanted to move on from the tape-delay-based instrumentals to something more rhythmic, but for once their ideas didn't gel, and the project was abandoned. Some of their recordings were included in the 1994 *Essential Fripp and Eno* compilation, in the form of variations of a track called *Healthy Colours*. Although these are less than essential, they illustrate Eno's changing direction from writing song lyrics to using taped voices, something he'd soon explore more fruitfully with Byrne. Another brief diversion found Fripp noodling energetically on a cover of *Hound Dog* by punk violinist and CBGB regular Walter Steding. Steding's arrangement of the Leiber and Stoller song bore little resemblance to the famous 1956 Elvis Presley version, or any other for that matter, being released as a B-side the following year.

While Fripp was otherwise gainfully occupied, June 1979 brought the release of his much-delayed solo album, now entitled *Exposure*. The images of Fripp used on the cover, which were stills from the *Alphaville* screen tests, showed that this was now a very different-looking Fripp, albeit captured in the role of Lemmy Caution, the beard long gone and sporting a slick, short haircut and smarter clothes. It can be dangerous to read too much into titles, as often they are just something convenient to identify an album, but with *Exposure* there are connotations of Fripp putting himself back in the public eye, as well as his own comment that he wanted to shine a light into the nooks and crannies of 'family customs'. In the sleeve notes, as well as thanking his managers for 'following despite disbelief', he explains that this had been intended as part of the ill-fated trilogy with the Hall and Gabriel albums. His intention now was for it to be the first part of his own trilogy, with plans for albums of 'Discotronics' and 'pure Frippertronics'. Fripp had been free to use the name King Crimson if he'd wanted to, and he would later have a failed attempt to get the core band from *Exposure* together as the next Crimson. However, making this a 'solo' album was another way of highlighting that this was a New World Fripp, not Old World Crimson. Related to this, scratched into the vinyl around the label on side two, are the words, 'The aim is freedom, conscience and truth'. Nobody knew what to expect as regards the contents, and the album can be hard to get to grips with, its seventeen tracks zigzagging between spoken word, ambient, light rock, heavier rock and manic blues. It takes a great deal of unravelling, but its contents are a product of many factors, the main ones being Fripp's (musical) relationships with Hall and Gabriel, his experiments with Frippertronics, the influence of Bennett, his relationship with Walton (who contributes lyrics for five songs) and the inevitable influence that came simply from being in New York. Something that passes a lot of people by is that, while it has its more serious moments, this is anything but a po-faced or preachy record. Given the prophesies of doom that had been consuming Fripp, there is a surprising amount of humour here, a lot hidden in plain sight and easily mistaken for something deep and meaningful. The personnel list is equally mind-boggling, as beyond Fripp and bassist Levin, there are ten others, four of whom are vocalists. The original cover unhelpfully neglected to say who was on which track, leading to a lot of confusion. The whole record is also liberally sprinkled with taped voices, or 'indiscretions' as Fripp termed them, of the likes of Eno, Gabriel, Bennett, Fripp's mother and aged Nepalese holy man Shivapuri Baba. [8]

The opening track of sorts, *Preface*, tries to alert us that we shouldn't necessarily take what we are about to hear too seriously. It starts with a taped clip of Eno talking about his own new material, cut with a few seconds of a choir—actually a multi-tracked Hall—with Gabriel also edited in to sound like an indecisive band leader. Fripp is just having a bit of a laugh, and the use of the choir is his gently poking fun at his old pal and his recent ambient release, *Music for Airports*. A ringing telephone—probably meant to be in a despised record company exec's plush office—is eventually answered and in bursts the first proper track, *You Burn Me Up I'm a Cigarette*. With vocals and piano by Hall, on the surface this is surprisingly straightforward rock, and one of the highest-tempo tracks Fripp would ever do. It's otherwise notable for the fact that Fripp penned the lyrics himself, his first entire set since GGF. Supposedly a love song about him and Walton, these are anything but straightforward lyrics however, filled as they are with clever rhymes and with a gentle Fourth Way reference slipped in. If we hadn't entirely got down to the business of serious music yet, we do with *Breathless*, a weighty instrumental performed by the fascinating combination of Fripp, Levin and Walden. The main riff is not too far removed from that of *Red*, and there are echoes of the *Larks'* era in the angular climbing sequence in the middle, signs that this new Fripp hadn't entirely jettisoned the past. It's also here that we're introduced to his use of simple Frippertronics as a sort of orchestration (later referred to as Applied Frippertronics), something that would be a feature throughout the album. After a short intro of Frippertronics and Fripp's mum apparently talking about his potty training, we then enter unique territory with *Disengage*. As one of the songs originally sung by Hall that had to be re-done, this features Hammill's gloriously disturbed delivery of Walton's lyrics, which are written from the viewpoint of someone in therapy. Fripp has shifted to an even heavier mode here, with Phil Collins as drummer on what is the punkiest piece of music he would ever play on. Hammill was thrown in the deep end for this, being handed a sheet of lyrics by Fripp and asked to improvise with them over the existing backing, guzzling a 'fair amount of brandy', according to Barry Andrews, to get into a freed-up state of mind. He was allowed a few runs at it, but the result is something that could never have been written, which was probably the point, and the overall feel is of a nervous breakdown captured in musical form. This fades abruptly, and while the listener is considering the need for counselling, *North Star* drifts in to soothe the soul, with Hall's second permitted vocal. Walton's lyrics here are more of a gentle wordplay than a song, Hall getting to demonstrate his remarkable vocal range in expressing them. *Chicago*, another of the songs where Hall's vocals had to be replaced, lumbers in as a menacing, grinding blues. Hammill snarls the words inspired by an enigmatic comment from Walton to her boyfriend about his smile, as Fripp overlays sections with Frippertronics, and all parties take liberties with the time signature. Continuing the uneasy-listening feel, *NY3* is a blazing family row turned into a short, heavy rock track. Fripp cheekily replaced Hall's forbidden vocals in this case with lines he'd taped from a raging argument he overheard from his Hell's Kitchen neighbours, the unrelenting tension of the music matching that of the row. With one final handbrake turn in mood, side one closes with *Mary*, the most stripped-down piece on the album, with its simple chords and touches of Frippertronics. Sticking to the vocal melody developed by Hall, here Roche gives a passionate-yet-delicate interpretation of a song Walton had written about a troubled friend. [9]

Though much patchier, side two starts strongly enough with the title track, co-written by Fripp and Gabriel. The last of the tracks where Hall's vocals had to be replaced, this is an alternate version to the one which had featured unobtrusively on *Gabriel II*. While the same basic track is used, the slow funk is now dramatically supplemented by Roche snarling and screaming the title—and by the end she is simply screaming—while Eno slowly and repeatedly spells it out. The *Gabriel II* version had taken exposure to mean getting out into the open, however Roche's delivery of this single word instead suggests the revealing of something sleazy. A tape of the Bennett aphorism, 'It is impossible to achieve the aim without suffering' (a reference to an aspect of Gurdjieff's teachings known as Intentional Sufferings) is repeated mantra-like, while Frippertronics provide the melodic backdrop. The effect is unsettling but stunning. One of the tracks that fails is *Häähden Two*, which sounds like a Mahavishnu Orchestra reject. Fripp is, however, just being perverse and is aware of the music's inadequacies, inserting Eno's voice midway to tell us it's an 'incredibly dismal, pathetic chord sequence'. The music, in fact, is little more than something to hang a few indiscretions on, including a backwards voice that (played the right way round) tells us 'One thing's for sure. A sheep is not a creature of the sky', and Eno telling Fripp to 'abandon it'. The first of three minimalist Frippertronics pieces, *Urban Landscape*, is a refugee from *Sacred Songs*. It's a slightly longer version here and serves as an introduction to pure Frippertronics. The serenity is shattered by another of the less-successful tracks, *I May Not Have Had Enough of Me, But I've Had Enough of You*. For this, Fripp set Hammill and Roche the task of improvising around a repeated line over recycled music from *NYCNY* (on *Sacred Songs*). It must have seemed like an amusing idea at the time, but the result is just annoying. This ends with the sound of a needle being scraped across vinyl, followed by three seconds of interference entitled *First Inaugural Address to the IACE Sherborne House*, a piece credited to Bennett. Some writers have been taken in by a light-hearted Fripp comment that this was a Bennett speech raised by countless octaves, however that would have been inaudible. *Water Music: Parts One and Two* are Frippertronics pieces wrapped around an alternative version of *Here Comes the Flood*. *Part One* is short and melodic, overlaid with clips of Bennett talking of impending sea level rise and a new ice-age. Up to this point, Bennett had been deployed by Fripp to humorous ends, but here the message is serious, even though Bennett was perhaps confusing issues. *Part Two* shimmers beautifully for several minutes, like something you can't quite make out on the horizon, before gently vanishing. The song which these passages act as bookends for is something of an oddity, insomuch as it's a Gabriel song largely performed by him but on a Fripp album. Gabriel had felt that his original version was rather overblown, and took the opportunity to rework it here, stripping it back to the basics of piano and voice, with just a few notes of guitar from Fripp and touches of synth from Eno. Ending the album in the gently humorous fashion it began, is *Postscript.* A taped clip of Eno tells us, 'So the whole story is completely untrue, a big hoax, ha-ha-ha', Fripp looping the last phrase in mockery of the Eno/Frippertronics style. Then to tie up the loose ends, the phone that had been picked up in *Preface* is hung up, footsteps walk back across the executive's office floor and the door is closed. [10]

Fripp was overjoyed with his output, declaring that he saw it as 'tweaking the vocabulary of . . . rock music . . . expanding the possibilities of expression and introducing a more sophisticated emotional dynamic'. Certainly, the return to vinyl of one of the great figures of prog-rock attracted a lot of attention and would do more than just tweak the vocabulary for the swathe of musicians who worshipped at the Fripp altar. While some music journalists considered the album bold and forward-looking, others wondered what all the fuss was about, seeing it as little different to what had gone before. For all its flitting around and occasional annoyances, *Exposure* was a mostly successful mishmash, and Fripp was definitely back, with ideas and inspiration bursting out of him, and still relevant in the post new-wave world. The jury was still out as to whether he knew where he was going, as based on the evidence, he was heading in half-a-dozen directions simultaneously. His 1979 Frippertronics tour had, in effect, acted as a low-budget promo tour both for Frippertronics itself and obliquely for *Exposure,* and while no one was expecting sales of the latter to hit the levels that Crimson albums had, it did sell reasonably. It was also helped that October by a rare Fripp appearance on mainstream American TV, his notoriety earning him a slot on NBC's *Midnight Special.* Choosing to perform a solo Frippertronics piece, presenting it as a sort of demonstration, it would be by far the biggest audience that he would ever get for the format. Fripp had to admit in sleeve notes penned in 2005 that the dinosaurs, for all their wrong motives, actually did him a favour in forcing him to re-do a big chunk of the album. The tracks originally recorded with Hall's vocals have since been added as bonuses on various re-releases. Hall's vocal talents were undoubtedly remarkable, but what came out of the other side of Fripp's rework was far better, even if side two felt awkwardly cobbled together. Amusingly, two years later Phil Collins would consider calling his debut solo album *Exposure*; remembering in time that it was the name of the Fripp album he'd played on, he switched his to *Face Value.* [5]

By the time *Exposure* had reached the record shop shelves, Fripp was already assembling a second solo album. Again filled with bold experimentation, the dinosaurs found nothing to object to this time and it was released in January 1980, uniquely presented in its vinyl form, as if it were two half-albums stuck together. One was named *God Save the Queen* and consisted of three Frippertronics tracks; the other, *Under Heavy Manners*, contained two long, upbeat, full-band tracks. To indicate the equal standing of the two halves, both had front covers and the sides were labelled 'One' and 'A'. Fripp's original intention hadn't been for half-albums, these being the manifestations of pure Frippertronics and Discotronics he'd talked about, but without enough material for a whole discotronics album, the master plan had again taken a diversion. The upbeat-downbeat split wasn't in itself unique, loosely resembling Bowie's *Low*, but presenting it in this manner was Fripp's quirky way of emphasising the two distinct lines of his work. Other than the unusual format, after the scattergun approach of *Exposure*, this seemed far more focussed and was much easier to get to grips with.

Frippertronics had been out in the wild for a couple of years, but *God Save the Queen* was a clear sign of Fripp's confidence in the pure version of it, and a full half an hour of it at that. He'd gone through a few changes of mind between the conception and finally compiling it, his earlier notes stating it would be made up of his 1977–1978 studio experiments, while in the end its tracks were all from gigs in California during the 1979 Frippertronics tour. While the music is undeniably a close relation to Fripp's work with Eno, in having no overdubbed solos, no taped voices and no added keyboards, it is distinct, and had also noticeably evolved even from the Frippertronics tasters on *Exposure*. As before, Fripp's sound is based on variations of a fuzzed/sustained guitar sound, sometimes with wah or attack/decay pedals, creating sounds that could be mistaken for synthesisers. The Fripp pedalboard, in fact, became a source of fascination for musicians who were able to get a much closer look at Frippertronics gigs, considering it the height of sophistication for guitarists. Fripp varied his method a little for each piece, but the basic pattern was that phrases or sequences were constructed a note or two at a time, either followed by adding in harmonies, bass parts or rippling higher notes that could resemble strings. There's never any risk of a tune breaking out, but the beauty and power comes from the interplay of the phrases and the lush textures that appear. Once he had taken a sequence as far as he could, he would leave it to begin fading away, then begin to construct another, continuing in this way until he felt ready to allow the piece to fade away completely. Depending on the repetition interval used—usually around four seconds—and the lengths of notes, unconventional or even ambiguous time signatures could be called into existence, further complicated if stereo delay was added in. But far from making it challenging to listen to, this is part of the charm of the music, and part of why Fripp found it such fertile territory to explore. While the process might sound as if it's just being clever, and might create mechanical, unemotional results, the art that Fripp was developing was in creating highly evocative pieces, something which took immense skill despite how simple he made it look.

The opener, *Red Two Scorer*, is a slightly eerie but gentle introduction to Fripp's longer, more developed pieces. As would often be the case, its construction is laid bare, as you can hear each new note added, the audio equivalent of seeing every brushstroke added to a painting. The track titles are ultimately of little importance but this particular one is a clunky leftover from Fripp's original intention to call the album *Music for Sports*. His circuitous logic was that, with the smaller-scale audiences at Frippertronics gigs, there was a healthier relationship between performer and audience. He also felt that the music itself could be used 'as an accompaniment for a wide range of healthy activities or as a field for active listening'. In the end, he decided not to intrude on Eno's line of *Music for . . .* titles. The second piece, *God Save the Queen*, drones and bleeps away pleasantly for almost ten minutes, with an almost classical elegance, as Fripp's response to an audience member requesting the American national anthem, *The Star-Spangled Banner*. The final piece, *1983*, begins with more of an edgy feel to it. This is where Frippertronics diverts from being strictly ambient, as this demands the listener's attention. Its tone early on indicates that something dramatic is going to happen, and after a couple of minutes it does, as an ominous, rumbling, two-note figure rolls in, followed by snakelike wah-pedal notes rearing their heads. This sets the tone for the rest of this thirteen-minute epic, building up to giant sweeps of noise that wouldn't be out of place on a sci-fi soundtrack. [11]

Opening the *Under Heavy Manners* side is the title track, which possibly set a record for being recorded in the most countries. The backing consists of Frippertronics from a live performance in Calgary, Canada, and a disco-ish rhythm track of Fripp's guitar, Paul Duskin's drums and Busta Jones's bass, recorded in New York. On top of this is a vocal from David Byrne, recorded in London, the Talking Heads frontman for no apparent reason having himself listed in the credits as Absalm El Habib. The bulk of what can only loosely be described as a song is a long list of words ending in . . .*ism*, interspersed with such fripperies as an anagram of the title and an obscure religious reference inspired by a visit to a monastery in Greece. The chimes of Wimborne Minster's bells also put in an appearance. After six minutes, with Byrnes' vocal getting increasingly manic, proceedings are brought to an abrupt halt by a voice-over, followed by further Byrne warblings. As ever, we must beware of looking for meanings that aren't there, as at a pinch you could interpret the . . . *isms* as a look at the diverse nature of people's beliefs and activities, and how we label them. Otherwise, the piece is packed with references that may mean something in themselves, but when you put it all together, it's just an exercise in wordplay. The title, *Under Heavy Manners*, shared with a 1976 reggae album, is a Jamaican term for a state of emergency, adding another layer that in the end has no discernible meaning here. *The Zero of the Signified* begins almost as if it's a continuation of the first track, the title referencing the work of French philosopher Roland Barthes (who died later in 1980) and his thoughts on repetition, which is what this track is all about. Musically, its roots are traceable to Terry Riley's minimalist experiments in the sixties and early seventies, *Zero*, in effect, being a post-punk equivalent of Riley's *A Rainbow in Curved Air*. Fripp hypnotically weaves a fast-repeating guitar arpeggio in and out of the punchy rhythm track, all of which is played over a slowly building backdrop of Frippertronics. It's a simple setup, but with its elements repeating in different cycles, it's ever changing. Up to a point it's an experiment set in motion just to see where it goes. However, with Fripp adding in harmonies of the guitar line, and the rhythm track eventually being faded out to leave a lingering Frippertronics ending, the artist takes back some control from the scientist to shape the end-result.

Sales were moderate. But considering how far Fripp was now venturing into arty experimentation, that was only to be expected, the market for this being a specific subset of his existing fans. And fascinating though it was, it was hard to see where Fripp saw himself going after this. Sleeve notes alone were not enough for him this time, and if anyone examined their vinyl closely, they'd find that the outer edge of the label had been used to outline part of his Bennett-inspired philosophy. It states that 'the future unit of organisation is the small, mobile and intelligent unit, where intelligence is defined as the capacity to perceive rightness, mobile is the capacity to act on that perception, and small, the necessary condition for that action in a contracting world'. While the collapse-of-society aspect had rapidly faded from his thinking, Fripp's stance was increasingly in opposition to the bloated scale of things in the music business, and its general lack of interest in the music or creativity. He had tried to turn himself into the musician equivalent of a small-scale craftsman (as far as Frippertronics was concerned at least) rather than be a willing part of the machinery of mass production. While the likes of ELP had needed to mobilise a fleet of articulated lorries, employ an army of roadies and take months to plan a tour, Fripp could pretty much just jump in his ageing green Volvo and slot into the smallest venues at the drop of a hat. [11]

In amongst the albums and preaching of his philosophy, Fripp was called up again by Peter Gabriel, for a session for his third solo album. His involvement would be relatively minor this time, only playing on three tracks and with no big solos or production duties. However, there would also be the unintended consequence that what Gabriel was doing would act as a signpost to Fripp as to where he could go with his own music. With Gabriel having already been influential in getting Fripp back involved in music, in a role reversal from 1969, Fripp was now metaphorically standing in the crowd, watching Gabriel show how it should be done. Gabriel's record company were trying to push him in a more chart-friendly direction, but he was standing firm in pursuing his own unique line and trying out new things. In particular, he was embracing cutting-edge electronics, in the form of samplers, and beginning to incorporate influences we would come to call World Music. All in all, he was demonstrating how an ex-prog rocker could make it in the eighties, while still maintaining credibility. Fripp is most present on *No Self Control,* with several layers of guitar drones and phrases, some looped to sound mechanical, acting as a counterpoint to Gabriel's very human, angst-filled lyrics. As with Bowie, Gabriel had also fallen under the spell of Steve Reich's gamelan-style pieces like *Music for Eighteen Musicians*, an influence that found its way onto *No Self Control* in the form of interlocking synth-marimba patterns. Another ingredient of the track (and the album as a whole) was Gabriel's approach to the drumming, instructing his drummers not to use cymbals or hi-hats. This strategy prompted Phil Collins to make more inventive use of the rest of the kit, giving the track a different texture to what it would otherwise have had. Fripp would make a mental note of all of the above for future reference. *No Self Control* was put out as a single, but even with the added attraction of young Crimson fan Kate Bush on backing vocals, its unsettling feel made it poor chart fodder. *I Don't Remember* is the combination of many simple parts to make a glorious whole. It features Fripp using a synth-like, filtered-guitar sound, reminiscent of that on Bowie's *Blackout*, as Gabriel's pleading vocal tackles the pain of memory loss and identity. The track is underpinned by a driving bass line from Levin on his Chapman Stick, Levin fast becoming the best-known exponent of this recently invented instrument. With twelve strings covering the tonal ranges of a bass and a guitar, it only requires them to be touched rather than plucked, so a player could use both hands to cover a greater range or, if needed, a bass and rhythm part. This was later put out as a single but only troubled the lower regions of the U.K. chart. Fripp's third—and relatively unobtrusive—contribution is on *Not One of Us*, Gabriel's attack on casual racism. Released in May 1980, *Gabriel III* went to No. 1 in the U.K., achieving a more modest No. 22 in the U.S. An otherwise-identical version, with Gabriel having re-recorded the vocals in German, was also put out.

Aspects of the philosophy that had caused Fripp to disband Crimson were still important to him, but there was a huge downside that was also becoming increasingly apparent to him. Recording solo albums with the help of musician friends was all well and good, but if he adhered too rigidly to his principles, he would be unable to perform live other than Frippertronics, and that was not enough. He realised what he had to do and set off once more down the road of forming a band. Prompting some to say that he was trying to prove he could hold his own in this post-punk era, the thirty-three-year-old sought out a younger crew, enlisting Barry Andrews (who had played on *Exposure*) on organ, Sara Lee on bass, and Johnny Toobad on drums. Fripp asked Lee and Toobad to join, having seen them play live with a band called Baby and the Blackspots (Lee also being a member of staff at Polydor Records). Fripp's aim with the band was to continue with his line of Discotronics begun on *Under Heavy Manners*, and for this he chose to resurrect the name The League of Gentlemen from his teenage band years. While he was having to row back a little from the small, mobile concept, the new LoG would still be a relatively stripped-down affair. Having moved back to Wimborne, into a flat above a shop, in March 1980 he summoned his recruits to Fripp Central, holding the early rehearsals nearby in a former hunting lodge overlooked by the woods and ancient remnants of Badbury Rings. Just three weeks later, with the set raw and embryonic to say the least, they were on the road, playing a handful of gigs in Southern England. Traffic jams, engine problems and a van door slamming on one of Fripp's hands nearly put paid to their attempts to set off for Western Europe in May, but they eventually made it, subsequently flying across to North America in June. It was easy to forget, with the Frippertronics tour and his having been onstage with other bands, but these were the first gigs of a Fripp band since he'd broken up Crimson six years earlier. Older fans eagerly flocking to see him again would find there were no concessions whatsoever to the past, while for the new wave generation, it was their first chance to see a Fripp band in the flesh. What they found was an enjoyably lively and energetic act, despite Fripp still playing seated and there being no vocalist. The music was upbeat, with bass, drums and organ complementing Fripp's jangly arpeggio guitar riffs and soloing, and with no odd time signatures in sight. With only a handful of ideas that were anything approaching fully formed, for the first few months their set contained a large proportion of improv, based around loose ideas, and therefore with plenty of the hazard element that Fripp relished. One thing he increasingly didn't relish, though, was people taking photos while he was playing, even trying to kick cameras out of people's hands at gigs if they came within range. It would be such a bugbear for him in the coming years that he would try to ban photography at his gigs. As they toured, while Fripp's head may have been full of his personal politics, he still had other urges. Andrews remembers him being 'up for some action', but all too often being cornered by male fans seeking guidance, 'instead of basking in the oestrogen waves of well-deserved post-show girly adulation'. [9]

In a space in the early LoG schedule, an event to file under bizarre was Fripp's participation in what has become known as The Stranglers and Friends gig in April 1980. Hugh Cornwell, frontman of the massively successful punk band, had been caught in possession of drugs and was sentenced to a few weeks in Pentonville Prison. The band had a gig lined up at The Rainbow in North London and, wanting to defiantly stick two fingers up at the authorities, instead of cancelling, called on the goodwill of a whole host of musician friends who took turns filling in for Cornwell on the night. Fripp wielded his guitar on the songs *Tank* (with vocals by his friend Peter Hammill), *Threatened* and *Toiler on the Sea*. He also crossed paths that evening with Toyah Willcox, who he would marry six years later. Then at the peak of her own pop career, she sang on four songs, including *Peaches*, The Stranglers' single that had put them on the map, sharing vocal duties with Ian Dury and Hazel O'Connor. Fripp and Toyah wouldn't properly meet until a music industry event three years later however, where they were photographed together with Princess Michael of Kent. The Stranglers and Friends gig was later released on CD, sounding like a lot of fun but also a bit of a shambles, as many of the participants hadn't really had time to learn their parts.

Fripp's regular magazine articles in this period gave him a good platform to reiterate and expand on his views on the music business, as well as diverting into aspects of touring and his opinions on current fads in production. His underlying message, however, was the immorality and destructiveness of the business and how it didn't operate for the benefit of musician kind. As well as his push for more of a Schumacher-esque approach, he also suggested that they should cater more for 'an intermediate level of performer'—presumably, himself included—who didn't fall into the mainstream of pop but who could be reasonably successful at their own level, with a lesser level of financial backing. In one article, Fripp suggested that 'it is a human requirement to make music, to express all that a person would wish to say but lacks the words', linking this to his more spiritual beliefs, saying 'music is a cosmic requirement. It is a direct language common to God and man'. In this religious context he then added a line that would be quoted to death in the internet age: 'music is the cup which holds the wine of silence'. This is, however, usually quoted without the vital context that Fripp believes that 'silence is an echo of the presence of god'. On a more down-to-earth level, discussing ideas and inspiration, a particular Fripp gem from his articles was 'we cannot govern the breeze, but we can learn how to raise the sail'. While he hit several nails beautifully on the head in these articles, Fripp's style tended towards the intense, sometimes to the point of discouraging the reader. Tamm described him as being 'not entirely without craft', but the results as being 'not what one would call graceful, elegant or flowing'. [12] [13] [4]

Early in June, Fripp also renewed his partnership with Bowie, albeit just for one day, for what would become the album *Scary Monsters.* Bowie's *Lodger* album, and the tour that followed, had featured guitarist and future Crim Adrian Belew, his highest-profile contribution being a feedback-filled solo on *Boys Keep Swinging.* Belew had been under the impression he was a shoe-in to play on his next album, so he was surprised to hear that Bowie had called in Fripp instead. Fripp plays lead guitar on six tracks, including the hit single *Fashion*, Bowie's danceable mocking of the fickle nature of what's in or out from one day to the next. The other highlight, from a Fripp angle, is his spine-tingling fuzz/sustain guitar on Bowie's cover of Tom Verlaine's *Kingdom Come.* Fripp repeats the feat over the *Heroes*-like intro to *Teenage*

*Wildlife*, also playing on the title track and the gently political *Up the Hill Backwards*, both of which became minor hit singles. For the weird concoction that is *It's No Game (Part 1)*, with vocals half-spoken in Japanese by actress Michi Hirota, and half-shouted in English by Bowie, Fripp's instruction had been to play in an exaggerated B. B. King style. It ends with Bowie yelling in mock anger at Fripp as he carries on playing after the rest of the band have finished. On a couple of tracks, you get the feeling that Fripp could have done with another take or two, and he later admitted that he wasn't in the best state to play that day, having dived straight in after a long, early-morning drive from where the LoG had been playing the previous night. The album was released in the autumn, with Bowie's record company for once being pleased, as this was a return to form in commercial terms for their man. From a Fripp perspective, he once again found himself on a U.K. No. 1 album, as well as some hit singles.

After a moderately ambitious twenty-eight-night summer tour of the U.S.—a new and exciting experience for Lee and Toobad—Fripp tried to get the LoG down to the serious business of recording an album. He soon began to realise the difficulty of what he'd taken on. He'd done it very deliberately—but teaming up with musicians who were not at the level he was used to was starting to feel frustrating, and ideas were just not gelling in the way he'd hoped. Andrews later said that he'd had his doubts from the start but he needed the work as he'd been living in a squat. It seemed to him that Fripp was working through a theory or a vision 'to revolutionise rock 'n' roll, [that] just wasn't grounded in reality'. Their first week in Arny's Shack Studio, near Poole in Dorset, proved to be very disappointing, with only two tracks completed to Fripp's satisfaction. In the meantime, the workaholic guitarist was also continuing to slot in Frippertronics gigs when time allowed, and at London's ICA in September 1980, the aspect of hazard and unpredictability went a stage further than usual. Keith Tippett had been due to appear alongside Fripp but his piano wasn't delivered to the venue in time. Fripp decided to fill the extra time available by using a synth that

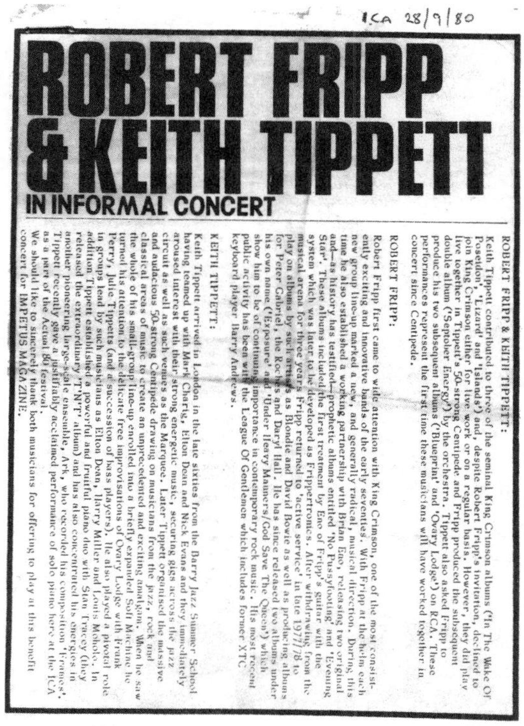

ICA 28/9/80

# ROBERT FRIPP & KEITH TIPPETT

IN INFORMAL CONCERT

ROBERT FRIPP & KEITH TIPPETT:

Keith Tippett contributed to three of the seminal King Crimson albums ('In The Wake Of Poseidon', 'Lizard' and 'Islands') and, despite Robert Fripp's invitation, declined to join King Crimson either for live work or on a regular basis. However, they did play live together in Tippett's 50-strong Centipede and Fripp produced the subsequent double album ('Septober Energy') by the orchestra. Tippett also asked Fripp to produce his two subsequent albums ('Blueprint' and 'Ovary Lodge') on RCA. These performances represent the first time these musicians will have worked together in concert since Centipede.

ROBERT FRIPP:

Robert Fripp first came to wide attention with King Crimson, one of the most consistently exciting and innovative bands of the early seventies. With Fripp at the helm each new group line-up marked a new, and generally radical, musical direction. During this time he also established a working partnership with Brian Eno, releasing two original and—as history has testified—prophetic albums entitled 'No Pussyfooting' and 'Evening Star'. These albums included the first treatment by Eno of Fripp's guitar with the system which was later to be developed as Frippertronics. After withdrawing from the musical arena for three years Fripp returned to 'active service' in late 1977/78 to play on albums by such artists as Blondie and David Bowie as well as producing albums for Peter Gabriel, the Roches and Daryl Hall. He has since released two albums under his own name ('Exposure' and 'Under Heavy Manners/God Save The Queen') which show him to be of continuing importance in contemporary rock music. His most recent public activity has been with the League Of Gentlemen which includes former XTC keyboard player Barry Andrews.

KEITH TIPPETT:

Keith Tippett arrived in London in the late sixties from the Barry Jazz Summer School having teamed up with Mark Charig, Elton Dean and Nick Evans and they immediately aroused interest with their strong energetic music, securing gigs across the jazz circuit as well as such venues as the Marquee. Later Tippett organised the massive and audacious 50-strong Centipede drawing on musicians from the jazz, rock and classical areas of music to create an unprecedented and exciting amalgam. When he saw the whole of his small-group line-up enrolled into a briefly expanded Soft Machine he turned his attention to the delicate free improvisations of Ovary Lodge with Frank Perry, Julie Tippetts (and a succession of bass players). He also played a pivotal role in groups lead by such musicians as Elton Dean, Harry Miller and Louis Moholo. In addition Tippett established a powerful and fruitful piano duo with Stan Tracey (they released the extraordinary 'T'N'T' album) and has also concentrated his energies in another pioneering large-scale ensemble, Ark, who recorded his composition 'Frames'. Tippett recently gave a justifiably acclaimed performance of solo piano here at the ICA as a part of the Actual 80 festival.

We should like to sincerely thank both musicians for offering to play at this benefit concert for IMPETUS MAGAZINE.

*Frippertronics gig flyer, ICA, 1980.*

had made it there to play keyboard-based Frippertronics. The event had been billed as an informal concert, and this was the perfect illustration of the flexibility made possible by the smaller and less formal nature of these shows. In contrast to when he was onstage with his bands, Fripp was always much more open to interaction with the audience at such events, talking between tracks and lingering afterwards to sit and chat to audience member (and, as at the ICA, receiving demo cassettes from teenage wannabees). [9]

Back with his troubled LoG, the U.K. touring and attempts at recording continued into the autumn. Tensions were growing, however, and the sessions were unproductive. One issue was with drummer

Toobad, who Fripp realised was not interested 'in adopting the life of a professional musician'. He later put a positive spin on this, remarking that it was 'a sure sign of a man to be trusted in life's fundamentals', although this attitude was not good for the task at hand. At the same time, Toobad was developing health problems, treatment for which naturally took priority over band concerns. On a more positive note, that November the band recorded a BBC session for *The John Peel Show* on Radio One, a show that had the power to boost interest in a band. Sadly, the positive feeling didn't last, and a few days later, after playing in Manchester, tensions came to a head, resulting in Toobad leaving the band. They still had a few gigs to play and an album to finish, but luckily, Kevin Wilkinson from Restaurant for Dogs (who had been supporting the LoG in the U.K.) was able to occupy the drum stool. With no time to rehearse, he bravely winged it on the basis of having seen them play several times!

When the ordeal of the LoG was finally over, December 1980 brought Fripp the more pleasurable diversion of guesting on stage once again with Blondie for the encores of their eight-night stint at London's Hammersmith Odeon. Merely passing through on a world tour, Blondie were themselves now a massive, international success, and the days of roughing it at CBGB had long gone. With Iggy Pop also guesting on encore versions of his song, *Funtime*, Fripp added his distinctive tones to versions of *I Feel Love* and *Heroes*. [14]

The LoG's eponymously titled studio album was released in February 1981 to expectant fans, only to receive decidedly lukewarm reactions. Fripp's aim had been valiant but the idea had not translated well into a finished product. Not only was the material patchy but the frustrating studio sessions hadn't produced enough useable material to fill an album, several of the embryonic tracks aired on tour having been jettisoned along the way. To fill it out, Fripp had knocked up three short keyboard Frippertronics-style pieces and, as with *Exposure*, added in several spoken-word passages, some taken from Bennett lectures. For added spice, these were mixed in with taped excerpts of women, including the Roche sisters, discussing sex or, in one case, possibly having sex. This wasn't a completely random element as it tied in with Fripp's idea that this was dance music, and for the pelvis rather than the brain, and therefore inherently sexual. After some initial indiscretions, *Inductive Resonance* opens the album. A prime candidate for being the highest-tempo track Fripp would ever do, this is what the LoG were for, with Fripp playing variations on a joyful arpeggio riff, supplemented by Andrews's organ swirling and bouncing its way around the chords beneath. The album's only song, and a highlight of the album, *Minor Man*, features Danielle Dax, of the experimental post-punk band Lemon Kittens, on vocals, the song being about how drearily unromantic relationships can be. It's a lot of fun and wouldn't have been out of place on *Exposure*. It is also the only Fripp track to ever include the word *arse*. Dax also contributed a drawing for the front cover, with three mischievously grinning cat-like creatures peering round a fence post. While the band's music may have been deliberately lowbrow, this didn't stop Fripp from indulging in highbrow track titles, the epitome of these being *Heptaparaparshinokh*, a word borrowed from Gurdjieff's writings on chaos and hazard. The track itself is based around a shockingly jaunty riff, played over something close to a tango rhythm, giving the whole thing an oddly old-fashioned feel. This was also put out as a single, with the bonus for anyone bravely attempting to ask for it at a record counter, of a lengthy Frippertronics B-side called *Marriagemuzik*. *Dislocated*, one of only two tracks featuring Toobad, goes some way to enjoyably repeating the formula of *Inductive Resonance* but suffers from the undercooked, under-produced feel that permeates the album. Fripp had not totally left his Audio Verité ideas behind, and the band tracks had largely been recorded without overdubs. After this, the album simply runs out of inspiration. The three keyboard Frippertronics pieces are forgettable and the remaining four band tracks are unsuccessful attempts to squeeze tracks out of half-ideas and improvs. The only points of interest are where Fripp tries out his newly acquired guitar-synth, and on *Trap*, where there are the germs of ideas that would find better homes in the future. [14]

Fripp had long realised that this was no League of Extraordinary Gentlemen and was himself unhappy with the album. There was nowhere left to go, however, and so he called a halt to the LoG, and with it, Discotronics, and instantly started looking to form his next band. Regarding the LoG's personnel, Sara Lee would go on to more satisfying experiences with Gang of Four and the B52s; Barry Andrews with Shriekback; and Kevin Wilkinson with The Waterboys, China Crisis and Squeeze. Tragically, Wilkinson, who suffered from severe depression, would take his own life in 1999 at the age of forty-one. The LoG's original drummer, Johnny Toobad (real name Johnny Elichaoff), would subsequently ditch the music to become a company director and, in 1999, married Sarah Jane Woodall, known to the world as Trinny on the TV fashion-advice programmes *Trinny and Suzannah* and *What Not to Wear*. Sadly, he too would die young, taking his own life in 2014.

Now all hitting their mid-thirties, it was a time of mixed fortunes and much uncertainty for all in the Crimson world. McDonald was back out in the cold again and Lake was having to try to establish himself outside ELP. Wetton was looking for something new, with UK having run its course, the same applying to Bruford, who had also had to abandon his own band to stop it from bankrupting him. Fripp was still optimistic, even though the LoG hadn't really worked. He was back in full flow again and still pushing on into new territory, creating his own musical vocabulary and genres. He just needed a more appropriate vehicle.

# 7

# It Is Impossible to Achieve the Aim Without Suffering

## *1981 to Late 1984*

The League of Gentlemen was a rare, relative flop for Fripp, being based on a passing whim that just didn't have enough mileage in it, or what Barry Andrews has since characterised as 'a Gurdjieffian social experiment gone wrong'. Fripp's dissatisfaction with the LoG, who he undiplomatically termed a second-division band, led him to look again to form a first-division outfit. He was in it for the art rather than to showcase technical ability but having dipped into the pool of new-wave musicians, he knew he needed people who could cover both bases. To do this, not only would he have to reject youth for its own sake in favour of quality, but he would have to accept that things would return to being much bigger and less mobile, ditching a significant plank of his post–Fourth Way approach. Forming a new band would lead Fripp somewhere that nobody, including him, had expected, and surprise, in fact, would be a common theme across the wider Crimson family in the early eighties. This phase would be at least as eventful as the seventies for Wetton, not to mention being a whole lot more lucrative, and there would even be an unexpected U.K. No. 1 single, featuring lyrics by Sinfield. [1]

A message scratched into the vinyl of the LoG album had informed us, 'The next step is discipline', and sure enough it was, as *Discipline* was the name Fripp chose for his new band. With earlier thoughts of an *Exposure* spin-off line-up with Hall, Levin and Marotta being a non-starter, as Fripp set about finding personnel, to move forward, he started by looking back, contacting Bruford. The pair met up and, although the drummer was overjoyed at the prospect of linking up with Fripp again, he made it clear that this new venture would need to be a lot more fun and not something that you needed a Ph.D. to enjoy. He was also a little wary because of how it had ended in 1974, saying, 'I didn't want to be jilted again'. But having had to give up on his own band for financial reasons, Bruford could see that life back with Fripp promised much, whatever the difficulties. This was far from being the only change in approach, as Fripp then contacted American guitarist and Crimson fan Adrian Belew. Fripp had seen Belew as part of Bowie's live band in 1978, and when they subsequently crossed paths at a Steve Reich concert in New York, Fripp asked Belew and his band, GaGa, to support the LoG for a few nights of their tour. Asking Belew to join Discipline was a big deal for Fripp as up to this point he had scrupulously steered clear of working alongside *any* other guitarist. In an interview with one of the few guitarists he admired, John McLaughlin, Fripp would later state that he simply didn't like other guitarists. Back in 1974, he had been less than complimentary about several widely worshipped rock guitarists, being particularly scathing about Eric Clapton, who he described as 'banal' and 'excessively tedious'. The change of heart was the result of ideas he was now developing, inspired by Indonesian Gamelan music and Steve Reich, which would need two guitars, and the younger American had the necessary qualities. [2] [3] [4]

Plenty of others had noticed Belew's self-taught talents and, as a result, he was always in great demand. Following his stint with Bowie, in 1980 he had been conscripted into the recording of Talking Heads' *Remain in Light*, the album that would see them break through into the wider public consciousness. They were already a two-guitarist band, but Belew took them to places the others could not reach, especially his inimitable soloing on *The Great Curve*. He then stayed with them as part of their expanded touring line-up, and it was during the tour's

U.K. leg that Fripp approached him about joining Discipline. Belew felt that he couldn't make a snap decision because of his commitments with Talking Heads, and events could easily have taken several turns. Bad feelings were brewing in the band's ranks, and there were informal discussions of Belew either fully joining, or even replacing Byrne as frontman. Belew diplomatically turned down the offers however and, once the tour was over, instead joined the Heads' spinoff project, The Tom Tom Club. There was another factor causing Belew's hesitancy about joining Fripp, as: despite his CV, he was suddenly doubting his own abilities. With Fripp pressing him for a decision, Belew realised that Talking Heads looked likely to be on hiatus for a while, so he put his self-doubt to one side and took Fripp up on his offer.

According to Talking Heads biographer David Bowman, Belew had a reasonable idea of what he would be letting himself in for. He knew 'Fripp was a complex guy', but wasn't the 'strange deity' some made him out to be. In some ways he was better suited to working with Fripp than Talking Heads; being very dedicated to his music and, being a married man with a small child, he was not into the rock 'n' roll lifestyle. When looking back on his time with Talking Heads, Belew later commented, 'I think I was seen as probably being a little naïve and square', steering clear of the 'drugs and party favours' that some of the others in the expanded Heads setup indulged in. In terms of personality, teaming with Fripp looked more awkward though. The American was, onstage at least, irrepressibly extroverted, while Fripp would just sit quietly on his guitar stool. The Kentucky-born guitarist (born Robert Steven Belew) had talents beyond being a much sought-after guitarist, and would double as vocalist for Fripp's new band, with a passion for singing that could be traced as far back as age five when he would sing along to jukebox records at a neighbourhood bar. Having been a drummer in his school's marching band and in teenage bands would also come in handy. He brought a big range of influences with him, from Hendrix to Gershwin to Stravinsky. His love of The Beatles, since seeing them on *The Ed Sullivan Show*, would also be clear for all to see in the coming years. With everything seemingly going his way, while in the Bahamas working with the Tom Tom Club, Belew also found himself being offered a solo deal by Chris Blackwell too. [5]

Fripp still needed to fill the role of bassist, and a promising early candidate was Bruford's previous bandmate Jeff Berlin. After some consideration, Fripp felt he just wouldn't get on with Berlin's style and decided to look elsewhere. Tony Levin, from Boston, was now at the top of Fripp's list, having worked with him several times already. Fripp had initially assumed he would be too much in demand elsewhere to commit himself to a major band, but while Levin still wanted to fit in working with Gabriel, he was fully prepared to sacrifice much of his session work and commit to Fripp. After walking his audition, he was welcomed on board. There is no such thing as being just a bassist in a Fripp band, and in addition to having an input into the material, Levin would do backing vocals. He also had a rare virtuosity on the Chapman Stick, which opened up some interesting possibilities. Levin's post-*Exposure* time had been eventful for him, in good ways and bad. He already had a reputation for delivering the goods, but he had also shown he was unphased by working alongside the biggest names on the planet or being dropped into some very unusual situations. As well as continuing to work with Gabriel, he had been called up again by Paul Simon, not just to record with him but also to play a role in Simon's 1980 film, *One Trick Pony*. It was an appropriate role for Levin, playing a bassist in a band! Oddly, Simon's character had the surname Levin, while Levin himself played John De Batista. The bassist was also part of what started out as a highly secretive project, with John Lennon and Yoko Ono. Released in November 1980, *Double Fantasy* was Lennon's big comeback after a five-year gap, so it was already a significant album despite receiving decidedly mixed reviews. Tragedy would give it a whole new significance when, just three weeks later, on 8 December Lennon was shot dead outside his Manhattan home, devastating fans across the world. There turned out to be one notable difference between Levin and the others Fripp had enlisted, in that he wasn't a Fripp fan as such, confessing in a 1984 interview, 'I'd never listened to King Crimson'! [6]

With the line-up of Fripp, Belew, Levin and Bruford in place, Discipline began sessions together in Dorset. As well as his own unique brand of guitar playing, Belew would also add what you could loosely call Byrne-esque vocals. What Fripp had also seen in him was his writing ability, including lyrics, and he was to be a significant contributor in this department, Fripp's short phase of lyric writing now over. Belew soon found that the multiple roles he'd taken on weighed extremely heavily on his shoulders, and by week three he 'was a nervous wreck'. Interviewed in 1982, Belew revealed that his crisis of confidence returned and for the first few weeks he was lost as to what his approach should be and even whether he was up to the job. 'When I came into the band, I was insecure', he admitted. 'I thought everything I was doing was a load of crap'. Something clicked in week four, though. He stopped trying to fit in with Fripp and started doing his own thing. Commenting on his colleague's change, in his diary Fripp referred to 'AB's wild and weird sounds . . . [being] . . . all over the place now'. But it still wasn't plain sailing for Belew, and as they prepared for their first tour, he told Fripp he felt the band was 'pushing him to the limits of what he can do'. It was working, however, and there seemed to be a rich collective vein of new ideas for them to mine. Being so close to home, Fripp was able to completely relax, and would spend most of his evenings back at his parents' house in Wimborne. Their only collective discomfort came after they all went out to see a local band and got caught in a blizzard that was so bad it caused a power cut across the area, Levin subsequently coming down with a terrible cold.

All in their mid- to late-thirties, they were at an interesting age, being old enough to be considered veterans but still young enough to have another serious go at some kind of biggish time. By the end of April, ready or not, they took to the road, starting with a warmup in a Bath restaurant called Moles, followed by trekking around some of the south of England's college circuit. Next up was the first sizable venue of the tour, London's Her Majesty's Theatre, where things ran so smoothly that the only real fan complaint was about the lack of a bar. Following this, the band headed for mainland Europe.

For their live sets, the only concessions to their collective back catalogues were the Crimson tracks *Red* and *Larks' Two*, the former only getting its first live airings seven years after its appearance on vinyl. Other than that, the band's sound was markedly different from that of Fripp and Bruford's Crimson era, feeling instead like a progression from Fripp's recent solo work and liaisons with Gabriel. While all four had an impact on the direction of travel, some interestingly contradictory personal dynamics soon developed. Fripp still saw himself as more of a facilitator than band leader, and left space for the others to put forward their ideas. As he put it, 'I wish to determine the parameters, not to be a dictator'. However, as the others were extremely wary of triggering another Fripp retreat, they were initially reticent to push their views too much. [7] [3]

Discipline was to be a band of technological innovation, and in addition to Levin's stick, Fripp and Belew would develop their use of guitar-synths, while Bruford would incorporate a set of Simmons electronic drums into his armoury. Onstage they were, as a consequence, quite a sight, without the need for any added visuals. Quietly in command, a suited Fripp sat to one side with his growing array of pedals and devices laid out at his feet. With guitar-synths still being a new thing to most audiences, his use of one would take a bit of getting used to. We could see he was playing guitar, but some kind of electronic trumpet or synth-strings sound would be coming out of the amps. Front-middle was a bouncing Belew, often in a red or pink suit, singing and doing extraordinary things with his guitar. Ivan Eastwood has described him as 'a pioneer in creating his own unique palette of sounds', his party piece being, through a mix of effects, feedback and guitar-synth, to extract very un-guitar-like noises out of the instrument. As David Bowman put it, 'Belew had discovered the mammal lurking in his guitar'. He would also be responsible for onstage introductions and announcements. At the other end of the stage was the striking, bald, moustached Levin, alternating between his bass and grappling with the weird but decidedly cool-looking Chapman Stick, also an unfamiliar sight to audiences. At the back was Bruford, his conventional kit supplemented by electronic drum pads. Not only were all four definitely first division, but Fripp had assembled a genuinely exciting blend of musicians. That said, as the tour progressed, never has so much attention been paid to a man sitting quietly on a stool to one side rather than the energetic frontman! As well as the technological advances, Bruford noted that comfort levels for the touring musician had also moved up a notch or two. 'By the 1980s, European chain hotels had sprung up, modelled on the U.S. Holiday Inn, guaranteeing a certain level of quality and uniformity, and the worst of the Mrs Miggins digs, family-owned hotels faded into the past'. [5] [8] [9]

People say there's a lot in a name, and that was certainly true with what happened next. After just a handful of gigs performing as Discipline, conversations with band members led Fripp to decide that they were, in fact, the new King Crimson, and they immediately switched to using the name. His only real consideration was that, as he saw Crimson as a vehicle for certain types of music, he had to decide if what Discipline were doing was worthy of the name. He decreed that it was, and with two of the three members from the Crimson that ended in 1974, there was at least some semblance of continuity. More significantly, the use of the name would draw that extra bit of attention from fans and media alike. This wasn't just a new Fripp band but the return of the mighty Crimson—an extremely big deal, despite the fact that it was the same four men playing the same music. The name change also meant that Belew and Levin were the first non-Brits in Crimson, and that this once-English band was now 50 percent American. With Belew being the vocalist, the tradition of Crimson's dual bassist/vocalist role had also ended. Having plied his trade in relative obscurity up to the age of twenty-eight, his rise over the past four years had taken him from thinking that he'd missed the boat, to finding himself as frontman of a world-renowned rock band, likening it to 'joining The Beatles'. Met by a mix of excitement, curiosity and cynicism about reviving the name, Fripp set out his reasoning, starting by neatly summing Crimson of 1969 to 1974 as 'that eclectic, forward-looking band of an unsettling nature'. He explained that 'the musical movement, of which King Crimson was a founding force, went tragically off course', suggesting that his group was the only one with 'the intelligence to withdraw'. While the latter point is something of a re-spinning of what actually happened, he rescues things by adding: 'It's a very different world from seven years ago [and] there is useful work to do which requires a powerful instrument'. Going on to say, 'King Crimson has a life of its own', he was deflecting from his somewhat decisive role in what happens, however, he then came up with a phrase that would serve to draw a decisive line of continuity between all Crimsons past, present and future: 'King Crimson is a way of doing things'. [3] [10]

Twelve years on from the heady days of 1969, Crimson Mk IV would be flaunting its wares in the post-punk era. U2 were emerging as a major force, helped by having Eno as their producer, while the singles charts were dominated by the likes of Madonna and Wham! This was also the era of the New Romantics, typified by Duran Duran and Spandau Ballet, while Kraftwerk, The Human League and Heaven 17 would take electronic pop to new heights. It would be a mixed time for some of the prog artists of the seventies, perhaps the biggest surprise being the chart-friendly reinvention of Crimson's former admirers, Genesis, their frontman, Phil Collins, also launching a massively successful solo career. Echoes of early Crimson were still to be found, such as from: rising stars Talk Talk as they evolved from electro-pop with an edge to deeply moody pop. The Crimson influence would be most apparent on *Tomorrow's Started*, with a pastiche of *Court* also slipped into a section of *Today*. Nevertheless, the revolutions had left a different landscape in their wake, and prog of the early seventies had run its course. The new Crimson were innovators and returning to early prog was never going to be on their agenda, the four all still embracing a deep desire to be different from the herd. To Bruford, this was simply part of their natural instinct. As he rhetorically asked: 'Don't we all want to be different from the man or woman next door?' Mocking his own wish to be different in such a public way, he added, 'Some deranged folk, possessed of a potent cocktail of arrogance and vanity, seek to express that difference through artistic endeavour. These megalomaniacs believe they can do it not just well but do it better'. [9]

A message etched into the vinyl of *Exposure* had predicted that 1981 was going to be 'the Year of the Fripp, and April of that year brought the release of his third solo effort, *Let the Power Fall*, a whole album of pure Frippertronics. It is also an album of contradictions. While it showed Fripp's confidence in this line of music, it would also mark the end for pure Frippertronics albums. And although it was beautiful music that more than justified the record's existence, it was time to move on. The average listener would take it on its merits simply as music, but to Fripp it carried with it a mass of Gurdjieffian philosophy and the political weight of his battle with the music industry. Even before the album reached the shelves, that phase of Fripp's life was coming to an end. He'd already come up against the limitations of his small, mobile-unit concept, and it was now just a useful alternative approach, rather than an essential one for surviving the future. The album's six tracks were, again, all from the 1979 tour, which seemingly had been his Frippertronics purple patch, and following on from *GSTQ*'s *1983*, they are numerically titled from *1984* to *1989*, although this is simply for cataloguing purposes rather than anything deep and meaningful. While they are all further variations along the lines of *GSTQ*, we have the chance to hear those avenues explored at much greater length, the eleven minutes of *1989* being a fitting culmination for the album, with Fripp squeezing a great deal of beauty and emotion out of the format. [11]

While the music is wordless, the back cover goes to the other extreme, Fripp using the space to set out some of his business and work philosophy. Although his intense style of writing clashes somewhat with the dreamlike music within, it is nevertheless a fascinating window into the thought processes that were driving him. It was now five years on from his IACE retreat, and enough time had passed for him to have thought things through a lot more. While aspects of the philosophy were quietly falling away, as the articles he'd been writing in recent months had been detailing, he still had a deep distrust of the music industry, and that was the root of the views he was expressing here. The mini essay is also partly a summing up of The Drive to 1981, with the album itself being its final musical output. With a photo from a Frippertronics gig to show us the smartly dressed, clean-cut Fripp addressing us, he explains that The Drive was a modern version of 'blasphemy and heresy', quoting former High Court judge and minister in Winston Churchill's cabinet, Viscount Simmonds. In simpler terms, Fripp's small-scale tour was, in its own way, politely controversial. He was doing it very gently but was doing things you weren't supposed to and getting in under the radar to ask probing questions. [12]

As the world was getting used to the era of Prime-Minister Thatcher and President Reagan—the economic right having taken control on both sides of the Atlantic—many musicians were attaching themselves to left-wing causes. Still very much a man on a mission, Fripp, however, stayed away from anything overtly party political although you could perhaps read his criticisms of major record companies as criticisms of the nature of capitalism. However, as the album title suggests, he saw what he was doing as being (non-party) political in the sense that he was seeking to change dinosaur society and its organisations from within. He believed that the only realistic way to bring about significant change was from the inside, or as he puts it, 'All political activity directed towards changing the means of working is ineffective without a change in our way of working, and this is essentially personal'. He reiterated that 'the next step is discipline', this time adding that it would be 'the first step of the incline to 1984, [his] second three-year campaign in the marketplace'. The word *discipline* here refers specifically to using *self*-discipline as a method of changing our way of doing things and, in so doing, causing 'structural change' around us. Other than this, the closest he got to politics was talking about 'the erosion of a wide range of small personal liberties to which we have become accustomed'. He didn't specify which liberties, but he was critical of the 'control' exerted by 'authoritarian organisations', which, in this context, was a reference to a lack of freedom for artists due to the pressures and narrow commercial priorities of the big record companies. After this he then added a bewildering list of twenty-one points, setting out his logic about change. In the end, this amounted to a long way of saying that people can adapt to working in different circumstances, that different circumstances work for different people, and that organisations can be transformed by bottom-up action. It's hard to know who all this was aimed at, as it felt as if Fripp had simply written down a mental exercise he'd been working through. Helpfully, though, he ended with 'Now, forget all of this'. While to him the music and the politics were all part of the same bundle, he did at least realise that the latter wasn't a prerequisite to enjoying the music. [12]

Having tested and tweaked their new material live, Crimson Mk IV went into Basing Street Studio in May 1981, emerging a few weeks later with a wonderfully coherent package for the eighth Crimson studio album. Once again, the sound had radically changed, and was now bright, upbeat—and even fun! The structures were more straightforward than before but instead there was often a complex interplay of guitars and stick. The entire album is credited as having been written by the band, with Belew as lyricist. It was the first time the main lyricist for Crimson had been a playing band member, though Belew's style differed greatly from his predecessors, going for quirky ideas and even straying close to love songs at times. Despite the band-name change, the next step was still *Discipline*, with that being the title of the album, which was released in October 1981, a Fripp aphorism on the back cover informing us that 'discipline is never an end in itself, only a means to an end'. Still feeding through from his Fourth Way experiences, he felt that (self-)discipline was a vital ingredient in the approach to music he was now adopting. The approach was clearly working, and to an extent, this had rarely been the case since 1969; there was a crystal-clear sense of direction and purpose. The process of translating their ideas into the finished product on vinyl had been greatly aided by the presence of Rhett Davies, brought in as co-producer. As well as having been a studio engineer for Eno, Fripp and Talking Heads, Davies's recent credits as a producer included Roxy Music's U.K. No. 1 album, *Flesh and Blood*, and their cover of Lennon's *Jealous Guy*, which topped the singles chart. He therefore came with a thorough understanding of the creative needs of bands like Crimson but was no stranger to chart success. [13]

*Elephant Talk* opens the album, giving us a taste of the playful style of Belew's lyrics, or 'elephantosity' as the cover credits would have it. His words here however, seem to take their cue from Fripp's style of word play on *Under Heavy Manners*, being a thesaurus-like listing of alternative words for *talk*. We also get a good cross-section of what to expect musically from the quartet, with a Stick intro from Levin, guitar interplay from Belew and Fripp, overdubs of elephant impressions from Belew's guitar, and a Fripp guitar-synth solo. Bruford is listed on the credits as playing '*batterie*'—the French for drum kit—and here, as would be the case throughout the album, he avoids playing the hi-hat. Evolving out of aspects of Fripp's recent solo work, *Frame by Frame* features an archetypal Fripp riff of this period in 7/4, and the first full-blown outing for the Gamelan-style interlocking guitar ideas, as he and Belew play sequences that shift in and out of phase. For this track, Belew went for minimal but ambiguous lyrics, leaving us drowning in our own analysis as we once more look for deep meanings that aren't there. Some fans would find the new frontman's style a bit brash, although the third track, *Matte Kudasai*, shows a different side to Belew, introducing a tenderness that didn't often find expression in Crimson's customary output. The Japanese title translates literally as *wait please*, though it was interpreted by the band as 'will you wait for me?' With its gentle, romantic, slightly bluesy feel, musically it's a recycling of

Fripp's *North Star* but with a magical change to a minor chord added in. Belew's passionate vocal evokes his longing for a lover that's far away, enhancing the mood by also conjuring up some seagulls from his guitar. Fripp needlessly called a second version into existence a few years later, after taking his soloing out of the mix, deeming it excessive. He later relented, and subsequent editions of the album reinstated the original. Side one ends with a return to the playfullness with *Indiscipline*, switching between spoken-word sections and the band breaking loose with distortion boxes set to eleven. Searching for appropriate lyrics, it was only on the final day of pre-tour rehearsals that Belew found inspiration in a letter from his wife, which he turned into something wonderfully ambiguous by removing any reference to what it was actually about (which was a painting). He will also be congratulating himself forever for repeating a line that refers to repetition! On an album filled with tracks that would become crowd favourites, this would be especially popular, and a song that the band could have fun messing around with in live shows. [13]

Complete with jagged rhythm guitars, variations on a three-note bass line and faux-African vocals, *Thela Hun Ginjeet* incorporates the story of a Belew misadventure while out seeking inspiration for lyrics. In a similar way to Deep Purple's *Smoke on the Water*, it became circular, in that the song is about the making of the song. The story, which he would happily recount for years, was that while wandering in South London, not long after the Brixton riots, and speaking ideas into a portable tape recorder, just as he'd been saying what a dangerous place it was, he was accosted by a group of aggressive youths. He was genuinely scared, especially when they played back his tape and accused him of being an undercover cop. 'I thought I was going to die', he would later explain to audiences. Then, as he was wearing a Talking Heads T-shirt under his Hawaiian shirt, he tried to convince them he was in that band and was doing the recording for them, but they just didn't believe him. Tiring of their captive, they eventually let Belew go, and he scurried round the nearest street corner, in doing so running straight into two actual cops, who promptly searched him for drugs. Levin's bass riff and Bruford's hi-hat-avoiding percussion add to the African feel, while the African-sounding title is actually an anagram of the track's original title, *Heat in the Jungle.* All in all, the track is essentially an exploration of how musicians can create something that sounds deep and meaningful, when all they're actually doing is playing around with a few words and sounds. What was quite a wordy album up to this point ends with two contrasting instrumentals. First is *The Sheltering Sky*, a long, mellow track with Fripp going to town with a guitar-synth trumpet sound over simple chords from Belew and organic stick oozings from Levin. For this, Bruford abandoned his conventional drum kit altogether, instead using a set of African slit-drums, which sound like a cross between congas and marimbas. The title was taken from a 1949 novel by Peter Bowles, who was part of the Beat Generation movement, something they would further explore. Closing with the mid-paced title track, *Discipline*, it was on this occasion literally an end in itself. Here they return to the interlocking guitars, with a particularly cute Fripp riff in amongst the clever-clever sequences. For Bruford, playing this particular track live could be hit-or-miss, but on a good day, when they were collectively in a disciplined frame of mind, there was nothing to beat it. He found that 'all the hours of practice and struggle are validated in such moments of pure pleasure'. His twist on what discipline meant in the band context was self-restraint, referring to containing the ego and just playing your part. Essentially it was a musician's take on the workplace aphorism, 'There's no "I" in team'. [14] [15]

Despite the injection of fun into the formula, its relative accessibility and even an appearance on a popular ABC TV show, *Fridays*, *Discipline* only got into the lower reaches of U.K. and U.S. top fifties for a handful of weeks. Seven years on from *Red*, the album nevertheless marked a triumphant return, proving popular with much of the Crimson faithful and gathering many new disciples. Bruford later said of the album and the tour that followed: 'We knew we were on to something. We were the right band in the right place at the right time'.

With the help of the extra attention drawn by the band name, they were still relevant and influential. Bruford felt that 'with its introduction of elements drawn from minimalism and ethnic music, elements new to rock', the album in effect launched a post-prog movement. It was stretching things a bit to say those elements were new to rock but, as with *Court*, Crimson again crystallised where the more thinking person's rock was going, and *Discipline* would rank highly amongst their most influential albums. While he certainly wouldn't deny their ongoing influence, Fripp would thoroughly disagree about eighties Crimson being anything to do with prog. Whether or not he was right would depend on whether you view prog as being that style of music played by the likes of Crimson, Yes and ELP from 1969 to the mid- to late-seventies, or more of an ongoing approach, with Crimson of 1981 now moving the genre on. Semi-seriously, Bruford also points out that 'the musicians frequently don't quite know what they're doing'. Being on the inside, they just do what they do, leaving it to the critics to look at the bigger picture and genre labels. [15]

The album would have a profound impact on many young people who didn't necessarily know much about of earlier Crimson, approaching them without the baggage of expectation older fans would have. One new fan for whom eighties Crimson would become an obsession was an American teenager named Ronan Murphy. Going on to become a studio engineer, he would get to work directly with his hero, Fripp, on many occasions. Eighties-era Crimson would, however, remain a touchstone for him, and discussing this in 2020 he said, 'To me, the *Discipline* album stands as a seminal work of art and will always be my favourite King Crimson album'. *Discipline* had one other unexpected impact, its titles and lyrics creating a whole new, highly quotable vocabulary for Crim-heads. The front cover is a design by Peter Saville, who had previously designed covers for Joy Division. It's mostly a darkish red, with a Celtic-style symbol in the centre, known as The Discipline Knot. This was to be an appropriate name in more ways than one: it turned out that it was similar to a copyrighted design from the 1950s.

To avoid a knot of legal battles, they had to pay for its use, and for later re-releases used a different version designed by Steve Ball. The original cover managed to have a minor part in a high-profile film in 2000, being visible in some of the record shop scenes of *High Fidelity*, which starred John Cusack and Jack Black as music obsessives. [16]

Buoyed by his recent achievements, between the release of *Discipline* and a Crimson tour of North America, Belew headed back to the Bahamas, thinking he would be helping to finish off the Tom Tom Club album. A sizeable fly suddenly appeared in his ointment when he learned it had been finished without him and was about to be released. Worse still, some of the parts he'd recorded had been erased. Where his contributions had been used, he felt that he hadn't always been given the writing credits he'd expected, others having decided his contributions were those of an arranger. Communications between the parties broke down over this, and Belew decided to just move on and work on his other projects. Although the situation was resolved more to his liking years later, following the success of *Wordy Rappinghood* and *Genius of Love* as singles in the U.K., the album unexpectedly took off and was given a much wider release than had originally been planned. Belew still had a lot going for him, and in addition to working on ideas for the next Crimson album, he finished off his first solo album. With assistance from his former GaGa bandmates, *Lone Rhino* gave him free rein to use his own ideas, unfiltered by the other Crims, and even to incorporate some piano doodlings from his four-year-old daughter, Audie. It would be released in 1982, avoiding clashes with Crimson albums, the cover featuring Belew in his bright-red suit, posing with his guitar, and standing alarmingly close to a (lone) rhino. It sold only moderately, setting the frustrating pattern for much of Belew's solo career.

While Fripp had been busy reinventing Crimson one more time, Sinfield's career took an unexpected turn. Post-ELP, the lyricist had set up home in Ibiza and took a break from the music biz. However, the breakdown of his marriage and realising that he wouldn't be getting as much income from his ELP work as he'd thought, led him to return to the U.K. in the early eighties to urgently rethink his future. Looking to make new contacts, he was put in touch with writer/producer Andy Hill and ended up penning the lyrics for a song that would see him at No. 1 in the U.K. singles charts. This wasn't with a rehabilitated prog outfit though, but with Eurovision Song Contest winners Bucks Fizz, the song being their second chart-topper, *The Land of Make Believe.* They were kept off the Christmas 1981 top slot by The Human League's *Don't You Want Me*, reaching No. 1 in the new year. While his Crimson lyrics had been full of impenetrable layers of meaning and coded references, *Land of Make Believe*, at least on the surface, seemed much more straightforward. The lyrics are not quite as fluffy as the style of the music suggests, however, and Sinfield's has claimed that they were a subtle dig at the U.K.'s then-prime minister, Margaret Thatcher. With the ex-Crim also contributing lyrics for three other tracks on the Bucks Fizz album of 1982, this was a lucrative linkup for him, compensating for the worthy, if less lucrative, earlier years. The radical change of style for Sinfield initially took some work, but promising new avenues were opening up as his fortieth birthday loomed, even if what he was doing was beyond the pale to his prog following. as his fortieth birthday loomed. Having got the hang of writing pop hits, later that year the Sinfield/Hill partnership, along with John Danter, conjured up a sizeable hit for Leo Sayer, with *Have You Ever Been in Love.* This reached No. 10 in the U.K. and won Sinfield an Ivor Novello Award, the prestigious annual prize for U.K./Irish songwriters. With his cash-flow situation much improved, Sinfield headed back to the Balearics, where he bought a home in Mallorca. There he would also meet a model and Miss Spain runner-up, who would become his second wife.

Crimson may have been back and staying highly relevant but in terms of commercial success this period belonged to hard-working, ambitious Wetton. After UK, he had a few months as bassist with bluesy rockers Wishbone Ash, following this up with a solo album, *Caught in the Crossfire*, which ran headlong into a common problem:

no matter how big the band is that you are in, there's no guarantee that fans will follow you across to a solo project. Determined not to resort to being a jobbing bassist again, in the spring of 1981 he set about forming another band of his own. After an attempt with Rick Wakeman, Trevor Rabin and Carl Palmer was scuppered by Wakeman leaving before they had really begun, Wetton's manager Brian Lane arranged for him to link up with ex-Yes guitarist Steve Howe. After an initial session together went well, they called up a willing Palmer. He was keen to have a keyboard player involved, so Geoff Downes was also contacted, which turned out to be a key decision. Downes had had memorable chart success with the very un-prog Buggles with *Video Killed the Radio Star*, then making the unexpected move of joining Yes. Yes had subsequently disbanded, so Downes was open to Wetton's offer. Adopting the band name Asia, they were snapped up that summer by the new record company, Geffen, and instantly tagged as a supergroup. It would take them five months in London to put an album together, but Geffen were convinced they had something huge on their hands. The big surprise to those on the outside was that, despite their collective credentials, Asia would have more in common with the commercial rock sound of Foreigner and Boston than any of their former bands. With Wetton and Downes dominating the writing, the material was upbeat, and the songs all featured big choruses. This turned out to be a winning formula. They hit the road in the U.S. in March 1982, just as the album came out, giving it the momentum to reach No.1 on that side of the Atlantic, ultimately selling millions. It was less of an instant success in the band's home nation, but it still spent months in the chart, peaking at No.11. A few months earlier had seen the launch of MTV—Music Television—a cable and satellite channel aimed at the youth market. Their repertoire largely consisted of pop-and-rock videos, with *Video Killed the Radio Star* being the first one screened on the channel. Asia's music fitted their bill perfectly, and with their management recognising the power of this new medium, videos were shot to accompany their singles *Heat of the Moment*, *Only Time Will Tell* and *Sole Survivor*. All subsequently became big hits in the U.S. and, to a lesser extent, in the U.K., meaning that, at thirty-three, he had become a full-fledged pop star! It could be said that Asia were everything that Crimson weren't, although for Wetton that was the point. His view was that 'in order to survive the eighties you have to stop being a band of the seventies. You have to condense more . . . cut the soloing . . . play for four minutes instead of the eight you used to play'. It wasn't just moving with the times though; as they were operating in a completely different market, one of the buyers who largely didn't know or care about the likes of King Crimson. Some were rather cynical about Wetton's venture, Bruford describing Asia as 'bland, radio-friendly pop', feeling that they symbolised the end of 'the idealistic impulses of the sixties'. Wetton and his bandmates could not have cared less. Having tapped into an international desire for such rock, they were on the airwaves everywhere, the tills were ringing, and their gigs were selling out. [17] [15]

Having conquered the world with The Police, Andy Summers had begun to look for work outside the force. He'd heard some of his old friend Fripp's recent work and wrote to him to suggest they get together. Although they had crossed paths frequently in Bournemouth as teenagers, the pair had never actually played together. Having seen him with Crimson in the seventies and having the occasional chance to chat at places like The Speakeasy, Summers was seriously impressed by Fripp. 'He's different', he explained. 'More intelligent and more aware than the average rocker, or most people. He gets it'. With Fripp now at ease about working with other guitarists, the two met over mince pies and stuffing at Summers's parents' home at Christmas 1980, to discuss the possibilities. They found some space in September 1981 and May 1982 for some relaxed recording, covering all the instruments between them. These sessions, which were mainly at Arny's Shack in Dorset, produced *I Advance Masked*, which was released late in 1982. It was an interesting mix of experimentation and indulgence that hit on some moments of brilliance, which, on the whole, was far more satisfying for Fripp than Summers, giving him a chance to explore some different

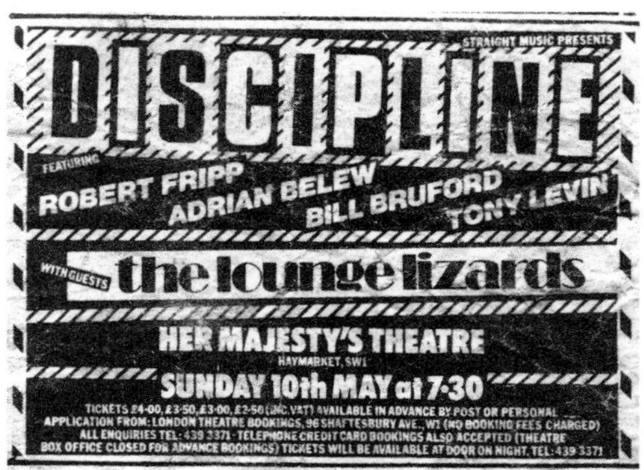


*Discipline gig ad, 1981.*

avenues. The title track is the standout piece, with a driving rhythm and a simple-but-uplifting melodic sequence in 7/4. Over this, Fripp interjects lightning-fast guitar-synth solos, which sound like a crazed electronic take on *Flight of the Bumble Bee*. A promo video was made for this, featuring the two guitarists smartly dressed and playing seated, with exotic dancing girls swirling around them. It didn't get much of an airing at the time, although it became better known in the internet video age. A similar, but softer, piece of Frippery is *Hardy Country*, the title harking back to their shared Dorset youth, while the gentle chords and guitar-synth of *Girl on a Swing* imaginatively evoke the soft-focus, dreamlike scene of the title. The pair's September 1981 sessions had unknowingly marked the end of the three years of Fripp's Drive to 1981, with no event of apocalyptic import other than the alignment of two acclaimed guitarists. [18]

The good vibes around Crimson in 1981 were too good to last, and in the months following the release of *Discipline* something began to change for the worse. Tensions had begun to surface in the writing-and-recording process for the follow-up album, and Fripp's Incline to 1984 was in serious danger of tipping into decline. That follow-up would be much more reliant on Belew as the engine room of inspiration; however, this was an increasingly unhappy Belew, and that unhappiness inevitably filtered through. While Bruford had demanded more fun in the band, and for them 'not to take themselves too seriously', Belew, who was normally their bringer of joy, revealingly said in 1982, 'Fun didn't seem like the right thing for King Crimson'. One key issue was his growing annoyance with being the frontman and under pressure to come up with ideas, while the media still endlessly pandered after Fripp, who was doing his best to shun the attention. Fans didn't help either, tending to put everything down to Fripp's genius and his mythical master plan. Despite being seen as an extrovert onstage, Bruford noted that Belew had 'surprisingly low self-esteem'. And it wasn't only Belew who was experiencing pressure. Although he relished, and perhaps needed, the challenge, Bruford gave some interesting insight into the difficulties of this Crimson and their creative processes: 'It starts out as a string of negatives [from Fripp] . . . which cracks many a lesser man', also comparing Fripp's directions and restrictions to being like a prison you have to find your way out of. It was clear that the happy, dynamic and productive Fripp that had emerged from New York was getting lost again, fast. But what had for a while been a tolerable level of difficulty was now taking nastier turns. Bruford describes the atmosphere in these sessions as becoming 'poison', as they all tested the limits of Fripp's authority. Discipline dissolved into indiscipline, if not a little ballyhoo and brouhaha, and things came to a head at one session as Belew's frustration with Fripp boiled over to the point that he told him to leave the studio! Fripp duly left and, for a while, it seemed like he might not come back. After a few days of silence from 'The Great Leader', as Bruford came to refer to him, the band's management brokered a peace deal that allowed them to finish the album. It was still a struggle, and they only ended up with thirty-five minutes of material. With emotions running high, Fripp would have nothing to do with the album's mixing. The dispute came close to breaking up the band, and Belew in particular found it a hideous experience. They managed to laugh a little at themselves afterwards, adding 'Social Services' (a.k.a. Tex Read, from their management team) to the credits on the back cover. Even so, Fripp felt that a divide had appeared between himself and the others, one illustration of this being that Belew, Levin and Bruford all felt that the new album was an improvement on *Discipline*, when he felt the opposite. The roots of this souring of relations were seemingly not fully broached by the four. While *Discipline* had had the feel of a natural, easy creation, joyously teetering on the border between populist and experiment, the good feelings generated were vanishing fast, and Fripp's flow of ideas was diminishing. With the band not having a shared vision of what would constitute success for them, things became muddled and, with Belew in particular still gushing with inspiration, Fripp increasingly felt he was being pushed in a more commercial direction than he could stomach. While all the studio shenanigans had been going on, Crimson had managed to land a rare TV appearance on BBC Two's worthy rock showcase, *The Old Grey Whistle Test*. In one of the stripped-back studio settings the show favoured, they opted for two tracks from the previous album, performing *Frame by Frame* and *Indiscipline*. The show was broadcast in March 1982. [1] [3] [15] [19]

Released in June 1982, *Beat* was the ninth Crimson studio album. With Rhett Davies again co-producing, remarkably, this was the first time two consecutive Crimson albums had been recorded by an identical line-up. Although it would do marginally better commercially than its predecessor, it got a very mixed reception, lacking the easy accessibility and consistency of *Discipline*. Many fans had inevitably fallen into the trap of expecting more of the same, and while on first inspection it was superficially a continuation, beneath the surface were important differences. With Crimson moving in two directions at once, roughly half of the album's material was reasonably accessible, while the rest was a lot more challenging. With its minimalist blue cover and a pink musical note (a beat) in the centre, the album took much of its inspiration from the Beat Generation writers of the post-war era in the U.S. The theme is most apparent in the opener, *Neal and Jack and Me*, a reference to Neal Cassady and Jack Kerouac, the album coming twenty-five years after Kerouac's landmark novel, *On the Road*. Sadly, the track illustrates how the easy flow and sense of purpose of *Discipline* was getting lost. The opening riff is a poor relation to *Frame by Frame*, and while the lyrics are fine, they sound forced into the space available, giving it a much more contrived feel. In contrast, *Heartbeat* is a surprisingly straightforward rock track, with Bruford even rediscovering his hi-hat. While the title is borrowed from a book by Cassady's wife, Belew in this case simply took it as a prompt to go off in his own direction, singing about love, sex and intimacy. For Crimson this was quite a radical change, as while Sinfield had begun to put in sexual references, Belew was edging more closely towards the kind of love song that would previously have been verboten. It was an idea he'd offered up almost fully formed during a writing session at their Illinois rehearsal room and, in its finished form, it flows well. But on an album of behind-the-scenes frustrations, even here Belew was annoyed by how it ended up sounding after it had been tweaked by the others. As a fairly commercial piece of rock, not really that far removed from what Asia were doing, *Heartbeat* was selected as the single from the album. For once it got a decent airing on FM stations, and there was even a video made, but inevitably it failed to chart.

The real gem of *Beat* is the moderately upbeat instrumental, *Sartori in Tangier*. As well as the reference to the Moroccan port city, a popular hangout for the Beat Generation writers, this is mixed in with the title of a Kerouac novella, *Satori in Paris*. This is led by a Stick rhythm from Levin, overlaid with Fripp's best guitar-synth-playing to date, and tinged with Middle Eastern scale leanings. Fripp also playing some simple synth-organ, mellotrons having been rejected by this Crimson. There must have been some prog fans in useful positions in the BBC, as for several months part of the track was used as a backdrop to BBC TV programme trails. Returning to the faux-African line, *Waiting Man* opens with a Bruford-written Reichian riff in rock-waltz time, played on a blend of guitar, stick and tuned electronic percussion. When Belew's vocals appear, the frontman is at his exuberant, expressive and celebratory best. Having switched to 4/4 in the slightly awkward middle section, Bruford again throws in his trick of playing 4/4 while the music does something different, in this case switching back to 3/4 for climax of the final verse. It's another track they would enjoy doing live, with Belew as a second percussionist for the intro, playing a second set of electronic drum pads opposite Bruford.

Lulled by a short intro of recycled Frippertronics, the riff-laden *Neurotica* hits you with a cityscape of noise and chaos. Summing up the change in mood from the previous album, the elephants and gulls have fled Belew's guitar, to be replaced by car horns and police sirens, and in one of his wordier songs, he extrapolates his own fantasy from the title of an American magazine of the fifties. With an impenetrability to rival Sinfield, the verses are a rapid-fire commentary in the manner of a radio announcer, in which Belew paints a string of surreal images of city characters as assorted, exotic wildlife. His inspiration came simply from looking out of a New York hotel window one day. From his perspective, the scene resembled a jungle, prompting him to hunt through a book about animals and fish and picking out the ones with which he was unfamiliar. The tone may seem deceptively light, but Belew is, in effect, describing North American urban life as tipping over the edge into madness. In something of a Belew family piece, the frontman's wife, Margaret, contributed the lyrics to *Two Hands*. This album's parallel of sorts to *Matte Kudasai*, the song is sung from the unusual perspective of a picture hanging on the wall of a couple's bedroom, where it witnesses their passionate love for each other and feels their every intimate move. Bruford gets the slit-drums out again, while Fripp adds a misty guitar-synth solo. In amongst the riffs, time-signature changes and awkward key changes of *The Howler* lurks a great track. What made it onto vinyl, though, is a mishmash of sections and unfathomable lyrics, that is unnecessarily hard to listen to. It's dark, intense and stuffed full of interesting ideas, but the arrangement needed more care and attention than the band could muster under the circumstances. At Fripp's suggestion, Belew took his inspiration here from Allan Ginsberg's epic poem, *Howl*, a stream-of-consciousness that mixes social comment with themes of madness and people not fitting in with conventions. In contrast to his light observations in *Neurotica*, Belew has us looking into the more dangerous, seedy corners of the city, with cryptic references to that familiar Crimson theme of the devil and hell, or hell on earth. For good measure, there's a diversion into forty-five seconds of funk à la Crim in 15/8 time, before an appropriately howling, discordant guitar-synth solo from Belew. Soft Machine's second album had contained an improv named *Out of Tunes*, a title which may have been appropriate for the final track of *Beat*, actually called *Requiem*. Its six-and-a-half minutes are the result of the cupboard of useable ideas being bare, and neither terrible nor memorable, it's the product of people needing it all to be over so they can get away from one another for a few weeks. It opens with Fripp improvising over some 1979 Frippertronics, then as his solo gets wilder and more discordant, the rest of the band join in for a few minutes of unstructured track. It soon runs out of steam, Fripp resorting to throwing in phrases from other solos, before it ends with some reflective, appropriately funereal bass from Levin. The Frippertronics section was later sampled by British DJ Sasha in 2002 for a track called *Cloud Cuckoo*, raising knotty questions over copyright, as it could be deemed to have come from two separate sources.

Matters small and mobile were taking an increasingly back seat in this period, and though Fripp was still a believer in some of the principles of the Fourth Way, his musical expression of this, Frippertronics, only had two outings in 1982. The first was a one-off in New York, Fripp having escaped from the *Beat* sessions; the other being in the weeks between the release of *Beat* and Crimson's autumn tour, at Peter Gabriel's inaugural WOMAD (World of Music and Dance) Festival. The ill-fated event, held in July in Shepton Mallet in England's West Country, failed to attract enough of a paying audience despite a glorious array of U.K. and world musicians. In fact, Gabriel lost so much money that a hurriedly reformed six-piece Genesis was got together to hold a fundraising gig at a rain-sodden Milton Keynes Bowl later in the year to bail him out. As far as the Frippertronics was concerned, there would only be one more short tour of U.S. and Canada in the spring of 1983 before Fripp pulled the plug on his two-tape-machine live performances, though not the small, mobile unit as such.

A bit of session work in 1982 quietly lodged Levin on yet another piece of music that will get played forever. Mark Knopfler was working on the soundtrack to the comedy-drama film, *Local Hero*, but using session musicians rather than his usual bandmates in Dire Straits. Levin was called in to play on a couple of tracks, one of which was the closing instrumental, *Going Home*, which would become as well-known as the film. That original version, with its distinctive sax melody played by Michael Brecker, was soon adopted by Newcastle United FC as their walk-on music-at-home games. With the track being so popular, it became part of Dire Straits live set in 1983. With Brecker being unavailable, Mel Collins was brought in, as a result appearing on the much-acclaimed 1984 album *Alchemy Live*. For Collins, having played on Camel's stunning 1981 concept album *Nude*, in the spring of 1984 Collins toured with them for the last time, a tour that resulted in the live album *Pressure Points*. While this was highly regarded, Decca dropped them, causing Andy Latimer to call a halt to the band. Another ex-Crim, Peter Giles, would also crop up in some unexpected places. After getting disillusioned partway through a law degree, he had concluded that he was 'unemployable' in terms of conventional jobs and needed to return to music. Starting back at the bottom in a pub band, he quickly worked his way up to being band leader at the prestigious Royal Garden Hotel's Roof Restaurant in the upmarket London district of Kensington. This would last for six years, a time he would regard as a proper completion of his 'musical apprenticeship'. It would also lead to him meeting wife-to-be and fellow musician Yasmine. [20]

Wetton's Asia aimed to build on the staggering success of their debut album, going into the studio in Canada in the spring of 1983. That was always going to be a difficult task, but with Wetton developing a serious alcohol problem, the follow-up, *Alpha*, had to be completed with the super-egos of this supergroup clashing terribly. Wetton and Downes dominated the writing, some describing Howe and Palmer as being treated like little more than session musicians as they honed down their winning formula to its key elements. As a result, even the minimal elements of creative adventure that had found their way onto the first album were squeezed out. An ambitious broadcast of a gig in Tokyo on both MTV and BBC Radio 1 was set up for that December. However, with *Alpha* struggling to match the sales of the first album,

Wetton felt personally under fire, and with everyone overreacting instead of preparing to take the world by storm in Tokyo, Wetton stormed out of the band. Rather than cancel a show to the biggest audience of their lives, Palmer called on his former bandmate Greg Lake to fill the vacancy. Though happily engaged with his own solo career and only having weeks to prepare, Lake willingly stepped up to the plate. It was quite a feat of preparation, with songs having to be transposed to different keys for him and, as he didn't have time to fully learn the lyrics, he had to sing using an auto-cue. All things considered, other than some dubious examples of eighties fashion, it was a slick, high-energy performance on a massive stage set in the shape of the Asia logo. It's also quite likely that much of the audience didn't even realise that one ex-Crimson vocalist/bassist had been substituted for another. Wetton would return to the fold the following year, but only on the condition that Howe leave. It was becoming hard to avoid seeing the pattern of his developing problems with the guitarist in each of his major bands, shedding a different light on the Crimson of 1973–1974 and where at least some of the blame lay.

With much trepidation, Crimson reconvened at intervals through the second half of 1983 for sessions for the third album of this phase, choosing to produce this one themselves. Given the band's history, a third album by exactly the same line-up was a significant achievement; however, they were now being held together by sticky tape, or rather, by the efforts of their management. For the time being at least, they were persuaded that what they had together was too good for them to give up. Belew was certainly not going to walk away, although the pressure on him for fresh ideas was just as bad, and the others found Fripp at least as awkward to be around. Bruford, for his part, has described the band's creative process by this point as 'argy-bargy' and 'everything that the general public thinks it isn't. Crimson sort of scuffles for its music'. With alarming echoes of the *Islands* era, Fripp found himself increasingly unhappy with the direction things were moving. Inspiration was thinner on the ground and the dynamics between the four were just not working well anymore, with the album ending up being recorded twice. Rather than there being a useful level of creative tension, their collective mood was seriously damaging their output. Recognising this, they took a break from each other after the first attempt; they reconvened a few weeks later to have another go. Even so, such was the struggle that they ended up relying on partly improvised pieces to bring the album up to a reasonable length. [6]

Released in March 1984, *Three of a Perfect Pair* was the tenth Crimson studio album, its cover being a striking yellow with a blue symbol in the centre. That symbol, designed by Peter Willis, depicts the *Three of a Perfect Pair* theme in minimalist line form, although some have interpreted it as something more phallic. The first four of the album's nine tracks are the more fully written ones, and work well, but inevitably the argy-bargy had an impact, and the remaining five are varying degrees of half-ideas fleshed out by improvs. Unintentionally, although taken from one of the better tracks, the album's title could be read as saying that it was an album too far for this line-up. Putting a positive spin on things, it was presented as a deliberate split between the more accessible 'left side' and more challenging 'right side'. The lyrics gave away more than the band realised about the behind-the-scenes situation, Belew's chirpy word play and amusing tales by this point being ancient history and his themes instead being despair, nightmares and mental illness!

For the title track, which opened proceedings, there was still plenty of inspiration, exploring the difficulties of a couple coping with each other's habits and with one of them being schizophrenic, in effect having three people in the relationship. Part of what could loosely be described as the *Frame by Frame* family, it shifts between rock waltz verses and 7/4 time choruses, with a unique guitar-synth solo from Belew flitting crazily between the octave settings. *Model Man* opens with a riff reminiscent of *Brass in Pocket*, signalling further flirting with more accessible song territory. The chorus diverts into more characteristically Crimson-esque timings as Belew pleads for the world, or perhaps his band leader, to understand he's just a normal, flawed human being. The band were rightly pleased with themselves for coming up with *Sleepless*, with its slap-bass riff and swooping guitar-synths, as Belew's reverb-soaked vocal takes us into his dramatic dream/nightmare world. This started life as a much slower piece and was about to be dropped when, according to Levin, he came up with the bass idea and 'it just took off to a different place'. Even after it seemed to be finished, aspects of Bruford's drumming were felt to be an issue, so Levin and engineer Bob Clearmountain decided to take samples of his drum sounds and use them to construct a simpler, more regular drum track. This was the clearest manifestation of a growing issue for Fripp with Bruford, the latter's jazzier urges making him want to put the beat all over the place, while Fripp wanted him to play more straightforwardly. Belew had initially tried to persuade Bruford to 'simplify' but had changed his mind, saying, 'I prefer Bill being Bill . . . the random schizophrenic drummer', although 'that way is guaranteed to irk Fripp'. About as upbeat and commercial as this Crimson was to get, *Sleepless* was put out as a single, getting a little airplay but still failing to make any real impression, despite band members (minus Fripp) touring the radio stations to plug it. Bruford concluded that Crimson could no longer get the level of airplay they deserved, as those who took the decisions about playlists for the radio stations were reacting negatively to the name King Crimson, afraid of playing anything too original or imaginative. With a catchy guitar riff and a wo-oh-oh-oh vocal line, *Man with an Open Heart* is another Belew idea that leans in a more populist direction and even sticks to 4/4 time. Its message is for men to be more accepting of the moods and quirks of the women they meet—the things that make them individuals—rather than seeing them as difficulties. [6]

Sadly, from here on the album goes into a decline. Their move towards a more industrial sound was a conscious decision, using a method Belew characterised variously as 'freeform' or 'not playing together', which meant going in an agreed direction but not really paying attention to each other! Two of the results were the loosely structured, part-improvised instrumentals, *Nuages* and *Industry*, which each contain the germ of an idea, and on both Fripp solos over mildly interesting rhythms. However, the results were not entirely convincing. In the midst of the semi-improvs is the more solidly written *Dig Me*. The concept here at least is promising, Belew's imagination having gone into overdrive as he sings from the perspective of a once-loved classic car that finds itself at the dump. He was developing a talent for writing lyrics from unusual perspectives, but you could also read into this that he was feeling he personally had gone from being held in high regard to not feeling valued at all. Being part of what Belew would introduce live as 'the weird stuff', he got the others to play around his 'very awkward guitar'. But while it holds together in the brief chorus sections, the verses are too ragged and everything is overly plastered in effects, even Belew conceding that 'the song sounds like it's falling apart'. By the time we get to the final semi-improv of *No Warning* and the tightly structured *Larks' Tongues in Aspic: Part Three*, the well of inspiration is getting very dry, although, surprisingly, the former is a personal Bruford favourite. Inspired by *Larks' Two* still being popular in their live set, while there would be further worthwhile mileage to be found in the *Larks'* idea, what they came up with for *Part Three* sounds almost throwaway, based around a reshaping of the familiar 5/4 riffs into something closer to 4/4. Steve Hackett had already done this better, slipping a funky 4/4 *Larks'* pastiche into the middle eight of *The Show*. One unusual idea that didn't make it through was Levin's suggestion of a Barbershop Quartet piece. It was a style he loved, and he went as far as multi-tracking himself singing one evening after the others had left to create a demo. The idea got short shrift from Fripp. [6] [21]

The album only charted moderately, reaching No. 30 in the U.K., previously loyal fans being wary of the weakening output of this incarnation. Three months of world touring followed, and if some in the band were sick of the sight of some others, onstage it didn't show, a tribute to their high level of professionalism, not to mention Belew's natural showmanship. It was hard to read too much into Fripp's placid demeanour, but the other three at least looked as if they were enjoying themselves, getting as much out of the experience as they could while it lasted. In fact, they had developed a strong alliance onstage. Some insight into this came in response to a slightly barbed fan question at a Belew gig, asking about how he coped with Bruford's 'syncopation-from-hell method of playing'. Belew responded with nothing but praise for the drummer's talent, and talked about how they would all, in effect, have each other's backs. They might, for example, all be playing in different times, building up to 'the classic Bruford drum roll'. He would be confused as to where they were [but] Levin would then look at everyone else as if to say, 'Is anyone hurt?'—and all would be okay. While the line-up had stayed the same, their stage set and fashions had evolved. Bruford's drum kit and his many other percussion items were raised to make him more visible to the auditorium, his electronic drums also now arranged vertically behind him for added dramatic effect. Belew had moved away from the colourful suits, going for a wilder, swashbuckling look with baggy trousers. The fashion faux-pas of Fripp's white suit jacket and white shoes can be blamed on the styles of the mid-eighties! As the tour progressed, their semi-freeform opener, *No Warning*, evolved into an even more flexible improv, *Entry of the Crims*. Starting with some loops and soloing from Fripp, the rest of the band would emerge to cheers, one by one, Levin by this point experimenting with a device that allowed him to mix his stick with synth bass live. Raucous and wild, on a good night this could truly blow the socks off an expectant audience from the outset. Bruford was in his element when given the freedom of moments like this. While he set the bar high for himself, making his performances 'effortless, economical and elegant', playing the unexpected was just as important to him, feeling that it was part of what fans were after. 'Call me old-fashioned, but that, I thought, was what you were paying me to do!' He would later add, 'I like best those performers who convey the impression that what they're playing is being invented right there on the spot for this particular audience. It's never been played quite like that before'. [14] [9]

As ever, perceptions from outside and inside the band were markedly different, something that was perfectly illustrated in a gap between songs at the final gig of the tour, in Montreal, when a fan shouted, 'Four of a perfect group!' Sadly, those onstage no longer felt this was the case, and little did that fan or indeed anyone else know but this would be the last Crimson gig for ten years. That certainly hadn't been the intention, with a further tour being planned and all four giving interviews in August, discussing their future direction and how they might overcome their current difficulties. These interviews revealed an extraordinary state of affairs, a veritable case study in miscommunication, together spelling out that the writing was on the wall for Crimson due to deepening issues between Bruford and Fripp, and Belew and Fripp. The bassist, while not being able to explain how the band was holding together, had bought a drum machine to keep the beat in place of the actual drummer. At the same time, the lead guitarist/vocalist was considering becoming the core drummer. He had no doubt Crimson would be continuing, saying, 'I think about the future of the band all the time'. The actual drummer was aware of all this and happy to shift to being a percussionist. He had grown to resent the standard role of a drummer, describing it on the one hand as being 'the carpet' and on the other as 'like being shat on'. Stemming from this, he said he'd given up trying to accommodate the others, preferring to be 'an irritant at rehearsals'. He also admitted, 'I've been deliberately changing my part . . . which really gets them going'. Not reading the mood at all, he went on to say, 'It's easier to be in Crimson now . . . Robert and I are both a lot calmer'. His instincts and personal direction were now pulling too strongly in a particular direction to be contained within this Crimson. [22] [6]

In the meantime, Fripp resorted to using the press to speak to his bandmates. He said he regretted reforming Crimson 'because it is excruciatingly painful'. It particularly grated on him that while he laid out the space for the others to 'find themselves', that courtesy wasn't reciprocated. He expressed his hope that the penny would drop for the others, saying 'Dear Guys, if you're reading this, your guitarist is frustrated!' Concerning Bruford's not wanting to be a drummer that keeps time, Fripp said that, up to a point, he didn't mind. The issue was, as he put it, 'My personal pulse is being disturbed so often . . . for so long, that I'm not going to handle it anymore'. At the same time, he felt that he was keeping his role much more limited than he'd have liked, in order to allow Belew space for his more expansive wailing and soaring. [6]

Was there a way for them to continue, perhaps pursuing the more industrial route? Fripp took some time to unwind and reflect but concluded that there wasn't and pulled the plug. Society was not about to collapse this time, but the sky was falling in on Crimson again. In the space of just four years, it had gone from being unimaginable that Fripp would reform the band, to the agony of it being disbanded a second time. He'd gone from not being able to live without being in a first-division band, to again not being able to live within one. While that was perhaps just the way it had to be, thankfully this breakup was done with much less drama than in 1974. In fact, it was done with so little drama that Belew said that he only found out about it by way of the media. To a lot of fans, Crimson of this period were a real joy, if somewhat flawed and a bit frustrating, but as the four went their separate ways with very mixed feelings, Belew, Bruford and Levin at least all knew that they were losing what could still have been a bright part of their futures, and time was now against them. None of them would be short of work, but little if anything would be as good as being in Crimson, and with this disbanding turning into an even longer hiatus than the first, that was effectively the end in terms of them being part of a mainstream-ish big time. Despite all the difficulties, Bruford especially loved this period, later singling out the 1984 tour as a career highlight. He sums up this Crimson in four words: 'Damn, we were good!' [15]

# 8

# The Crafty Guitarist and the Crimson Queen

## *Late 1984 to 1993*

'I've come to realise that my life changes radically every seven years', Fripp would state profoundly some years later. Despite the awkward implication of there being other forces at work shaping his life, and the theory only loosely fitting the facts over the longer term, 1984 was indeed seven years on from his return to music, and the demise of eighties Crimson did indeed lead to a markedly different phase in his life. As before, he would go on a period of retreat and spend a few years away from the mainstream, but the vital difference this time was that, while again having no specific plans, he knew that he would return at some point. In fact, what is inescapable is that the underlying story of this period is of Fripp missing being in a major band and finding all sorts of alternatives until he could have the real thing again. As with Hiatus I, there would be some occasional musical output, but it would be eight years before his full-blown return. While this withdrawal was done without the drama of 1974, Fripp was still walking away a second time from the career he'd worked so hard to achieve, which to the outside world was hard to understand. From the inside, though, it looked very different. He was deeply unhappy with where he found himself, and his earlier sense of purpose was vanishing fast in the rear-view mirror. There is no rule book for what rock musicians should do at each age, especially intelligent and unconventional ones, and for the sake of sanity and replenishing his sense of self, it seems Fripp just had to periodically get completely away. But while he could be confident that there would still be a sizeable Crimson faithful around whenever he chose to return—a Crimson faithful that were used to his eccentricities—a second long absence would cause damage, and commercially things would never be quite the same again. As ever, his ex-Crimson cohorts wouldn't be taking any such break, there being lots of activity from Belew, Bruford, Lake, Sinfield, Wetton and Haskell, sometimes in musical backwaters but sometimes with unexpected returns to the big time. All in all, there would be no shortage of gigs and albums to keep the Crim-heads happy. [1]

Before retreating there was still a little business for Fripp to deal with in the shape of promo work for his less-than-essential second collaboration with Andy Summers. Released in autumn 1984, *Bewitched* lacks even the intermittent magic of their first collaboration and has a very different feel. It was an ill-focussed affair, or perhaps just badly timed, Fripp having to leave Summers to it after a couple of weeks to join the next leg of a Crimson tour. As a result, the finished product was much more Summers than Fripp, this time also featuring other musicians, including ex-LoG bassist Sara Lee. Summers had considered reproducing some Bartok pieces with his guitarist friend, but they ended up going for original material again, the highlight being the moody, faux-African title track, one of the few pieces that feels like a properly considered collaboration. Ultimately, the album just amounted to a bit of light relief for the Police man, after the chaos that had accompanied the global success of *Every Breath You Take* and the album, *Synchronicity*. For Fripp, it seemed less than incidental, and after getting through the U.K. publicity work, he headed straight for America, life in the coming years set to involve regular trans-Atlantic commuting. While he'd now ditched or toned down aspects of the philosophy, Gurdjieff and Bennett would still feature strongly in this second hiatus, with Fripp having booked himself onto a further course, this time at the American Society for Continuing Education. Set up by Bennett shortly before his death to promote the Fourth Way, the ASCE's base was at a colonial-era mansion called Claymont Court, on the outskirts of Charles Town, West Virginia. This would be Fripp's home for the next three months.

Having given up on the three-year plans, Fripp reverted to the strategy of waiting for the future to present itself to him. That was the theory at least. When a music-related future tried to present itself, however, he was initially reluctant to go with it. This happened when others at Claymont suggested that he run residential music seminars. He declined, but the others persisted, and Fripp eventually agreed to give it a try. Back in 1974, Fripp had said that he felt that rock-guitar playing was hopelessly inadequate and that a new kind of teaching was needed. A decade on, this would be his chance to meet that need, extending the principles of the Fourth Way into guitar teaching. To do this he set up what he called a Guitar Craft course, which started in March 1985. He intended this as a one-off, but it went so well that the concept evolved into an ongoing set of courses. His approach was much more holistic than conventional guitar teaching, blending it with aspects of personal development and yoga, and basing it on what he described as connecting the heart, hands and head. As the courses developed, they incorporated a mix of daily group and individual sessions, with lessons including relaxation, how to sit, how to hold a plectrum, the Alexander Technique, concentration and sensitivity. Actual playing and music theory would come later. Fripp would also introduce his students to New Standard Tuning, his own alternative way of tuning a guitar. This uses C-G-D-A-E-G as opposed to the 'old standard tuning' of E-A-D-G-B-E, increasing the instrument's range by seven semi-tones and lending itself to different styles of playing. The downside is that it requires a big commitment to re-learning all the chords and using special sets of strings to avoid the bottom string being too saggy and the top string being too strained. Courses were open to guitarists of all levels of ability, but every student would start at the bottom of Fripp's seven levels, working their way to the top. During Fripp's stint at the ASCE, in recognition of his lasting commitment to the work of the organisation, he was offered the post of president, which he graciously accepted. Music would provide Fripp with another link to the Fourth Way that year, through his producing an album by American concert pianist Elan Sicroff, who had also been through the IACE course at Sherborne. Entitled *Journey to Inaccessible Places and Other Music*, it consisted of sacred music composed by Gurdjieff and De Hartmann and would be released in 1987. Sadly, just as Fripp's life was taking these exciting turns, in April 1985 his father died at the age of seventy-four, and the guitarist returned home immediately to attend the funeral in Witchampton, just a few miles from his childhood home of Wimborne.

In the summer of 1985, only a year into this hiatus, Fripp began to dabble again in the more formal music business. Having been unhappy with aspects of the League of Gentlemen album, he went back to the original tapes and remixed a selection of tracks from it. In the process, he decided to jettison around half of the album, including the keyboard Frippertronics tracks and the taped-voice interludes. This meant that there wasn't an album's worth of material to re-release, so to fill the void, the two tracks from *Under Heavy Manners* were recalled to action. The *Under Heavy Manners* song was left more or less in its original form, however *The Zero of the Signified* became a mere backdrop for a no-holds-barred guitar-solo overdub, with dynamic extra Frippertronics and Belew-esque screechings added to the ending. This may have been a throwaway idea, but it turned out to be the highlight of the compilation. Recognising its distinct identity and to distinguish it from the original, Fripp named it *God Save the King*, which also served as the new album's title. While this was also perhaps just a throwaway variation on *God Save the Queen*, coming so soon after he'd ended Crimson, he was also being playfully perverse. To do some typically Fripp-style promotion, he did a three-day tour of record shops in England, performing a little and answering questions. The performances were Frippertronics of sorts, however the tape machines had been retired in favour of an Electro-Harmonix device that gave him up to sixteen seconds of delay, and he was using his guitar-synth rather than the old pedalboard. Confusingly, at a West London music shop, in response to a fan's question about the future of Crimson, he said that he'd told the other three that they were free to continue without him, which would have raised some interesting questions had they chosen to do so. Afterwards, as he walked the few yards to his Volvo, he was handed a demo cassette by a young Fripp wannabee. Pocketing the tape, he told him it was unlikely he'd get to hear it. As he then drove away, that marked the end of any kind of small, mobile solo performances for the next nine years.

Back in 1983, Fripp had first properly met singer and actress Toyah Willcox, the pair being thrust together at a music-biz charity lunch through being under the same management. Two years on they met again, both being picked up by the same chauffeur-driven car en route to that year's charity event. During the journey, Fripp asked Toyah if she would do the narration for a story project he was aiming to put together soon, to raise money for a school in America, and she said yes. Born in Birmingham and twelve years his junior, Toyah was best-known as the highly expressive singer with brightly coloured dyed hair in the group bearing her name, with a string of hits in the early eighties. She'd also had a varied acting career, most notably as a young punk in Derek Jarman's 1978 film *Jubilee*, the soundtrack to which included a small Fripp contribution through him being on to Eno's *Slow Water*. Fripp's ASCE activities would keep him otherwise engaged for a while, but when an opening appeared for that October, he arranged to meet Toyah for a week's recording at Arny's Shack. This was to be a significant few days for the pair, marking the beginning of their relationship. Speaking about that period in a 1992 interview, Fripp said, 'Within that week I realised that she was to be my wife. I was completely bowled over by this wonderful little woman'. Also interviewed in 1992, Toyah described feeling an 'immediate attraction', seeing Fripp as 'instantly adorable' and a 'gentle, traditional, old-worldy gentleman'. 'I'd been in a relationship where I'd been unhappy and didn't feel safe'; she would later reveal, while Fripp was 'reliable and dependable. A Perfect English gent . . . and everything I wanted'. [1] [2]

Business was still business despite the new relationship, and Fripp flew back to America to run his next Guitar Craft course. This time he came up with the idea of setting a challenge for his students to perform a concert at Claymont as part of their learning experience. As the available repertoire for a group of (in this case) eighteen acoustic guitarists was very limited, Fripp had written a few ideas for them to work with. For most of these, the parts were divided up almost orchestra-like between them, some playing in unison, while others played complementary parts, sometimes with Fripp soloing on top. As it hadn't been done before, one thing that no one had foreseen was just how striking and original the sound of so many acoustic guitars playing together could be, and it made for an interesting and unusual show. That December, Fripp arranged another challenge for his students to perform a live radio broadcast in nearby Charles Town, following that up with three shows at a university in Washington, D.C. As they now needed a band name, Fripp came up with The League of Crafty Guitarists, a name he would continue to use for each subsequent crop of students. Challenges of a similar nature would become a regular feature of future courses, with his students only getting a few days' notice of when and where they were to play. Some of their performances were recorded for wider consumption, with an album entitled *Live!* released in November 1986. The opening piece, *Invocation*, is by far the most memorable, starting in a highly original way, with numerous guitars playing harmonics, creating a shimmering, rippling effect. Eventually a simple-but-evocative chord sequence takes over, with Fripp playing a fluid mix of melody and solo over the top. The rest of the album is quirky and varied but weak overall, with a so-so Frippertronics track thrown in to bring it up to a reasonable length. Fripp would introduce other unusual elements to the live performances, as at their first U.K. show, at London's Queen Elizabeth Hall in 1987, where the fourteen strong line-up entered via the auditorium rather than onto the stage. Led by Fripp and carrying their guitars, they weaved their way up and down the aisles of bemused fans for a few minutes, before eventually heading for the stage. Then, for an hour or more, fans were engaged by this rare chance to see Fripp live, and the novel spectacle he was presenting. It was easy to forget but while Fripp was perfectly at home playing venues of that scale, most of his Crafties were playing in front of the biggest crowd of their lives, simply as a test! Unlike his appearances with Crimson, where Fripp let Belew do the talking, with The Crafties he spoke so much that these shows were almost as much seminars as concerts.

November 1985 saw the release of the third Asia album, *Astra*. With Wetton's return to the band requiring the departure of Howe, the vacancy had been filled by ex-Krokus guitarist Mandy Meyer. Only reaching the sixties in the charts on both sides of the Atlantic was a massive slump for a band that was all about big sales, and Wetton's bubble had burst, with the businessmen clipping fat cigars now looking elsewhere. The singles from the album, *Go* and *Too Late* (some unintended irony there), did well but this was not enough to save them. Geffen pulled the plug on their forthcoming tour and promptly dropped Asia, leaving them little choice but to disband. For the third time Wetton, now thirty-six, was back out on his own after being in one of the biggest bands on the planet. Asia had been that cliché of a roller-coaster ride for him, but one that in the end had only lasted about as long as his stint with Crimson. On the plus side, he'd established himself a second slot in rock's history and taken care of the pension—but set against this was a great deal of personal turmoil and damage to his health from alcohol abuse.

Considering the tangled interweaving of band line-ups elsewhere, there were surprisingly few crossings of paths for Crims with Pink Floyd. One occurred in 1985, when Mel Collins toured the U.S. as part of Roger Waters' band, promoting his *Pros and Cons of Hitchhiking* album. Following one of the greatest splits in modern music history, the ex-Floyd frontman was heavily embroiled in a legal battle over whether the others could still use the Pink Floyd name, feeling that without him there shouldn't be a Pink Floyd, and concerned that while he was trying to establish himself as a solo artist, an active Floyd without him would steal all the attention. Collins also appeared on Waters' contributions to the soundtrack of the animated film, *When the Wind Blows*, in October 1986. With the Cold War dominating world affairs, the film brought to life Raymond Briggs's tale of a couple's futile attempts to survive the aftermath of a nuclear attack through following government guidance. Another crossing of Crimson and Floyd paths came shortly after, with Levin briefly filling the enormous shoes of Waters, as regards his bass playing, joining David Gilmour and a cast of friends and session musicians in assembling the first Floyd studio album since Waters' departure. Released in the autumn of 1987, *A Momentary Lapse of Reason* had a different feel to earlier Floyd, while still being recognisably Floydian, was a marked improvement on 1982's tortured *Final Cut*. Levin's most prominent contributions were on the upbeat-but-reflective *One Slip* and the anthemic, air-guitar-inducing *On the Turning Away*. He had to turn down Gilmour's offer to be part of the tour that followed, already being too heavily booked elsewhere.

16 May 1986 was a somewhat eventful day for Fripp. It was his fortieth birthday, and that morning the sale went through for his purchase of Red Lion House in the village of Cranborne, ten miles north of Wimborne. This wasn't a rural idyll for Toyah and him to enjoy though but was to be a base for Guitar Craft in the U.K. Just a few hours later, after nine months together, he and Toyah were then married at St. Mary's Church in Witchampton. From Fripp's perspective it was the only place to hold the event, the church entrance being overlooked by his father's grave, the churchyard also being the resting place for several Fripps from earlier generations. It was a remarkably small affair for such a well-known couple—and would have been even smaller if Fripp had his way. Of the few guests, there were notably no ex-Crims, and they also tried valiantly to keep the event under the radar of the media. They nearly succeeded but, by chance, a photographer who was in the village spotted what was happening and spread the word. Fripp and Toyah

got away relatively lightly on the day, due to Witchampton being so far from anywhere, but their plans for a quiet time together were shattered. The following day a media circus was on their doorstep and they had to make a hurried escape, laying low elsewhere until the paparazzi lost interest. While there's no avoiding that ugly term, celebrity marriage, this was still a case of two people in love tying the knot. Toyah would later say, 'I got married because I had found my soul mate, not because I wanted to get married'. It's amusing to find that at the time they had little understanding of each other's fame. Toyah admitted in the coming years that she 'knew nothing of King Crimson', despite being a huge Bowie fan and hubby being on two Bowie albums. For Fripp, the penny only dropped as to how famous his wife was, when they were in a supermarket together and he saw how people reacted to her. Just a week after the wedding, Fripp was back in America, setting the pattern for the coming years of mostly living apart. [1]

The fundraising narration project that had brought Fripp and Toyah together made for a strange release for the unwary purchaser in 1986. Named *The Lady or the Tiger?* it consists of Mrs Fripp telling two long, winding and ultimately inconclusive stories over backdrops of guitars. These are supplied on one just by hubby, and on the other by his then-crop of Crafty Guitarists. First is the thirty-minute title track, the text for which was taken from an 1882 story by Frank Stockton, an American engraver with a side-line in writing. Fripp had encountered Stockton's writing through the ASCE, Claymont having once been his home (in fact, Fripp now held tuition sessions in what was once Stockton's study). Set vaguely in the distant past, it tells the story of a ruler who would judge an accused person's guilt or innocence through the use of chance. The accused would be given a choice of two doors to open. Behind one was a tiger that would instantly kill him, deeming him guilty, while behind the other was a beautiful lady he would marry, whether he was already married or not, deeming him innocent. The tale takes us through a particular person's case, although his fate is not revealed. The text for the second story, *The Discourager of Hesi-*

*tancy*, is from a follow-up piece by Stockton, where a group of people from another land call on the ruler to find out what happened to the accused man of the first story. Instead of getting a simple answer, they are told the tale of a visiting foreign prince who wished to marry one of the famously beautiful women of the land. Thinking that he has been granted his wish, the prince finds that he has also been set a task based on chance, which again carries the potential outcomes of either instant death or marriage, the Discourager of the title being a guard who would speed up a person's decision making through the unspoken threat of extreme violence. What the prince decides is not stated, and this story is also left unresolved to leave questions stirring in the listener's mind about love, jealousy and human nature. The cover shows Toyah and Fripp as a decadent, filthy-rich couple, lounging around in evening dress beside the kind of art-deco fountain you might find outside the mansion of an American millionaire. Bearing no relation to the subject matter within, they were simply having a bit of fun and playing on the fact that people would initially assume the album title referred to them.

More conventional signs of life on Planet Fripp appeared later in 1986 as he contributed to David Sylvian's solo album, *Gone to Earth*. Sylvian was best known for having been frontman of New Romantics, Japan, and more recently for providing vocals for the single version of Riuichi Sakamoto's *Forbidden Colours*, a spinoff from the *Merry Christmas, Mr Lawrence* film soundtrack. He was now moving away from his New Romantic past and broadening his interest in religion and other philosophies, including those of Gurdjieff, so linking up with Fripp was not as strange as it initially seemed. Fripp added a mix of solos and Frippertronics to five of the seven tracks on the original release, *River Man*, *Silver Moon* and *Taking the Veil* in particular all oozing with atmosphere, and with influences pulled in from all over the place. The first two also feature Mel Collins on sax. Perhaps through being out of the loop for a couple of years, some of Fripp's contributions sound a bit 'phoned in'. In fact, for the title track, with its ugly, discordant clash of guitar and voice, they seem to have crossed a line. A 2003 re-release included an entire second album's worth of ambient instrumentals that had initially been shelved, with Fripp appearing on two tracks.

In 1986, Bruford again turned to jazz and formed another band of his own. For this he scoured the rising talent of the U.K. scene and enlisted the much younger crew of Iain Ballamy on sax, Django Bates on tenor horn and keyboards, and Mick Hutton on bass. As well as the abilities of the individual members, a key element for Bruford in this setup would be the latest version of his Simmons electronic drums, the drummer aiming to take their use much further than with Crimson. As a drummer who always wanted to be part of the composing, he aimed to boldly take his role where no drummer had gone before, using a mix of electronic and acoustic kits to not only play the parts you would expect, but also to play some chord-and-melody parts. As well as drawing on the examples of Cobham, Collins, Peart and DeJohnette, as drummers who were taken seriously as music writers, Bruford also put his instinct to go down such radical avenues to his time alongside Fripp. Answering an interview question about his approach, and whether some of the vital element of feel was lost in using the new technology, he replied, 'Yes, jazz is made up of feel, but more importantly it's made up of innovation, of guys thinking of interesting ways to do things . . . trying to look under stones that have not been looked under'. Being one of the biggest names in the drumming world, he got his Simmons kit more or less for free, the trade-off being that he had to agree to demonstrate them at a series of international music-tech trade fairs around the world each year. He found that they weren't always the most reliable of instruments but felt that they were worth pursuing, despite the accompanying stress. To avoid being The Bill Bruford Quartet, he came up with the usefully ambiguous band name Earthworks, their eponymously titled debut coming out in 1987 to a predictably mixed reception, being experimental jazz from someone best known as a prog-rock drummer. Listening to *Bridge of Inhibition* in particular, with its in-your-face use of electronic drums and Arabic scales, you can feel how feathers would be ruffled amongst those not keen on having their boundaries pushed. The album sold reasonably, though

Bruford put this down to his prog following giving it a try before spotting that there were no guitars. He was probably right, as sales on subsequent albums would be much poorer. Jazz is not immune from personnel difficulties, and tensions between two of the band erupted into a violent incident on tour. Hutton, who Bruford would describe as 'a dark and extremely intense man', subsequently left to be replaced by Tim Harries on bass. The amended quartet produced the 1989 album, *Dig?* which includes the charming and jaunty *Gentle Persuasion*, where the e-drums play a more discreet role, and *Stromboli Kicks*, another piece from the more challenging end of their spectrum. [3] [4]

Being in a healthy financial situation, in December 1987 Fripp and Toyah treated themselves to an eighteenth-century manor house in the village of Broad Chalke, near Salisbury. Known as Reddish House, it was a moderately grand affair, once owned by war photographer Cecil Beaton, and listed by English Heritage. This was to be more of a quiet, rural retreat than a place for rock-star partying, and as it needed to have quite a lot of work done on it, the Fripps ended up spending a lot of time and money on improving it. In fact, such was the poor state of the building that Fripp was said to be afraid to fill the bath too much in case it caused the end wall to collapse! For such a small village, Broad Chalke was no stranger to well-known residents, former prime minister Sir Antony Eden living there after leaving office in 1957, and at the time the Fripps moved in, science-fantasy novelist Terry Pratchett was living close by. Despite buying such a grand home together, as Fripp and Toyah lived apart so much, the early part of their marriage didn't run particularly smoothly. Fripp spent much of his time in America, returning home every two weeks, while Toyah was mostly in the U.K. He would ultimately admit that 'there were enormous adjustments to be made', knowing he had to change from his bachelor lifestyle, but it would take him a few years more to actually do so. There were other issues too, Toyah later telling journalist, Nina Myskow, 'I married this wonderful man and spent two years threatening ex-girlfriends. There were just so many'.

In other interviews she put an end to discussions about whether they planned to have any children, revealing that a year after their wedding she had undergone sterilisation. She also added that neither she nor Fripp particularly wanted children, and as a result of childhood illnesses, she was physically unable to carry a child to term. [1] [2]

With a singer and a guitarist living together (sometimes, at least), the inevitable happened, and Fripp and Toyah formed a band. Fripp missed being in a proper touring band; he also wanted to help his wife's career, as she hadn't toured for five years. Together with Guitar Craft graduate and new Stick maestro on the block, Trey Gunn, and Dorset drummer Paul Beavis, they opted for the name Fripp Fripp, setting off for a short tour of England. For a couple who hadn't spent more than a few weeks a year together up to this point, this was quite a contrast. While there were some lingering elements of eighties Crimson in their sound, the band shaped the music around Toyah's ideas, sticking to tightly structured songs, largely in standard time signatures. Feeling there was definitely some mileage in the project, a second round of touring commenced in autumn 1989, this time billed as Sunday All Over the World, the name taken from one of their songs (Toyah's alternative suggestion of Strange Girls had been rejected). They got good turnouts and a favourable reception, playing moderate-sized venues like the Town and Country Club in North London. While it felt as if some Fripp normality was being restored, many of his fans wondered just how they came to be at a Toyah gig!

Taking a break from his worthy but not so lucrative Earthworks, in 1988 Bruford was tempted over to the Caribbean island of Montserrat to record with Jon Anderson. He'd assumed it was for an Anderson solo album, but when he met Rick Wakeman and Steve Howe en route, he realised that it was a reunion of early-seventies Yes personnel. As they lacked a bassist, Bruford suggested they call Levin, who flew out to join them. There was one major complication however, in that they were legally unable to use the name Yes. After countless personnel changes over the years, there was a version of the band in existence that didn't include any of these four, and they didn't take kindly to Anderson's plans. For this project they therefore opted for the cumbersome but informative name, Anderson Bruford Wakeman Howe, leaving their fans to join the dots, assisted by the clue of a Roger Dean fantasy landscape album cover. The mixture of late-eighties trends in sounds and production gave the music a bright, lively feel, although that would prove to be a double-edged sword, anchoring them rather too firmly in the passing fads of that period. The album was a commercial success, though, reaching No. 14 in the U.K., and was followed by a major tour in the summer of 1989, again with Levin. The big names involved, along with big money sloshing around, prompted some tabloid stories of their supposed excesses on tour, such as a customised 747 and taking over hotels. While Bruford has suggested that some of this was a bit exaggerated, they had definitely reached the other end of the scale compared to his early days of touring. 'ABWH in 1989–1990 came to a sponsorship arrangement for accommodation with the Ritz Carlton [hotel] chain in the U.S. That came complete with tea and sandwiches on bone china at 4.00 p.m., and was, I can assure you, extremely comfortable'. Two years on, with the sound of arena-sized crowds still ringing in ABWH's ears, Arista Records decided it would be a great idea for them and the official version of Yes to do an album together. The result of this, *Union*, Bruford has described variously as a 'Frankenstein' album and a 'preposterous, directionless enterprise', the album proving more popular with fans than the participants. A promo tour followed, which was also a big-money spinner, Bruford participating but feeling it was part of the 'ever more preposterous and bloated world of stadium rock'. Although it was a good pay day for him, the good feeling that had come out of ABWH had been killed off. [4] [5]

Although Fripp had, in the meantime, sold his Crafty HQ in Cranborne after just three years, Guitar Craft was still an ongoing success in 1990, attracting plenty of students wanting to learn the Fripp way. That year, instead of just the occasional concert set as a challenge, Fripp toured the U.S. and Canada with his Crafties, playing over fifty shows. After having encouraged them to try writing, he also felt it was time for a studio album, assembling them at New York's Manhattan Center Studios that June. Amongst his crop of personnel were several who would go on to greater things, most notably future Crim Trey Gunn, but also Hideyo Moriya, Bert Lams and Paul Richards; they would form The California Guitar Trio, despite none of them being Californian. The album, *Show of Hands*, took a year to get released, and is a mix of occasional brilliance and beauty, with the customary quirkiness of The Crafties. The only Fripp composition this time was *Eye of the Needle*, sounding like an acoustic leftover treasure from *Discipline*. Of the rest, *Chiaria* and *Asturias*, both composed by Lams, are highlights, the latter using the massed acoustic guitars to full effect. With this album also in need of a little padding, there are also five rather grating a cappella interludes, written and sung by an American friend of The Crafties, Patricia Leavitt, who had also performed at several of their gigs. With all this following on from Fripp's band work with Toyah, you didn't need to be a psychologist to see that it was all to try to fill a distinctly Crimson-shaped hole in his life!

While Belew was perhaps feeling that he was drifting back into obscurity as he approached forty, 1989 took some interesting turns for him. He released his fourth solo album, *Mr Music Head*, which included the song *Oh Daddy*, on which he sang a duet with his daughter, Audie, now eleven, with her asking him when he was going to have a big hit. This was put out as a single, with accompanying video, and did indeed give him a surprise hit in the U.S., albeit of the novelty variety. While this was going on, Belew received an unexpected phone-call from Bowie, asking him to again be part of his touring entourage. This was a surprise, as not only had it been ten years since *Lodger*, but because The Thin White Duke had been occupied with his hard-edged band, Tin Machine. However, on the back of a greatest hits package his record company had put out, Bowie wanted to tour, not only to promote the album but also to draw a line under his back catalogue, the material starting to feel like an albatross around his neck. The dynamics of Belew's relationship with Bowie had changed, the guitarist's status having been raised by fronting Crimson, while Bowie's status as rock deity had taken a battering after some weak eighties albums and the much-derided Tin Machine excursion. Reflecting this, Belew was also asked to be the tour's musical director and would spend weeks preparing track arrangements with Bowie in the build-up, before the ambitious seven-month *Sound and Vision Tour* got going in March 1990. Visually stunning and with a crowd-pleasing set list, it was generally well received. The only major criticism was that the relatively minimal band—Bowie, Belew and just three others—did not sufficiently fill the aural space. Onstage it was predominantly a two-man show, with Bowie and Belew up front, while the others were partially hidden behind the stage set and screens, a fact that grated on them as the tour progressed. For Belew, it would be a mixed experience. On the one hand, you don't get much more high-profile and prestigious than touring the world beside Bowie. On the other hand, his memories were tainted by being on the end of some sniping in the music press for his guitar style and even for his smart, pony-tailed appearance. In addition, he was having an emotional roller-coaster ride with his marriage breaking down. On the plus side, during the tour he met Martha, who would become his second wife.

Belew had been putting together his latest solo album just prior to the Bowie call up, and as a spinoff to the pair working together, Bowie joined Belew in his studio to put down a couple of new songs, adding an unexpected extra dimension to the guitarist's project. With Belew's star rising again and the Bowie tour in full swing, that new album, *Young Lions*, was released in May 1990. Bowie contributions apart, for Belew, solo did actually mean his doing pretty much everything, and it's packed with the former Crimson man's exuberance and imagination, such as *Phone Call from the Moon*, a piece you can take at face value, and *Small World*, inspired by how the world looks on a mini-TV. His reworking of *Heartbeat* is disappointing but was something that he just needed to get out of his system. More than making up for this are the two tracks featuring Bowie. Firstly, he duets with Belew on the wonderful *Pretty Pink Rose*, a relatively straightforward Bowie-penned rock track, with lyrics littered with political references. This was put out as a single and, assisted by being included in Bowie's live shows, reached No. 2 in the U.S. The second, a Bowie/Belew co-write called *Gunman*, rounds off the album. With some lingering Tin Machine showing through, this is a punky number about media glamorisation of gun-crime, Bowie's manic rendering of the words mingling with interjections of Belew's solo guitar. Frustratingly, other than becoming better known amongst Bowie fans, Belew still didn't break through in any lasting way into the wider public consciousness as a solo artist.

With just about an album's worth of material to use, Fripp and Toyah's Sunday All Over the World went into the studio, the resulting eleven-track album, *Kneeling at the Shrine*, being released in May 1991. Toyah's ideas are imaginative, and she sounds distinctly Kate Bush-like in places, rather than the more brash post-punk pop style of her eighties material. The album, however, suffers from being neither fish nor fowl, as Fripp had stepped back to allow the others space, while Toyah was not being full-on Toyah. Ending up for Fripp as patchy hiatus material, there were a few echoes of the *Discipline* era and some faint future echoes of Crim to come, the stronger ideas coming where they kept it short and sweet, such as *Don't Take It Away* and *Storm Angel.* Almost in parallel, much the same personnel recorded Toyah's next solo album, *Ophelia's Shadow*. Another Crafty Guitarist, Tony Geballe, was the main guitarist here, Fripp playing on just two tracks, with passing ex-Crims Tippett and Haskell also guesting. On meeting Fripp again after a long interval, Haskell belatedly got to hear some of eighties Crimson, and was quite impressed by it. As for his opinion of Fripp the man though, he thought 'he was his usual peculiar self'. [6]

With Toyah's solo effort being more commercial, and her career suitably re-launched, she headed off to tour the U.S. for the first time. SAOTW had been rendered redundant, and that would be the end of Fripp and Toyah working together for many years. Giving an interview to a Connecticut radio station while away, Toyah casually lifted the veil on her private life rather more than Fripp perhaps would have liked. Speaking to the station's DJ, Joel Krutt, she said, 'Robert has been through the sixties when there was sexual freedom . . . [his] kind of perception of women, as far as I'm concerned, is that they give free love'. Her view was that, whether women want to have children or not, 'We're going to have a career and we're not going to be sexually exploited. Robert and I came together in love instantly but we're such kind of opposites and we've such problems kind of relating to each other'. Explaining how their contrasting views of gender roles fed into her lyrics, she went on to say, 'I think our conflicts have made us very creative together . . . I won't do his washing. I won't cook for him and he won't tolerate this in me. It makes for fascinating conversations . . . and yet we're so utterly in love and we can't be separated'. Fripp's old-fashioned gentlemanliness was proving to be a mixed blessing it seemed, although Toyah certainly wasn't putting all the blame on him for their disagreements, admitting to being 'madly possessive and madly angry', while Fripp was more 'free-wheeling'. [7]

The hectic level of live Guitar Craft performance challenges continued into 1991. By then, Fripp had had enough of a break from the real thing and began moves to re-form Crimson again, contacting the others from the eighties line-up. But while they were willing in principle, they were all heavily involved with other commitments for some time to come. Fripp then instead approached David Sylvian, with a view to his being Crimson's vocalist, and started to think of others he could approach for the rest of the line-up. Though flattered by the offer, Sylvian declined, not wanting to end up as a name in the next chapter in the endless turmoil of the band. As he was working through a bundle of deep personal issues at the time, he in any case, couldn't face the prospect of the intense touring he'd have had to commit. He did, however, suggest that they do a full collaboration in the near future. Fripp reverted to the idea of recalling the eighties Crimson line-up, and resigned himself to having to wait, with plans pencilled in for 1994.

Being unable to re-form Crimson would prove to be one of Fripp's lesser problems of 1991, however, with E. G. collapsing after a series of ill-judged investments in the property and insurance markets. Enthoven and Gaydon were long gone, and the company's nature had changed greatly in the intervening years, Fripp feeling that they hadn't been paying him his full royalties, instead diverting artists' income into assorted financial adventures, through loans to a partner company, Athol and Co. The subsequent demise of E. G. led to the sale of his back catalogue to Virgin and the publishing rights to EMI. After writing countless letters to E. G. executives filled with a mix of 'venomous abuse, abstruse legal arguments and bitter wit' but getting nowhere, Fripp turned to the courts to contest the sale and the issue of royalties. He had a big fight on his hands in trying to prove his case, as in the early years there had been a high level of trust between the parties, and Crimson's original arrangements with E. G. had literally been on the basis of a handshake. Things had been further complicated when Fripp went on his seventies sabbatical, where E. G. asked him to sign a document that allowed them to manage his royalties on his behalf. He explained in a 1994 interview why he was so angry and had to go down the legal route. 'I felt a deep sense of personal violation. E. G. was set up as a partnership between artists and managers . . . and to see the power and quality of that relationship violated so thoroughly, left no alternative'. It would take him the next six years to get anywhere, a process that nearly bankrupted him. [8]

Sylvian's promise of a collaboration with Fripp became a reality late in 1991, as the pair got together for some initial jamming and writing. They also called up Trey Gunn, the thirty-one-year-old Texan having worked his way into becoming a regular Fripp sideman. They stopped short of enlisting a fuller band at this point, Sylvian having only agreed to the project on the condition that their touring was kept low-key. He was an interestingly contradictory person, seemingly 'delicate, effete and introvert', according to Steve Holtje of *Creem Magazine*, while at the same time 'stubborn' and 'used to getting his own way', his record company, Virgin, keeping the faith and allowing him much artistic freedom. As was the custom for Fripp bands, in the spring of 1992 after just a few weeks together they were on the road, notably being billed with Sylvian's name first. This was a partnership of two very strong individuals in their own different ways. Sylvian was certainly no adjunct to Fripp. Their itinerary consisted of short tours of Japan and Italy, playing new material supplemented by tracks from *Gone to Earth.* [9]

Following this, after Fripp gigs in New York in May 1992, accompanied on separate nights by Gunn and The Californian Guitar Trio, he thought it would be an interesting idea for them all to get together as a sort of elite Crafty Guitarists spin-off, and by the end of the year they were gigging as The Robert Fripp String Quintet. Although inescapably dominated by the presence of Fripp, this was much more of an equal partnership in terms of the material and arrangements, the group gigging in November that year, squeezed in between further legs of Sylvian and Fripp's tour. Back with Sylvian, Fripp decided the time was right to flesh out the band, with Jerry Marotta joining on drums, and another American, Marc Anderson, enlisted as a second percussionist. It's interesting to consider that, had Sylvian not turned down the offer, this could have been the new Crimson! As their material took on a more solid shape, the alliance leant in an unexpectedly heavy funk direction, with Fripp's *Exposure* getting an unlikely airing in their live sets, as it fitted their bill. Undoubtedly glad not to be attempting to belt out the likes of *Schizoid Man*, Sylvian's more restrained deep tones, channelling Bowie with a Ferry-esque vibrato, would add a laid-back warmth to their sound too. As they began studio sessions, the nature of their roles in the partnership became clearer. 'I'm being chaotic, and David is more organised', Fripp would tell Steve Holtje. Sylvian becoming something of an obsessive perfectionist for the project.

1992 was an exceptionally busy year for Fripp. As well as being musician, teacher, husband and being involved in major litigation, motivated by his anger at his former management company and the music industry in general, he set up his own record company, Discipline

Global Mobile (DGM). For this he went into a partnership with David Singleton, a thirty-one-year-old musician and ex-teacher-turned-sound engineer, who shared his principles. The pair had met in 1990 when Fripp needed a sound engineer in a hurry for some Crafty Guitarist gigs, employing Singleton, and keeping him on afterwards. Based in Salisbury, near to where Fripp was now living when on this side of the Atlantic, DGM was to be a small, mobile and independent company. More importantly, its aim was to be ethical, unlike conventional record companies, which Fripp saw as exploitative, short-sighted, immoral and having a fundamental conflict of interest. He saw the standard practices of the music industry as depriving the creators of music of their authority and their right to benefit from their own work. This is because the agreements artists often sign stipulate that the record company owns the copyright to their work. The costs of the recording, promotional work and videos that may never get broadcast are also recouped from an artist's royalties. All in all, an artist could end up with a very low percentage of the royalties their work has generated. Fripp has summed this up as being like an artist 'constructing a work to be stolen, paying for its construction, agreeing to it being stolen and then meeting the costs involved for its theft'. As it's normally the only deal in town for a new artist, they tend to accept it. To counter all this, Fripp wrote a set of business aims for DGM. Predictably, these were lengthy, but he begins with some guiding principles. 'The first aim of DGM is to help bring music into the world which would otherwise be unlikely to do so, or under conditions prejudicial to the music and/or musicians'. The second aim was to attempt the interesting balancing act of operating 'in the marketplace while being free of the values of the marketplace'. DGM also aimed 'to be a model of ethical business in an industry founded on exploitation, oiled by deceit, riven with theft and fuelled by greed'. They would also operate with the key Fripp principle that 'artists have the right to own the copyright in their own recorded work'. [10]

Fripp also found a few days to get together with Eno for the first time since their abandoned *Music for Health* project. Brain One was, by this time, known as much for being a successful producer of his own music, somehow being both well-known and obscure simultaneously. The albums he produced for the likes of U2 were selling shed loads, while his own work, though widely influential, rarely threatened the charts. Neither fully ambient or instrumental nor a full return to songs, 1992's *Nerve Net* was a different concoction, Eno not retreating from being cutting-edge in his chosen territory despite having reached middle-age. Fripp appears on four of the eleven tracks, some of his guitar parts again given unusual descriptions. On the opener, *Fractal Zoom*, which David Sheppard describes as 'electronic art-funk', Fripp plays 'pin-trumpet guitar' around Eno's dramatic vocodered vocal harmonies. On the simultaneously futuristic and retro *Juju Space Jazz*, Fripp's part is down as 'early fifties club guitar', his other contributions being more mundanely listed as just 'solo guitar' on the less-memorable *Distributed Being*, and the enticingly tense yet ambient *Web*. [11] [12]

In 1992, after a brief phase with initially compatible Cozy Powell in place of Carl Palmer, the original ELP returned after their own fourteen-year hiatus, with the album *Black Moon*. This included an interestingly rocked-up version of Prokofiev's *Dance of the Knights* from *Romeo and Juliet*, but while they were perhaps thinking in terms of another *Fanfare*, it failed to register with the common man. Despite a loyal core following, ELP's brand still felt a bit lost, the album selling poorly and getting poor reviews. They would only produce one additional studio album, *In the Hot Seat*, in the early nineties, but personal differences and Emerson struggling with a nerve problem in his right hand convinced them to call it a day in 1998. While it wasn't on the scale it had been in the seventies, there were still other ex-Crims to be found in many places in the early nineties. ELP's former colleague, Sinfield, continued to produce lyrics for mainstream-pop artists, including another Eurovision Song Contest winner Celine Dion, who had taken the world of MOR pop by storm. Sinfield's song, *Think Twice*, co-written with Andy Hill, was put out as a single in 1994, reaching No. 1 in the U.K. and across much of Europe, winning him a second Ivor Novello Award. Elsewhere, Mel Collins and Michael Giles were part of an all-star cast backing Bryan Ferry on his album *Taxi*, one of his periodic indulgences in covers, while Haskell would get an unexpected extra trickle of income from his song, *Almost Certainly*, topping the South African chart being covered by Caribbean reggae singer Judy Boucher.

In the summer of 1993, while both were back in England, Fripp and Haskell were invited to a reunion with other ex-members of their teenage bands, the others feeling it was time for a bit more hatchet burying. Since their acrimonious parting after *Lizard*, their lives had taken very contrasting paths. From Haskell's perspective, while Fripp had been sailing through life, he'd become hardened by decades of misfortune and being ripped off by 'little Hitlers'. Haskell had now found himself 'financially ruined, completely heartbroken' and back living with his mother. He also hadn't released an album for ten years but maintained his self-belief and kept working at his craft. Looking back on those years he explained, 'You can glamorise it as struggle if you like but I was playing great, singing great and getting tons of money in tips and wages. Better than anything the record business has ever done for me'. Playing six nights a week for much of that period, 'It was what a real artist does, not a fabricated pop or rock star. I was face to face with real people with real feelings, in bars all over Europe'. Feeling it was time to have the courage of his convictions, he set up his own label, Wilderness Records, to enable him to take the plunge back into recording his own music. He'd learnt a lot from his mixed bag of experiences in the intervening years, and his subsequent album, *Hambledon Hill*, was an accomplished product, mixing commercial, full-band tracks with his love of stripped-down folk and blues. The title track gently weaves together hints of Simon and Garfunkel and Gordon Lightfoot with elements of nursery rhyme, its lyrics having been inspired by the break-up of a relationship. The title itself came from the picturesque site of an old hill fort where he and his girlfriend had romantic walks when they first met. The best of the full-band tracks, however, is *Pelican Pie*, for which the man from the rural backwaters of Dorset conjured up some sleek, American-style bluesy pop crossed with a sea shanty. The big breakthrough still eluded Haskell, things not helped by distribution nightmares that meant he had to fall back on direct sales at gigs. While Fripp was now contemplating returning once again to his personal world stage, Haskell had recently resorted to playing on cruise ships, performing a tiring schedule of sets for weeks on end to boatloads of heavily partying Scandinavians. Reflecting on meeting up with Fripp again, he self-effacingly compared how their lives had been going. 'He [Fripp] was in his twentieth successful year as a world-renowned musician. I was in my thirtieth successive year as a complete screw-up'. At least now having his own record label, Haskell finally had some sense of being on par with Fripp. As he put it, in a tangled mix of resentment and admiration, 'I had attained the confidence level that Robert Fripp had been born with, and it had only taken me forty-seven years'. [13] [6]

Although there hadn't been a Frippertronics album since 1981, Fripp hadn't lost interest in working with layered repetitions. He'd abandoned the Revoxes years ago, and even the devices with longer delay that he'd been using now seemed primitive, with technology having moved on a great deal. Fripp could see that the latest digital devices—some of which were introduced to him by Sylvian—would allow him to use much greater lengths of loops, with digital recording greatly increasing the clarity of the sound. Adding in his proficiency with guitar-synths, he could now produce sound loops and solos with his guitar, using pretty much any sound he cared to try. With some initial experimenting on a stack of equipment he nicknamed The Lunar Module, in the privacy of a studio, Fripp confirmed to himself that there was indeed a rich vein of possibilities to explore. Even more so than with Frippertronics, it would become a significant side-line for him in the coming years, both in its pure form and as an extra dimension on other tracks. Fripp eventually christened this new format 'Soundscapes'.

After some studio sessions, the RFSQ took to the road again in the spring of 1993, their tour finale and only U.K. gig coming at Nottingham's Playhouse Theatre. On the tour, Fripp took the opportunity to try out some live soundscapes as a support act to his own band, eight years on from his last Frippertronics outing. After that it was back once again to working with Sylvian, and the release of their one and only studio album, that July. Recorded the previous winter in New York and New Orleans, *The First Day* featured the same line-up as the tour band, supplemented by co-producer David Bottrill, a Canadian with tendencies towards the heavier side. The title, which derived from a Sylvian song that didn't make the final cut, suggested some kind of new beginning, mixed with biblical references, both parties wanting to portray that they had changed. The album's otherwise less-than-thrilling cover is a rarity, not only for featuring a photo of Fripp, but a laughing Fripp. Alongside is a grinning Sylvian, sporting long, blonde, Robert Plant-esque hair. The former Japan frontman was responsible for the lyrics, vocals, keyboards, some guitars, co-writing and co-production, but nevertheless it was musically much more likely to appeal to the established Fripp market than Sylvian's former following. Fuzz boxes and wah pedals abound, with a core sound of thoughtful metallic-funk, and while the titles and lyrics are filled with religious overtones and undertones, it never feels as if you're being beaten over the head with any message.

The formula works well on the opener, *God's Monkey*, which has the best of the rather cryptic and unfathomable lyrics on the album, sung over layers of guitars, percussion and a deep, funky stick-bass. *Jean the Birdman* repeats the feat, with a bit more cynicism thrown in. Going for heavy without the funk, *Firepower* is burdened with over-complex interplays and timings, Sylvian singing to a different pattern than the other instruments, making its verses too awkward. It's rescued by a seven-minute ending where Fripp solos over the rhythm track and a shimmering soundscape backdrop. The cleverly titled *Brightness Falls* hangs on a funked-up, slightly soured *Foxy Lady*-like riff. Sylvian's vocal here mixes his understated world weariness with despair, and again, after the vocals end, the track shifts into a lengthy, atmospheric wind-down. *20th Century Dreaming: A Shaman's Song* starts as a heavy bluesy song, with the twist of being in 5/4. Even more so than on the previous two tracks however, it's the end sequence that steals the show. Over a repeating bass line and sparse vocals, Fripp again builds layers of sounds, and after the vocals and rhythm instruments die away, a towering, industrial landscape lingers on for a few glorious minutes more. This section is powerful in its own right but was also significant as it captured Fripp in transition from Frippertronics to Soundscapes, using longer loops and adding guitar-synth strings in amongst the layers of droning guitars. The final track by the full band, *Darshan: The Road to Graceland*, shifts back to the heavy funk, clocking in at an unnecessary seventeen minutes. The Eastern religious theme is upfront here, albeit given a trippy flavour, its minimalist lyrics about facing difficult choices in life and the fear of making mistakes. The Sanskrit term, *Darshan*, which refers to a state of meditation that induces a vision of God, is repeated mantralike throughout, while Graceland refers to a spiritual destination rather than Elvis's mansion! Unfortunately, this is where the formula fails, as it feels like a seventeen-minute search for an idea. Although it starts promisingly, with a rhythm lifted from the nineties club scene, it relies on an insubstantial riff and is a step too far for Fripp down the heavy-funk path, as he plays little more than throwaway noodlings. *Bringing Down the Light*, the actual final track, is the first album release of a pure soundscape, though it is not listed as such. This is eight-and-a-half minutes of passionate, yet serene, swirling layers of guitar-synth, somewhere between classical and ambient, and somewhere between pre-meditated and improvised. Startlingly original and inspired, especially for a forty-seven-year-old big-name musician, it signified that the transition in this area of the guitarist's work was complete.

Even more so than with The Crafties and SAOTW, we can safely read into this venture that it was a stand-in for Crimson, and for that reason alone it was destined to be a one-off, even if the pair were talking about there being more to come. As a near-Crimson experience, it was eagerly lapped up by fans who had been waiting for a 'proper' album from Fripp since 1984, and it has numerous high points despite never completely taking off. That said, the project certainly carried some musical weight, attracting attention way beyond people's initial curiosity as to how the two would combine, and was an album of integrity that experimented with bold new twists on rock formats. The pair would reveal that it was Sylvian who spent the most time worrying about getting the finished product as perfect as possible. 'Robert was forever telling me that a track was fine. It's finished!' he told *Creem Magazine*, having had to be persuaded to stop picking away at what he perceived to be imperfections. The album itself only really tells half the story of the collaboration, there also being three EPs and, later, a live album and religious-themed installation. The two *Jean the Birdman* EPs featured some early Fripp soundscape experiments and embryonic Sylvian songs, while a third EP, *Darshan*, came with a remix of that track by The Grid and, far more interestingly, *Darshana*, where electro-ambient duo The Future Sound of London constructed a trippy ten-minute piece out of Sylvian and Fripp samples and *Zero of the Signified*. A photo shoot and interview for *Vox Magazine* to promote the album that July took a bizarre turn, with a playful Fripp blowing into Sylvian's ear, pulling faces and doing silly voices, while Sylvian was trying to take it seriously. Eventually Sylvian got so pissed off that he stormed out and had to be coaxed back. While they were only twelve years apart in age, the photos taken that day made Fripp look more like a middle-aged uncle with dubious dress sense, standing with a rebellious young nephew, Sylvian looking even younger than his thirty-five years. [9]

Whatever pleasure Fripp had from the release of this latest work was horribly cut short just days later by the death of his mother, Edith Fripp, who had died of cancer at the age of seventy-eight. Fripp gave a eulogy at the funeral service, the text of which he later published in sleeve notes, giving perhaps the deepest insight we would ever get into the feelings of this high-profile, but often very private, man. We are left in no doubt about his affection for his mother and how vital her support had been to him when he was finding his way in the music business. Finding humour in his darkest moments, he talked affectionately about her poor sense of direction when driving, and how they had put a pack of cigarettes in her coffin, describing her as an 'unrepentant smoker' and hoping that wherever she was now, there would be a smoking section. She was buried alongside Fripp's father in Witchampton. [14]

Devastating though the loss of his mother was, the Fripp show would go on, as he embarked on several months more touring with Sylvian. Under the banner of *The Road to Graceland Tour*, their band again included Gunn, but with Marotta dropping out, they were joined by thirty-eight-year-old Californian drummer Pat Mastelotto. Mastelotto had previously been with the bands Page and Mr Mister, appearing on two No. 1 singles in the U.S., and was a self-taught drummer who couldn't read music. On hearing of a vacancy in a Fripp band, he did everything he could to get an audition, and then made sure he got the gig. Forty-two-year-old Canadian Michael Brook also joined the live setup, playing 'infinite guitar'—a guitar with modified pickups to make a feedback loop. As a third guitarist, and with a background in ambient music, he would enable greater exploration of the atmospheric aspects of the material in the live performances. The tour ended in December 1993 with a two-night grand finale at London's Royal Albert Hall, with a live album, *Damage*, recorded at those gigs and put out the following year. As well as reprising much of *The First Day*, it includes three tracks that didn't make the album but which, between them, capture what was lacking from it. *The Blinding Light of Heaven* leans further to the heavy side, with some Hendrix-like guitar from Fripp, while *Damage* and *The First Day* are downbeat, passionate Sylvian songs, unlike anything else on the studio album. *Damage* wasn't entirely the end of the pair's work together, as they also assembled an installation called *Redemption—Approaching Silence*. With music by Sylvian and smatterings of text written and spoken by Fripp, this meditative, ambient piece was created specifically for an exhibition held in a Tokyo temple. Other than the music, the installation included a room full of screens, a floor of mirrors and candles blowing in an artificial breeze. A second room displayed Fripp's text on video screens, while his reading of it was played through hidden speakers. The 'silence' of the title is, as before, what Fripp feels is 'an echo of the presence of god'. While its message was religious, Sylvian's hope was that people seeing it would 'find within it some catalyst to a greater experience'. He was aiming to 'bring the listener or observer to a place where they're comfortable with silence'. A version of the music, including Fripp's voice, was released in 1999 as part of a Sylvian album called *Approaching Silence.* [15] [16]

The culmination of the RFSQ's work together came with the release of the instrumental album *The Bridge Between*, in November 1993, the first Fripp album put out by DGM. The obligatory, ambiguous title seemed to refer to the guitar bridges that connected the quintet, however, in the sleeve notes, which included another outpouring of Fripp philosophy and his text from *Approaching Silence*, we would find that there was a religious meaning to the phrase. Writing in relation to the human race seeking redemption in order to approach the gates of paradise, Fripp referred to building 'the bridge between' our world and the 'new world' that is 'struggling to be born'. To him, it is a bridge that we are currently crossing, with music being one of the possible actions a person can take through which God can enter our lives and through which we can achieve redemption. With echoes of 1974's doom-and-gloom, he refers to our world collapsing, criticising those in power for 'abrogation of responsibility towards those who are dependent on them'. Musically, it's a diverse affair, with Fripp taking more of a back seat in the writing and arranging. It opens with *Kan-Non Power*, written by Moriya, which is the kind of track you'd probably expect from this mix of personnel, with its driving rhythm, unusual time signatures and some powerful Frippery. The sombre and beautiful *Hope* is filled with fuzz/sustain solos from Fripp and Gunn, weaving their way around the spidery chords. While this is reminiscent of Fripp circa 1975, it is, in fact, a cover, with an arrangement by Gunn. There are also three covers of Bach pieces, one played with distortion, the others using acoustic guitar sounds to loosely resemble harpsichords. As with *The First Day*, the album closes with a soundscape, this time by Fripp and Gunn. Its title, *Threnody for Souls in Torment*, is another reflection of Fripp's intense religiosity, threnody meaning a lament for the dead. In contrast to *Bringing Down the Light*, this is an exploration of a line of distinctly uneasy listening that Fripp would dip into at times over the coming years. In his sleeve notes, Fripp's DGM partner, David Singleton, said that he had found working with the quintet 'challenging', bluntly stating that they 'may have seemed to be lacking in integrity'. The album's release drew a line under the project. [15]

On a solo tour in the U.S. that autumn, while answering audience questions in Boston, Belew had confirmed that Crimson would be back when all parties were free, and, in fact, his set had included a couple of new songs which he announced were intended for a reconvened Crimson. Rather than a straight-forward reuniting of the eighties four-piece Crimson, Gunn was now in the frame as a fifth member, and Fripp was looking to Marotta to be the drummer rather than Bruford. With his characteristic openness, in an earlier interview Belew had already lifted the lid on how things were between individuals saying 'I don't think Robert wants to have Bill involved. There was a lot of conflict built into that situation'. Dates were now firmly in diaries, though, and some jamming of the potential new Crimson (minus Belew) had already taken place in the summer. There was no doubt as to what would be following shortly, but it seemed that elements of the new line-up were still up for discussion! [17]

9

# Dinosaurs?

## *1994 to 1999*

Middle-age was never going to be pipe-and-slippers time for Captain Bob, and instead of putting his feet up, in the mid-nineties he would not only get another new King Crimson line-up together but would take soundscapes on the road and continue to develop DGM. He wasn't a man to worry overly about how he was perceived but in the late nineties would again demonstrate his uniqueness both as a musician and as a human being. For many of the others in The Greater Crim, with all concerned being that much older, calmer and more mature, this was to be a remarkable period of reconciliations, reunions and re-emergings, leading to a series of pleasant surprises, just when it looked like they might all be quietly fading away. It helped somewhat that after a couple of decades of hostility to those associated with prog, music trends were shifting back in their favour.

The once-simple act of a few like-minded musicians getting together had, for Fripp and Co., mutated into a tortuous, diary co-ordinating exercise, coupled with negotiations and diplomacy so tricky you might expect to find the U.N. involved. However, ten years on, Fripp's great entity that lived and died at his whim, was finally resurrected. Plans had re-evolved since 1993, and despite Fripp having been prepared to ditch both Belew and Bruford, by the spring of 1994, as the pieces of the latest Crimson jigsaw fell together, both were to be in-

*Sylvian and Fripp ticket, London, 1993.*

volved. While pressure from Belew and Levin had caused Fripp to recall Bruford rather than go for Marotta, the reunited members of eighties Crimson were to be supplemented by two others from the Sylvian and Fripp band. These were Trey Gunn, on Stick, and a second drummer, Pat Mastelotto, making this once-English band two-thirds American. This looked like an overload in some departments, now with two drummers, two bassists/Stick-players and two guitarists, but the idea that had been forming in Fripp's mind was not for a straight-forward sextet but a double-trio, adapting ideas from the jazz world.

Being much younger than the others, Gunn hadn't even heard of Crimson until being blown away by *Discipline* in 1981. He'd already been combining playing in punk bands and studying classical composition, but his direction was shifted by hearing this album, while at the same time discovering the Mahavishnu Orchestra. Having tried guitar and bass, by the mid-eighties he had concluded that the Stick was to be his instrument, and he impatiently drove to the manufacturer's home in an attempt to buy one. It wasn't that easy, and he would have to wait, but a couple of years on he would manage to get his hands on one. Belew had been enjoying his solo career in the meantime but his albums were not selling well, so a new phase of Crimson was most welcome to him. There was an important creative factor for him, too, telling *Fender's Frontline*, 'King Crimson can take me in lots of directions that I can't go by myself'. He would also reveal that they had collectively agreed to a change in their approach to avoid self-destructing again, telling Cleveland's *Scene Magazine*, 'One of the requirements of us not hating each other is that we spend short, intensive bursts of time together, then go away and do other things'. Other than that proviso, he felt Crimson were now more confident and mature, and boldly asserted that 'this band will be fun to be in and will have a longer life together if we're smart about it'. With tour planning under way, first on the agenda for Crimson Mk V was a short spell of writing and studio sessions in May 1994, in Woodstock, U.S., and signs were positive, with these producing enough work-in-progress material for a mini-album to be planned for later in the year. [1] [2]

Having worked his way into a world-famous rock band, Mastelotto would soon drum his way into a bit of TV history in 1994. As a session drummer with The Rembrandts, he played on *I'll Be There for You*, which the world and its life-partner came to know as the theme to the extraordinarily successful U.S. sitcom *Friends*. The first series came out in 1994 (with the last in 2004) using a short-theme, tune-length version of the song. As the series took off, the band recorded a fuller version, along with a video featuring the stars of the show one by one taking over the instruments from the band. In this, the character of Monica, played by Courtney Cox, playfully bonks Mastelotto on the head in order to take his place behind the drum kit. With the series being so immensely popular across the world and continually re-run ever since, it's quite possible that the theme is being played somewhere in the world every minute of every day.

After a live performance with FSOL on BBC Radio One in May 1994, Fripp took soundscapes on the road in their own right for the first time, with a mini tour of Argentina. He understood from the start that the format was never going to be mainstream, but that wasn't the point. He was doing what he did best, exploring something that fascinated him, and taking his guitar playing somewhere new, which wasn't something that too many big-name guitarists would be attempting with their fiftieth birthday looming. At this stage, his audiences wouldn't have known what to expect, beyond it being some sort of modernised Frippertronics, and with the music being improvised, beyond the basic setup, to an extent Fripp himself would also turn up not knowing quite what would happen. This is what he loved about the format though, each piece to him being a product of 'time, place and person', all having 'the characteristic of being true to the moment in which they are performed'. Using a lot of sweeping synth-strings and the mellower end of the brass spectrum, pieces would build up from gentle openings, some developing into deeply sombre pieces, while others would take an edgier or unsettling turn. Either way, they were full of drama that demanded attention from the listener, rather than being simply a pleasant backdrop. Just four days in, though, after the first of two shows in a Buenos Aires theatre, a section of the audience noisily demanded their money back, unhappy at how short the show had been and at the music not meeting their expectations. After the commotion reached such a level that a TV crew turned up, the mini riot was quelled by people being given free admission to the second show. [3]

In similar vein to his passing liaisons with FSOL, a Fripp collaboration with The Orb was released later that summer under the name FFWD>>. The Orb was another band that revolved around one person, in this case Alex Paterson, with a revolving door of other members. They were at the peak of their commercial success at this point, their 1992 album, *UFOrb*, having topped the U.K. chart, producing music inspired by the likes of Kraftwerk and Eno, to accompany the drug-fuelled clubbing scene, mixing trippy electronics, ambience and a hefty dose of samples. The band and album name, FFWD>>, came from the abbreviation for fast forward, also serving as a contrived combination of their initials, if you count Paterson as D for Doctor, the nickname by which he liked to be known. His two colleagues here were Thomas

Fehlmann and Kris Weston, both of whom dealt with the electronics, while Paterson himself was sound manipulator-in-chief. Having recorded Fripp improvising in the studio the previous summer, using the guitar-synth sounds he was now favouring, the others took notes and phrases of his and added their own material to construct the album's twelve instrumental tracks. Around half are downbeat, such as *Can of Bliss* and *Hempire*, with the titles clearly in the hands of The Orb crew! Others, like *Colossus* and *Klangtest* are more rhythmic, the latter with layers of sequenced synth-marimbas. The album scraped into the lower reaches of the U.K. charts but slipped completely under the radar of many Fripp fans. Now considered a good example of nineties chill-out music, its only negative is that promising ideas are at times drowned in samples and effects. While FFWD>> was just a one-off, Fripp would make an appearance of a similar nature, on *Terminus*, on The Orb's 2001 album, *Cydonia*, marking the end of his flirtations with the electro-ambient crowd for many years.

Nothing if not diverse, the familiar sound of Fripp's guitar could also be heard in 1994 on *Sidi Mansour*, an album by veteran Algerian rai singer Cheika Rimitti. Rai, which mixes traditional chants and songs with Asian influences, was given some interesting twists here, not only with touches of Fripp, but also contributions from Flea from the Red Hot Chilli Peppers and East Bay Ray from The Dead Kennedys. In the meantime, there also turned out to be an element of truth in rumours that had been circulating about a Fripp reunion, of sorts, with Wetton, with his contributing to Wetton's 1994 solo album, *Battlelines*. Aimed more at his Asia following, it failed to reignite his career however, and Wetton himself was dismissive of it in years to come. Only the title track had broader appeal, tackling his reflections on his personal life and his battles with alcohol. His 1998 follow-up, *Arkangel*, also with contributions from Fripp, would be a significant improvement. Fripp and Wetton had found they were now able to put the conflicts of their Crimson time together behind them, and actually became good friends. With twenty years having passed, Wetton had actually come to look back on their Crimson material as being the best thing he'd been part of. The pair would avoid actually discussing the band, and on seeing the new version live in the coming years, Wetton would have mixed feelings, feeling that they lacked the kind of balance that he'd provided in his era.

The world may have thought it had seen the last of Fripp's lumbering behemoth, but with the release of their mini-album, *Vrooom*, in October 1994, they were back, and once more heading down the road of creating new music. The material didn't seem aimed particularly at drawing in new fans but what was the first release of new Crimson material by DGM, gave notice of their return, as well as providing clues as to where the nineties band would be going. Some fans would baulk at buying two versions of some of the same tracks quite close together, when the full album came out, but Fripp felt it was a valid approach, and there would be similar EPs in the coming years. The title track echoed *Red* in sound, pace and structure, but was a touch more bluesy. It was also an early illustration of the double trio in action. As well as other early versions of tracks that would be on the forthcoming album, there was the very short *Cage*, where Belew sings at breakneck speed about the state of the world. His mood had changed from having a relieved laugh about such things on *Thela Hun Ginjeet*, and the city is now a far more dangerous place, as he fears mugging and car-jacking, and sees freaks everywhere. Belew has never been coy about his love of The Beatles, and the piece of sleazy, bluesy rock that is *Sex Sleep Eat Drink Dream* has us firmly back in Walrus-esque territory. It was the only piece created from scratch in the studio, Belew taking home recordings of a jam, to nail down a structure for it, then sitting in the car park outside the studio to knock out some last-minute lyrics. The release of *Vrooom* was timed to coincide with a series of loosening-up gigs in Argentina, the band trying out their new material live and having a bit of fun with episodes of improv. This being eighties Crimson at its core, several tracks from their albums stayed in the set, the only nods to the more distant past being the ever-popular *Red*, *Talking Drum* and

*Larks' Tongues: Part Two*. With David Bottrill as co-producer alongside the band, they next checked into Peter Gabriel's highly civilised Real World Studios near Bath, from October to December, to record the long-awaited new album. Everyone would contribute ideas and credits would be equally shared, but Belew soon found that one thing that hadn't changed was the heavy reliance on him for lyrics and song structures. For the time being at least, this was working.

After the tasters tagged on to other albums, the first full exploration of soundscapes was *1999*, released towards the end of 1994. All live tracks, though not presented as such, this was the product of the June mini tour of Argentina. The album mimicked *Let the Power Fall* in mostly having years as token track names but, other than being based on layered repetition, that's where the similarities with Frippertronics ended. Here, the sound loops were much longer, allowing more structure and melody to be developed, and the guitar was now acting simply as a trigger for Fripp's pallet of sounds, rather than anything recognisable as a guitar. Although you would put this, and other soundscape albums to follow, on the shelf beside Eno's ambient albums, this music doesn't want to be left in the background or just flow over you, the five pieces straddling a broad range of moods. The opener, *1999*, slowly lures you down a path of deceptive serenity into darkness and fear. In a more filmic way, *2000* plays with your emotions for several minutes before you find you've been led back to the doubt and uncertainty lurking within yourself. Fripp next included the sombre twelve minutes of the piece that preceded the mini-riot in Buenos Aires, naming this inner-space odyssey, *2001*. *Interlude* is four minutes of relatively light relief, being more sound-effect-like, before we return to the sombre reflectiveness with *2002*. Sales were low, but Fripp himself acknowledged that 'soundscapes aren't much in the way of a product line which accommodates itself to a hard sell'. However, being so well established with a worldwide following, he could afford the luxury of indulging in an uncommercial side-line for his own satisfaction. In fact, he'd reached the point where he could say that 'as a musician, I am unable to perform where the performance is only a piece of promotion'. Where he was able to control the situation, these days he preferred a soft sell, so that 'the music reaches its audience gently'. Not letting the grass grow under his new line of work, Fripp then embarked on a ten-date soundscapes tour of California in winter of 1995. He was supported on this by Guitar Craft off-shoot The Californian Guitar Trio, who he would describe as supplying something 'more recognisably musical'. A few weeks later he headed south for another short tour of Argentina, enlisting the support of local guitar quintet Los Gauchos Allemanes to perform a similar role to that of the CGT. That was to prove all the more necessary this time, as the soundscapes Fripp was creating leant sharply towards the challenging. Often unsettling and at times more like sound-effects, even for the usually receptive Fripp audiences of Argentina, what he played was so difficult to sit through that Fripp himself couldn't avoid being aware of the audience's discomfort. He has talked about the music as if it were out of his control, saying 'soundscapes were developing in a way which was alarming to me . . . but [I] went with them'. The implication was that there was something spiritual happening and that the soundscapes were creating themselves, using him as a conduit. In years to come, Fripp would put this type of thing down to the intervention of 'the good fairy', his way of referring to God without saying the word. A more down-to-earth explanation might be that the sum of his knowledge and experience was combining with something in his imagination and his inclination to explore these possibilities. [3] [4]

More reassuringly, the eleventh King Crimson studio album, *Thrak*, was released in April 1995, a mere eleven years on from the tenth. There was a lot to absorb, with not only the fifty-six minutes of music it contained, but all that had changed through the expanded personnel. As well as the double-trio arrangement on some tracks, Bruford's use of electronic drums had been toned down, and where Frippertronics had peppered earlier albums, soundscapes now featured. Going the other way, a mellotron had been dusted down for Fripp to use, though just to confuse everyone, Belew was also using a very convincing mellotron strings sample on his guitar-synth. Overall, the album had a familiar-yet-different feel, with steps into the unknown being juxtaposed with echoes of the past. There was still much playfulness in the track titles, but there were darker, more intense moods lurking behind than before. Where there were words, Belew was again sole lyricist and the source of the darkness, despite his recent wave of personal success and his second marriage. With little conscious concession to commerciality or populism, *Thrak*'s appeal was largely to those existing fans who had kept the faith. This, and the impact of the on/off nature of the band for so long, meant that the album only crept into the lower reaches of the U.K. chart for a short period, although over the longer term it would fare reasonably well. The band certainly didn't intend it, but *Thrak* and the *Vrooom* EP would turn out to be the only new, written Crimson material (as opposed to improv) between 1984 and 2000!

A reworked *Vrooom* opens proceedings, using the double-trio format, with a trio in each speaker. Listening closely, you can pick out the complementary guitar roles, although the clearest split is between Bruford playing the main beat on one side, and Mastelotto playing assorted percussion on the other. Although the track is distinctly in the vein of *Red*, there are sections that are reminiscent of a twangy fifties-style guitar, only with this being Crimson, they are in one of Fripp's angular climbing sequences and in 7/4. This segues into a coda, *Marine 475*, which creates the effect of endlessly descending for several minutes, like a rock version of the famous Escher drawing, its title coming from the only clearly distinguishable taped words overlaid from a long, unexplained list of numbers. A guitar-synth mellotron intro, followed by a riff resembling part of *Cirkus*, opens the first song, *Dinosaur*. The imitation of *Cirkus* was accidental, Belew having been aiming more for *Larks'* territory, as he took a self-effacing look at his over-confident, naïve youth being such easy prey that he should be extinct. There's another layer, as the band are light-heartedly reclaiming the word *dinosaur*, which was being liberally thrown round as a term of abuse for older artists who had the cheek to still be around.

*Walking on Air* captures a beautiful-yet-sombre mood, our seemingly troubled lyricist reflecting on a lover's ability to be carefree. With the double-trio-setup redundant here, we instead get layers of gentle, almost weeping guitar and stick, over a melodic bass line. Belew was in fact quite dismissive of the idea that they were a double trio, describing it as 'a nebulous term' That he didn't see much evidence of. Putting his spin on what was actually going on, he explained, 'What it is meant to imply is that the band can break down into different factions'. While the concept name would be permanently appended to this line-up, the theory hadn't had much mileage in practice and was abandoned beyond a couple of tracks. Up to this point you could describe the album as being reasonably accessible, and perhaps even lacking in true adventure, but that ended here, and the next eight minutes were the band at their most original. *B'boom*, a percussion-based, mutant relation to *Talking Drum*, is a bold adventure that abandons chords and melody. Initiated by Bruford and Mastelotto, it steers clear of the dinosaur drum solos of prog-past, being instead a sophisticated, inter-locking, poly-rhythmic percussion duet, played over a swirling soundscape that suggests images of a twenty-third-century traffic jam. Avoiding the need for an ending, this crashes straight into the raw and raucous interplay of guitars of the title track. This intro and the track's closing section were the only written sections and were only there to serve as bookends for a lot of dramatic, discordant, noisy improv. They would have fun with the track in their subsequent live shows, the album version proving to be quite mild in comparison. [2]

*Inner Garden I*, opening the original side two, is a short piece of vaguely Shakespearean loneliness and regret, sung over simple arpeggio guitar chords and bass/stick rumblings, the even shorter *Inner Garden II* continuing the theme further into side two. Lyrically, these are something of a departure for Belew, being reminiscent of *Moonchild*, and giving the impression that we are dipping into sections of a story without knowing the beginning or ending. Between the two parts, *People* does what it says on the tin, with Belew's upbeat observations of the astonishing range of things that people get up to, and which make the world what it is, good or bad. It is the only (relatively) light mood on an otherwise sombre album, and the closest they get to a conventional rock song. *Radio I* and *Radio II* are short soundscapes that threaten to turn melodic but then vanish. These are wrapped around another Belew-initiated song, *One Time*, which dives headlong back into his darkness within. It's a song the frontman had been developing on tour, which ponders human emotional frailty, reflecting on how the chaos of life can easily overtake and overwhelm you. Musically, the track is made more interesting by the rhythm instruments trying to convince you it's being played in fours, while it's actually in waltz time. A fuller version of the raucous, bluesy *Sex Sleep Eat Drink Dream* has Belew channelling Lennon, the lyrics perhaps being more observation and comment than the band's own daily 'to do' list! The final two tracks are alternative versions of the opening two. *Vrooom Vrooom* contains variations on the riffs of *Vrooom* that feel a little unnecessary, and in case anyone hadn't already noticed the parallels, has a middle section that pastiches that of *Red*. Its coda, an electronically slowed-down, looser rendition of *Marine 475*, is a wander back down the road to the weird stuff.

After the long second hiatus, Crimson had re-materialised into a much-changed world. British politics had been turning grey under Prime-Minister John Major, however rock music in the nineties had taken a colourful turn, and quite a useful one from the point of view of older artists. The charts and music press were being filled by the likes of Blur, Suede, Oasis and Jamiroquai, all of whom unashamedly took their cues from the sixties and seventies. There were also the likes of Mercury Rev and Radiohead (the latter just commencing their path to world domination), successfully merging new wave, prog and pop influences, rather than seeing them as being in opposition to each other. The future was, in fact, the past—for a while anyway—and the record-buying public were happy to lap it up. After years of derision from some quarters, the early years of rock were being reappraised and rehabilitated, and courtesy of the swaggering Gallagher brothers and others, it was cool to like and to play like the older bands. It felt as if young people had been given permission to explore older music, instead of there being a constant push to move on and to forget the past. You didn't need to be too cynical to realise that plundering the past was merely the latest fad the music industry was happy to run with to make their next buck, but it was a godsend for older artists and had the effect of stimulating a rash of re-formings and re-emergings. As well as Crimson, looking through the gig listings in London's *Time Out Magazine* could make you think you'd travelled back in time, with names like Caravan, Curved Air and Camel all to be found again, and even a massive Pink Floyd tour. So, as well as being happy to raid their dad's record collections for 'classic rock', kids could actually see some of the original bands live. The dinosaurs were alive and kicking.

*Thrak*'s release was followed by bursts of touring in North America and Europe, culminating in two nights at London's prestigious Royal Albert Hall. Playing at such venues illustrated that Crimson were still able to draw large crowds, the previous year as a whole demonstrating that they were still relevant. While the *Thrak* tour was under way, in a surprising move, DGM put out a double CD of live material called *B'boom*. Rather than being a hasty attempt to cash in, this was a response to a poor-quality bootleg from the 1994 Argentina tour. The thinking was that if there was a market for a dodgy bootleg, DGM could head it off at the pass with their own, better quality, reasonably priced, official version. This proved to be right, with the album briefly poking its nose into the lower reaches of the U.K. chart. Drawn from the same pre-*Thrak* tour, its lasting value is that it breaks many of the unwritten rules that seem to govern live albums. A conventional live album would be compiled from a promo-tour following the release of a studio album, and the band would be aware that they were being recorded for this purpose. Here, Crimson are captured loosening up pre-album after a ten-year gap, and in mid-flow of developing new material. It's also compiled from recordings taken directly from the mixing desk, with different panning and mixing from what you might find on a more considered recording. Of the tracks that would form the backbone of *Thrak*, there are two enjoyable versions of *B'boom*—another live album rule broken—with more melodic soundscape intros than would end up on the studio version. Of the variations on older tracks, *The Talking Drum* stands out, with Belew and Gunn improvising joyously in the space occupied on the original by the violin of Cross, before Fripp brings it all to a climax. Sound engineer and big Crimson fan Ronan Murphy would later work on other live material from this period of the band, discovering for himself the huge complexities of the setup. Looking back on the experience he said, 'Trying to mix the double trio was like getting a doctorate in mixing. It was the most challenging thing I'd ever mixed up to that point, and I think going through that made me a better engineer'. Touring conditions for Crimson Mk V didn't quite match up to the high standards Bruford had enjoyed with ABWH, however they had continued to move in the right direction. The drummer recalled, 'I'm the only musician I know who only slept one night on a tour bus. I didn't sleep a wink, of course, being entirely unused to it. In King Crimson's later years, we had a luxury bus with bunks, to ferry us from city to city in the daytime, but then a hotel room at the other end, so we had the best of both worlds'. There was now also much less reliance on road managers making the band's itinerary up as they went along, especially for overseas touring. To his relief, 'some of the efficiency of high-level international touring [had] percolated down, so even beginner bands know roughly where they're going and why they are going there'. [5] [6]

Audience difficulties in Argentina notwithstanding, Fripp had faith in his soundscapes, and that July put out a second album of them, entitled *A Blessing of Tears*. Compiled from the mini tour of California earlier in the year, this is a collection of beautiful, melodic pieces, and what would ultimately be widely regarded as the most accessible of the pure soundscapes albums. Mood-wise, it's the audio equivalent of gazing into the middle distance, coloured by the guitarist's lingering, intense feelings over the death of his mother. Fripp's achievement here was that, for all the variety of his output over twenty-seven years, he had still found somewhere new to go. The opening piece, *The Cathedral of Tears*, is a suitably towering construction of interweaving layers, and you have to remind yourself that this is live, improvised, solo music, albeit with some degree of pre-meditation in terms of timings and sounds. Similarly, *Midnight Blue* and the title track build into sombre, near-classical-sounding dramas that insist that the listener shares in Fripp's emotions. The album ends less intensely, with two serene, reflective pieces, both incorporating a bit more studio tinkering than the rest. *Returning I* is a piece run backwards and *Returning II* is a re-mix of the same piece run forwards. The extensive sleeve notes include the text of Fripp's eulogy at his mother's funeral service at Wimborne Minster, giving us some rare insight into the man. His most poignant words are, 'Life is what we are given. Living is what we do with it and then we die. The death of one's mother is about as close to home as we get, but the death of friendship and trust remind us of the richness which both give to life and our living of it'. The impressionist-style John Miller painting on the cover shows the shimmering figure of an elegantly dressed woman on the horizon, amidst shades of mauve and blue in fading evening light. Given the sleeve notes, this seems to have been chosen to portray Fripp's mother, remembered in her prime.

In August 1995, still keeping several other plates spinning, between legs of the *Thrak* tour, Fripp returned to the spinning plate of Guitar Craft for the latest course he was running at Claymont. Twenty-one years on from his encounter with the philosophies that led him to set up Guitar Craft, Fripp's beliefs had continued to evolve, and he was now following a much more conventional line of belief. Partly as a consequence, although Guitar Craft would continue, once this course was over, he announced the formal ending of his relationship with Claymont. He would also cite having to spend much more time running DGM as a reason for this. [7]

Fripp's third soundscapes album, *Radiophonics*—assembled from the shows in Argentina where the music had taken an abrupt left turn—was released in March 1996. Unlike *Blessing*, this is a difficult listening experience, as other than two sombre, melodic pieces, it's made up of unsettling rumblings, whirring noises and rapid panning. Short extracts of this had worked well on *Thrak*, but on the much longer pieces here the basic idea that music should be enjoyable on some level has been forgotten. Such indulgences only have limited audiences, and Fripp himself describes soundscapes from this phase as 'sometimes unpleasant' and 'not a music which of itself would claim to be entertaining'. Nevertheless, even this album gets an occasional airing on shows such as BBC Radio Three's *Late Junction*, a showcase for music that starts leftfield and keeps going. The album's cover came with another essay's worth of notes, explaining where Fripp was in terms of his approaches to performing and business. Returning to soundscape performances that month, as part of the four-day *Music and Dance for Tomorrow* event on London's South Bank, Fripp settled in for the duration, giving free shows in the foyer of the Queen Elizabeth Hall. Crowds of anything from handfuls to a hundred would gather round, disciple-like, including the occasional thirty-something male fan with a distinctly unimpressed girlfriend. Because of the location, many others passed by on their way to or from shows, ticket booths or cafés, loving or hating what they caught snippets of, with no idea who they had just walked past. Such was the setup that the guitarist himself could periodically get up from his playing position, leaving loops of sound running, and wander away either to get his own perspective on his performance or even to nip to the bathroom, much to the amusement of the audience. With a bewildering array of seven Fripp or Crimson albums, plus a few EPs, all released in the space of eighteen months, fans certainly couldn't complain about any lack of new material. Concluding this sequence was the May 1996 release of *THRaKaTTaK*, compiled from the improvised adventures

*South Bank Soundscapes flyer, 1996.*

MARCH 96

**Thu 7 to Sun 10**

**Foyer, Queen Elizabeth Hall RFH ❷**

## Robert Fripp South Bank Soundscapes

**Now You See It**

Continuous live performance of Fripp's solo guitar work based on combinations of delay, repetition and hazard. Schedule of performances: 7 Mar (7-10pm); 8 Mar (6-8pm); 9 Mar (1-10pm) & 10 Mar (6-10pm)

Admission free

Other *Now You See It* events: 7 Mar RFH2; 9 Mar RFH3 (page 30); 9 & 10 Mar RFH2 (page 30)

Cultural Industry in association with *SBC

Soundscapes Magazine *listing, 1996.*

Crimson went on in each night's version of *Thrak* on the recent tour. This is, to say the least, a challenging listen, with fifty-seven minutes of unrestrained, often discordant improv, rather than the few minutes that would form part of a Crimson set. As the double trio then set off on their next round of touring, they didn't realise that *THRaKaTTaK* had, by accident, heralded the next phase of the band. [2]

The second half of the nineties would see the re-emergence of several ex-Crims and some interesting, if fleeting, partnerships. The first of these was a temporary super-group of the kind that middle-aged prog fans might dream up during an evening in the pub. Twenty years into his highly acclaimed solo career, former Genesis guitarist Steve Hackett returned to some of the Genesis material he'd left behind. He realised that fans still had great affection for it, much of which he had co-written, and he put together an album of new versions. Assembling an extraordinary range of musicians, including Wetton, Levin and Bruford, most significantly he also persuaded his friend McDonald to get involved sixteen years after he'd largely vanished, post-Foreigner. With all the Genesis-Crimson links over the years, the collection of personnel seemed very natural, and under the title *Genesis Revisited*, with Wetton filling Peter Gabriel's vocalist shoes where appropriate. As a follow-up, Hackett got together several of the same musicians, including Wetton and McDonald, to play for four nights live in Tokyo in December 1996. Although this was essentially *Genesis Revisited* live, in honour of his guests, Hackett also got them to tackle *The Court of the Crimson King* and *I Talk to the Wind*, with Asia's *Heat of the Moment* given an unplugged rendering and Wetton's *Battlelines* also thrown into the mix. Given the broad-ranging set and having only had ten days of rehearsals, it was quite an achievement, a double CD of those nights later put out as *The Tokyo Tapes*.

This period also proved fruitful for Toyah's TV career, with Mrs Fripp cropping up as a presenter on a whole host of programmes, such as the BBC's travel show *Holiday*, consumer rights show *Watchdog Healthcheck*, and Channel 4's *The Good Sex Guide Late*, the latter of

Wetton gig flyer, late 1990s.

John Wetton gig, with David Cross as support, 1996.

which would have got Fripp followers curious! It was, however, an edition of *This is Your Life* in October 1996 that really got the Fripperati chattering. The long-running BBC show featured a different celebrity each week, with friends, relatives and colleagues brought out one by one to illustrate aspects of the person's past. For this edition, the subject was Toyah, and the first guest was hubby Robert. This was a surprise to Toyah, as he was on tour in Germany at the time and had flown back specially for the show. Overflowing with emotion for his wife's career being acknowledged in this public way, our hero couldn't hold back the tears as he tried to answer host Michael Aspel's questions. In contrast to her husband, Toyah was rarely out of the media, and the flow of behind-the-scenes details of their life together kept coming, sometimes just for the sake of sensationalism. After touring in a *Live Bed Show* and hitting forty, Toyah spoke to the *Daily Mirror*'s Nina Myskow, who found her 'fun, brave and oddly vulnerable'. In amongst the more mundane facts, she dropped in that Fripp 'finds me very sexually exciting now . . . every time we meet it's a dirty weekend!' In a very different sphere, in 1997 Toyah acquired herself an unlikely piece of something close to immortality, doing part of the narration used in each episode for the BBC pre-school kids programme *The Teletubbies*. This beautifully assembled idea, with brightly coloured characters with TV sets in their bellies, became a worldwide success, its episodes repeated endlessly for each new crop of toddlers. [8]

Despite the relatively luxurious conditions, Crimson's touring was causing a mix of old and new niggling problems to build up. According to Bruford, Fripp was unhappy about many things, such as the lack of privacy on tour, the state of the venues they played and the poor sound quality. In turn, Bruford was simply getting aggravated by Fripp's whingeing. The guitarist's insistence on having no specific lighting on him onstage, rendering him barely visible to the audience, he also found grating. After all, for all the affection fans had for the other members of the band, it was Fripp who most came along specifically to see. It did nothing to help Bruford's mood when Fripp decided to have sound

*King Crimson ticket, Shepherd's Bush, 1996.*

screens put around the drummer's kit, as he was finding two drummers to be too loud. This meant that, during their shows, Bruford could see little more than his own reflection in the screens. He read all this as signs that the band was once again falling apart, and that he needed to be elsewhere. To add injury to insult, he began to develop a wrist problem while in the U.S. He ended up playing what turned out to be his final Crimson gig, with the assistance of ice packs and pain killers.

While still under the impression that his future was with Crimson, after the tour Bruford turned his attention to a couple of short-term diversions. The first came about after the seed of an idea was planted in his mind by a fan, and Bruford subsequently had a post-gig drink with an American businessman who agreed to fund the project. This was with two legends from the jazz world: guitarist and keyboard player Ralph Towner, and acoustic bassist Eddie Gomez, who Bruford would describe as the greatest musician he ever worked with. Getting together for five busy days in February 1997, although they were recording in a winter, in a rural part of New York State, the drummer had in mind a 'softer, hazy, autumnal' feel. The result was the album, *If Summer Had Its Ghosts*. Varied and gently experimental in places, the autumnal feel was most apparent on the Gomez composition, *Amethyst*, while Bruford's briefly resurrected electronic drums were used in a less-obviously electronic way on *Splendour Amongst Shadows*, where a set of melodic East-Asian bell sounds were reproduced. Staying in the U.S., he got a second jazz-inclined group together, this time with Levin, along with two more Americans, Chris Botti on trumpet, and David Torn on guitars and looping devices. To contrive the acronym BLUE, they named themselves Bruford Levin Upper Extremities and put together a partly improvised album with hints of Miles Davis and plenty of Crimson-esque time signatures, called *Upper Extremities*. These albums were signs of where Bruford would go if left to his own devices, but although well received, both passed by almost incidentally. [9]

On top of all the original material being released, there was another significant project in 1997, the release of the boxed set *Epitaph*, consisting of live material from the Crimson U.S. tour and radio sessions of 1969. The result of years of tracking down recordings of one sort or another, and much painstaking work using the possibilities created by digital technology, it gave new life to that remarkable year of the original band. Fripp has often said that he feels live performances represent the material better than the studio versions, but while not everyone would agree, with versions of *Schizoid Man*, *Mars*, *A Man A City* and *Court*, these recordings go some way to capturing the live feel of that Crimson, as well as letting us hear other ideas that were floating around that would be abandoned or recycled down the line. Through sleeve notes contributed by each of the original five, plus roadie Dik Fraser, it was clear that whatever issues they'd had with each other had been resolved. Mistakes were forgiven and youthful impetuousness forgotten. Its cover, a picture by British artist P. J. Crook, called *The Four Seasons*, uses a stylised classical theme, showing a widow visiting the mausoleum of a loved one in the grounds of a mansion. The analogy is clear: we are revisiting a long-lost loved one, the grand surroundings echoing the music. With the original band's thirtieth anniversary on the horizon, McDonald then mentioned in an interview that he'd had the idea of getting a gig together involving all Crimson line-ups to mark it! 'There's definitely talk, but it's just talk. At least everyone is talking and friends, so there's always a possibility of something happening'. While they were now friends, McDonald and Fripp hadn't entirely resolved their issues over the 1974 break-up, McDonald remaining convinced that Fripp had taken his chance to take 'a little revenge' on him. 'I think he only asked me if I would tour with them to see what I would say, before he disbanded the group', also adding, 'who knows what goes through Fripp's mind. He's hard to figure out, that one'. [10]

1997 also brought a welcome re-emerging from the wilderness for violinist David Cross, with his album *Exiles*. After Crimson, he'd worked as a producer and director in a theatre, going on to become a university lecturer. Although he had put out a handful of low-key albums in the interim, this new CD brought his music back to the attention of a wider audience. With twenty-three-years' worth of water having passed under the bridge, and everyone feeling able to work together again, it included contributions from Fripp and Wetton, as well as lyrics from Palmer-James and Sinfield. As you'd expect, given the title, it included a reworking of the song *Exiles*, complete with Wetton reprising his vocal role. To avoid reproducing the original, Cross gave it a makeover, turning it into a much rockier track. With a new synth-and-violin opening section, and the melody from the original's opening section being shepherded into a new rhythmic arrangement, it's by far the highlight of the album. Fripp plays guitar on *Troppo* and *Tonk*, both

**● DAVID CROSS**
**Timely return for the electric violinist with 60s adventurists King Crimson. Sheila Mahoney handles the keyboards, free jazz rocker Dan Maurer (ex-Hazard Profile) plays drums and John Dillon supplies the cultured bass.**
**Willesden Green Library Centre** 95 High Road NW10 (081-451 0294) Today 8.30, £4.50, concs £3.50. Tube: Willesden Green.

*David Cross gig ad, September 1990.*

*David Cross and band warm up in Guildford, July 2010.*

*ELP at the High Voltage Festival, 2010.*
Courtesy of Tomoko Okamoto

*Roadies pack up after Travis and Fripp gig, Barcelona, 2010.*

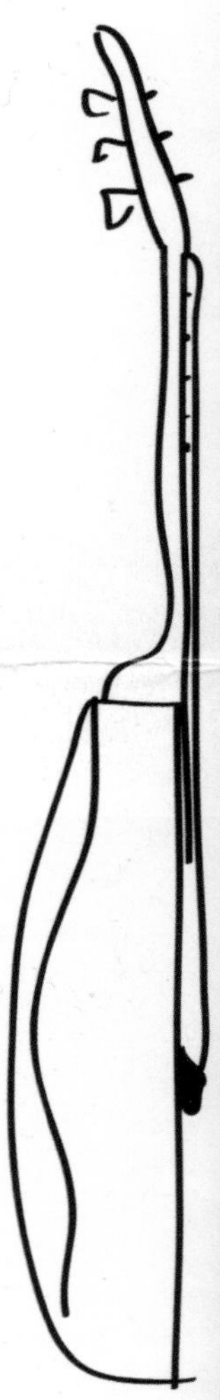

# TALLER INTRODUCCIÓN A LA NEW STANDARD TUNING

SÁBADO
22 DE MAYO DE 2010
CURSO INTENSIVO
BARCELONA, ESPAÑA

Imparte Luciano Pietrafesa
*(The League of Crafty Guitarists & ZUM)*
asistido por Marco Moreira
*(The League of Crafty Guitarists)*

Informes e inscripción
nst@zumguitars.com
++34 - 627704779

*NST course flyer, Barcelona, 2010.*

*Crimson's equipment pre-gig, London, 2015.*

*David Cross live in London, 2016.*

Richard Palmer-James live in London, 2016.

Crimson fans entering the London Palladium, 2018.

*Crimson's equipment pre-gig, London, 2018.*

*The 50th Anniversary Tour reaches London's Royal Albert Hall, 2019.*

*Levin, Stacey, Bruford, and Mastelotto backstage, Royal Albert Hall, July 2019.*

*Gordon Haskell live in London, 2019.*

*Toyah in London on her Court of the Crimson Queen Tour.*

*David Cross gig ticket, September 1990.*

of which also feature Peter Hammill giving his vocal cords a pounding, and harking back to 1974's *Trio*, Fripp contributes a soundscape for Cross to solo over, on *Duo*. The rock world had become a secondary career for the violinist, however, the positive reception *Exiles* received encouraged him to set up his own label, Noisy Records. His gigs would still have to be fitted into university holidays, however.

While everyone was wondering what would happen next with nineties Crimson, so were they. Fripp had successfully developed an updated version of his small, mobile unit with soundscapes, however the six-piece version of Crimson had become the opposite, and now seemed too large for its own good. Worst of all, the musicians were not functioning well together. When they reconvened at great expense in Nashville, Tennessee, in the autumn of 1997, it was a particularly grim experience, as they collectively ran into a brick wall. They were there to knock about ideas for a new album, but found those ideas were painfully hard to come by, and anything that did begin to surface from the others was vetoed by Fripp. Bruford voiced his feelings—something that he says wasn't really done in the band—and an upset Fripp hastily departed from the session. Bruford apologised and the next day Fripp returned, but that was the beginning of the end for him in Crimson. While Fripp had a well-established, if not always deserved, reputation for being Mr Awkward, this time the ill feeling was a manifestation of the band collectively running headlong into some uncomfortable questions. Where does a band go after twenty-eight years when they no longer have that innate, indefinable youthful understanding of where to go next and the ideas are just not flowing? What do they do when, although still well respected, they are no longer leaders in the way they once were? There was undoubtedly still a big audience out there for them, and there was still desire from the band members, but they had ground to a halt creatively after just one album in this phase!

Fripp didn't want to disband again but didn't have a solution, and in the end, it was Bruford who, despite having blotted his copy book, came up with the suggestion that would allow them to get round this impasse, floating the idea of going for total improvisation. They all enjoyed having space for improv in their live sets, so perhaps they should take that aspect further and remove the pressure to come up with workable ideas in the studio. It would, of course, replace it with the pressure of playing everything off the cuff, but they might find that more exhilarating. Fripp mulled the idea over and came back with the unexpected decision to split the band into a variety of improv-only sub-groups. He termed these ProjeKcts, heralding a phase of putting a capital 'K' before every 'c' in titles for a while to come, scrupulously avoiding the word split, instead referring to this as 'fractalisation'. Four ProjeKcts were planned, all of which would include Fripp and Gunn, along with one or two of the others, Fripp considering them to be 'research and development units' that would loosen up 'the band's view of itself' and its 'sense of possible futures'. The line-up planned as ProjeKct Two, consisting of Fripp, Gunn and Belew, was the first to get down to some recording, in November 1997, convening at Belew's studio in Nashville. Although he didn't initially realise it, Belew would be this line-up's drummer.

That was never likely to be his role in a future Crimson, but he accepted it as part of the loosening-up process and, more to the point, simply because he enjoyed the opportunity to be a drummer again. His drum kit was no ordinary one, however, but a newly purchased set of Roland V-drums, which operate as electronic triggers to a wide variety of programmable sounds, as well as being able to trigger programmed bass sequences. When they subsequently played live, this latter aspect could initially be confusing for the audience, as they wondered where the bass was coming from. Fripp was in his customary role on guitar/guitar-synth, trying out every setting he could find, with Gunn wielding his latest Touch Guitar. [11]

ProjeKct One, a four-piece of Fripp, Gunn, Bruford and Levin, was next up, performing a four night-stint at London's Jazz Café in December 1997. It was an interesting choice of intimate venue, as not only were they almost within touching distance of the diners on the upper level, removing any possibility of playing the distant rock star, but they had also stripped themselves of the protection of playing any well-worn Crimson music, also choosing to enter the venue through the crowd, after their local pre-gig meal out together. The improvised music, with no connection to any Crimson of old, was a shock to the unprepared fan. While many were happy to witness their heroes doing this, with all

*ProjeKct 1 ticket, 1998.*

the hit-and-miss that came with it, there were some for whom it was all too much, and who took the opportunity to vanish at the interval. According to Levin, the four went to great lengths to ensure they were spontaneous onstage: 'The day before the first gig we had a rehearsal just to check that all the gear was working. No two of us played at the same time to avoid falling into any groove that we might repeat later'. The only rule was that there were no rules, except a default position for when no one seemed to want to get the next piece going, 'in which case Bill starts'. Tellingly, Levin also commented that the level of tension that normally existed in Crimson was absent that week! Fans were unaware, but these gigs were to be Bruford's last in any Crimson-related capacity. After a Crimson career spanning twenty-five years, other than Fripp, he would ultimately be the band member to appear on the most Crimson studio albums. Having felt like he'd been released from prison after the ending of the disastrous Nashville sessions, he'd already decided to leave, only agreeing to stay involved for this final outing as it didn't involve any lengthy flights. Crimson had felt like his home, but it was a home with 'a bed of nails'! The decision meant he'd be leaving of his own accord this time, rather than one of Fripp's traumatising disbandings, which felt a lot better. [12] [9]

The ProjeKct Two threesome reconvened in February 1998 to begin a five-month world tour, performing what would to be the most gigs of any of the sub-groups. While they were on the road, the fruits of their studio sessions were released as the double CD *Space Groove*, the space of the title serving the dual purpose of meaning the freedom to go anywhere and to allow them to indulge in light-hearted space-themed track titles. With ideas flowing in a way that 'normal' Crimson had ceased to, the trio were pleased with what they'd recorded and, as Belew's trekkie-like sleeve notes put it, 'even Mr Fribble seemed elated'. However, critics felt that it had too much of the feel of musicians working out material, which was a fair-enough reaction, as that's what it was. The opener, *Space Groove II*, is a nineteen-minute workout over a suitably jazzed-up, ever-shifting rhythm. Fripp solos away at length,

T.O. 15/4/98

Ballroom, plugging excellent new single 'Don't Stop' (Mother Records) as part of this kitsch 'n' balmy club night.

★ **John Foxx** Subterania W10, 8pm-2am; £10, adv £8.50.

The leader of the original Ultravox brings his cold and arty brand of synth-pop back from the land of 'whatever happened to them?' A must for fans of Gary Numan, who always cited Foxx as a major influence.

★ **Projekct Two** Jazz Café NW1, 7pm; £15, adv £12.50.

The second King Crimson sub group project, featuring Adrian Belew (vocals, drums), Robert Fripp (guitar) and Trey Gunn (touch guitar). The music will be spontaneous and improvised in the aim of 'researching and developing for the greater Crim'!

*ProjeKct 2 listing–Time Out, 1998.*

switching in the guitar-synth midway to use piano and vibe sounds. The track is especially impressive when one considers that it was a warmup jam that happened to be recorded. They had caught themselves out before they knew they were improvising for a possible album. That is quite telling as the rest is decidedly patchy, and someone should have taken a firm hand and edited it down, rather than treating every note as sacred. ProjeKct Three (Fripp, Gunn and Mastelotto) and ProjeKct Four (as Three plus Levin) would subsequently have fleeting existences, Four playing seven gigs in November 1998, with Three rounding off this phase with a five-night tour of Texas in March 1999. [11]

A lot of individual ProjeKct material was put out for the most dedicated followers to buy, much involving sound engineer, Ronan Murphy, who had become involved with the Crimson 'family' through meeting Crafty Guitarist Steve Ball and subsequently working with Gunn and Mastelotto. He recalls, 'It was an amazing experience. I absolutely loved it. Mostly because I was getting to work with a band

I loved, where I got to be involved with the creative process'. Over the coming years he would work on a lot of live Crimson material, but he singles this out as being particularly enjoyable: 'The ProjeKcts stuff was a lot of fun, but far more than just mixing a live album, I was doing a lot of work, choosing strong parts of live improvs and editing parts together, essentially creating new tunes from cool parts of different pieces'. Often working in conjunction with David Singleton, his creations would then be edited into pieces for release, and he would also take great pleasure in hearing some ideas evolve into things that the band would work on again later. Prior to the mixing work, Murphy had toured with ProjeKcts Two, Three and Four, and being around Fripp and the others meant that he was privy to some of their discussions about the future of the full band, which, he alarmingly remembers, included 'the possibility of there not being anymore Crimson!' Notably he came away with far more positive feelings about Fripp as a person than some had in earlier years. 'I know some have talked about Fripp being tough to work with, but I certainly did not experience that', he recalled years later. 'I loved working with him. The thing about Fripp is that he is a cool and fun guy, but when it's time to be serious about the work, it is *really* serious! Robert and I got along really well, and I do not have a single bad thing to say about my time with him'. As regards the day-to-day details of the work, Murphy found that 'Fripp was not super hands-on. He would mostly let me do my thing, but he did have some specific ideas about things like panning and a few tonal issues. Of course, he had final say on everything we did, and it was never done until he liked it'. A more manageable compilation, *The Deception of the Thrush*, was also released in 1999, its title coming from T. S. Eliot's 1938 poem, *Burnt Norton*, where the bird appears to know something the observer doesn't—but this is just an illusion. The ProjeKcts had been a daring way to try to throw off the conscious or sub-conscious, self-imposed shackles that had been getting in the way. However, while many found the gigs enjoyable in themselves, there was a widespread longing for a 'proper' Crimson album. [5]

Released in the spring of 1998, *The Gates of Paradise* was another of Fripp's more challenging soundscape albums, and the religious expression that had been easing its way in before, had become unambiguous and unavoidable. As well as the album title itself, this manifested itself in track titles such as *Pie Jesu* and *In Fear and Trembling of the Lord*, and in the latest mini-essay of sleeve notes. While it contains a real gem of a track, elsewhere it repeats the indulgences of *Radiophonics*, illustrating the downside to owning your own record company—there's no one to act as a filter to what is released. Comprised of a mix of Fripp's early studio experiments and some live pieces, again much is unsettling, and unrelenting in pursuing this feeling. Fripp was immersed in thoughts of death, the afterlife and the tortuous journey to heavenly paradise, and the music was intended to reflect this. The mood is somewhat lightened by *Sometimes God Hides*, recorded live during Fripp's 1996 South Bank stint and arguably the best soundscape he would ever create. For this he lays out a backdrop of floating ambience, as if you've walked into a mystical East-Asian dreamscape, then adding several minutes of dazzling guitar-synth piano solo, before gently depositing you back in the dreamscape.

Music aside, it's the sleeve notes that again give us insight into what was going on in Fripp's mind. He had not only changed greatly from the intense rock musician of the seventies but had also gone through an evolution in terms of his beliefs. Writing as if it had always been this way, he was applying his intense intellectual mind to his religion. But while some people find solace from their beliefs, for Fripp there was a new doom-and-gloom element that profoundly concerned him. Reprising and expanding on his text from the Sylvian installation, he explains that the world is still going down the pan and gives us his views on the possibilities for the redemption of humankind. Some things hadn't changed, as there's a healthy swipe at the 'cynicism, greed and violation upon which the music industry has been based'. He then broadens out the criticism to the rest of the world and, without ever going into anything specific, writes, 'The world with which we are familiar is collapsing. Something has gone terribly wrong . . . We have abused our inherent and natural freedom, even forgotten it'. He feels that humankind is 'living in the red' and racing down erroneous pathways, with little or no effort to pay back its debts. It is in dire need of redemption, which is 'a process of repair'. No soul is barred from seeking redemption. We all just have to find our path, our gate into paradise. Connecting this with the music, he believes that 'music is one of the many possible actions through which the inexpressible benevolence of the creative impulse may enter our lives'. Beyond vague allusions to souls or angels, religion in any deeper sense can sit rather uncomfortably with the rock world. For this particular guitarist, who'd made his name with a band whose name was a term for the devil, there was an additional irony, although he was keeping the more overt religious expression to his work away from Crimson. Other than the general difficulty of expressing profound religious belief in the face of developing scientific knowledge, one problem with *The Gates of Paradise* notes is that they lack any context. Fripp's is a particularly intellectual take on religious belief, yet we're not given any sense of the basics of where these beliefs come from or the assumptions that his belief is built on. His lesson ended with a light-hearted indication that God shares his despair at the failings of humanity. With current humankind considered by this philosophy to be the sixteenth creation, when faced with the breakdown of the fifteenth, he suggests that God said, 'Oh well, here we go again'. [13]

By coincidence, a religion-related book by a Robert S. P. Fripp was also published in 1998. With different editions called *The Becoming* and *Let There Be Life*, it discusses what he feels has happened to religion in the age of science. Over the years this 'other', slightly older Robert Fripp has occasionally been confused with his guitarist namesake, despite moving to Toronto. The funniest mix-up he recalled was, 'Way back when the other Robert Fripp had an event in Toronto, we got a phone call in the small hours one morning from a man who was obviously very drunk. He insisted that I needed to hire him as a drummer for my concert!' On another occasion he was mistakenly sent a bouquet of flowers by one of Cher's assistants. In more recent years he's picked up social media followers who have assumed he was the musician, despite a complete absence of reference to music. On the other hand, he believes he has probably lost sales through people wrongly going to the guitarist's web pages rather than his. Having spoken to Patricia Fripp by phone and corresponding with the guitarist Fripp's father years earlier, the author Fripp established that there wasn't any obvious family connection, despite their both coming from southern England, although he believes there might have been a connection much further back in history, when Fripps populated the Bristol area. [14]

Back down on earth, 1998 had found Gordon Haskell working hard to promote his latest album, *Butterfly in China*. After the briefest of airings on BBC Radio, it 'sank without trace' and he had to fall back on sales at his gigs around Hampshire and Dorset. Even so, he felt it was his best yet and managed to break even, the record even getting the praise of a certain Fripp. He'd found a new level of happiness, welcoming the fact that performing at this level was 'a million miles away from egotism and yearning for fame and fortune'. His philosophy was that 'if I could make three hundred people happy every week, I felt that I wasn't wasting my life after all'. Of his audiences, he said, 'None of us knew where we were going but we drew comfort from a certain camaraderie that existed between us'. Having generally tried to distance himself from his Crimson past, he discovered that the association could sometimes work in his favour. Preparing to fly to Los Angeles with the idea of doing a few gigs in the area, he phoned up a Crimson-loving friend to see if he could stay with him. That friend was happy to put him up, but he took it upon himself to fix up a string of gigs for Haskell around Hollywood, and to spread the word around Crimson fans across America, Haskell ending up with fifteen shows to perform. It was far from glamorous, and at one point he found himself smoking a hubble-bubble pipe with a whacky fan at whose dodgy Kansas City flat he was staying. Surviving the experience, Haskell moved on to Chicago, where he was supposed to be a support act. When the main act pulled out belatedly, he agreed to play a double set for the Crimson-loving audience; he even gave in to requests for *Cadence and Cascade*. It was a good night's crowd-pleasing work, and he'd perhaps laid a few ghosts to rest in the process. He was still quite wary of an element of Crimson fans though, describing them as 'special people', meaning a bit mad and probably on drugs. [15]

Having parted company with Crimson, Bruford focussed on forming a new band, and, seeking out more up-and-coming talent, he established a line-up with Patrick Clahar on sax, Steve Hamilton on piano and Mark Hodgson on bass. He decided to resurrect the name Earthworks, but this second version would be very different, in particular being without the electronic drums. These had been a nightmare to programme and he found them too inflexible, so having freed himself from Fripp, he also freed himself from that burden too. After thirty years of being known as a rock drummer who took occasional diversions into jazz-fusion, he felt the time was right to get back to his musical roots, and the new band would be a relatively traditional acoustic jazz quartet, with the aim of being an antidote to the empty, overly processed music filling the airwaves. Bruford had just hit fifty, but his aim was not to play it safe and plod through jazz standards. Creativity and adventure were still very much on his mind. Their first studio album, *A Part and Yet Apart*, released in 1999, while not beating you over the head with trying to be ground-breaking, showed that the new Earthworks was an imaginative enterprise, with strong, purposeful output. The youthful ability of the new three was encouraged and channelled by their experienced band leader, and they pulled off the feat of indulging in what they loved, while producing something quite accessible. The quartet's combined influences were many and varied but, as the title track and *No Truce with the Furies* best illustrate, the end product had something of the melodic feel of Weather Report and *Aja*-era Steely Dan, with occasional almost Crimson-esque passages. With plenty of structure and compelling melodies, this was jazz that could draw in otherwise-wavering rock lovers—*if* they got to hear about it, that is! Bruford knew all too well that without the budget of a large record company to promote it, he simply had to accept that sales would be on a much-smaller scale. With no studio overdubs, the material was easy to reproduce live, and given the limited equipment needed, touring would be more manageable than in his previous bands. In fact, this was Bruford's relatively small, mobile, intelligent unit!

The nineties had one last big surprise to spring before they were done, as motivated by the reception given to the *Epitaph* archive release, McDonald released his first solo album in the summer of 1999, at the ripe old age of fifty-three. Called *Drivers Eyes*, it comprised ideas he'd been collating over the previous decade, being put out by Hackett's record company, Camino. Mostly recorded in New York, McDonald made full use of his multi-instrumental talents but also called on an extensive list of friends for guest appearances, old wounds having been healed. He even attempted to get Fripp involved, but that proved impossible to arrange. Polished and accomplished throughout, although his tastes had shifted more towards classical and jazz, there are several homages to aspects of McDonald's past. As if to signal from the outset that this was not going to be an album of Crimson-like doom-rock, it opens with the happy, upbeat instrumental, *Overture*, followed by *You Are a Part of Me*, a commercial, mellow, relationship break-up song with its roots in the softer end of the Foreigner spectrum. One of several songs with guest vocalists, the latter was sung by John Waite, another Englishman who'd relocated to New York, best known for his 1984 hit, *Missing You*. Michael Giles doubles up on drumming duties here with the album's main drummer, Steve Holley, a veteran of stints with Wings and Elton John. The first piece of Crimson revisited is *Forever and Ever*, which is a pastiche of the end section of *Epitaph*. With lyrics written and sung by Wetton, it also features McDonald's son, Maxwell, on acoustic guitar. On the punky, guitar-riff-based *Saturday Night in Tokyo*, McDonald stepped up to the vocal mike himself, having been working hard at improving his technique. The style changes continue as we reach *Hawaii*, the album's best track overall, and a decidedly cool guitar- and piano-driven instrumental that doesn't tie in with any aspect of McDonald's past. It also doesn't have anything particularly Hawaiian about it, McDonald having originally considered calling it *The Scenic Route*. Had McDonald been twenty years younger, *If I Was* would have made a commercial single. Another softish rock song, this is the best of the album's vocal tracks, McDonald also singing this one, while seventies rock legend Peter Frampton guests with a guitar solo. The mildly jazzy, near-instrumental *Demimonde* is a fuller reprise of the McDonald-and-Giles partnership, the pair covering all instruments and voices between them. After the largely breezy and upbeat nature of the album to this point, the darkness of the final piece, *Let There Be Light*, is quite a contrast. Also, with echoes of *Epitaph*, it's a one-off revisiting of the McDonald-Sinfield writing partnership. With the album being mellotron free, here McDonald calls on a ten-piece string section to add the drama, while Gary Brooker, from Procul Harum, provides a deep, grainy vocal performance. Dark though it is, this is what Crim-heads buying the CD were hoping for. Having got the taste for gigging again after Tokyo, McDonald aimed to tour with his new material and was even talking about doing another McDonald-and-Giles album. Both plans would fall by the wayside though, as events soon took an unexpected turn.

It had been an astonishingly good few years for The Greater Crim, and all in all, with the new millennium approaching, there was much cause for optimism. No one expected the intensity or innovation of the early years to be rekindled but, other than the Nashville incident, inspiration and creativity was still flowing, and it seemed reasonable to think that the instruments and mikes would stay plugged in for a few years longer. But despite hatchets being buried, and with reunions and reappearances happening all over the place, there was still much uncertainty as to what kind of Crimson would follow. Fans had been playing the game of guessing which ProjeKct line-up was to be the new Crimson—

*Schizoid Band, 2002. Courtesy of Alex 'Bomber' Harris.*

the answer in the end being none of them—but that would have to hang in the air for a while longer. Fripp had another distraction to sort out first, as the costs of his legal battles had been heavy and maintaining a manor house was expensive. That meant that before getting down to band business he had to sort out a major house move in the summer of 1999, selling Reddish House, although he and Toyah would leave it in a much better state than they found it.

# 10

# Uneasy Money

## *2000 to 2010*

As the twenty-first century arrived, there was a distinct absence of flying cars and shiny jumpsuits. However, there was still a recording and touring King Crimson, something no one would have forecast during their early incarnations. The touring was less intense and the gaps between albums were longer, but we were just glad they were still around doing what they do. While they were no longer going to significantly impact on the mainstream of rock, they were still creating original music and plenty of people were still paying attention. Inevitably it wouldn't last too long, but things would at least hold together long enough to allow a couple of albums before it would all grind to a baffling halt yet again. Fripp's occasional output for the rest of the decade would largely be soundscapes; however, others would fill the spaces. In particular, a revival of early Crimson tracks by several early Crims was an unexpected bonus, while Wetton would reform the original line-up of Asia, and Bruford would continue with his enjoyably reinvented Earthworks. The biggest surprise of all however, would be the singles chart success of Gordon Haskell, his persistence finally paying off.

If we accept the positive spin that The ProjeKcts were research and development teams for the next Crimson, then *The ConstruKction of Light*, released in May 2000, was the first full product to result from them. For those who had found the period since *Thrak* frustrating, the first non-improv album in five years was a welcome relief, especially on hearing that the level of quality and originality had remained high. With Bruford exiting for good, and Levin being too heavily committed elsewhere, Crimson were, for the time being, the quartet of Fripp, Belew, Gunn and Mastelotto. It transpired that there had been other significant discussions going on behind the scenes too, and when comments appeared in Fripp's diary that Belew was having doubts about his future in Crimson, the frontman felt the need to go public, explaining 'King Crimson is never easy. It's challenging. That's why I like it'. Belew is nothing if not sincere but sounding rather like a politician having to tow the party line here, added 'I'm very happy with the band now and plan to continue dedicating some of my best work and full enthusiasm to King Crimson'. Commenting on the effect of Bruford no longer being there, Belew said rather tellingly, 'I'm glad to see the tension gone. [Bruford and Fripp were] just two guys who don't really see music in the same way and probably shouldn't be working together. It's a relief to me that I'm not stuck between them . . . I was taking a lot of punches'.

What's notable about the material produced for *TCOL* is that despite the untethered explorations of the last few years, they were, for the most part, back in familiar territory. It was a case of evolution and not revolution, as while they had cleared their writer's block, they had essentially just freshened up and heavied up the sound from *Thrak*. Being labelled Prog-Metal by some, Crimson Mk VI was described by Belew as having 'more of a heavy rock band sound . . . dense and menacing. Pat and Trey have devised a unique landscape for me and Robert to explore'. Aspects of that landscape came about through Fripp having fallen in love with the V-drums during the ProjeKcts, subsequently asking Mastelotto to use a set of them for the recording. Although it was hard to gauge the impact, there was one other notable difference in the process of creating this album compared to many of the earlier ones, in that they didn't get a chance to try out the material live before hitting the studio. [1] [2]

The opener, *ProzaKc Blues*, is a bit of Belew darkness beneath a veil of humour, expressed in the form of a heavy blues in an awkward time signature. Belew's slowed-down voice growls in mock-blues fashion, including a light-hearted reference to the Crimson fan website, *Elephant Talk*, which you'd suspect had been getting him down. The title track then jangles its way through six minutes of inter-locking guitar intro, where we get more of a feel for the change in drumming style and Mastelotto's entirely electronic kit. Belew eventually makes his vocal entry with what sounds like a word-association therapy game crossed with a nursery rhyme, his words suggesting that while he may have dealt with the subject of depression through humour on track one, he still needed to get a lot more off his chest. His skill here is in giving an innocent beauty to negative feelings but joining up the dots of the album's themes as a whole, you didn't need to be a psychologist to realise that Belew had been battling some personal issues. The rest of the song is a collection of lines that sound like they could mean something deep but probably don't, as in amongst verses about such things as dinosaurs becoming talking birds, Belew bizarrely sings about Warhol, male genitalia and Venus! Still pondering the difficulties life throws at us, for *Into the Frying Pan* Belew is back once more in Beatle-esque mode as regards his vocals. Quirks of timing make the track hard to follow in places, but a great riff comes to the rescue as the band gets heavier. The album sags a little in the middle, starting with *FraKctured*, the title playing on *Fracture* from 1974, but musically more of a follow-on from the title track. It's full of pleasant, inter-locking riffs but ultimately it feels as if it's going through the motions without any real sense of purpose. The low point, though, is *The World's My Oyster Soup Kitchen Floor Wax Museum*, an ugly wordplay-derived title with a suitably ugly heavy blues track attached. Things pick up markedly with *Larks' Tongues in Aspic: Part Four*, a gloriously heavy nine-minute instrumental workout, and perhaps the heaviest Crimson would ever get. The opening few minutes are an interplay of Fripp and Belew's guitars over the customary mix of time signatures. They then move through several sequences of weighty riffs and solos, being in their fifties clearly no hindrance to displaying and enjoying their metal abilities. A more melodic coda, *I Have a Dream*, echoes the famous words of Martin Luther King, Belew listing high-profile tragedies the human race has been guilty of during his lifetime. The final track, *Heaven and Earth*, credited to a mysterious ProjeKct X, appears after a long interval that emphasises its separateness. An album highlight, it's the only obvious spin-off from the ProjeKcts phase, but even so is a semi-structured instrumental, mixing a rocky riff and solos with more reflective sections, and touching on more emotion than any of the previous ProjeKcts output had. A ProjeKct X album was put out simultaneously, and mostly sold at gigs, revealing that it was simply the same four personnel captured in improv mode during rehearsal sessions, with Gunn and Mastelotto taking more of the initiative.

Not everyone was happy with *TCOL*. Tom Johnson, of *Something Else*, describing it as 'dreary, dismal and at times downright boring', suggesting that the band had a bad case of 'cold feet' when it came to the recording. Fripp himself would gradually fall out of love with the album for different reasons, particularly the drumming. Mastelotto agreed, and years later did a wholesale re-recording of his parts using the hybrid kit he'd have preferred to use in the first place. The album was reissued as *The ReconstruKction of Light* in 2019. By the time of *TCOL*'s original release the band had already been on tour for three months, with several months more lying ahead. Focusing largely on the new album and *Thrak*, the only pre-nineties material left in the set was *Sleepless* and a cover of Bowie's *Heroes*, which both guitarists felt they had enough association with to legitimately use. Something that wasn't intended at the time was that the gig at London's Shepherds Bush Empire on 3 July 2000, as well as being their first U.K. show in four years, would also be their last in the country for a very long time. The *Guardian*'s Adam Sweeting reviewed that night's show, characterising the

ıestra, Baka
oruba Jazz
:alls, work-
ıer activities.
ıseum, London
o-8699 1872)
'ree. [WA]
**Villie And**
**›ys**
cabilly and
utfit fronted by
extraordinaire
s.
›use, Lodge Ln,
4710) 8.30pm, £6.
**'eekend**

by Jesus And Mary Chain singer Jim Reid's new scuzz-rock supergroup.
*The Monarch, Chalk Farm Road, NW1 (020-7916 1049) 8pm, £5, concs £4.*

**King Crimson**
Robert Fripp's errant prog rock heroes return to scatter the pretenders with a show of polyrhythmic might.
*Shepherd's Bush Empire, Shepherd's Bush Green, W12 (020-7771 2000) 7.30pm, £18.*

**Knoxville Girls**
Former members of The

**The Oil**
Sexagena
bluesmar
powerful
*The Princ*
*Princes Sq*
*2221) 8.30*
**Instrum**
Unique fu
string sex
21st centu
*Festival C*
*Naval Col*
*(020-8858*
**Moussa**
**Kevin B**

*King Crimson gig listing, Guardian, July 2000.*

*King Crimson London gig flyer, 2000.*

*King Crimson London gig ticket, 2000.*

music as 'a heady mix of steamhammer rhythms, howling mutant funk and passages of seething noise'. Conjuring up the words that many observers were grappling for, he described Fripp in his slightly removed and unlit position as being 'like a technician monitoring a complicated experiment', and Gunn on his Warr Guitar (a touch guitar in similar vein to the stick), 'like an octopus tormented by fleas'. Most of this no doubt pleased the band, however Sweeting drew some minor negatives, questioning Belew's vocals in places, and ending with the comment that the current Crimson were 'only slightly ludicrous'. [3] [4]

Toyah and Fripp saw so little of each other at this time that she was driven to tell him that things just couldn't carry on as they were! Her words had an impact, and in the coming years they would be together a little more, although it would still only be around twelve weeks a year. In one of their periods together in 2000 they found themselves mixing in very high-powered circles, when just a few days after Crimson's Shepherds Bush gig, they attended the eighty-fourth birthday dinner of former prime minister, Sir Edward Heath. Taking place at Arundells, Heath's mansion in Salisbury, to the outside observer this might have seemed rather a surreal event. Not only was it an unlikely mix of people, with Sting and Andrew Lloyd Webber also there, but Heath ended up on the phone to Libyan dictator, Colonel Gaddafi, the ex-P.M. still being involved in behind-the-scenes diplomacy in his later years. Having moved into the area just a couple of years after Heath, the Fripps had met him through Toyah and Heath both being patrons of the Salisbury Festival. Heath and Fripp had sort of crossed paths through the festival three years before, when Fripp had played a soundscape set in the city's cathedral. Parking restrictions imposed on the area to allow the movement of artists had drawn the ire of Heath, who phoned the organisers to complain that his VIP guests that day couldn't park by his home. This didn't get in the way of the pair being able to discuss their shared love of music at their subsequent meeting, Heath having also been the conductor of an orchestra in his heyday. When Heath died in 2005, Fripp and Toyah would be amongst vast numbers of the great and the good—from government, military and elsewhere—who attended his memorial service.

The next Fripp release, with Jeffrey Fayman, was *A Temple in the Clouds*, a variation on the soundscapes format and an album whose creation was deliberately shrouded in a fantastical tale. Released in 2000, Fayman, an American drummer and producer with an interest in ambient music, had met Fripp in the nineties, an album of his band, Ten Seconds, being released by DGM. Although *Temple* is again based on layered repetition, here it is taken in a much more meditative direction, especially in the longer pieces. According to the sleeve notes, Fripp had linked up with Fayman for a rather unusual recording method, and the pair, along with large amounts of equipment and a sound crew, travelled to a 'half-forgotten' temple called Anapraxis. This is on an isolated island, where legends are said to state that in ancient times a pilgrim could lie on the temple's altar and, through dreaming or God-like intervention, recall their past lives. Fayman and Fripp's aim was to record music while in this state, and despite the huge practical difficulties, they succeeded. Or did they? It's a wonderful story, which many of those buying the album would take at face value, but reality gets in the way. Most importantly there is no Anapraxis on any map or referenced in archaeology. The clunkily vague description of its location as being 'off of the southern Mediterranean coast' is also a big clue, as is the idea that any beautiful temple in the Med could be even half-forgotten, rather than swarming with tourists. With other unlikely elements in the story, ultimately you have to conclude that it's an elaborate invention, and the reality was that Fripp left Fayman with some recorded guitar extracts, from which he created loops and added other sounds. To the musicians there was clearly an important spiritual aspect in what they were creating, but the music has a grandeur and an epic quality to it, even if the recording methods were more prosaic than the sleeve notes would have us believe. [5]

There are four pieces on what is perhaps the most consistent and satisfying of all the soundscape albums. *The Pillars of Hercules*, the first piece, washes over you for fifteen minutes, with its intensely layered flow of drones, strings, waves and other Fripp-derived guitar phrases. Here we are in Atlantis or somewhere similar, the title being an ancient term for the entrance to the Mediterranean between modern-day Morocco and Gibraltar, used in Plato's description of the location of Atlantis. On first hearing, after a couple of minutes you expect more to happen, with perhaps a solo or melody emerging. None appears, though, and the only variations are minor shifts in the mixing, your attention instead being drawn to how the sounds and sequences ebb and flow around each other. The second track is a shorter, more melodic interlude, *The Sky Below*, the title suggesting that we are in the heavens looking down on earth. This feels relatively incidental though, coming before the thirty-one minutes of the title track. This opens with a minute of eerie sounds, as if we've intruded on a madman in a cave, before something more conventionally soundscape-ish rolls in, like a giant but gentle wave. In this sea of sounds is one that harks back to Eno's squawking synth on *Swastika Girls*, only easier on the ear, the piece also drawing inspiration from Cardew's *Paragraph Seven*, as had Eno. Again, there are no solos or melodies, just subtle changes, and it's this that gives it its meditative quality. The short, final track, *The Stars Below*, is a Fayman remix of an earlier Fripp soundscape, *2006*, the new title indicating that in our meditational state, we have risen even higher, so that we are able to look down on the stars. The original had a spacey, sci-fi feel, which Fayman accentuates by adding more strings and choral sounds, creating a powerful, eerie sadness.

Back at the other end of the Fripp spectrum, in 2001 Crimson toured North America promoting *TCOL* and giving a live airing to the material they were developing for album thirteen. Reflecting where they were musically, for nine nights they were the opening act for American metal band Tool. Formed in 1990, while their name lacked subtlety, Tool's particular brand was variously described as alternative metal or prog-metal, so there was some affinity between the two bands. Fripp and Belew revelled in being in such company and playing to a younger audience, with members of Tool even joining Crimson onstage for a couple of their weightier tracks. Live versions of Crimson tracks from the Tool support slot were then released as the mini-album, *Level Five*, previewing ideas that would appear on the next album, with a brave choice for its lead track. This was *Dangerous Curves*, a long, slow-building instrumental that sounds like a sped-up version of Led Zep's *Kashmir* crossed with *The Devil's Triangle*. This was followed by the title track, which was, in all but name, a fifth part of *Larks' Tongues*, with some of the mathematical nature of *Fracture* mixed in. Elsewhere on the tour, Crimson were supported by another artist from the thinking person's end of heavy music, former Led Zep bassist/keyboardist John Paul Jones. With a Zeppelin reunion looking unlikely, despite Page and Plant working together, Jones was enjoying a solo career and releasing albums through DGM.

Older Crimson fans could hardly believe their ears in the run-up to Christmas 2001. In the customary media-hyped battle to be the U.K.'s Christmas No.1 single, this year there was a strangely familiar, yet unlikely, name amongst the contenders: that of Gordon Haskell, with his song *How Wonderful You Are*. The media dubbed him 'the pub singer', picking up on a deliberately gimmicky phrase his PR manager had used, but once we had rubbed our eyes, we found that this was actually the one-time Crimson vocalist. That detail seemed to bypass some of the media but, given Haskell's feelings over that troubled episode, he was not too bothered, preferring people to just take him for what he was now. Life wasn't so terrible for him by this point, with a home in a picturesque part of Dorset and a long-term relationship with a woman half his age. While he was still having to play in bars most nights to make ends meet, suddenly, after decades of struggle, things finally seemed to be working out for him musically too. For a while he was in the frustrating position of having the most-requested song on BBC Radio Two but unable to get it distributed on a big scale. Through a mix of skill, management bargaining and luck, the situation was flipped, and major record companies came in to bid big money for a slice of the

Haskell action. He even found himself getting appearances on TV chat shows. In the end, the song made it to No.2, only being kept off the top slot by Robbie Williams and Nicole Kidman's cover of *Somethin' Stupid*. The irony wasn't lost on Haskell that Williams's manager was none other than Crimson's former manager David Enthoven. Haskell's song's title would be taken by many at a simple level, with people buying it for their partners as a love song. However, it actually took its inspiration from all the people he had met over the years who had struggled against the odds, as he had. Whether or not people took on board its deeper meaning, it opened up a different market for Haskell, a million miles from Crimson, couples holding onto it as 'their' song. Publicity generated by the single, which sold 400,000 copies, also did wonders for Haskell's album, *Harry's Bar*, which expanded on the theme of the myriad of people, good and bad, he had encountered on his long journey, and the double-dealing and personal sacrifices he'd endured. In interviews the fifty-five-year-old simply thanked his mother for always believing in him, even though it had taken rather longer for him to make it than he'd hoped. There was to be another unfortunate twist in the tale though, when Haskell got a lawyer to look at his contract, he was told he'd 'been had', and that most of the royalties would be going elsewhere. He concluded he'd 'been robbed along the way' and claimed that his success had left him 'not a penny richer'. His follow-up album, *Shadows on the Wall*, just made it into the U.K. top fifty, but after that, other than some lingering success in Poland, normality was resumed for Haskell. [6]

Twenty-two years on from *Scary Monsters*, Fripp, sadly, had to turn down the chance to play on what would become Bowie's 2002 album, *Heathen*, because of other commitments. The main commitment in the way was starting sessions for the thirteenth Crimson album, sessions that resulted in the mini-album, *Happy With What You Have to Be Happy With*. As was now their habit, the band took this as an opportunity to preview new ideas, hoping that fans would appreciate buying early versions that may or may not go anywhere. While it's not specifically referenced, this was put together as the world was still reeling from the 9-11 attacks. Crimson had been in North America at the time, in a break between legs of tour, and some of their writing sessions indeed took place in the traumatic weeks following 9-11, and it would have been impossible for them not to have felt some kind of emotional impact. The title track is a compact, heavy piece, derived from experiments with timings based on counts of eleven and a tongue-tying chorus designed to fit with the pattern that materialised. Its verses had temporary lyrics about the writing of lyrics, left in for a laugh while Belew thought up some proper ones, while the music seemed to be tip-toeing along the boundary between serious heavy rock and a mocking of heavy metal clichés. Elsewhere, as well as some brief Belew vocoder experiments, there was a stunningly beautiful two-minute soundscape, *Mie Gakure*, the Japanese title translating approximately as hidden and seen. Another Japanese-titled piece, *Shoganai*, which translates as such is life, is a multi-tracking of melodic bell-like percussion sounds. A more sombre Belew-initiated song was a semi-unplugged *Eyes Wide Open*, another of his line of does-what-it-says-on-the-tin songs, reminding us that we should keep alert so as not to miss life's opportunities. The cover is a piece of social comment that links to the EP's title, in the form of a P. J. Crook painting, her first, other than on archive releases. This depicts a family watching TV, waiting for the lottery results, the implication being that they are unhappy—or being made to feel dissatisfied—with their lot in life, desperately hoping for that remote chance to win.

While fans had grown used to Fripp's uncompromising belief in moving on and not risking Crimson becoming mired in nostalgia, that policy left a gap in the market. Encouraged by the success of *Epitaph*, a group of ex-Crims got together to fill that gap in 2002. It was Michael Giles who took the initiative and, with brother Peter also interested, called up Mel Collins, who was enthusiastic despite having moved to Germany. The coup de grace was getting Ian McDonald involved, as after his solo album he was now on a similar-enough wavelength to want to give it a try, and he flew over from New York. This made for an interesting mix of people who had played in various versions of early Crimson but never all at the same time. To fill the Fripp-shaped hole of guitarist and the Lake/Haskell/Burrell–shaped hole of vocalist, they only had to look as far as Michael Giles' son-in-law, Jakko Jakszyk. More than a decade younger than the others, Jakszyk had spent much of his career to date in low-profile bands but had also had spells in the early nineties with the funk band Level 42. As well as marrying into the wider Crimson family, Jakszyk was also a lover of prog.

Opting for the name the 21st Century Schizoid Band, they got together for some relaxed and friendly rehearsals, and planned their first tour. While the band would probably have gone ahead anyway, it received Fripp's blessing, and he sent along some champagne to mark the beginning of that initial tour. Venues were at the more moderate end of the spectrum, but they drew in highly appreciative crowds, mostly of middle-aged men, along with a few inquisitive, younger fans. For those who came, this was a chance either to relive memories or to hear tracks played live by some of the original musicians for the first time. As well as material from *Court*, *Poseidon* and *Islands*, it was also a long-overdue chance for tracks from the *McDonald and Giles* album to get played live, with *Tomorrow's People* and parts of *Birdman* included in their sets. That album had just been remastered and, having been largely overlooked in its time, could now belatedly reach a wider audience. McDonald had made some minor tweaks, mostly just to tidy it up, however he'd also felt the need to overdub one word on *Suite in C*, changing *pussy* to *kitten*! Because of the smaller scale, the Schizoids gigs were all the more personal, with time afterwards to chat with fans, autograph covers and answer questions. At London's Queen Elizabeth Hall, though, the band weren't allowed to do this inside the venue, and like naughty schoolboys, band and fans instead arranged to meet outside the stage door afterwards. It said a lot about the character of band members of such stature that they were perfectly willing to do this. What it said about middle-aged men bearing album covers however, is another question! The only

*Schizoid Band ticket, 2002.*

other venue-related issue arose when McDonald ordered a baby grand piano for a gig at The Limelight Club in Crewe—a converted church. McDonald only realised quite how small the stage there was when he arrived and, so that the whole band could actually play on the stage, had to hastily cancel the order and revert to using his electric piano. In the intervening years, Peter Giles had taken up competitive long-distance running, and, although finding the level of touring quite hard in itself, would vanish for a run each day while the others did the sound check. By the following year, Michael Giles, now over sixty, felt he no longer wanted to put himself through the rigours of even this level of touring, and he dropped out. His place was soon ably filled by another ex-Crim, Ian Wallace, who was overjoyed to be back playing with his friend Mel Collins. He had already rekindled his friendship with the wider Crimson family in recent years, the current Crimson even dropping in for dinner with him whenever they were anywhere near his home in Nashville. The 21CSB touring soon resumed, with the set developed further to include *Cirkus* and even the occasional new composition.

While the Schizoids were breathing new life into Crimson past, Crimson present were finishing off album thirteen, *The Power to Believe*. Released in January 2003, with much having been previewed on mini albums, only about half the material was completely new to fans. Mixing echoes of earlier Crimson with newer ideas, it showed that they hadn't yet lost their interest in heavier music—the album's

*Schizoid Band flyer, 2003.*

CKET NUMBER : 64 0 AO
RESERVED PLACE 31
7.50 MEAN FIDDLER PRESENTS MF
21ST CENTURY SCHIZOID BAND 1
7.50 AT LI
DOOR MEAN FIDDLER WC2H TI
Z511 * AGE RESTRICTIONS APPLY *
OCT3 FRI 31-OCT-03 7:00PM 3

*Schizoid Band ticket, 2003.*

working title having been *Nuovo Metal*, but also that there was no danger of them sacrificing variety and sophistication. Interviewed at the time, Belew was bursting with enthusiasm for what being in Crimson meant: 'It's all about challenging and working at a high level of intensity. It has nothing to do with the normal machinations of a rock band . . . the whole idea of the game is to play something remarkable together'. The cover features a P. J. Crook painting entitled *Fin De Siecle*, her first to be used on a full Crimson studio album. In contrast to the album title's feeling of hope, her image is a bleak vision of the future, with a baby on a drip feed being attended to by a nurse wearing an oxygen mask. Through the windows of the room, we can see a heavily polluted city, and immediately outside are military figures with guard dogs. Joining the dots, the baby represents the future of humanity that we must have *The Power to Believe* in, but he needs to be carefully protected to be kept alive. [1]

The album opens with *Part One* of the title track, which is simply a vocodered a capella piece using a short set of Belew's lyrics that would crop up through the album. Vocoders are often used to create robot-like vocal sounds, but here Belew uses his to give his voice a delicate, vulnerable quality. The *Power to Believe* title on the surface is ambiguous and could be taken as a religious reference. Belew's few lines however, say enough to tell us he's referring to self-belief, his words being extracts from a solo song of his from 1996, called *All Her Love is Mine*, which is about a supportive partner helping him through difficult times. As previewed on the live EP, *Level Five* is essentially *Larks' Tongues: Part Five*, or as Tom Johnson put it, 'Black Sabbath meets [Philip] Glass', with inter-locking guitars thrown in for good measure. Based on geometric riffs and key changes—the ideas of Schillinger, Persichetti et al. still alive and well in Fripp's mind—it's a little colder and more mechanical feeling than its predecessors but is not without power. With tongue firmly in cheek, Tom Johnson also noted the difficulties of rocking out to tracks like this, with odd time signatures: 'Dancing to King Crimson, while not entirely improbable, is generally unlikely and would certainly have to be a free-form, aimless, interpretive dancing'. A fully plugged-in *Eyes Wide Open* is another impassioned Belew song, giving us his personal philosophy on life about being open to possibilities, and in the process perhaps having a gentle dig at someone he knows who doesn't follow his approach. There are a couple of disappointments, the first being *Elektrik*, an overly mechanical-sounding instrumental that goes through Crimson-esque motions at length but without a strong enough idea at its core. *Facts of Life* opens with a short, atmospheric soundscape that may have escaped from *The Gates of Paradise*, but in mood-shattering contrast, a harsh, little-loved song crashes in. Once again, we are in *Red/Level Five* territory, while Belew expresses environmental and anti-war messages, likening the human race to ants on a plate. [3]

*The Power to Believe: Part Two* incorporates a reworked *Shoganai* between passages of ProjeKcts-like improv, Belew also reprising the lyrics from *Part One*. This is followed by the sleek studio version of the instrumental *Dangerous Curves*, the masterpiece of the album. Full of twists, turns and what sound like anguished cries, this is somehow original sounding while simultaneously being classic Crimson. The meaning of the title is left hanging in typical ambiguity, but clues may lie in the 1988 film of that name, featuring fast cars and bikini-clad young women. With the track's pace and air of tension, it feels as if it's aiming to conjure up images of driving in Bond fashion on a winding mountain road. A slightly reorganised *Happy with What You Have to Be Happy with* follows. While this is fun, it's a little disappointing in that Belew's throwaway verse lyrics were left in. You could take the view that they are poking fun at aspects of heavy rock or even at themselves, combining anti-lyrics with music that flirts with the clichés of heavy rock, however, lyrical jokes soon wear thin, and they could have done better. *The Power to Believe: Part Three* is another ProjeKcts-style, improv-derived piece. With hints of industrial and ambient in the mix, it falls into the OK-but-hardly-memorable category. The album closes with *The Power to Believe:*

*Part Four*, a serene soundscape with Belew's four lines of vocal used one more time. It's unusually tender for Crimson, but that's due to the band as such not having anything to do with its creation, Fripp's contribution being a piece recorded in 1997, and Belew's vocal being a cut-and-paste job. It was nevertheless a powerful and appropriate way to close the album, lyrically bringing it back full circle.

Despite there being a strong, world-wide market of fans who still believed in Crimson, the album failed to chart. While some artists of a similar vintage were continuing to be commercially successful, Crimson were paying the price for having had such an erratic existence since 1984 and, highly principled or not, for Fripp's aversion to playing the game at all. One-time fans who weren't so actively following Crimson's comings and goings no longer necessarily noticed when a new album appeared or had simply lost that youthful sense of urgency to acquire these straight away. As far as the material itself was concerned, there were suggestions that Crimson 2003 were just too weighed down by their own past. A simpler explanation was that ideas were just running low again, especially for Fripp. While the end product was strong—and for each track you could argue that what they were doing was perfectly valid—when you analysed the album as a whole, there were clearly problems. Belew, in particular, was deeply immersed in the band's philosophy, but there was no great sense of moving on anymore, and the curves Crimson found themselves on now were indeed dangerous, as they were close to leading them in circles. Much-loved *Larks'*-era tracks had now been revisited several times, which suggested that new ideas were thin on the ground, and the ongoing reliance on hit-and-miss improv to flesh things out was also not a healthy sign. Add in the extrapolation of multiple parts of the title track from one set of already-recycled lyrics, and you get the distinct impression that large cracks were being papered over. For the tour that followed, they presented a professional and positive face, as did the album's marketing, but were they a spent force in terms of inspiration? Sadly, the band's management had been unable to reach agreement with U.K. venues, which meant there weren't any

U.K. gigs this time. Courtesy of the Channel Tunnel and budget airlines though, some dedicated British fans made pilgrimages over to the nearer parts of Europe to combine catching the band with a bit of sightseeing. They would have been glad they went to such lengths, as once the tour ended that November, the band quietly slipped into another hiatus, and as things stand, *The Power to Believe* was the final Crimson studio album. As to whether the struggle for ideas and material caused Fripp to feel he'd reached the limit of how much of Crimson he could cope with again, or vice-versa, is hard to say, but it seemed that no version of the band could exist for more than four or five years.

While Crimson had been on the road, in May 2003 they had received an unexpected high-profile name check, courtesy of Labour Prime Minister Tony Blair. It started with a Blair interview for *Saga Magazine* (for readers over fifty) as the PM reached his fiftieth birthday, where he commented that he still much preferred rock music to classical. A BBC Radio Four programme picked up on this and, with the PM having famously been in a band called Ugly Rumours in the early seventies, interviewed former bandmate Mark Ellen. Ellen, who went on to present the BBC's *Old Grey Whistle Test*, told them that Blair still loved King Crimson and Free from those days, and that they would still discuss *Schizoid Man* and rave over Fripp's playing. *The Guardian* also picked up on the story and decided to have a bit of fun with it, reproducing the lyrics to *Schizoid Man* in order to draw parallels to the modern day, particularly the Iraq War. This gave them an excuse to revisit Sinfield's claim that his Bucks Fizz lyrics had been anti-Thatcher. The newspaper tried to contact both Fripp and Sinfield but, perhaps strategically, both managed to be uncontactable. The initial Blair article was all about political spin, to make him seem like a normal guy to middle-aged voters, and to seem less stuffy to younger voters. Nevertheless, it seems likely that the core of the story is genuine, with Blair having been sixteen when *Court* came out and clearly interested in rock music. Given Blair's reputation in years to come, it was probably wise for Fripp and Sinfield not to get drawn into this passing brouhaha, and just hope that it would give their sales a boost. Another event that got Crimson fans rubbing their eyes in disbelief came when the worlds of Robert Fripp and twenty-first-century popular culture briefly collided. In 2003, Toyah was a contestant on the ITV show, *I'm a Celebrity Get Me Out of Here*, where contestants live in a jungle and are given unpleasant tasks, such as eating grubs. On getting voted off the show, Toyah did the customary interview with presenters Ant and Dec, and was met by hubby Fripp, who had been flown out for the occasion. Not knowing or caring who Ant and Dec were, let alone which was which, in typical Fripp fashion he wouldn't play ball with the presenters and give them the type of interview they were hoping for, preferring just to be with his wife.

For the rest of the noughties Fripp's musical activity was typical of his hiatuses, with sporadic, unusual output and small-scale tours. In the summer of 2004, he was invited to take part in the annual tour known as G3, which perhaps he should have declined. G3, which had been running since 1996, was organised each year around New York–born guitarist Joe Satriani, with two other rock guitarists invited along. Each year they also slotted in a handful of guests for particular shows, Fripp amongst them. As well as Satriani and Fripp, 2004's twenty-night tour of Europe also included another New Yorker, Steve Vai, their shows consisting of the three playing solo sets, followed by a short set together. It was perhaps foreseeable that Fripp was in the wrong company here, performing sets of soundscapes to an audience who were there for a head-banging, rock-god-worshiping, air-guitar fest. As the first one onstage each evening, he was often just met with indifference, but on a couple of nights reportedly had to play through booing and jeering. When the three played together at the end, Fripp was much better received, with sets including Crimson's *Red* and Neil Young's *Rocking in the Free World*. The experience could not have been great for Fripp's spirit and is unlikely to have contributed much to Crimson album sales. That summer there was an unexpected follow-up to the Fripp-and-Eno albums of the seventies, with the release of *The Equatorial Stars*. The

*King Crimson ticket, Paris, 2003.*

technology had changed drastically in the intervening years, but otherwise the setup was largely as before, with Fripp soloing over Eno's backdrops. With the cover of a star chart, the album title was clearly to position it as a belated follow-up to *Evening Star,* but while Eno could still conjure up unique new ideas, Fripp struggled to find anything new or interesting to say with his guitar, and the inspired magic of their original collaborations is thin on the ground. The opening piece, *Meissa,* encapsulates the problem, as over Eno's minimalist backdrop, which is like listening up close to the vibrations of a pin dropping, Fripp seems to run dry midway through the track's eight minutes. The next five pieces are largely unmemorable, including two that could be ProjeKcts outtakes, however the closing piece, *Terebellum,* goes somewhere different, achieving an unsettling, nightmare-in-space tone.

One of Fripp's more unusual sessions in this period was in Seattle, where he was enlisted by Microsoft to record some snippets of sound for the latest Windows operating system, something Eno had done a decade earlier. It's a strange concept that we've all grown to accept, that onscreen messages, or even just the starting up or closing down of a computer, are accompanied by a short fanfare or musical phrase. The software giant had now infiltrated many people's home and work lives, and for a while there was a bit of Fripp in there too, at least until everyone moved on to the inevitable upgrade. Fripp and co. would start to appear more on our computers in another way too, as this period would also see the eruption of social networking sites on the internet. These opened up possibilities for bands and musicians to market themselves worldwide for free, with the great benefit that they could keep their existing fan base up to date to an extent never before imagined, while also attracting new fans. There were plenty of people around who would set up fan pages for their favourite artists too, and word could spread to an entirely new market through people following links from friends' pages. The cyber world would prove to be fickle and faddist, and as the years passed the 'in' site would shift from one to another, but the internet changed things for musicians forever. But while the possibilities for cheap worldwide marketing were opening up, Fripp was discovering that ethics and business didn't necessarily mix conveniently. Running DGM without resorting to the methods he'd loathed in standard record companies left them barely afloat without him putting in his own money. Staff were overworked and underpaid, and while the main Crimson albums still sold well, he found that releases of digitally cleaned-up archive material struggled to break even. He would persist, though.

While Fripp was pottering around in the margins again, Cross continued to keep up his music side-line in the gaps between university terms, carrying the mantle of the 1972–1974 Crimson in his recordings and live sets. In fact, in the absence of Crimson, he had become an enjoyable alternative for those fans who were aware that he was still active. In 2005, he produced his best album to date, *Closer Than Skin*, the highlights of this confident set being *Are We One?* and *Only Fooling*, with the extra Crimson connection of having Richard Palmer-James lyrics. His unsettling angles on relationships are given an extra twist of angst by being delivered in Hammill-esque style by vocalist Arch Stanton. The album also proved that Fripp's recent Crimson were not the only ones who could do heavy, and that Cross would no longer have been blown offstage by the Wetton-Bruford rhythm section. He would follow this with the equally strong *Alive in*

*David Cross ticket, 2005.*
Courtesy of Tomoko Okamoto

*the Underworld,* showcasing the best of his recent material, along with versions of Crimson's *Exiles*, *Schizoid Man* and *Starless*, Cross's violin on the latter still having the ability to make the hairs on the back of the listener's neck stand up. Although the album name stemmed from its mostly being recorded live at The Underworld in Camden, Cross was also pointing out that he was still around and producing the goods, even if it had to be on the margins.

Crimson's original lyricist, Peter Sinfield, had in recent years moved back to the U.K. Although lyric writing had become a lesser part of his life, he didn't remove himself from culture, settling into Aldeburgh on the Suffolk Coast, a place famous for its annual arts festival. He had also begun to suffer from serious heart problems, resulting in his having quadruple bypass surgery in 2005. After that scare, he made a slow-but-sure recovery, and got involved with social media, styling himself as Peter the Sailor. Elsewhere, as well as being in the Schizoid Band and releasing what would be his only solo album, Wallace began another inspired off-shoot project, The Crimson Jazz Trio. Teaming up with a pair of accomplished American musicians—bassist Tim Landers and pianist Jody Nardone—this was not so much to breathe life into old material but to take the basics and see where else they could go with them. In 2005, their first collection was released as *The King*

*Crimson Songbook: Volume One*, its feel being that of sitting in a bar or restaurant with a jazz band playing in the corner. Instead of hearing pleasant-but-bland standards, you can pick out familiar-but-jazzed-up riffs and melodies. With Fripp's blessing, and with the band name being his suggestion, the trio were ambitious in what they chose to do, not limiting themselves to Wallace's era in the band, going from *Schizoid Man* to *Three of a Perfect Pair*, via *Red* and *Starless*.

With no end in sight for the Crimson hiatus, Fripp had room for other projects, and those he settled on tended to be at the gentler end of things. Combining ambient and improv, he linked up with American multi-instrumentalist Bill Rieflin and four other musicians, under the banner The Slow Music Project. Taking a less-is-more approach, they performed a series of gigs in the U.S. in May 2006, just as Fripp turned sixty. Using a rejigged tower of electronics, nicknamed the Solar Voyager, created for him by his tech genius John Sinks, Fripp followed this up with a short soundscapes tour of Estonia that August, the arrangements for which involved Toyah and Estonia's ambassador in London. With all the venues being churches, the highlights from these and some gigs in England were put out the following year as *Churchscapes: At the End of Time*. Although they were at the melodic end of his soundscape spectrum and have moments of inspiration, such as his use

*David Cross Band ticket, London, 2006.*
Courtesy of Tomoko Okamoto

of layers of delicate bell sounds, on the whole it feels as if something is lacking. This, and Crimson's latest hiatus, may be explained by Fripp's state of mind, as amidst the pleasantries and technical info in the cover booklet, he expresses his ongoing general unhappiness with music and performing. When he writes that 'live performance in contexts mediated by commercial culture, increasingly become a depressing exercise in futility' and 'despair has been an almost constant companion', he's expressing a deeper level of personal pain than before, and he leaves us in no doubt that the pleasure of live performance has been lost for him. There was also the stark reality that small expeditions like this, without any great promotional hoo-ha around them, were loss making. He also talks about 'a period . . . when rock music held a door open . . . then it closed', that period being the two or three years after the release of *Court*. He says he's subsequently had to make do with 'side doors', but even to get to use these you had to know 'where to find them and hold a key'. While you might read into this that he was feeling regret for not having gone through that original door, it's actually an expression of his ongoing disappointment that commercial interests and his chosen line of work haven't coincided to a greater degree. You could argue that it was actually the original band themselves who had forced that door open, or even that they created their own door. Once McDonald, Lake and Giles had left, Fripp deliberately chose not to go through that door, deciding instead to pursue his art whatever the consequences, or perhaps believing that the initial level of sales and interest would simply continue whatever he did. These sleeve notes would only have been read by the most hard-core Fripperati who came across this particular album, but for those who did, it was devastating to find that the man we had always applauded for his pursuit of his art rather than sales had come to feel this way. Fripp hasn't exactly struggled to have ongoing deals over the decades, but he has had to exist, relatively speaking, in a sort of outer mainstream. His main complaint therefore boils down to his not receiving the publicity, profile and sales that others got. Perhaps this just comes with the territory, and realistically, you have to sell a little of your soul to keep up your profile—or accept that side doors are the best you're likely to get. Managing to throw in a little self-effacing humour, Fripp added, 'There are small technical flaws in the recording and major functional flaws in the performer'. On a lighter note, while Fripp didn't get many mentions in radio comedy shows, an unlikely one came in December 2006 on BBC Radio Four. In an edition of a show called *Personality Test*, where a celeb—in this case, Rick Wakeman—is quizzed about their own life, somehow the unlikely line, 'Have you tried Robert Fripp's chutney?' was heard from one of the participants! [7] [8]

After working together on lower-profile projects, in 2006 Wetton and Downes decided to reform the original line-up of Asia. There were legal complexities to be sorted out first, but once these were resolved, and with Howe and Palmer willing and able, the original band were back. Their strength lay in their early material, especially with an eighties revival beginning to brew in the U.K., but as well as focussing on their own hits, being free of the pressures of their earlier existence, and understanding what their audiences were there for, they devoted a sizeable chunk of each night to their individual pasts away from Asia. This included playing Crimson's *Book of Saturday* and a full-length take on ELP's *Fanfare*. Wetton even found himself singing *Video Killed the Radio Star* to the appreciative and healthy-sized crowds they still attracted. Alarmingly, during their 2007 tour, he was found to be suffering from a serious heart condition, and that August had to undergo urgent surgery. The surgery was successful, and he made such a good recovery that he was back on tour within a matter of months. In September 2006, Boz Burrell was the first of the Crimson family to leave us, at the age of just sixty. Living in Marbella in southern Spain in his later years, Boz had suffered a heart attack during a rehearsal session for his latest project. Another blow came early in 2007 when Boz's former bandmate Ian Wallace also passed away, having been battling oesophageal cancer for some time. Understandably, The Schizoid Band came to a halt after this, however a second Crimson Jazz Trio album was finished, with contributions from Wallace's Schizoid Band colleagues, Collins and Jakszyk, and released in 2009.

Although they had never completely lost contact, the most unlikely musical reunion was in 2006 between Fripp and Judy Dyble. After three decades away, Dyble had resumed her musical career a couple of years earlier, and over the next three years would release a series of albums called *Spindle*, *The Whorl* and *Talking with Strangers*, each with contributions from Fripp, and on the latter also from McDonald and Mastelotto. In amongst the original material, *Whorl* included a version of *I Talk to the Wind*, Dyble having been the original vocalist on the song for the GGF demo. There was also an interesting cover of Lake and Sinfield's *C'est La Vie* on *Talking with Strangers.* Understanding the value of social media, Dyble found she still had a loyal following, despite having been away for such a long time. Though not a fan of playing live, in the coming years she would perform occasional solo gigs, incorporating *I Talk to the Wind* into her set, as well as taking part in periodic Fairport Convention get togethers.

Still preferring to keep things gentle and in the margins, Fripp saw the opportunity to take soundscapes in an interesting new direction, linking up with flute-and-sax man Theo Travis. Though more than a decade younger, Englishman Travis was himself a veteran of assorted prog and psychedelic bands, having had stints with Soft Machine and Gong, as well as playing alongside ex-Caravan cousins, Richard and David Sinclair. In the last few years, he'd become more interested in ambient music and using digital looping, so teaming up with Fripp was an ideal move for him. From Fripp's perspective, as he was five years into what was looking like another writing drought, bouncing ideas off a compatible musician offered a new way of bringing some buried inspiration to the surface. As a result, on a cold January day in 2007 they got together for a relaxed improvised session in DGM's studio in Wiltshire to see what might happen. The setup loosely echoed Fripp's partnership with Eno, though here Fripp took on the role of sound-shaper, creating loops either from his own guitar or phrases played by

Travis. The pair would then add elements of solo or melody, with the emphasis on atmosphere rather than drama. With a couple of overdubs from Travis and further treatments from Steve Wilson, the session was eventually turned into the 2008 album *Thread*. While some falls into experimental-noodling territory, the longer pieces, *As Snow Falls*, *Pastorale* and *The Silence Beneath*, are interesting, sombre, ambient explorations, showing that the pair were on to something.

With clamour from fans for some kind of glorious amalgam of past line-ups to mark Crimson's approaching fortieth anniversary, in 2007 Fripp did indeed announce a new line-up. Never one to pander to nostalgia however, this was more of a shuffling of the pack than anything else, with Belew and Mastelotto remaining, while Levin re-joined in place of Gunn, who had left to pursue other commitments. The biggest change was that, for the first time since 1994, there was a new recruit: drummer Gavin Harrison. Originally from Harrow in North-West London, the forty-four-year-old had clocked up an impressive list of session credits. He'd also had a stint with folk-rock band Renaissance, and for the last few years had been with Porcupine Tree, which is where he'd come to the attention of Fripp and Belew. With there being no gigs for this line-up for an entire year, in the interim, Belew went off to form The Adrian Belew Power Trio, with talented and versatile young bassist Julie Slick and her equally talented drumming brother, Eric. They incorporated some Crimson into their sets, prompting *All About Jazz*'s Justin Smith to pour the highest of praise on them: 'I can't believe that two players so young could take the Bruford and Levin parts . . . and more or less reinvent them'. Levin also went away to record a solo album, *Stick Man*, with contributions from Mastelotto. They enjoyed it so much that they formed an ongoing band under the name The Stick Men, enlisting a second stick player, Michael Bernie. [9]

Not wanting to repeat his 2006 experience, Fripp turned down a second invitation from the Estonian Embassy to play in their country. To make the most of the opportunity, Toyah instead assembled a new band of her own, calling on family friend Bill Rieflin; she also recruited

Chris Wong, another multi-instrumentalist she had worked with on her solo albums. Under the name The Humans they played three gigs in the Baltic State that October. On turning fifty in 2008, Mrs Fripp gave some rather frank interviews, revealing that she'd had cosmetic surgery in Paris despite Fripp's disapproval, and felt that this had helped in reviving her TV career. She had asked him to fly back from America to be at her side as she came round from the anaesthetic, and then spent a week together in a Paris hotel room, a time she later likened to 'the honeymoon we never had'. Disagreements with Fripp over other surgery she wanted would persist. As she told the *Daily Mail*'s Lester Middleton, 'I'm begging my husband to let me have a hysterectomy, because it would get rid of . . . problems with my hormones. But he won't let me. If it was up to me, I would have my boobs completely removed . . . but again he says no. but While Fripp would probably not have wanted such things aired in public, as Middlehurst points out, Toyah is 'by her own admission a bit of an attention seeker'. She also changed tack on what she had said previously about not wanting to have kids, now feeling that if something happened to Fripp, she would possibly adopt a child. Now being quite wealthy—as much through investments as music and TV work—she would be able to give a child a good upbringing. She also revealed that in their wills the couple had left their combined fortunes to the setting up of a children's music education trust. As if to remind the wider world of her connection to Fripp, Toyah named her next album, *In the Court of the Crimson Queen*, although there was no appearance by him on it. [10]

The Crimson clouds of gloom parted briefly in August 2008, as the latest five-piece version of the band played an eleven-night tour of the U.S. This was intended as part of the warmup for a Crimson fortieth anniversary tour in 2009, but with plans for that subsequently falling apart, those few gigs turned out to be just a brief interruption of the hiatus. The reason given was of diary clashes, but given the significance of the anniversary, these would surely have been foreseen, and the real reason was perhaps the unwillingness of one of the parties. It was particularly frustrating for new drummer Harrison, with what looked at the time like potentially the shortest active spell with the band. There had, in fact, been signs in their tour sets that all was not as it should be. Whereas fans had grown accustomed to hearing new works in progress, the only new pieces this time were two drum duets, and the emphasis had shifted back to tracks from *Thrak* and before. Interviewed for *All About Jazz*, after the tour Belew clearly believed that Crimson had a future and that he was undoubtedly part of it. Interviewer Justin Smith, having seem Crimson on the mini tour, observed, 'Belew appeared very much the leader, guiding the band through its labyrinthine arrangements with a sure hand'. As things would pan out, that short tour was his Crimson finale, though he would only find that out five years later. Twenty-seven years after joining, and with six studio albums under his belt—the most for any Crimson vocalist—he wouldn't have wanted to have had such a low-key exit. [9]

Without a tour, Crimson's fortieth anniversary year instead began with Fripp announcing that Guitar Craft would end the following year, on its twenty-fifth anniversary. He'd already handed over much of the running of courses to other instructors, but while the techniques he promoted still had validity, he needed to draw a line for himself under this project. While the public at large still knew nothing about Guitar Craft, it had quietly created its own sizeable legacy, with over three thousand pupils having been taught. In the coming years, many of those disciples of The Fripp Way would form their own groups, called Guitar Circles, to continue the work in a different way and to perform arrangements of Fripp and Crimson material. In the end, the only real marking of Crimson's fortieth came through the release of a remastered *In The Court of the Crimson King*, with all sorts of bonus material. For this, a 'play-back event' was held in Highbury, North London, at what had been the recording studio used for the album, which was attended by the original line-up and other Crims. All in all though, the possibilities that could have been exploited for such a landmark Crimson year were lost, and it was something of a damp squib!

Turning sixty, while continuing with his Power Trio, Belew persisted in lobbying for Fripp to reconvene Crimson again, even suggesting a revival of the eighties line-up. Fripp was not interested. His outlook had, if anything, now worsened, having embarked on legal action against the Universal Group over what he considered to be unauthorised releases of his work and unpaid royalties. In addition, a decade on from having made his decision to leave, Bruford felt that any idea of a reunion involving him was a bad one. That however turned out to be as he was soon to announce his retirement. After more than forty years of often-gruelling touring, Bruford felt it was time to hang up his drumsticks and spend more time with his family and promoting his own substantial back catalogue. He would be glad to be out of it, later commenting, 'These days you have to shout very loudly, with as much money, as many social platforms and a very loud hailer to attract a pair of ears at all. Modern music invention is not for the shy and retiring. Making music, they say, is easy (although I never found it so). Getting it to others is much harder, and getting someone to pay for it harder still, now that music is effectively free'. Musicians now, he believes, have to spend more time on communicating about what they've created than actually creating it. But while Bruford Senior wanted a quieter life, there was still a Bruford behind a drum kit, his son Alex following in his footsteps and playing with a band called The Infadels. [11]

Fripp was still tempted to put in some typically hiatus-like appearances, including guesting with Toyah's band, The Humans, when they returned to Estonia in May 2009. As part of a festival to mark the twentieth anniversary of the nation's independence from the U.S.S.R., this also served as a launch event for The Humans album, *We Are the Humans*. They followed this up with the release of a lively cover of Sandi Shaw's sixties hit, *These Boots Were Made for Walking*, calling it simply *Bootz*. Covering a fifty-year-old pop song was hardly breaking new ground, but it had energy and scored high on the bizarrometer, accompanied by a video featuring Toyah performing in a brightly coloured leotard and Fripp spinning on his guitar stool. That same month, belatedly following on from *Thread*, Fripp also played a short tour of southern England, with Theo Travis taking in Coventry and venues in his homes of Wimborne and Broad Chalke.

After the demise of ELP, since the late nineties Lake had again been pursuing his solo career. In May 2010, feeling finally mellowed, he reunited with Emerson for the first time in twelve years, to play two gigs in the U.S. McDonald also joined them as a special guest for a couple of tracks on both of those nights. A few weeks later the full trio of ELP were back together to mark the fortieth anniversary of their formation. They would only play the one gig, though, at the High Voltage Festival in Victoria Park in London, as part of a two-day event packed with 'Classic Rock' bands, And, despite age and health problems intruding, they worked through a crowd-pleasing set that included *Karn Evil 9*, *Tarkus*, *Fanfare* and *Pictures at an Exhibition*. There was to be no new material played or recorded, and ELP would perform only one more gig after this, in November 2011 at the O² Arena (the former Millennium Dome) in London. It wasn't intended as their farewell performance, but subsequent events would cause it to be just that.

In the continued absence of Crimson, and with distinct echoes of his 1975 tour with Eno, in the spring of 2010 Fripp set about a leisurely mini tour of Spain with Theo Travis, performing improvised soundscape duets. With no U.K. gigs, this again provided an excuse for some British fans to indulge in a city break while catching a Fripp gig. And on the unseasonably soggy final night of the tour, at Sala Apolo in Barcelona, a fair portion of the five-hundred-strong audience were actually from the U.K. Beforehand the venue's ticket office had been confused by the event, which was part of a guitar festival, believing that what people were asking about was impossible, and that there was instead some kind of flamenco gig that night! Thankfully, it *was* possible, and other staff who were aware of what was going on turned their pre-gig announcements about safety and not taking photographs into a multi-lingual piece of performance art over pre-recorded soundscape backing. Travis and Fripp then emerged from the backstage darkness to perform ten improvised pieces—a real larks' tapas in aspic of a set—but with no flamenco. There was little direct communication with the audience, while communications between the pair relied on instinct, understanding and the occasional barely perceptible glance or hand movement. The musicians then took their bows and vanished back into the darkness. A CD of their 2009 show in Coventry Cathedral was released at the time, and having had more time to develop the partnership, this made for a more consistent collection than *Thread. In a Field of Green* in particular ranks highly amongst Fripp's more ambient works, while *The Offering*, underpinned by a slowed-down, pitch-shifted, bluesy flute line, illustrates how working with Travis took Fripp to places he wouldn't have gone on his own. There's also a very different take on *Moonchild*, based around loops reprising the 1969 track's chords and melody.

As Fripp returned home from Spain, he was confronted with the release of the single *Power* by hugely successful hip-hop artist Kanye West. It was unexpected and controversial from Fripp's perspective, as it contained samples from *Schizoid Man*, approved by the record company but which Fripp knew nothing about in advance. Videos of the song were uploaded to the internet and had clocked up many thousands of views by the time Fripp was formally consulted. Still in the middle of his other legal dispute, this did nothing to improve his frame of mind. Other Crims were more pragmatic, with Lake in particular being quite upbeat about it, using *Power* as his own walk-on music on his next tour, segueing into his singing *Schizoid Man*. English Premier League football club, Bournemouth, would later adopt the track as their walk-on music too! *Power* became a world-wide hit, but while sampling like this is just the way of the modern music world, especially in hip-hop, it can be grating to fans of the original tracks when the 'using' artist gets plaudits for riding on someone else's genius, their fans often unaware that it's a sample. *Power* would also crop up in TV ads for aftershave, perhaps rubbing salt into Fripp's wounds, but nevertheless good for the flow of royalties!

With the new century having started so optimistically for Crimson, by the end of 2010 all looked lost. A cold, hard examination of the facts told us that there had been just a handful of gigs in the last seven years. Fripp was now approaching Bus Pass age, was deep in legal action and had told us in no uncertain terms about his unhappiness with performing and the state of the music business. There was still intermittent, low-key activity from him, but in their hearts a lot of fans had concluded that they had seen the last of Crimson. On the other hand, while the Schizoid Band had been and gone, there was usually something going on with other Crims if you looked hard enough. In fact, every time things started to seem a bit too quiet, something would usually materialise!

11

# Summoning Back the Fire Witch

## *2011 to 2021*

As we reached 2011 all was disappointingly quiet and, given Fripp's age, we had to wonder if this hiatus was going to be a terminal one. It had also fallen unusually quiet amongst the Greater-Crim too. Fripp's online diary showed that he was still doing a fair amount of travelling, but that was for all sorts of non-touring reasons, and when not enjoying one of Toyah's homes on the Cote D'Azur, he was simply spending time back in rural England, the couple having bought a home in the market town of Pershore in the Vale of Evesham. At first, he veiled his exact location by using the semi-made-up name of Bredonborough, but after a while he let the veil slip, especially after their home was featured on the TV show, *Through the Keyhole.* Having lived in London and New York, and having toured the world countless times, he was content to enjoy countryside walks alongside his wife, living in a place that was not that different from his childhood home. The eagle-eyed would have spotted a rare prime-time TV appearance for Fripp in March 2011, not performing but supporting Toyah as she took part in a charity fundraiser, *Let's Dance for Comic Relief.* At around the same time, but slightly more highbrow and illustrating a little piece of the Crimson legacy, there were some U.K. TV performances of folk band The Unthanks, with their ethereal cover of *Starless.* For a while, it seemed as if

*Travis and Fripp ticket, Barcelona, 2010.*

such incidental events were all we should expect from now on. Luckily, there were still a few twists, turns and surprises to come.

The quiet was briefly interrupted in the spring of 2011 by the unexpected release of an album with Fripp's involvement. Under the billing of Jakszyk, Fripp and Collins, *A Scarcity of Miracles* was the result of a melding of recent Crimson and Schizoid Band members, which they had been quietly working on behind the scenes. While this was not considered to be a new Crimson, given the personnel involved, Fripp decided to bestow upon it the status of a ProjeKct. It evolved out of Jakszyk and Fripp having a relaxed jam together, Jakszyk then developing their ideas into fuller songs. He ran these past Collins, who contributed sax and flute parts, and finally, to underpin them with a rhythm section, Levin and Harrison were drafted in. With a much mellower sound, the album's style bears no resemblance to any incarnation of Crimson past, each track incorporating elements of soundscape with a Jakszyk song breaking out at some point. The title track, which opens the album, has the strongest guitar parts and melodies, and has some warmth in the sound. With lyrics that reference historical invasions and battles, it goes beyond Jakszyk's wistful imagery and middle-aged relationship angst elsewhere. *The Price We Pay* also carries off the formula well, with Collins demonstrating that he's lost none of his dynamism and fluency. Unfortunately, after these the miracles are rather scarce, and the remaining tracks reflect the disjointed nature of their creation, with simply too much optimistic throwing together of ingredients in the hope that something of substance would form. Playing on the biblical connotations in the title, a painting from P. J. Crook, *Christian Children, Marching, Singing*, fills the cover, showing ranks of young people carrying loaves and fishes. With a low-key release, no promo tour and a lukewarm critical reception, the album made little impact, and while Fripp was happy with it, a lot of fans were left hoping that this wasn't the damp, squib-ish finale of his recording career.

On the other side of the Atlantic, Belew, Levin and Mastelotto were not done playing Crimson music, and after running a series of seminars incorporating the line-ups of Belew's Power Trio and Levin's Stick Men, in 2012 they decided to form a sort of Frippless Crimson. With Fripp's blessing they named themselves The Crimson ProjeKct and landed themselves a support slot on tour with American prog-metal band Dream Theater. As well as being a weighty combination, it was notably an all-American line-up that was keeping alive the legacy of what had started as an English band. Performing variations on the kind of sets Crimson had been playing in the nineties, as well as going for the easy wins like *Indiscipline* and *Elephant Talk*, they didn't shy away from the more challenging pieces like *B'boom* and *Industry*. With the concept safely anchored in the repertoire of a particular period, Belew could relax and just enjoy reprising his frontman role, without the pressure to come up with new ideas and all the other frustrations that had accompanied working with Fripp.

It probably didn't cross too many people's minds at the time but at the London Olympics in the summer of 2012—in amongst the celebrations of British culture and appearances by Paul McCartney, Mike Oldfield and others—Fripp's guitar could frequently be heard reverberating around the stadium. Courtesy of Bowie's *Heroes* being used as Team GB's entrance music in the opening ceremony and for each medal ceremony, thirty-five years after its creation, this almost casually knocked-out bit of Frippery became a spine-tingling part of the backdrop to the biggest sporting event ever hosted in Britain. Off the back of this, *Heroes* became a staple of sporting events, attaining the status of 'anthem', and in a sense Fripp did, after all, record some *Music for Sports*. While the Olympics were on, he gave a rare press interview announcing that he had retired from the music business. Years ago, this would have been a shock, but now it only really confirmed what Fripp followers already suspected. The interview wasn't with the music press or even one of the trendier newspapers, but with the *Financial Times*, the FT claiming it was the only paper Fripp would now buy. Having been involved in his latest legal dispute for six years, Fripp felt that he needed to devote so much of his energy to his battles that he could no longer continue with being a professional musician, and he sadly described music for him now as 'a joyless exercise in futility'. He was still fighting a principled fight, but this wasn't the way anyone wanted such an extraordinary music career to end. [1]

Retirement didn't prevent confusion from reigning in March 2013, in relation to Fripp and an album he had no involvement with. Bowie had surprised everyone by releasing his first new material for ten years, and his first since developing serious health problems in 2005. All well and good. However, parts of the media accused Fripp of having almost given the game away prematurely through his online diary, the recording process having been kept secret. Bowie's producer, Tony Visconti, also suggested that Fripp had turned down an offer to play on the album. Fripp said it was simply a coincidence that he'd referred in his diary to a dream he'd had about Bowie working on new material, and he didn't know this was actually happening in real life, so couldn't have revealed it. He also said he hadn't received a request to play on the album, and therefore could not have turned it down. Had he been asked, he would have considered breaking his retirement for Bowie. He emphasised that nobody was hurt by this episode and, as with pretty much the whole world, he was pleased for Bowie.

We moved from confusion to the surreal that May, as Fripp appeared with Toyah on *All Star Mr and Mrs*. This show, on ITV in the

U.K. has couples competing in a gentle and mildly humorous way to prove how much they know about each other. The host, Philip Schofield, probably didn't know anything about the man in front of him called Robert—his surname never being mentioned—other than what was written on his auto-cue, and the show's general cringe-worthiness was only mitigated by the fact that it was raising money for charities chosen by the celebrities. The Fripps didn't win, fluffing a couple of questions, including one about which of them had more fans, Mr Fripp going for the modest answer rather than the real one. While this appearance was essentially part of keeping up Toyah's media profile, many who saw it found the sixty-seven-year-old Fripp endearing and surprisingly old-fashioned, rather than any kind of stereotypical ageing rock guitarist.

Early in 2013 there were serious moves to form another Frippless Crimson—tentatively termed Crimson DNA—which would have involved Jakszyk, Harrison, Collins and Wetton. Events soon overtook them, with word then beginning to spread on social media amongst the Fripperati that Fripp was after all going to get King Crimson together one more time! It was hard to know if this had any substance or not, but that didn't stop a lot of speculation about who was to be in the band. After some fairly cryptic postings in Fripp's online diary, DGM put everyone out of their misery in September 2013 by announcing that, with his legal dispute approaching settlement, it was indeed true that Fripp had reconsidered his retirement, and that there was going to be a new Crimson. The line-up was to be a magnificent seven-piece of Fripp, Jakszyk, Collins, Levin, Mastelotto, Harrison and Rieflin. This was the line-up from *Scarcity of Miracles* with two additions, making Crimson more British than American for the first time since 1974, and the largest-ever line-up. The biggest shock was that there was no Belew, particularly shocking to Belew himself, who was having a difficult few months all round, not only rejected by Fripp but also having an abortive stint with Trent Reznor's Nine Inch Nails. He subsequently posted on social media that he hadn't been asked if he wanted to join the new

Crimson, but that this wouldn't affect his friendship with Fripp. This all seemed quite amicable, although some observers suggested that Fripp's dealing with the situation lacked diplomacy. The contents of an email from Fripp to Belew conveniently later surfaced via social media, where he explained, 'This is not a Crim I see for you', but 'this doesn't mean you are no longer a member of the Crimson brotherhood', clarifying that there had in fact been some attempt at softening the blow. [2]

On the more positive side, as well as creating more of a link back to early Crimson, there was a recall for Collins, thirty-nine years after last being on a Crimson album. The first of the new Crims, Jakszyk, would be vocalist/guitarist, his Schizoid Band years meaning that he'd already covered some of the groundwork. But while he was to an extent replacing Belew, this was to be a band of a different nature. The other new Crim, Rieflin, was a fifty-three-year-old American, with Nine Inch Nails, REM and The Humans on his CV. He would take on the unusual, combined role of drummer and keyboardist. The other big talking point was speculation as to what the three drummers would do. A Fripp comment, that the backline would become the frontline and vice-versa, only raised more questions. Significantly, he also announced that there was no intention to go into the studio to do new material. Instead, they would tour, playing what was described as reconfigured existing material, starting towards the end of 2014. This was something of a sea change for Fripp, from continually trying to move on, but no one was going to begrudge him finally leaning on his own glorious past. That also meant steering well clear of any potentially difficult writing-and-recording sessions. There was still a desire within Fripp to perform, and it was perhaps a case of finding a workable and satisfying enough way of doing this. With The Rolling Stones having just headlined at Glastonbury, despite Jagger being about to hit seventy, and Hackett successfully touring the world performing a set of revived seventies Genesis, if Fripp needed any indications as to whether there were audiences out there for more mature artists playing their back-catalogue, he need look no further.

In February 2014, Toyah's social media mentioned that they had picked up Rieflin from Heathrow, having just flown in from America. Levin's posts across social media, as well as showing how grim the winter was in England, confirmed that he was also on this side of the pond. The new Crimson—dubbed The Seven-Headed Beast—were gathering, ready to dive into rehearsals in Elstree, just north of Greater London, a location formerly famous for the recording of TV shows. Amongst the band's pre-tour social media posts were photos of the line-up dressed so smartly they looked more like bank staff or a firm of solicitors than a rock band. Understandably, with their average age being sixty, there was noticeably a lot of grey hair on display too. As regards how this band would revisit tracks by earlier Crimsons, according to Levin, Fripp's guidance was 'to look at them as if they've just been written'. Levin would also reveal that Fripp set his trio of drummers a rather daunting task, telling them, 'I want you to reinvent rock drumming'. They were happy to take on that challenge, but Levin knew that this also meant he would have to adapt his style to fit in. Even with his versatility and experience, the seemingly ever-cool bassist said, 'I took a deep breath and, as I always do in King Crimson, I had faith in Robert's vision'. [3]

That same month, in amongst Mrs Fripp's media engagements and her own tour preparations, came an appearance with hubby on *The Fripps*, a show on satellite channel Vintage TV. The basis of the show was the couple choosing some of their favourite songs and videos, with Toyah taking on the role of interviewer. After discussing his work with Gabriel, Bowie and Blondie, they chose suspiciously populist songs such as Lennon's *Imagine*, Simon and Garfunkel's *Bridge Over Troubled Water* and *Angels* by Robbie Williams. The biggest revelation was that when he was missing his wife, Fripp didn't reach for Stravinsky, McLaughlin or even a Toyah album, but supposedly a bit of Whitney Houston! Although this latest appearance was on an obscure channel, they were becoming something of a quirky celebrity couple, something that came quite naturally to Toyah but wasn't such a natural fit for

Fripp. He did, however, seem to be enjoying this different kind of exposure for the sake of assisting his wife. While rehearsals were going on at Elstree, Toyah dropped another snippet of the mundanities of their home life into a media appearance. This came on the light-hearted *John Shuttleworth's Lounge Music*, on BBC Radio Four, where she informed us that Fripp is banished to the spare room if he snores, as it disturbs their agoraphobic rabbit, who shares the room with them. Snoring was perhaps a minor worry, as elsewhere Toyah said that she was convinced that their house was haunted by a small boy who only she and the rabbit could see, their pet following the vision when it appeared. Research, and the inevitable appearance on a TV show about ghosts, suggested that during an outbreak of plague in the sixteenth century, a group of children had been left in the building's cellar to die.

On 9 September 2014, a year after the reforming had been confirmed, the first tour of Crimson Mk VII got going, with an opening night in Albany, New York, followed by an additional nineteen nights across the U.S. Longer-term plans were still vague, and if this was to be some sort of final fling for the band, the big question was, just how long would the affair last? Prior to the tour they had put out a statement warning fans not to come expecting a populist set from start to finish. On one level it seemed unnecessary to say this, as fans would hardly be expecting a set of hit singles. However, the band clearly felt it was fair to give advanced warning that they would be delving into all sorts of corners of Crimson past, and not just playing the more obvious popular tracks. Their sets were ninety minutes long, each night opening with an uncompromising *Larks' Tongues: Part One*, as had been the case back in 1972–1973. It fitted the bill perfectly, setting the scene for what to expect, and making good use of the three drummers. Better still, it sounded stronger than it had when played live back in its own time. Other than wanting them to reinvent drumming, Fripp's instructions to his drum trio were surprisingly minimal. In fact, according to Mastelotto, he never actually explained why he wanted three drummers, and didn't—to any significant extent—tell them what to do.

When Fripp did give an element of guidance, it was more to do with the general feel he wanted. For example, on the heavier tracks, Mastelotto explained to *Music Radar*, that Fripp might ask for 'a fat, hairy ape on drums', which he interpreted as meaning that 'he wants that primal thing, but he still wants a sophisticated swing drummer as well'. The rest of the set was dominated by material from 1969 to 1974, including revivals of *The Letters* and *The Sailor's Tale*. Sets closed with *Starless*, with a full-blown *Schizoid Man* saved for the encore. There were no mellotrons as such onstage, but mellotron-strings sounds were programmed into Rieflin and Fripp's keyboards for use where we'd expect them to be. As usual, there was nothing resembling a stage show, but with the three drummers across the front and the other four musicians on risers across the back, it was a dramatic and unusual setup, and the lily didn't need gilding. The only minor concession to stage effects was that the otherwise-white lighting would shift to red during *Starless*. Other than the uniqueness of the stage setup, the one aspect that reviewers latched onto, was that for the first time in many years, Fripp had stage lighting on him. He was literally back in the spotlight, and it was a sign that he was happy being there, sitting stage left with his guitar, a stack of electronics and a keyboard, in quiet supervision of his colleagues. It would be fair to say that Fripp's creative well had now run pretty dry, the band's only new material initially coming in the form of polyrhythmic drum trios. It was his presence and willingness however, that allowed this Crimson to exist, and large audiences would turn up mainly because of him and the band name. What would soon become apparent was that, while Fripp had ultimate control, this Crimson was a chance for others to shine, and they would shine very brightly. Such was the scale and quality of the back catalogue that the lack of new material didn't seem to matter, as they breathed new life into the old tracks, with tweaked arrangements, different instrumentation and their collective abilities enabling stunning performances. It may well have been a more amicable banding together than previous Crimson incarnations, but that didn't mean they'd lost their edge. [4]

In October 2014, the *Daily Telegraph* published a rare interview with Fripp. Reporter Rob Hughes said that he found him to be 'eloquent, garrulous and frequently funny', rather than being the 'difficult . . . forbidding autocrat with exacting standards' he'd been expecting. He also found twenty-first-century Fripp to be very candid, agreeing with ex-bandmates' criticisms of him. 'I'm a very difficult person to work with', he confessed. On the other hand, he then went on to justify this by saying that he was honouring the standards set by the original Crimson. Things were different now, he said, adding, 'It's the first Crimson where I don't sense any animosity', undoubtedly helped by the fact that in this Crimson, 'the money is equally divided'. As far as his aims for this incarnation, he said he was 'looking for a sense of completion' and 'coming to a form of conclusion and satisfaction'. A final revelation was that one of the reasons for the latest reforming had nothing to do with music; he had done so because Toyah had told him he was 'in danger of becoming dull'. [5]

A mini-album, *Live at the Orpheum*, was the first release from this Crimson, in 2015, including familiar-but-different versions of *One More Red Nightmare*, *Sailor's Tale* and *Starless*. Compiled from a show in Los Angeles, at forty-one minutes it felt like something of a teaser; however, there would ultimately be no shortage of live material for us to digest in the coming years. Plans were constantly re-evolving, and whatever conclusion it was that Fripp was working towards luckily seemed to be some distance ahead, with dates soon announced for a European tour, followed by further dates across North America and beyond. These were signs of a happy camp and musicians who were confident in what they were doing. Sets continued to be broadened out in terms of older material, with a few more new ideas also creeping in. By the time they hit Europe, they had so much at their fingertips that they could perform markedly different two-hour sets on consecutive nights. Audiences were made up largely of middle-aged or older men, although there was also a surprising number of women and younger people too. This was, to an extent, due to the sons, daughters and wives

*King Crimson ticket, London, 2015.*

coming along to see what the men had been going on about for years, but also because the gap between the generations' tastes had narrowed and the gender divide over music was no longer so pronounced. There were a few niggles from audience members at the front at some venues, getting the full impact of three drum kits a bit too high in the mix. A few others just didn't get on with this line-up's style, which was settling into a weighty, jazz-tinged, *Larks'/Islands* hybrid, and was quite an intense experience. However, no one could complain about any lack of energy or entertainment, and all in all, the Seven-Headed Beast was a class act and something special to see. There was conspicuously little from the Belew era in the sets, and nothing at all that used his lyrics. Some initially assumed that this was because tracks from his era were not suited to this Crimson or Jakszyk's vocal style, but it would emerge that there was a dispute going on behind the scenes, and all was not sweetness, light and acceptance. Belew had been suggesting that many songs from that period were specifically his, despite being credited to the whole band, so Fripp decided it would be judicious and diplomatic for Crimson not to go there for the time being. Though deeply wounded by being excluded, Belew managed to successfully divert his creative energies to different spheres, in particular designing award-winning music and imagery software called *Flux*, and compositing the soundtrack for a short, animated Pixar film called *Piper*, which would come out in 2016.

A Fripp collaboration also appeared in 2015, in the form of the Cross-and-Fripp album, *Starless Starlight.* Released on Cross's Noisy label, it used Fripp's soundscapes as backdrops, and was scattered with extrapolations from the violinist's much-loved, original theme for *Starless.* As with anything that has the Fripp name attached, it attracted a fair amount of attention, making it a welcome bit of profile raising for Cross. His feet were still firmly planted on the ground, with a modest-scale launch event, held at The Bedford in South London before an audience of devotees. With Fripp only present on the backing tracks, Cross was instead aided by a band that included the irrepressible former Van Der Graaf Generator saxophonist, David Jackson, for an impressively varied evening at the arty end of the spectrum. It was a happy and busy couple of months all round for the ex-Crim, having also been gigging in Japan with Levin's Stick Men a few weeks earlier. He was soon also back in the studio with his usual band, now supplemented by Jackson, putting together *Sign of the Crow*, which would be released in August 2016. Its London launch gig was held at The Lexington in Islington, to a crowd of a hundred or so, though the David Cross Band's performance was worthy of an audience many times that size. At sixty-seven, Cross not only showed impressive levels of energy, with the heaviness ramped up even higher than before, but, remarkably, still appeared to be growing in confidence on his instrument and in terms of stage presence. A treat for those who got there was that the evening was opened by ex-Crimson lyricist Richard Palmer-James, accompanying himself on acoustic guitar to promote his first solo album, *Takeaway*, at the age of sixty-nine.

Early in 2016, Rieflin needed to take an extended break from Crimson for personal reasons, and at the suggestion of Harrison, Fripp enlisted Jeremy Stacey to cover his roles. Though he was London born, the fifty-two-year-old had (surprise, surprise) spent a lot of time living in the Bournemouth area. Inspired in his youth by Bruford and Phil Collins, he was largely unknown to the Crimson faithful but not to the drumming community, with a diverse CV that included working

*Adrian Belew Trio ticket, Firenze, 2016.*
Courtesy of Tomoko Okamoto

with Eric Clapton, Robbie Williams and Tom Jones. Most recently he'd been touring with Noel Gallagher's post-Oasis band, High Flying Birds. He was a remarkable find, being able to cover drums and keyboards, although he hadn't properly played keyboards for twenty years, so that aspect would be a steep re-learning curve for him.

With the 2016 Crimson tour in full flow, September that year saw the release of the live album *Radical Action (To Unseat the Hold of Monkey Mind)* with a package that thoroughly documented the Seven-Headed Beast. A live album from a band led by a seventy-year-old can hardly have been more eagerly anticipated, and it made a strong addition to fans' bulging shelves of Crimson material. With numerous new arrangements and a smattering of new ideas, this was certainly not Crimson as a tribute act to its former selves, Jakszyk ably channelling Wetton, Lake and Burrell. The highlights inevitably came from the reworked early material, including a spectacular *Easy Money*, as well as an unexpected interlude of serenity in the form of *Peace*, partly sung in Japanese. *The Sailor's Tale* improved on the textures of the original and was much more dynamic, as they cut loose in the end passage, emphasising a melody that had been all but lost in the 1971 mix. New ideas included *Meltdown* and *Suitable Grounds for the Blues*, which were Jakszyk-derived songs blended with a noughties-style Crimson feel. The only relatively weak points were the percussion trios which, though technically astonishing, didn't really go anywhere. The reference to *Monkey Mind* in the album's title is to a Buddhist concept that there is a part of the human brain that is easily distracted or acts as an inner critic. Either way it can be destructive and needs to be controlled in order to get on with things or to be creative, and the implication is that Fripp needed Crimson to stop himself from succumbing to his money mind! The cover features a disconcerting drawing by Rieflin's wife, Francesca Sundsten, of a chubby man with one big central eye, an image that had been used on promo material throughout the tour. As further tours were being planned, and *Radical Action* spent a few weeks in the lower reaches of the U.K. top 100, behind-the-scenes negotiations resolved the Belew song issue enough to allow a little more from his Crimson era to be considered for revival.

The music world had been coming to terms with the loss of David Bowie in the early days of 2016 and, given the age that many Crims from the earlier years were reaching, inevitably there were growing health problems for some of them. In July 2016 came the news that, having had a malignant growth removed the previous year, John Wetton was now undergoing chemotherapy. He kept up his usual active profile on social media and was still planning another tour with Asia. Those closest to him, though, knew he had a fight on his hands. That December came the sad news that Greg Lake had succumbed to cancer. He was the first of the original Crimson five to leave us, his long-term ELP bandmate Keith Emerson having tragically taken his own life in March of that year. Just weeks later, in January 2017, Wetton lost his fight with cancer at the age of sixty-seven. While not going public with his feelings at the time, having become great friends with Wetton, Fripp had been in regular contact with him and had visited him shortly before his death. We had lost some of our heroes far too soon, but they were much-loved, big names on the world stage, and their place in music history was assured.

When Rieflin was able to return to Crimson early in 2017, Fripp decided he'd like to keep Stacey around too, and so the band evolved once more, becoming an eight-piece, and again the largest-ever Crimson line-up. Four drummers would have been stretching things too far, so Rieflin would instead focus on keyboards—the first time Crimson had had a dedicated keyboard player—with a supplementary live-sound-manipulation role that Fripp described as 'sprinkling fairy dust'. A little tongue-in-cheek, Fripp characterised the eight-piece band as a double-quartet, even though they were not. While Stacey occupied the central drumming position onstage and in the panning, it was mainly Harrison who created the patterns that the three drummers used, his art being to write parts that contributed to the overall sound while not interfering with each other. Things seemed to be good for Fripp offstage as well, another window into his home life being opened by Toyah on the BBC Radio Four show, *Broadcasting House*, that March. Here she described her and Fripp as being 'chalk and cheese', and although they were two people who spent so much of their lives performing, as 'two complete, insular oddballs who made it work'. She also let on that she'd persuaded him to take up disco dancing to help him keep fit, though only in the privacy of their own kitchen. This also explained his signing his email to Belew as 'Boppin' Bob'! [6]

May 2017 brought the release of a live Crimson version of Bowie's *Heroes* as a single, having added it to their set after the great man's death. With an accompanying video release, it was timed to mark the song's fortieth anniversary, and appropriately enough, was taken from a show in Berlin. It was a much-changed Berlin from the divided Cold War city where the original had been recorded, Crimson's video using footage of the fall of the Berlin Wall mixed in with film of the band. In this brave new world of internet streaming taking over from physical sales, the video clocked up a healthy few hundred thousand views in its first year. The band's set had diversified so much since the previous tour that, by December of that year, they felt able to put out another album, *Live in Chicago*, from a performance in June 2017 that Fripp felt stood out from the rest. As well as being the first album to feature the eight-piece band, and in places three keyboards (Rieflin, Fripp and Stacey), the notable differences were the inclusion of Belew-era songs, *Neurotica* and *Indiscipline*, the latter featuring a new vocal melody from Jakszyk, avoiding the need to imitate Belew's spoken delivery. There were also seventies live rarities, *Fallen Angel* and *Islands*, with Stacey impressively taking on Tippett's role on piano on the latter. In fact, to crowds largely unfamiliar with him, Stacey was one of the great revelations of this tour. The other big surprise was an ambitious performance of *The Battle of Glass Tears* (renamed *Lizard Suite*), which had never been performed live but had plenty of mileage in it, that had been waiting decades to be exploited. Popular opinion was that the band were still improving, and in a review for *All About Jazz*, John Kelman described the album as 'fiery reinventions of older material'. During 2017, Rieflin found he needed to take a further break, his role covered for that autumn's touring by American ex-Crafty Guitarist Chris Gibson. [7]

While the current Crimson were now dipping a little into songs from Belew's period in the band, all was not, in fact, well concerning relations between the parties. Through August and September, Belew was busy doing the rounds of radio stations, promoting an album and tour by his new band, Gizmodrome, an unlikely sounding teaming-up with ex-Police drummer Stewart Copeland, and ex-Level 42 vocalist/bassist Mark King. During some interviews, Belew took his chance to publicly discuss his ongoing, deep resentment at not being in the new Crimson. This prompted further behind-the-scenes diplomacy from Fripp, and he subsequently announced that they had settled their disagreements. An *Uncertain Times Tour* was then announced for Crimson for Europe for the summer of 2018, when Fripp would be all of seventy-two years old, putting us tantalisingly close to the band's fiftieth anniversary year! A Fripp quote in tour publicity filled in the reasons for the tour name: 'In strange and uncertain times there are moments in which a reasonable person could despair. But hope is unreasonable and the power of music to unite people is a good reason to have some hope'. While this was a recycling of part of his earlier notes on redemption, with the religious connotation removed, in the era of Brexit, Trump and Putin, few would disagree that these were uncertain times. As that tour took place, the latest incarnation wowed substantial crowds everywhere they landed, tweaks to the set this time including partially rewritten lyrics for *Easy Money* by Jakszyk. Knowing he was unlikely to ever be on a Crimson studio album, he was making the material his own in other ways, and onstage was visibly putting his heart and soul into his performances. The back catalogue was then given a useful boost when parts of the original *Starless* were used in the moderately successful horror film *Mandy*, released in 2018. Set in the early eighties, with a plot involving flesh-eating bikers, notably its main character, played by Nicolas Cage, was named Red. Crimson influence is clearly lurking all over the place in the arts! [8]

During 2018 Crimson had put out a statement about how Brexit was making a 2019 tour unlikely, as it would cause problems with visas and work permits. No sooner was the 2018 tour over when *Celebration Tour* dates began to be announced for the following year, Brexit issues seemingly overcome. It was a moderately intensive schedule for artists of their age, aiming for fifty gigs spanning their regular haunts across the globe, including an impressive three nights at London's Royal

*King Crimson ticket, London, 2018.*

Albert Hall. As there had been little or no marking of any previous Crimson decade anniversary, this fiftieth-anniversary tour was a major achievement. Promo material featured a painting of a woman in nineteenth century–style clothing, with a disconcertingly Fripp-like face. Other than wondering what this was telling us, the big question was, would this be the big farewell? In April 2019, marking the fiftieth anniversary of Crimson's Speakeasy launch gig, a media event was held at a small London gallery. Its main purpose was to announce that, as well as the tour, DGM would be pulling out all the stops for that year, with two more boxed sets being released, and allowing Crimson's back catalogue to become available on streaming services, after years of resistance. It was also revealed that during 2018, Fripp had commissioned a documentary on the band, to be directed by British Toby Amies. This was to be called *Cosmic FuKc,* and the filmmakers were being given access to all the current Crims. Toyah would later give away in an onstage announcement during her own tour that, despite commissioning it, Fripp was reluctant to appear in the documentary himself, doing his best to vanish when the cameras started to roll! At the media event, Fripp also spoke at some length—to an extent that made his sleeve notes of old seem concise—about his and Crimson's aims, and his inner knots of philosophy on what Crimson is and has been. Although time was also allowed for questions from the assembled journalists, the feel was perhaps a bit too much like corporate PR, and beyond the announcements, for all the talking, true insights were few and far between. There's also the problem, as pointed out by Kevin Holm-Hudson in *Progressive Rock Reconsidered*, that 'Fripp is notorious for revising his own history', and Fripp 2019 puts a very different spin on things compared to the Fripp of decades past. [9]

Rieflin took a further sabbatical in 2019 following the death of his wife, Francesca, and because of his own health problems. To cover his keyboards and fairy-dust role, in April it was announced that Theo Travis would join the band on tour. There was some kind of hiccup, though, and by May this had been diplomatically abandoned, the band

*King Crimson ticket, London, 2019.*

reverting to a seven piece. As many Crimson tours of the seventies had, 2019's began with five gigs in Germany. This time, the opening night was in Leipzig, in the former DDR, something that would have been impossible back in the Cold War years. Next up were the three nights at the RAH in London, approximately fifty years on from Hyde Park, before they headed for warm welcomes across Japan and North America. This variation of the Seven-Headed Beast was by turns as powerful, delicate and disturbingly noisy as we'd come to expect. They were spine-tingling when the 'mellotrons' were in full flow—duties shared by Fripp and Stacey—and they truly relished the improvised passages. The only minor negative was that—other than a pre-recorded announcement from Fripp—there was no interaction with the audience. Crimson's music does plenty of talking, but it did make them seem a little distant at the larger venues. By now, crowds knew what to expect for the final tracks, *Starless* and *Schizoid Man*, audiences clinging on a bit more than usual to every note, in case this time really was the last. Each show would then end with the seven lining up to bow to the audience, to thunderous applause, before departing. The tour moved into its final leg, covering the major cities of South America, with the band getting in and out of Santiago for their last show, just days before the city was plunged into chaos by major protests and riots. With so much going on, one quirk in this odd, misshapen and unpredictable story that went under the radar was that Jakszyk had now been vocalist for longer than Lake, Haskell, Burrell and Wetton put together (though not Belew), and the seven/eight-piece band had overtaken the eighties line-up as the longest-lasting version.

*Was* that the end? In a truly creative sense the story had ended long ago, but as they had now tweaked and rearranged material from all corners of the back catalogue, was there a looming danger that, without any injection of new material, this version of the band could stagnate? We'd had the luxury of several, unexpected extra years of seeing several old hands running through music we loved and being introduced to highly talented new musicians. But had the beast gone as far as it could, especially after they'd thrown in the proverbial kitchen sink for the fiftieth anniversary? Fripp would no doubt love to enjoy more walks in the country with Toyah, or to sun himself on her Menton apartment's balcony, but would that be enough for him? Mrs Fripp was certainly not about to retire to be with him. In fact, as his tour was reaching its conclusion, she was just embarking on her *In the Court of the Crimson Queen* tour, a reissue of her album of that name having recently charted, notably featuring a song called *21st Century Super Sister*.

As things hung in a post-tour limbo, there was mixed news and, to say the least, a broad mixture of feelings about Fripp, around the wider Crimson family. Though one of the most genuine nice guys of the rock world, Belew was still angry behind the scenes about not being part of this Crimson, but still had his fingers in several other musical pies and had recently been promoting his latest solo album, *Pop Sided*. Elsewhere, Cross was touring with The Stick Men, when Levin and Mastelotto were not otherwise engaged, and McDonald, after a couple of years rocking with his neighbour Ted Zurkowski in Honey West, had been back onstage with a revived Foreigner. Haskell had also been gigging again, including a performance with the Polish Philharmonic Orchestra. He still harboured deep resentment for Fripp, saying 'the word c—- is too good for him'. In contrast, Peter Giles met up with Fripp at his Pershore home in December 2019, seeing him for the first time in nearly fifty years, and coming away bowled over by his former bandmate and his great integrity. When not doing long-distance running and breaking records for his age group, Giles was still involved with music and was planning to release an album written and performed with his wife, Yasmine. As for Crimson itself, it soon transpired that the end was probably not nigh. Firstly, towards the end of 2019, Levin told the *Boston Herald*, 'We're already discussing plans for 2020, so I'm hoping this is going on for a while'. However, they still had no plans for a studio album, the bassist saying, 'My assignment right now is to learn a few more classics'. Fripp's business partner, David Singleton, reportedly also told some fans that they were looking as far ahead as 2021, although he personally needed a break after the enormous demands of the anniversary year. [10] [3]

While deep breaths were being taken by everyone else, Fripp surprisingly announced that he would be running a Guitar Craft course in October 2020, near New York, and barely had we moved into 2020 when a short Crimson tour of North America that summer was also announced. Those plans were soon thrown into doubt however—as with everything else—by the Covid-19 pandemic! March then brought the terrible news of Bill Rieflin's death from cancer at just fifty-nine, bringing warm tributes from his friends across the world. It seems Crimson's 2019 tour had had to be conducted with a sadness in their hearts, knowing what was happening to their friend, as they performed without him. Fripp may have been content with tweaking the old stuff, but as Covid restrictions eased for a while in mid-2020, Belew was still filled with the creative spirit. When asked on social media if he was brewing more pots of ambiguity (a lyric reference) he responded, *'Oh you bet, Pete!'* While being excluded from recent Crimson was still a sore point, he could at least now reflect that, had he been part of it, history showed that it would almost certainly have collapsed again by now, with the danger of old issues resurfacing. Whether he'd been spared a difficult couple of Crimson years or not, through his solo work and Power Trio he could continue in safer, happier territory. [11]

Through that period there were more sad reminders of the age and growing vulnerability of the Crimson family. In June 2020, Keith Tippett succumbed to cancer, having blazed his unique trail for fifty years. The next month Judy Dyble lost her battle with the lung cancer she'd alerted her following to the previous year. In October we then also lost Gordon Haskell to cancer. He never quite managed to put the unhappiness of his time in Crimson behind him but was fiercely proud of his solo work right to the end.

As we all then waited again in our small, immobile units, on the bridge between the pre and post Covid worlds, Crimson's tour was inevitably pushed on a year. In the meantime, Fripp and Toyah made the best of things, and in the coming months posted regular videos, performing songs in their kitchen, attempting the tango and running around their garden in bee costumes. Profiles needed to be kept up! By far the most attention grabbing of their lockdown efforts came in January 2021, performing Metallica's *Enter Sandman*, a distinctly braless Toyah singing while riding an exercise bike. This mix of bizarreness and unavoidable nipples triggered coverage in the national press in a way Fripp's music hadn't done in years. Some reports suggested he had been angered by this, however, many similar posts followed.

Another TV car advert then cropped up using a sample of *Schizoid Man*. While it raised the same mix of annoyances versus royalties, it also showed that, more than five decades on, even the first track from the first Crimson album was still reverberating around culture, even if younger listeners didn't know exactly who they were listening to. The waiting had to go on, as Covid variants evolved, and we all did our best to advance masked, however, one positive we could hang onto was that Fripp was revelling in his role in this late era of Crimson far too much to call it a day just yet. And when it could, the Cirkus would still roll on!

12

# Tomorrow and Tomorrow

## *2022 to ?*

Fripp once said, 'Music is a very considerable friend to us at awkward moments', and he and his band have generously supplied us with a great deal of lasting friendship. Whether we have loved them from the word go or picked up on them somewhere along the line, we have become accustomed to this ever-changing band/concept/feeling that is King Crimson. Similar to the way people accept the ever-changing faces of James Bond and Doctor Who, we have come to terms with this periodically regenerating entity, accepting that each time it's still part of the same story. Paradoxically, while the ending of each line-up was lamented, it was this very instability that gave us the benefit of having markedly different eras of the band, as well as having many other strands of music to potentially follow. The trade-off for the disappointment of not getting more from each line-up was instead getting the likes of ELP, Foreigner, UK, Asia and Earthworks, as well as many more Fripp collaborations than we otherwise would have. [1]

The true scale of the legacy and influence of this roll call of ungraspable talent in the Crimson family is difficult to assess, and such a judgment is, in any case, highly subjective. Arguably, though, Crimson outstrips most others in rock, with only the likes of The Beatles, Bowie, Pink Floyd, Hendrix and a handful of others being comparable. In terms of output, most artists can think themselves lucky if they have one short purple patch they can trade on for the rest of their careers, but for Fripp alone you can identify several separate periods that were game changers. When you add in the likes of Lake, Wetton, Bruford, McDonald and Belew, we are off the scale. A look at the extensive discographies of all concerned, strewn with landmarks in music history, gives you some idea, but this is by no means the full picture. In terms of influence there are not only the obvious big examples such as Genesis, Gabriel, Hackett, Yes, Roxy and Camel, and those who subsequently took their cues from them, but you can also find signs in the music of other such luminaries as Kate Bush, Hawkwind, Nick Cave, Talk Talk, Mercury Rev and Radiohead. There have been countless others with a lower profile, for whom Fripp/Crimson were a significant influence, not just imitating the style from a particular phase, but acquiring that desire to want to go somewhere different. It must be acknowledged that the bulk of this influence came from their 1969–1984 output, but it continued to varying degrees beyond that time. To this day there are new musicians discovering one part or another of the Greater-Crim for the first time, even if the stop-start nature of the band itself has meant that they haven't enjoyed a higher ongoing profile.

More tangibly, as regards direct influence and legacy, for Fripp there are literally thousands of people who have passed through the ranks of the Crafty Guitarists, and even after the formal ending of Guitar Craft, ex-Crafties have continued to give lessons and set up Guitar Circles/Ensembles to give performances in the name of the Master, with an almost religious devotion to the cause. In a more literal sense too, in the absence of having any kids of their own, Fripp and Toyah have pledged to leave a substantial financial legacy to the establishment of a music-education trust for children. In this increasingly internet-based age, a casual trawl of major video websites is also a good indication of legacy and influence. As well as countless Crimson videos, official or otherwise, you find all sorts of musicians playing Crimson covers. Some of the gems to be found include a college orchestra doing an ambitious version of *Schizoid Man*; two pianists on one piano, filmed from above, demonstrating their own arrangement of *Red*; a Brazilian orchestra playing *Fallen Angel*; a young, female Italian guitarist (who has even been noticed by Fripp) playing *Larks' Tongues: Part Two*; and a piano-and-violin duet of *Moonchild* variations. What's really striking, though, is the great level of effort that has been put into these, and some of the arrangements can send shivers down your spine in the way the originals did. One amusing aspect of legacy is finding just how much Sinfield's term, Crimson King, has filtered through into the wider vocabulary far beyond music. It is, for example, the title of a Graham McNeil novel about inter-planetary warriors and sorcerers; the name of an immortal being in a series of Stephen King horror/fantasy books; varieties of basil, clematis and maple tree; a cocktail; an English cider; a financial management company in Bognor Regis; and, seemingly, an unpleasant 'urban' term!

Despite what some fans choose to believe—and sometimes Fripp's own spin on past events—there was no master plan as such, beyond that of aiming to make interesting and original music. In fact there is overwhelming evidence to the contrary, Fripp's attempted plans here and there, being blown off course. The older Fripp has believed that there's a good fairy who has a master plan that involves him, but that's a whole different matter! Nothing happens in a vacuum, and even geniuses have influences and learn from others along the way. For all his imagination and ability, triggered initially by everyone from Stravinsky to Hendrix, it's fair to say that Fripp would not have got to where he found himself at the beginning of 1970 without Lake, McDonald and Sinfield. It's also true that he would not have become the musician he evolved into had Lake and McDonald not then left. He was also shaped further down the line by working with Eno and Gabriel, by the very existence of McLaughlin and the massive jolt to his world from his Fourth Way encounters. None of this, however, diminishes what he came to be in his own right, pursuing his own paths and being that rarest of rarities: a true pioneer.

As to how this body of music will be regarded in the longer term, there is cause for optimism. Styles and genres go in and out of fashion, but the rehabilitation of prog that began in the nineties has continued. There is always a danger that the genre will tend to be reduced to a handful of tired clichés, most of which don't actually apply to Crimson, and Crimson's music itself will get reduced to a handful of tracks that are taken as representing them. However, there is also a good chance that Fripp, Crimson and others at the better end of prog will be regarded with the kind of reverence accorded classical music and early jazz. Changing attitudes to older artists, partly brought about by ways people access their music now, have made younger people less dismissive of them, taking an approach that most of us, now in middle age or older, would not have done to the music of our parents' generation. It's also a testament to the sheer quality of the music. Some albums will stay more high-profile than others—probably *Court*, *Red* and *Discipline*, and for different reasons, *No Pussyfooting*—but the rest will be unexpected pleasures for the uninitiated to discover through exploring a little further.

Celebrating this body of work inevitably raises questions about the music of today and to come. Fripp has taken a principled stand against aspects of the music business over the decades, and it would be hard to disagree with his aims. He has won some battles, but at times he has perhaps strayed into railing against the nature of the world and being too idealistic. While it's healthy to have a good whinge about the music biz, we live in a commercial world which isn't going away in a hurry, and it's not good to drown in cynicism. The commercial aspect is a necessary factor, and all but a fortunate few have to ride the gravy train to an extent if they want to earn a living from their art. It's all about trying to find a good balance between principles and business. That said, it's hard to avoid feeling that something is being lost and forgotten through the pressures that exist today. While there is always good, new music to be found if we look hard enough, the possibilities for artists to get enough exposure and to get time to experiment and grow seem much narrower, and genuine creativity struggles to find a mainstream platform. The GGF false start notwithstanding, Crimson were lucky to form in an era of changing attitudes, when so much was possible and it was far easier to be original, with so many unexplored avenues to try. It also helped that, through a mix of circumstances and talent, Crimson were able to hit the ground running. Other bands of that era and musical territory would take several albums to really perfect their craft, but importantly, were given time to do so. It helped that audiences back then were happy to be challenged, knowing that a little patience and openness would often be greatly repaid. Record companies were, even then, looking for trends and movements to profit by, but in the late sixties and early seventies the pressure for instant and sustained big success was not so great, and the amount of time and freedom they gave artists just wouldn't be allowed today.

Music radio has always been largely focussed on the more populist or throwaway end of things, but in Crimson's early years there was always room for DJs that showcased album tracks or 'underground' bands, supplemented by the occasional TV show that did the same. While we have many more music stations now, the bulk of these are focussed on a much narrower, safer range, and those TV shows have all but vanished. The recent dominance of TV talent/reality shows has not helped, filling the mainstream more than ever with a string of cash-cow puppets, churning out forgettable, generic pop. While some music with a real sense of adventure still gets through to a wider audience, in this environment true creativity is essentially unwelcome and therefore pushed into the margins. Developments in digital technology and the internet have been a double-edged sword. Recording and publicising music has never been easier; however, everyone is fighting to get themselves heard in a vast sea of good, bad or indifferent music, and without anyone to curate or filter for us, we are at the mercy of the algorithms and the sales-driven motives of their programmers. This could all leave you wondering just how any equivalents of Crimson would fare starting out today, though the darkness perhaps only serves to emphasise the light.

There's no doubt that most who have passed through Crimson have been happy about their career choice as a whole. Only Fripp's feelings on this have been in doubt, especially in the years before the final era of Crimson, when he was bogged down in legal battles and struggling to make the finances work. All things considered, surely even *he* is glad that he chose his brand of professional musicianship over a lifetime of showing people round three-bed semi-detached houses with potential in East Dorset. It's been a tortuous road at times, and Fripp has been a man of many contradictions, frequently displaying an unfathomable level of creative genius, while also being frustrating to fans and other musicians alike. There was always a queue of people wanting to work with him, but a lot of those who did found it a trying experience. Bruford, at one point, summed up Fripp as being 'one part Joseph Stalin, one part Mahatma Gandhi, one part Marquis De Sade', though adding that all of that was mixed with a 'wicked sense of humour!' There is a danger in discussing the history of Crimson in general, and Fripp in particular, in overly negative terms. The picture is far more nuanced than simply characterising Fripp as always being the baddie, when others were happy to join him, only to then try and drag his band in directions he did not want to go in. That said, whether the mostly glorious ends always justified the often-uncomfortable means is open to debate. When Fripp does finally vanish into the sunset, it's safe to say that, while the world may have been deprived of a legendary estate agent, he will be leaving it a far better place than he found it, for having instead chosen to follow that more powerful desire, with all that sprang from that choice. There has been no other band like King Crimson and its myriad members, and there will never again be a guitarist—or indeed a person—quite like Robert Fripp. [2]

# Discography

## KING CRIMSON & ROBERT FRIPP ALBUMS

*(The 13 King Crimson studio albums are highlighted)*

**The Cheerful Insanity of Giles, Giles & Fripp**—Giles, Giles & Fripp (1968)

**In The Court of the Crimson King**—King Crimson (1969)

**In The Wake of Poseidon**—King Crimson (1970)

**Lizard**—King Crimson (1970)

**Islands**—King Crimson (1971)

**Earthbound** (live)—King Crimson (1972)

**No Pussyfooting**—Robert Fripp & Brian Eno (1973)

**Larks' Tongues in Aspic**—King Crimson (1973)

**Starless & Bible Black**—King Crimson (1974)

**Red**—King Crimson (1974)

**USA** (live)—King Crimson (1975)

**Evening Star**—Robert Fripp & Brian Eno (1975)

**Exposure**—Robert Fripp (1979)

**God Save the Queen / Under Heavy Manners**—Robert Fripp (1980)

**Let the Power Fall**—Robert Fripp (1981)

**The League of Gentlemen**—The League of Gentlemen (1981)

**Discipline**—King Crimson (1981)

**I Advance Masked**—Robert Fripp & Andy Summers (1982)

**Beat**—King Crimson (1982)

**Three of a Perfect Pair**—King Crimson (1984)

**Bewitched**—Robert Fripp & Andy Summers (1984)

**Live!**—Robert Fripp & the League of Crafty Guitarists (1986)

**The Lady or the Tiger**—Toyah & Fripp (1986)

**Get Crafty**—Robert Fripp & the League of Crafty Guitarists (1988) *(cassette only)*

**Kneeling at the Shrine**—Sunday All Over the World (1991) (incl. Fripp)

**Show of Hands**—Robert Fripp & the League of Crafty Guitarists (1991)

**The First Day**—David Sylvian & Robert Fripp (1993)

**The Bridge Between**—Robert Fripp String Quintet (1993)

**FFWD>>**—FFWD>> (1994) (incl. Fripp)

**Damage** (live)—David Sylvian & Robert Fripp (1994)

**1999** (Soundscapes)—Robert Fripp (1994)

**Thrak**—King Crimson (1995)

**B'BOOM** (live)—King Crimson (1995)

**A Blessing of Tears** (Soundscapes)—Robert Fripp (1995)

**Intergalactic Boogie Express** (live)—Robert Fripp & the League of Crafty Guitarists (1995)

**Radiophonics** (Soundscapes)—Robert Fripp (1996)

**THRaKaTTaK**(live)—King Crimson (1996)

**That Which Passes** (Soundscapes)—Robert Fripp (1996)

**The Gates of Paradise** (Soundscapes)—Robert Fripp (1997)

**November Suite** (Soundscapes)—Robert Fripp (1997)

**Space Groove**—ProjeKct Two (1998) (Fripp, Belew & Gunn)

**Live in Mexico City**—King Crimson (1999)

**On Broadway** (live)—King Crimson (1999)

**The Repercussions of Angelic Behavior**—Rieflin Fripp Gunn (1999)

**The ConstruKction of Light**—King Crimson (2000)

**Heaven & Earth**—ProjeKct X (2000) (Fripp, Belew, Gunn & Mastelotto)

**A Temple in the Clouds** (Soundscapes)—Jeffrey Fayman & Robert Fripp (2000)

**Robert Fripp Unplugged: Intimate Conversations with Robert**—(spoken word)—Robert Fripp (2000)

**Heavy ConstruKction** (live)—King Crimson (2000)

**The Power to Believe**—King Crimson (2003)

**Elektrik: Live in Japan**—King Crimson (2003)

**The Equatorial Stars**—Robert Fripp & Brian Eno (2004)

**East Coast Live**—ProjeKct Six (2006) (Fripp & Belew)

**At the End of Time** (Soundscapes)—Robert Fripp (2007)

**Beyond Even (1992-2006)**—Robert Fripp & Brian Eno (2007)

**Love Cannot Bear** (Soundscapes)—Robert Fripp (2007)

**Thread**—Travis & Fripp (2008)

**San Juan Capistrano 12 May 2006** (live)—Slow Music Project (2009) (incl. Fripp)

**From Good To Great, Beginner To Mastery** (spoken word)—Robert Fripp with Patricia Fripp (2008)

**Live at Coventry Cathedral**—Travis & Fripp (2010)

**A Scarcity of Miracles**—Jakszyk, Fripp & Collins with Levin & Harrison (2011)

**The Wine of Silence**—Fripp, Keeling & Singleton (2012)

**Discretion** (live)—Travis & Fripp (2012) (limited edition)

**Follow**—Travis & Fripp (2012)

**Live at the Orpheum**—King Crimson (2015)

**Starless Starlight**—David Cross & Robert Fripp (2015)

**Live in Toronto: 20 November 2015**—King Crimson (2016)

**Radical Action (To Unseat the Hold of Monkey Mind)** (live)—King Crimson (2016)

**Live in Chicago: June 28th 2017**—King Crimson (2017)

**Between the Silence** (live)—Travis & Fripp (2018)

**Live in Vienna: 1 December 2016**—King Crimson (2018)

**Meltdown: Live in Mexico City July 2017**—King Crimson (2018)

**Leviathan**—The Grid & Robert Fripp (2021)

## COMPILATION & ARCHIVE ALBUMS (IN RELEASE ORDER)

**The Young Person's Guide to King Crimson**—King Crimson (1976)

**God Save the King** (remixes from Under Heavy Manners & LoG)—Robert Fripp / The League of Gentlemen (1985)

**The Great Deceiver** (live from 1973/74 tours—4 CDs)—King Crimson (1992)

**The Essential Fripp & Eno** (incl. previously unreleased material)—Robert Fripp & Brian Eno (1994)

**Thrang Thrang Gozinbulx** (live from 1980 tour)—The League of Gentlemen (1996)

**Epitaph Vols. 1 & 2** (1969 Live in USA + BBC radio sessions)—King Crimson (1996)

**Epitaph Vols. 3 & 4** (1969 Live in England)—King Crimson (1996)

**The Night Watch** (live in Amsterdam 23/11/73)—King Crimson (1997)

**Absent Lovers** (live in 1984)—King Crimson (1998)

**Cirkus—A Young Person's Guide to King Crimson Live** (1969 to 1998)—King Crimson (1999)

**The Deception of the Thrush**—A Beginners Guide to the ProjeKcts—King Crimson (1999)

**The ProjeKcts** (live CDs of ProjeKcts 1-4)—King Crimson (1999)

**The Brondesbury Tapes** (1968 home demos)—Giles, Giles & Fripp (2001)

**Vrooom Vrooom** (live from NYC 1995 & Mexico 1996 tours)—King Crimson (2001)

**Ladies of the Road** (live—1971/72 line-up)—King Crimson (2002)

**Live in Hyde Park, London 1969** (supporting The Rolling Stones, July 1969)—King Crimson (2002)

**Live at the Budokan 1983**—Asia (with Lake) (2002)

**Exposure** (remastered 1979 album plus previously unreleased original version)—Robert Fripp (2006)

**Rock Goes to College** (live at Oxford Polytechnic 1979)—Bruford (2007)

**The Collectable King Crimson Vol. 2** (Discipline live at Moles Club 1981 / Philadelphia 1982)—King Crimson (2007)

**The Giles Brothers 1962-67**—The Dowlands / Trendsetters / The Brain (2010)

**The Road to Red** (Box set 24 discs of 1974 live and studio material)—King Crimson (2013)

**Live in Paris 28 May 1975**—Fripp & Eno (2014)

**Starless** (Box Set 27 discs of 1973-74 live and studio material)—King Crimson (2014)

**Sailor's Tales** (Box set of 1970–1972 material)—King Crimson (2017)

**Heaven & Earth** (Box set of 1997—2008 live & studio material)—King Crimson (2019)

**The ReconstruKction of Light** (TCOL with new drum parts, plus original album/bonus material)—King Crimson (2019)

## KING CRIMSON & ROBERT FRIPP SINGLES / EPS

**One in a Million / Newly Weds**—Giles, Giles & Fripp (1968)

**Thursday Morning / Elephant Song**—Giles, Giles & Fripp (1968)

**The Court of the Crimson King (parts 1 & 2)**—King Crimson (1969)

**Cat Food / Groon**—King Crimson (1970)

**Easy Money / Exiles / Larks' Tongues in Aspic (part 2)**—King Crimson (1973) (US only)

**The Night Watch / The Great Deceiver**—King Crimson (1974)

**Epitaph / 21st Century Schizoid Man**—King Crimson (1976)

**North Star**—Robert Fripp (1979)

**Heptaparaparshinokh / Marriagemuzik**—The League of Gentlemen / Robert Fripp (1981)

**Dislocated / 1984**—The League of Gentlemen / Robert Fripp (1981)

**Elephant Talk / Matte Kudasai**—King Crimson (1981)

**Heartbeat / Requiem**—King Crimson (1982)

**I Advance Masked / Hardy Country**—Robert Fripp & Andy Summers (1982)

**Three of a Perfect Pair / Man with an Open Heart**—King Crimson (1984)

**Sleepless / Nuages**—King Crimson (1984)

**Parade / Train**—Robert Fripp & Andy Summers (1984)

**Network** (North Star / God Save The King / Under Heavy Manners)—Robert Fripp (1985)

**Jean the Birdman** (2 versions of single with different additional tracks)—Robert Fripp & David Sylvian (1993)

**Darshan / Darshan remix / Darshana**—Robert Fripp & David Sylvian (1993)

**Vrooom /Sex Sleep Eat Drink Dream / Cage**—King Crimson (1994)

**People**—King Crimson (1995) (promo only)

**Dinosaur / Walking on Air**—King Crimson (1995)

**Schizoid Man** (5 versions)—King Crimson (1997)

**Pie Jesu / A Blessing of Tears** (Soundscapes)—Robert Fripp (1998)

**Happy With What You Have To Be Happy With / Bude / Shoganai / Eyes Wide Open**—King Crimson (2002)

**Level Five / Dangerous Curves / Virtuous Circle** (limited edition)—King Crimson (2003)

**Heroes / Easy Money / Starless / Hell Hounds of Crim** (Live in Europe 2016)—King Crimson (2017)

**Uncertain Times** (Red/The Letter/Cirkus/Lark Tongues Pt2) (live) (10inch vinyl only)—King Crimson (2017)

## OTHER CRIMS SOLO ALBUMS, OTHER BANDS & COLLABORATIONS (AFTER JOINING CRIMSON)

**McDonald & Giles**—McDonald & Giles (1970) (incl. McDonald, Michael & Peter Giles)

**Emerson, Lake & Palmer**—Emerson, Lake & Palmer (1970)

**Septober Energy**—Centipede (1971) (incl. Tippett, McDonald, Charig, Evans, Robin Miller, Burrell, produced by Fripp)

**Tarkus**—Emerson, Lake & Palmer (1971)

**It Is and It Isn't**—Gordon Haskell (1971) (with Wetton)

**Pictures at an Exhibition** (live)—Emerson, Lake & Palmer (1971)

**Trilogy**—Emerson, Lake & Palmer (1972)

**Greenslade**—Greenslade (1973) (incl. McCulloch)

**Still**—Peter Sinfield (1973) (with Wallace, Wetton, Collins, Lake & Burrell)

**Brain Salad Surgery**—Emerson, Lake & Palmer (1973) (lyrics: Sinfield)

**Bedside Manners Are Extra**—Greenslade (1973) (incl. McCulloch)

**Accidentally Born in New Orleans**—Snape (1973) (incl. Burrell, Collins & Wallace)

**Bad Company**—Bad Company (1974) (incl. Burrell)

**Welcome Back My Friends . . .** (live)—Emerson, Lake & Palmer (1974)

**Spyglass Ghost**—Greenslade (1974) (incl. McCulloch)

**On Tour in Germany** (live)—Snape (1974) (incl. Burrell, Collins & Wallace)

**Return to Fantasy**—Uriah Heep (1975) (incl. Wetton)

**Straight Shooter**—Bad Company (1975) (incl. Burrell)

**Time & Tide**—Greenslade (1975) (incl. McCulloch)

**Viva** (live)—Roxy Music (1976) (incl. Wetton)

**Run with the Pack**—Bad Company (1976) (incl. Burrell)

**High & Mighty**—Uriah Heep (1976) (incl. Wetton)

**Burnin' Sky**—Bad Company (1976) (incl. Burrell)

**Raindances**—Camel (1977) (incl. Collins)

**Works (Vol. 1)**—Emerson, Lake & Palmer (1977) (lyrics Sinfield)

**Foreigner**—Foreigner (1977) (incl. McDonald)

**Feels Good to Me**—Bruford (1977)

**Works (Vol. 2)**—Emerson, Lake & Palmer (1977) (lyrics Sinfield)

**UK**—UK (1978) (incl. Wetton & Bruford)

**Double Vision**—Foreigner (1978) (incl. McDonald)

**Love Beach**—Emerson, Lake & Palmer (1978) (lyrics Sinfield)

**A Live Record**—Camel (1978) (incl. Collins)

**Breathless**—Camel (1978) (incl. Collins)

**In a Land of Clear Colours**—Peter Sinfield, Robert Sheckley & Brian Eno (1978)

**Danger Money**—UK (1979) (incl. Wetton)

**One of a Kind**—Bruford (1979)

**Serve at Room Temperature**—Gordon Haskell (1979)

**The Bruford Tapes** (live)—Bruford (1979)

**Head Games**—Foreigner (1979) (incl. McDonald)

**Night After Night** (live)—UK (1979) (incl. Wetton)

**Serve at Room Temperature**—Gordon Haskell (1979)

**In Concert**—Emerson, Lake & Palmer (1979)

**Gradually Going Tornado**—Bruford (1980)

**Caught in the Crossfire**—John Wetton (1980)

**Greg Lake**—Greg Lake (1981)

**Nude**—Camel (1981) (incl. Collins)

**Asia**—Asia (1982) (incl. Wetton)

**Lone Rhino**—Adrian Belew (1982)

**Alpha**—Asia (1983) (incl. Wetton)

**Manoeuvres**—Greg Lake (1983)

**Twang Bar King**—Adrian Belew (1983)

**Music For Piano & Drums**—Moraz Bruford (1983)

**Astra**—Asia (1985) (incl. Wetton)

**Emerson, Lake & Powell**—Emerson, Lake & Powell (1985)

**Flags**—Moraz Bruford (1985)

**Desire Caught by the Tail**—Adrian Belew (1986)

**Low Flying Aircraft**—Low Flying Aircraft (1987) (incl. Cross & Tippett)

**Earthworks**—Bill Bruford's Earthworks (1987)

**The Bears**—The Bears (1987) (incl. Belew)

**Wetton Manzanera**—Wetton Manzanera (1987)

**Arc Measuring**—Radius (1988) (incl. Cross)

**Rise & Shine**—The Bears (1988) (incl. Belew)

**Anderson Bruford Wakeman Howe**—Anderson Bruford Wakeman Howe (1989) (with Levin)

**Dig?**—Bill Bruford's Earthworks (1989)

**Sightseeing**—Radius (1989) (incl. Cross)

**Memos from Purgatory**—David Cross (1989)

**Mr Music Head**—Adrian Belew (1989)

**Hambledon Hill**—Gordon Haskell (1990)

**Young Lions**—Adrian Belew (1990)

**66 Shades of Lipstick**—Keith Tippett & Andy Sheppard (1990) (produced by Fripp)

**Union**—Yes (1991) (incl. Bruford)

**All Heaven Broke Loose**—Bill Bruford's Earthworks (1991)

**It's Just a Plot to Drive You Crazy**—Gordon Haskell (1992)

**Black Moon**—Emerson, Lake & Palmer (1992)

**The Big Picture**—David Cross (1992)

**Live at the Royal Albert Hall**—Emerson, Lake & Palmer (1993)

**Inner Revolution**—Adrian Belew (1993)

**Stamping Ground** (live)—Bill Bruford's Earthworks (1994)

**In the Hot Seat**—Emerson, Lake & Palmer (1994)

**Here**—Adrian Belew (1994)

**Testing to Destruction**—David Cross (1994)

**Battlelines**—John Wetton (1995) (with Fripp)

**Ghost Dance** (film soundtrack from 1983)—Michael Giles, Jamie Muir & David Cunningham (1995)

**The Acoustic Adrian Belew**—Adrian Belew (1995)

**Butterfly in China**—Gordon Haskell (1996)

**World Diary**—Tony Levin (1996) (with Bruford)

**The Third Star**—Trey Gunn (1996) (with Mastelotto)

**Oop Zop Too Wah**—Adrian Belew (1996)

**The Guitar as Orchestra**—Adrian Belew (1996)

**Monkey Business**—John Wetton & Richard Palmer-James (1997)

**Exiles**—David Cross (1997) (with Wetton & Fripp, lyrics Palmer-James & Sinfield)

**If Summer Had Its Ghosts**—Bill Bruford with Ralph Towner & Eddie Gomez (1997)

**The Caves of the Iron Mountain**—Steve Gorn, Tony Levin, Jerry Marotta (1998)

**Belew Prints: The Acoustic Adrian Belew II**—Adrian Belew (1998)

**Liquid Tension Experiment**—Liquid Tension Experiment (1998) (incl. Levin)

**Arkangel**—John Wetton (1998) (with Fripp)

**Upper Extremities**—Bruford Levin Upper Extremities (1998)

**Drivers Eyes**—Ian McDonald (1999) (with Wetton, Michael Giles & Sinfield)

**Raw Power**—Trey Gunn (1999)

**A Part and Yet Apart**—Bill Bruford's Earthworks (1999)

**Birth of a Giant**—Bill Rieflin (1999) (with Fripp & Gunn)

**Liquid Tension Experiment 2**—Liquid Tension Experiment (1999) (incl. Levin)

**All in The Scheme of Things**—Gordon Haskell (2000)

**Blue Night** (live)—Bruford Levin Upper Extremities (2000)

**The Joy of Molybdenum**—Trey Gunn (2000)

**Civilisation**—Radius (2000) (incl. Cross)

**Look Out**—Gordon Haskell (2001)

**The Sound of Surprise**—Bill Bruford's Earthworks (2001)

**Live Encounter**—Trey Gunn (2001)

**Car Caught Fire**—The Bears (2002) (incl. Belew)

**Harry's Bar**—Gordon Haskell (2002)

**Official Bootleg Vol. 1**—21st Century Schizoid Band (2002) (incl. McDonald, Collins, Michael & Peter Giles)

**Footloose & Fancy Free** (live)—Bill Bruford's Earthworks (2002)

**Live in Japan**—21st Century Schizoid Band (2002) (incl. McDonald, Collins, Michael & Peter Giles)

**Thunderbird Suite**—TU (Gunn & Mastelotto) (2002)

**Progress** (recorded 1978)—Michael Giles (2002)

**Wetton Downes**—Wetton Downes (2002)

**Shadows on the Wall**—Gordon Haskell (2002)

**Happiness with Minimal Side Effects**—Ian Wallace (2003) (with McDonald)

**TU**—TU (Gunn & Mastelotto) (2003)

**Random Acts of Happiness** (live)—Bill Bruford's Earthworks (2004)

**The Lady Wants to Know**—Gordon Haskell (2004)

**Official Bootleg** (live)—TU (Gunn & Mastelotto) (2004)

**The King Crimson Songbook (Vol. 1)**—The Crimson Jazz Trio (2005) (incl. Wallace)

**Volume One**—Fission Trip (2005) (incl. Wallace, Collins & Belew)

**Side One**—Adrian Belew (2005) (with Wallace)

**Closer Than Skin**—David Cross (2005) (lyrics Palmer-James)

**Icon I**—Wetton Downes (2005)

**Pictures of a City (live)**—21st Century Schizoid Band (2006) (with McDonald, Collins, Peter Giles & Wallace)

**Earthworks Underground Orchestra**—Earthworks Underground Orchestra (2006) (incl. Bruford)

**Unbounded**—David Cross & Naomi Maki (2006)

**Icon II**-Wetton Downes (2006)

**Greg Lake Live**—Greg Lake (2007)

**Stick Man**—Tony Levin (2007) (with Mastelotto)

**Eureka**—The Bears (2007) (incl. Belew)

**In Two Minds**—Bruford Borstlap (2008)

**Alive in the Underworld** (live)—David Cross Band (2008)

**Phoenix**—Asia (2008) (incl. Wetton)

**Music for Pictures**—Trey Gunn (2008)

**Live in Barcelona**—Asia (2008) (incl. Wetton)

**Icon III**—Wetton Downes (2009)

**The King Crimson Songbook (Vol. 2)**—Crimson Jazz Trio (2009) (incl. Wallace, with Collins)

**e**—Adrian Belew (2009)

**English Sun**—David Cross & Andrew Keeling (2009)

**The Adventures of the Michael Giles Madband** (2009)

**Omega**—Asia (2010) (incl. Wetton)

**Soup**—The Stick Men (2010) (incl. Levin & Mastelotto)

**One Day Soon**—Gordon Haskell (2010)

**Modulator**—Trey Gunn (2010)

**Live at High Voltage**—Emerson, Lake & Palmer (2010)

**Raised in Captivity**—John Wetton (2011)

**In the Moment**—The Michael Giles Madband (2011) (with Tippett)

**Absalom**—The Stick Men (2011) (incl. Levin & Mastelotto)

**Live in Russia**—TU (Trey Gunn & Pat Mastelotto) (2011)

**Live in Tokyo**—The Crimson ProjeKct (2012) (incl. Belew, Levin & Mastelotto)

**XXX**—Asia (2012) (incl. Wetton)

**Open**—The Stick Men (2012) (incl. Levin & Mastelotto)

**Songs of a Lifetime** (live)—Greg Lake (2013)

**Deep**—The Stick Men (2013) (incl. Levin & Mastelotto)

**Gravitas**—Asia (2014) (incl. Wetton)

**Live from Manticore Hall**—Keith Emerson & Greg Lake (2014)

**Power Play** (live)—The Stick Men (2014) (incl. Levin & Mastelotto)

**The Waters, They Are Rising**—Trey Gunn (2015)

**To Be Kind**—Swans (2014) (incl. Rieflin)

**Midori** (live)—The Stick Men & David Cross (2016) (incl. Levin & Mastelotto)

**Takeaway**—Richard Palmer-James (2016)

**Sign of the Crow**—David Cross Band (2016)

**Prog Noir**—The Stick Men (2016) (incl. Levin & Mastelotto)

**The Glowing Man**—Swans (2016) (incl. Rieflin)

**Bad Old World**—Honey West (2017) (incl. McDonald)

**Live in Piacenza**—Greg Lake (2017)

**Gizmodrome**—Gizmodrome (incl. Belew) (2017)

**Roprongi**—The Stick Men (2017) (incl. Levin & Mastelotto, with Collins)

**Another Day**—David Cross & David Jackson (2018)

**Crossing the Tracks**—David Cross (2018)

**Pop Sided**—Adrian Belew (2019)

**Panamerica** (live in Latin America)—The Stick Men & David Cross (2019)

**The Cat Who Got the Cream**—Gordon Haskell (2020)

**Crossover**—David Cross & Pete Banks (2020) (with Mastelotto & Stacey)

**Secrets and Lies**—Jakko M Jakszyk (2020) (with Fripp, Collins, Harrison & Levin)

**A Romantic's Guide to King Crimson**—The Mastelottos (2021) (incl. Mastelotto)

**Liquid Tension Experiment 3**—Liquid Tension Experiment (2021) (incl. Levin)

**Insight**—Peter Giles & Yasmine Giles (2021)

**Elevator**—Adrian Belew (2021)

## ALBUMS BY OTHER ARTISTS WITH SIGNIFICANT FRIPP/ KC CONNECTIONS

**H to He**—Van Der Graaf Generator (1970) (with Fripp)

**Fool's Mate**—Peter Hammill (1971) (with Fripp)

**Little Red Record**—Matching Mole (1972) (produced by Fripp)

**Blueprint**—Keith Tippett (1972) (produced by Fripp)

**Photos of Ghosts**—Premiata Forneria Marconi (1973) (lyrics: Sinfield)

**Ovary Lodge**—Keith Tippett (1973) (produced by Fripp)

**Here Come the Warmjets**—Brian Eno (1974) (with Fripp & Wetton)

**Another Time, Another Place**—Bryan Ferry (1974) (with Wetton)

**Another Green World**—Brian Eno (1975) (with Fripp)

**Let's Stick Together**—Bryan Ferry (1976) (with Wetton & Collins)

**Peter Gabriel (I)**—Peter Gabriel (1977) (with Fripp & Levin)

**Heroes**—David Bowie (1977) (with Fripp)

**In Your Mind**—Bryan Ferry (1977) (with Wetton & Collins)

**Peter Gabriel (II)**—Peter Gabriel (1978) (with Fripp & Levin / Produced by Fripp)

**Street Legal**—Bob Dylan (1978) (with Wallace)

**The Roches**—The Roches (1979) (with Fripp / produced by Fripp)

**At the Budokan** (live)—Bob Dylan (1979) (with Wallace)

**Scary Monsters**—David Bowie (1980) (with Fripp)

**Sacred Songs**—Daryl Hall (1980) (with Fripp / produced by Fripp)

**Peter Gabriel (III)**—Peter Gabriel (1980) (with Fripp & Levin)

**Are You Ready**—Bucks Fizz (1982) (lyrics by Sinfield)

**Keep on Doing**—The Roches (1982) (with Fripp / produced by Fripp)

**Alchemy** (live)—Dire Straits (1984) (with Collins)

**Peter Gabriel (IV)**—Peter Gabriel (1984) (with Levin)

**Gone to Earth**—David Sylvian (1986) (with Fripp & Collins)

**A Momentary Lapse of Reason**—Pink Floyd (1987) (with Levin)

**Journey to Inaccessible Places & Other Music** (Gurdjieff/De Hartmann)—Elan Sicroff (1987) (produced by Fripp)

**Ophelia's Shadow**—Toyah (1991) (with Fripp & Haskell)

**Nerve Net**—Brian Eno (1992) (with Fripp)

**Sidi Mansour**—Rimitti (1994) (with Fripp)

**Live in Concert** (1980)—The Stranglers & Friends (1995) (with Fripp & Toyah)

**Ten Seconds**—Ten Seconds (1996) (with Fripp)

**Genesis Revisited**—Steve Hackett (1996) (with McDonald, Wetton, Levin & Bruford)

**The Tokyo Tapes** (live)—Steve Hackett (1998) (with McDonald & Wetton)

**Approaching Silence**—David Sylvian (1999) (with Fripp)

**Trance Spirits**—Steve Roach & Jeffrey Fayman (2002) (with Fripp)

**Talking with Strangers**—Judy Dyble (2009) (with McDonald, Fripp & Mastelotto)

**We Are the Humans**—The Humans (2010) (with Fripp)

**Strange Tales**—The Humans (2014) (incl. Rieflin)

## DISCOGRAPHY NOTES:

While I've aimed to be reasonably comprehensive, for the sake of clarity and sanity, in places I have had to be selective, as to include too much would risk losing the important original releases and particular gems or curiosities in a fog of less significant albums. Except for GGF and a couple of others, I have not included Crimson members' albums from before they joined Crimson. In addition, as some Crims have been especially prolific or played on countless sessions, it would be impossible to attempt to catalogue them here. Since the 1990s digital technology has allowed a great deal of archive material to be cleaned up and put out in various forms. Some of this has only been for very limited releases, such as through DGM's Collectors Club or for digital download only. The result is that it has become hard to define what actually constitutes a 'release' in any meaningful sense. For the archive material I've therefore only listed those that are good examples of a particular period or line-up. I've also excluded re-issues, anniversary editions and compilations, unless there was significant new material included. I probably haven't been 100 percent consistent but c'est la vie.

## AUTHOR'S TOP TENS

### King Crimson tracks

Fracture

Lizard

Starless

Sartori in Tangier

The Court of the Crimson King

B'boom (live 1994)

The Sailor's Tale (live 2014)

Red

The Night Watch

Walking on Air

### Fripp solo or collaboration tracks

20th Century Dreaming—David Sylvian & Robert Fripp

Sometimes God Hides—Robert Fripp

Breathless—Robert Fripp

I Advance Masked—Fripp & Summers

The Stars Below—Fayman & Fripp

Invocation—Robert Fripp & the League of Crafty Guitarists

Exposure—Robert Fripp

Heavenly Music Corporation—Fripp & Eno

1989—Robert Fripp

North Meadow—Giles, Giles & Fripp

**Other KC members' solo or collaboration tracks**

Hawaii—Ian McDonald

Exiles—David Cross (with Wetton)

C'est La Vie—Greg Lake

Hell's Bells—Bruford

Wings in the Sunset—McDonald & Giles

Pelican Pie—Gordon Haskell

Pretty Pink Rose—Adrian Belew/David Bowie

In the Dead of Night—UK (incl. Wetton & Bruford)

One of These Days I'll Get an Early Night—Camel (incl. Collins)

A Part & Yet Apart—Bill Bruford's Earthworks

**Appearances on other artists' tracks**

Baby's on Fire—Brian Eno (Fripp—guitar / Wetton—bass)

St. Elmo's Fire—Brian Eno (Fripp—guitar)

The Great Curve—Talking Heads (Belew—guitar)

Heroes—David Bowie (Fripp—guitar)

Kingdom Come—David Bowie (Fripp—guitar)

I Don't Remember—Peter Gabriel (Fripp—guitar / Levin—Stick)

Listen Now—Phil Manzanera (Mel Collins—saxes)

The Last Three Minutes II—Ten Seconds (Fripp—guitar / soundscape)

Firth of Fifth (live) Steve Hackett (Wetton—vocals & bass / McDonald—flute)

Nightmare—Anthony Phillips (Michael Giles—drums)

# King Crimson Personnel Chart

The following thirty-three people have been members of King Crimson or have appeared on King Crimson albums as guests or as part of the live band. The distinction between those considered as members and those considered as guests is not always helpful, as some guests were with the band longer, and appeared on more albums than some members. Also, some guests became members, while some members became guests. David Cross had left the band by *Red* but is present through being on a track recorded live when he was still in the band. Eddie Jobson, though never in the band, did studio overdubs for what was the otherwise live album, *USA*. Peter Sinfield, as a non-playing lyricist also involved in production, was considered part of the band, while later lyricist, Richard Palmer-James, wasn't. As well as the thirteen studio albums, I've included five key live albums here. This is in order to give a more balanced picture, especially with several members only joining after the last studio album was released.

Key:

✓ = band member
G = guest
L = lyricist
(L) = lyricist for tracks on live album

| | *Court of CK* | *Wake of Poseidon* | *Lizard* | *Islands* | *Earthbound* | *Larks' Tongues* | *Starless & BB* | *Red* | *USA* | *Discipline* | *Beat* | *3 of a Perfect Pair* | *Thrak* | *B'boom* | *Constr. of Light* | *Power to Believe* | *Radical Action* | *Meltdown/Mexico* |
|---|---|---|---|---|---|---|---|---|---|---|---|---|---|---|---|---|---|---|
| **Robert Fripp**<br>Guitar / keyboards | ✓ | ✓ | ✓ | ✓ | ✓ | ✓ | ✓ | ✓ | ✓ | ✓ | ✓ | ✓ | ✓ | ✓ | ✓ | ✓ | ✓ | ✓ |
| **Ian McDonald**<br>Keyboards /flute/ saxes/ backing vocals | ✓ | | | | | | | G | | | | | | | | | | |
| **Greg Lake**<br>Vocals / bass | ✓ | G | | | | | | | | | | | | | | | | |
| **Michael Giles**<br>Drums / percussion / backing vocals | ✓ | G | | | | | | | | | | | | | | | | |
| **Peter Sinfield**<br>Words / VCS3 synthesiser | **L** | **L** | ✓ | ✓ | **(L)** | | | | **(L)** | | | | | | | | **(L)** | **(L)** |
| **Mel Collins**<br>Saxes / flute | | G | ✓ | ✓ | ✓ | | | G | | | | | | | | | ✓ | ✓ |
| **Gordon Haskell**<br>Vocals / bass | | G | ✓ | | | | | | | | | | | | | | | |
| **Peter Giles**<br>Bass | | G | | | | | | | | | | | | | | | | |
| **Andy McCulloch**<br>Drums / percussion | | | ✓ | | | | | | | | | | | | | | | |
| **Keith Tippett**<br>Piano / electric piano | | G | G | G | | | | | | | | | | | | | | |
| **Mark Charig**<br>Cornet | | | G | G | | | | G | | | | | | | | | | |
| **Nick Evans**<br>Trombone | | | G | | | | | | | | | | | | | | | |
| **Robin Miller**<br>Oboe / CorAnglais | | | G | G | | | | G | | | | | | | | | | |
| **Jon Anderson**<br>vocals | | | G | | | | | | | | | | | | | | | |
| **Boz Burrell**<br>Vocals / bass | | | | ✓ | ✓ | | | | | | | | | | | | | |
| **Ian Wallace**<br>Drums / percussion | | | | ✓ | ✓ | | | | | | | | | | | | | |
| **Pauline Lucas**<br>Soprano vocal | | | | G | | | | | | | | | | | | | | |

| | Court of CK | Wake of Poseidon | Lizard | Islands | Earthbound | Larks' Tongues | Starless & BB | Red | USA | Discipline | Beat | 3 of a Perfect Pair | Thrak | B'boom | Constr. of Light | Power to Believe | Radical Action | Meltdown/Mexico |
|---|---|---|---|---|---|---|---|---|---|---|---|---|---|---|---|---|---|---|
| **Harry Miller**<br>Acoustic bass | | | | **G** | | | | | | | | | | | | | | |
| **Bill Bruford**<br>Drums / percussion | | | | | | ✓ | ✓ | ✓ | ✓ | ✓ | ✓ | ✓ | ✓ | ✓ | | | | |
| **John Wetton**<br>Vocals / bass | | | | | | ✓ | ✓ | ✓ | ✓ | | | | | | | | | |
| **Jamie Muir**<br>Percussion / allsorts | | | | | | ✓ | | | | | | | | | | | | |
| **David Cross**<br>Violin / viola / keyboards / flute | | | | | | ✓ | ✓ | ✓/ **G** | ✓ | | | | | | | | | |
| **Richard Palmer-James**<br>words | | | | | | **L** | **L** | **L** | **(L)** | | | | | | | | **(L)** | **(L)** |
| **Eddie Jobson**<br>Violin / electric piano | | | | | | | | | **G** | | | | | | | | | |
| **Adrian Belew**<br>Guitar / vocals / percussion | | | | | | | | | | ✓ | ✓ | ✓ | ✓ | ✓ | ✓ | ✓ | | **(L)** |
| **Tony Levin**<br>Bass / stick / backing vocals | | | | | | | | | | ✓ | ✓ | ✓ | ✓ | ✓ | | | ✓ | ✓ |
| **Trey Gunn**<br>Bass / stick / Warr guitar | | | | | | | | | | | | | ✓ | ✓ | ✓ | ✓ | | |
| **Pat Mastelotto**<br>Drums / percussion | | | | | | | | | | | | | ✓ | ✓ | ✓ | ✓ | ✓ | ✓ |
| **Gavin Harrison**<br>Drums / percussion | | | | | | | | | | | | | | | | | ✓ | ✓ |
| **Bill Rieflin**<br>Drums / percussion / keyboards | | | | | | | | | | | | | | | | | ✓ | ✓ |
| **Jakko Jakszyk**<br>Vocals/guitar | | | | | | | | | | | | | | | | | ✓ | ✓ |
| **Jeremy Stacey**<br>Drums / percussion / keyboards | | | | | | | | | | | | | | | | | | ✓ |
| **Chris Gibson**<br>keyboards *(temp 2017)* | | | | | | | | | | | | | | | | | | |

## KING CRIMSONS I TO VII

| | | |
|---|---|---|
| I | 1969 | Fripp, Lake, McDonald, M. Giles, Sinfield |
| Ia | 1970 | Fripp, Sinfield, Lake(G), M. Giles(G), P Giles(G), Tippett(G), Collins(G), Haskell(G) |
| Ib | 1970 | Fripp, Sinfield, Collins, Haskell, McCulloch, Tippett(G), Charig(G), Evans(G), R. Miller(G), Anderson (G) |
| II | 1971 | Fripp, Sinfield, Collins, Burrell, Wallace, Tippett(G), Charig(G), Evans(G), H. Miller(G), Lucas (G) |
| IIa | 1972 | Fripp, Collins, Burrell, Wallace |
| III | 1972–73 | Fripp, Wetton, Bruford, Cross, Muir |
| IIIa | 1974 | Fripp, Wetton, Bruford, Cross |
| IIIb | 1974 | Fripp, Wetton, Bruford, Cross(G), McDonald(G), Collins(G), Charig(G), R. Miller (G) |
| IV | 1981–84 | Fripp, Belew, Bruford, Levin |
| V incl. ProjeKcts | 1994–99 | Fripp, Belew, Bruford, Levin, Gunn, Mastelotto |
| IV | 2000–03 | Fripp, Belew, Gunn, Mastelotto |
| IVa | 2007–08 | Fripp, Belew, Levin, Mastelotto, Harrison |
| VII | 2013–16 | Fripp, Jakszyk, Collins, Levin, Mastelotto, Harrison, Rieflin *(temp: Stacey in for Rieflin 2016)* |
| VIIa | 2017–19 | Fripp, Jakszyk, Collins, Levin, Mastelotto, Harrison, Rieflin, Stacey *(temp: Gibson in for Rieflin Oct/Nov 2017) (without Rieflin for 2019 tour)* |

# Sources

## QUOTE SOURCES BY CHAPTER

### Back Cover

A Special Sort of Awkward. Peter Sinfield interview with David Buckley, 17 June 2003.

### Chapter 1

1. CD sleeve notes, *A Blessing of Tears*. Robert Fripp. 1995.

2. Robert Fripp comment on Patricia Fripp's Facebook page, 2017.

3. *Lucky Man: The Autobiography*. Greg Lake. Constable, 2017.

4. Author's interview with Gordon Haskell, June 2019.

5. The Outer Limits: Al Stewart. Loudersound.com, 2 July 2014.

6. Author's email conversation with Al Kirtley, 11 January 2020.

7. *When Giants Walked the Earth: A Biography of Led Zeppelin*. Mick Wall. Orion Books, 2009.

8. Author's interview with Peter Giles, August 2019.

9. Ian McDonald comment on Ian McDonald Facebook Fan Page, 2017.

10. Peter Sinfield quote. Ladiesofthelake.com, original source unknown.

11. Author's interview with Judy Dyble, October 2019.

12. CD sleeve notes, *The Cheerful Insanity of Giles*. Giles & Fripp, 1968.

13. CD sleeve notes, *Epitaph* (Volumes 1 & 2). King Crimson. 1997.

14. *The Christchurch Herald Newspaper*, 1 December 1968.

15. *The Show That Never Ends*. David Weigel. W.W. Norton & Co., 2017.

**Chapter 2**

1. Without Friction You Don't Get Heat. Interview with Fripp, Sinfield et al. Uncut.co.uk, July 2012.

2. CD sleeve notes, *Epitaph* (Volumes 1 & 2). King Crimson. 1997.

3. *Lucky Man: The Autobiography*. Greg Lake. Constable, 2017.

4. Robert Fripp's Diary (23 & 24 April 1981). DGMlive.com.

5. *On Some Faraway Beach: The Life & Times of Brian Eno*. David Sheppard. Orion Books, 2008.

6. 40th anniversary edition CD sleeve notes by Sid Smith, *In the Court of the Crimson King*. King Crimson. 2009.

7. *The David Bowie Story*. George Tremlett. Futura Publications Ltd., 1974.

8. *The Show That Never Ends*. David Weigel. W.W. Norton & Co., 2017.

9. CD sleeve notes, *Live at Hyde Park 1969*. King Crimson. 2002.

10. Neil Armstrong. BBC TV broadcast of Apollo 11 moon landing, 1969.

11. Interview with Michael Giles by Aymeric Leroy. Elephant-Talk.com, 1997.

12. *Progressive Rock Reconsidered*. Kevin Holm-Hudson (ed). Routledge, 2002.

13. *Bill Bruford–The Autobiography: Yes, King Crimson, Earthworks & More*. Bill Bruford. Jawbone Press, 2009.

14. Interview with Ian McDonald. Big Bang Magazine, 25 August 1999.

15. Review of King Crimson concert, Fillmore East, 21 November 1969. *Billboard Magazine*, 6 December 1969.

16. Peter Sinfield interview with David Buckley. 17 June 2003.

**Chapter 3**

1. CD sleeve notes, *Epitaph* (Volumes 1 & 2). King Crimson. 1997.

2. Author's interview with Peter Giles, August 2019.

3. CD sleeve notes. *McDonald & Giles*. 2002 (re-release).

4. Robert Fripp's Diary (13 January 2000). DGMlive.com.

5. Author's interview with Gini Wade (née Barris). July 2019.

6. Robert Fripp's Diary (8 September 1999). DGMlive.com.

7. *The Road to Harry's Bar*. Gordon Haskell. Mainstream Publishing, 2006.

8. *The Thrill of It All: The Story of Bryan Ferry & Roxy Music*. David Buckley. Andre Deutsch, 2004.

9. CD sleeve notes, *Ladies of the Road*. King Crimson. 2002.

10. Article by Lester Bangs. *Rolling Stone Magazine*, 2 March 1972.

11. Unidentified music press article (16 October 1971) in CD booklet, *Islands*. King Crimson. 2009.

12. Without Friction You Don't Get Heat. Interview with Fripp, Sinfield et al. Uncut.co.uk, July 2012.

13. *Sounds*, 27 November 1971.

14. *Behind the Music Remastered: Bad Company*. VH-1, 2013.

15. Interview with Mel Collins by Chris Groom (1997). Elephant-Talk.com.

### Chapter 4

1. *Bill Bruford–The Autobiography: Yes, King Crimson, Earthworks & More.* Bill Bruford. Jawbone Press, 2009.

2. Interview with Richard Palmer-James in Calamity (March 2000). Elephant-Talk.com.

3. *Clothes, Music, Boys.* Viv Albertine. Faber & Faber, 2014.

4. *On Some Faraway Beach: The Life & Times of Brian Eno.* David Sheppard. Orion Books, 2008.

5. Article by Steve Peacock. *Sounds*, 30 December 1972.

6. Games of Thrones. Sid Smith. *Prog Magazine*, December 2012.

7. Author's interview with Bill Bruford, January 2020.

8. Article by Richard Williams. *Melody Maker*, 31 March 1973.

9. Article by Alan Neister. *Rolling Stone Magazine*, 30 August 1973.

10. Article by Chris Salewicz. *Let It Rock*, 8 September 1973.

11. Article by Ian MacDonald. *New Musical Express*, 8 September 1973.

12. Article by Ian MacDonald. *New Musical Express*, 1 August 1973.

13. The Talking Drum. Interview with Jamie Muir. *Ptolemaic Terrascope*, 1991/92.

14. Interview with Bill Bruford by Scott K. Fish. *Modern Drummer*, July 1983.

15. CD Sleeve notes, *The Night Watch*. King Crimson. 1997.

16. Stuff Happens & You Learn from It: Interview with John Wetton. Nick DeRiso. *Something Else*, 17 May 2012.

17. *Discourse on Method.* René Descartes. 1637.

18. Album sleeve, *Starless & Bible Black*. King Crimson. 1974.

19. Why I Killed the King. Interview with Robert Fripp. *Melody Maker*, 5 October 1974.

20. *Mountains Come Out of the Sky*. Will Romano. Backbeat Books, 2010.

21. Robert Fripp. Stewart Lee. *Sunday Times*, 30 November 1997.

22. Article in *Belfast Telegraph* autumn 1974 (featured on *Red* 40th anniversary edition cover).

23. The Anti-Dinosaur. Translation of interview with Robert Fripp. Jean-Gilles Blum. *Best Magazine*, January 1979.

**Chapter 5**

1. Author's interview with Ronan Chris Murphy, April 2020.

2. CD sleeve notes, *USA*. King Crimson. 1975 (vinyl).

3. CD sleeve notes, *Another Green World*. Brian Eno. 1975 (vinyl).

4. *On Some Faraway Beach: The Life & Times of Brian Eno*. David Sheppard. Orion Books, 2008.

5. Riding on the Dynamic of Disaster. Interview with Robert Fripp. Allan Jones. *Melody Maker*, 28 April 1979.

6. The Fourth Way. Wikipedia.

7. *Bill Bruford–The Autobiography: Yes, King Crimson, Earthworks & More*. Bill Bruford. Jawbone Press, 2009.

8. Author's interview with Gordon Haskell, June 2019.

9. *The Road to Harry's Bar*. Gordon Haskell. Mainstream Publishing, 2006.

10. *The Timetables of History*. Bernard Grun. Simon & Schuster, 1979.

11. Ian McDonald Talks About His Foreigner Days. YouTube, 2006 (original source unknown). https://www.youtube.com/watch?app=desktop&v=UrazLRZ27n8.

12. *Tony Visconti: The Autobiography: Bowie, Bolan & the Brooklyn Boy*. Tony Visconti. Harper Books, 2007.

13. *Heroes 40th Anniversary*. Zinc Media Productions for BBC Radio 2, 2017.

14. RCA marketing slogan, 1977.

15. The Anti-Dinosaur. Translation of interview with Robert Fripp. Jean-Gilles Blum. *Best Magazine*, January 1979.

16. CD sleeve notes, *Exposure*. Robert Fripp, 1979 (vinyl).

17. CD sleeve notes, *Breathless*. Camel, 1992 (re-issue).

18. *Robert Fripp: From Crimson King to Crafty Master*. Eric Tamm. Faber & Faber, 1990.

19. Author's interview with Bill Bruford, January 2020.

**Chapter 6**

1. *Village Voice*. John Piccarella. February 1978.

2. The Anti-Dinosaur. Translation of interview with Robert Fripp. Jean-Gilles Blum. *Best Magazine*, January 1979.

3. *Blondie: Parallel Lives*. Dick Porter and Kris Needs. Omnibus, 2014.

4. *Robert Fripp: From Crimson King to Crafty Master*. Eric Tamm. Faber & Faber, 1990.

5. Riding on the Dynamic of Disaster. Interview with Robert Fripp. Allan Jones. *Melody Maker*, 28 April 1979.

6. *Bill Bruford–The Autobiography: Yes, King Crimson, Earthworks & More*. Bill Bruford. Jawbone Press, 2009.

7. Let It Rock. Interview with Ian Wallace. Dmitry M. Epstein. Dmme.net, April 2003.

8. CD sleeve notes and notes on vinyl, *Exposure*. Robert Fripp. 1979 (vinyl).

9. How the League of Gentlemen inspired the rebirth of Robert Fripp's King Crimson. Sid Smith. *Prog Magazine*, December 2016.

10. Speech samples, *Exposure*. Robert Fripp. 1979.

11. CD sleeve notes and notes on vinyl notes, *God Save the Queen / Under Heavy Manners*. Robert Fripp. 1980.

12. The New Realism: A Musical Manifesto for the 80s. Robert Fripp. *Musician, Player & Listener Magazine*, 1980.

13. Vinyl Solution. Robert Fripp. *Musician, Player & Listener Magazine*, 1980.

14. CD sleeve notes, *Thrang Thrang Gozinbulx*. The League of Gentlemen. 1996.

**Chapter 7**

1. How The League of Gentlemen inspired the rebirth of Robert Fripp's King Crimson. Sid Smith. *Prog Magazine*, December 2016.

2. Notes scratched into vinyl. League of Gentlemen. 1980.

3. Old Cult Groups Never Die . . . Interview with King Crimson. David Fricke. *Trouser Press*, March 1982.

4. *Guitar Heroes of the '70s*. Michael Molenda (ed). Backbeat Books, 2011.

5. *Fa Fa Fa Fa Fa Fa: The Adventures of Talking Heads in the 20th Century*. David Bowman. Bloomsbury Publishing, 2002.

6. Crimson: Organising Conflict in Time and Space (interview). *Musician Magazine*, August 1984.

7. Robert Fripp's Diary (28 April 1981). Elephant-Talk.com.

8. Lessons in Hard Work. Interview with Adrian Belew. Ivan Eastwood. MyRareGuitars.com, 3 January 2018.

9. Author's interview with Bill Bruford, January 2020.

10. CD sleeve notes, *Discipline*. King Crimson. 2009.

11. Message scratched into vinyl, *Exposure*. Robert Fripp. 1979.

12. Vinyl sleeve notes, *Let the Power Fall*. Robert Fripp. 1981 (vinyl).

13. Vinyl sleeve notes, *Discipline*. King Crimson. 1981 (vinyl).

14. Discipline internet newsletter No. 110, 8 October 1993.

15. *Bill Bruford–The Autobiography: Yes, King Crimson, Earthworks & More*. Bill Bruford. Jawbone Press, 2009.

16. Author's interview with Ronan Chris Murphy, April 2020.

17. CD sleeve notes, *The Definitive Collection*. Asia. 2006.

18. *One Train Later: A Memoir*. Andy Summers. Portrait Books, 2006.

19. Vinyl sleeve notes, *Beat*. King Crimson.1982 (vinyl).

20. Author's interview with Peter Giles, August 2019.

21. Adrian Belew stage announcement, King Crimson concert, Montreal, July 1984.

22. Fan's shouted comment, King Crimson concert, Montreal, July 1984.

**Chapter 8**

1. How We Met 55: Toyah Willcox & Robert Fripp. Interview. Caroline Boucher. *The Independent*, 11 October 1992.

2. The Real Real Me. Interview with Toyah. Nina Myskow. *Daily Mirror*, 30 October 1998.

3. Introduction to Summerfold Records. Interview with Bill Bruford. 2003.

4. *Bill Bruford–The Autobiography: Yes, King Crimson, Earthworks & More*. Bill Bruford. Jawbone Press, 2009.

5. Author's interview with Bill Bruford, January 2020.

6. Author's interview with Gordon Haskell, June 2019.

7. Interview with Toyah. Joel Krutt. WHUS Radio, Storrs, Connecticut, 1991.

8. Interview with Robert Fripp. *Mojo Magazine*, May 1994.

9. Interview with Sylvian & Fripp. Steve Holtje. *Creem Magazine*, September 1993.

10. About DGM. DGM Live website, 2005.

11. *On Some Faraway Beach: The Life & Times of Brian Eno*. David Sheppard. Orion Books, 2008.

12. Cassette sleeve notes, *Nerve Net*. Brian Eno. 1992.

13. *The Road to Harry's Bar*. Gordon Haskell. Mainstream Publishing, 2006.

14. CD sleeve notes, *A Blessing of Tears*. Robert Fripp. 1995.

15. CD sleeve notes, *The Bridge Between*. Robert Fripp String Quintet. 1994.

16. Approaching Silence. Interview with David Sylvian. Craig Peacock. DavidSylvian.net. October 1994.

17. Discipline internet newsletter No. 110, 8 October 1993.

**Chapter 9**

1. Interview with Adrian Belew. Mike Keneally. *Fender's Frontline*, 1994.

2. Interview with Adrian Belew. Mark Holan. *Scene Magazine*, June 1995.

3. CD sleeve notes, *Radiophonics*. Robert Fripp. 1996.

4. CD sleeve notes, *Epitaph* (Volumes 1 & 2). King Crimson. 1997.

5. Author's interview with Ronan Chris Murphy, April 2020.

6. Author's interview with Bill Bruford, January 2020.

7. CD sleeve notes, *A Blessing of Tears*. Robert Fripp. 1995.

8. The Real Real Me. Interview with Toyah interview. Nina Myskow. *Daily Mirror*, 30 October 1998.

9. *Bill Bruford–The Autobiography: Yes, King Crimson, Earthworks & More*. Bill Bruford. Jawbone Press, 2009.

10. The Artist Shop/Talk City chat with Ian McDonald, 3 May 1998.

11. CD sleeve notes, *Space Groove*. ProjeKct Two. 1998.

12. Interview with Trey Gunn & Tony Levin. *Bassist Magazine*, April 1998.

13. CD sleeve notes, *The Gates of Paradise*. Robert Fripp. 1998.

14. Author's email conversation with Robert Fripp, August 2017.

15. *The Road to Harry's Bar*. Gordon Haskell. Mainstream Publishing, 2006.

**Chapter 10**

1. Caught by The Tail. Interview with Adrian Belew. Vintage Rock website, 29 January 2003.

2. Interview with Adrian Belew. George Khouroshvilli. *Music Box* (Russian Music Paper), 3 March 2000.

3. Power to Believe review. Tom Johnson. *Something Else*, 4 March 2015.

4. King Crimson gig review. Adam Sweeting. *The Guardian*, 4 July 2000.

5. CD sleeve notes, *A Temple in the Clouds*. Fayman & Fripp. 2000.

6. *The Road to Harry's Bar*. Gordon Haskell. Mainstream Publishing, 2006.

7. CD sleeve notes, *At the End of Time: Churchscapes*. Robert Fripp. 2006.

8. Personality Test. BBC Radio Four, December 2006.

9. Adrian Belew: Power Trios & Crimson Heads. Interview. Justin M Smith. *All About Jazz*, 10 November 2008.

10. I've Had A Facelift. Interview with Toyah Willcox. Lester Middlehurst. *Daily Mail*, 13 June 2008.

11. Author's interview with Bill Bruford, January 2020.

**Chapter 11**

1. Interview with Robert Fripp. *Financial Times*, August 2012.

2. Email from Fripp to Belew (September 2013), posted on social media June 2017.

3. Interview with Tony Levin. *Boston Herald*, 13 September 2019.

4. Interview with Pat Mastelotto. *Music Radar*, 8 March 2017.

5. Interview with Robert Fripp. Rob Hughes. *Daily Telegraph*, 31 October 2014.

6. Broadcasting House, edition featuring Toyah Willcox. BBC Radio Four, 4 March 2017.

7. Review of King Crimson Live in Chicago. John Kelman. *All About Jazz*, 12 October 2017.

8. Uncertain Times Tour, DGM Tour publicity. October 2017.

9. *Progressive Rock Reconsidered.* Kevin Holm-Hudson (ed). Routledge, 2002.

10. Author's interview with Gordon Haskell, June 2019.

11. Comment on Adrian Belew Facebook page in reply to author's question, 18 August 2020.

**Chapter 12**

1. CD sleeve notes, *At the End of Times: Churchscapes.* Robert Fripp. 2006.

2. *Bill Bruford–The Autobiography: Yes, King Crimson, Earthworks & More.* Bill Bruford. Jawbone Press, 2009.

# Bibliography

## Books

*Bill Bruford–The Autobiography: Yes, King Crimson, Earthworks & More*. Bill Bruford. Jawbone Press, 2009.

*Blondie: Parallel Lives*. Dick Porter and Kris Needs. Omnibus, 2014.

*Clothes, Music, Boys*. Viv Albertine. Faber & Faber, 2014.

*Discourse on Method*. René Descartes. 1637.

*Fa Fa Fa Fa Fa Fa: The Adventures of Talking Heads in the 20th Century*. David Bowman. Bloomsbury Publishing, 2002.

*Genesis: A Biography*. David Bowler and Bryan Dray. Sidgwick & Jackson, 1992.

*Guitar Heroes of the 70s*. Michael Molenda (ed). Backbeat Books, 2011.

*Lucky Man: The Autobiography*. Greg Lake. Constable, 2017.

*Mountains Come Out of the Sky*. Will Romano. Backbeat, 2010.

*My Own Time: The Authorized Biography of John Wetton*. Kim Dancha. Northern Line, 1997.

*Not Dead Yet; Autobiography*. Phil Collins. Arrow Books, 2017.

*On Some Faraway Beach: The Life & Times of Brian Eno*. David Sheppard. Orion Books, 2008.

*One Train Later: A Memoir*. Andy Summers. Portrait Books, 2006.

*Pigs Might Fly: The Inside Story of Pink Floyd*. Mark Blake. Aurum Press, 2007.

*Prince Rupert: Admiral and General-at-Sea*. Frank Kitson. Constable, 1998.

*Prince Rupert: Portrait of a Soldier*. Frank Kitson. Constable, 1994.

*Progressive Rock Reconsidered*. Kevin Holm-Hudson (ed). Routledge, 2002.

*Robert Fripp: From Crimson King to Crafty Master*. Eric Tamm. Faber & Faber, 1990.

*Roxy Music: Both Ends Burning*. Jonathan Rigby. Reynolds & Hearn Ltd, 2005.

*Starman: David Bowie—The Definitive Biography*. Paul Trynka. Sphere Publishing, 2012.

*Strange Fascination—David Bowie: The Definitive Story*. David Buckley. Virgin Books, 2005.

*The Complete David Bowie*. Nicholas Pegg. Reynolds & Hearn, 2009.

*The David Bowie Story*. George Tremlett. Futura Publications Ltd, 1974.

*The Living Years*. Mike Rutherford. Constable, 2014.

*The Show That Never Ends*. David Weigel. W.W. Norton & Co., 2017.

*The Thrill of It All: The Story of Bryan Ferry & Roxy Music*. David Buckley. Andre Deutsch, 2004.

*The Timetables of History*. Bernard Grun. Simon & Schuster, 1979.

*Tony Visconti: The Autobiography: Bowie, Bolan & the Brooklyn Boy*. Tony Visconti. Harper Books, 2007.

*Turn It on Again: Peter Gabriel, Phil Collins & Genesis*. Dave Thompson. Backbeat Books, 2004.

*When Giants Walked the Earth: A Biography of Led Zeppelin*. Mick Wall. Orion Books, 2009.

### Newspaper/Magazine Articles


Approaching Silence. Interview with David Sylvian. Craig Peacock, October 1994.

Article by Alan Neister. *Rolling Stone Magazine*, 30 August 1973.

Article by Chris Salewicz. *Let It Rock*, 8 September 1973.

Article by Ian MacDonald. *New Musical Express*, 8 September 1973.

Article by Ian MacDonald. *New Musical Express*, 1 August 1973.

Article by Lester Bangs. *Rolling Stone Magazine*, 2 March 1972.

Article by Richard Williams. *Melody Maker*, 31 March 1973.

Article by Steve Peacock. *Sounds*, 30 December 1972.

Article in *Belfast Telegraph*, autumn 1974 (featured on *Red* 40th anniversary edition cover).

Bowie: The Tracks of my Years Part 4. Stuart Hoggard. *Sounds*, 25 October 1980.

Crimson: Organising Conflict in Time and Space (interview). *Musician Magazine*, August 1984.

David Enthoven obituary. *The Guardian*, 12 August 2016.

Games of Thrones. Sid Smith. *Prog Magazine*, December 2012.

How The League of Gentlemen inspired the rebirth of Robert Fripp's King Crimson. Sid Smith. *Prog Magazine*, December 2016.

How We Met 55: Toyah Willcox & Robert Fripp. Interview. Caroline Boucher. *The Independent*, 11 October 1992.

I've Had A Facelift. Interview with Toyah Willcox. Lester Middlehurst. *Daily Mail*, 13 June 2008.

King Crimson gig review by Adam Sweeting. *The Guardian*, 4 July 2000.

King Crimson—An Observation. Robert Fripp. *Prog Magazine*, December 2012.

Newsletter One—Discipline Global Mobile, January 1997.

NME Consumer Guide to David Bowie Part 2. Charles Shaar Murray & Roy Carr. *New Musical Express*, 9 September 1978.

Old Cult Groups Never Die . . . Interview with King Crimson. David Fricke. *Trouser Press*, March 1982.

Robert Fripp. Stewart Lee. *Sunday Times*, 30 November 1997.

Sampling A Vintage. David Etheridge. 1986.

*Sounds*, 27 November 1971.

Sylvian's Fripperies. Steve Malins. *Vox Magazine*, July 1993.

The Anti-Dinosaur. Translation of interview with Robert Fripp. Jean-Gilles Blum. *Best Magazine*, January 1979.

*The Christchurch Herald Newspaper*, 1 December 1968.

The New Realism: A Musical Manifesto for the 80s. Robert Fripp. *Musician, Player & Listener Magazine*, 1980(?).

The Real Real Me. Interview with Toyah. Nina Myskow. *Daily Mirror*, 30 October 1998.

The Talking Drum: A Jamie Muir interview. *Ptolemaic Terrascope*, 1991/92.

Unidentified music press article (16 October 1971) in CD booklet, *Islands*. King Crimson. 2009.

Village Voice—gig report. John Piccarella. February 1978.

Vinyl Solution. Robert Fripp. *Musician, Player & Listener Magazine*, 1980.

### Web Articles / Interviews / Social media comments

About DGM, DGM Live website. 2005.

Adrian Belew interview: Lessons in Hard Work. Ivan Eastwood. MyRareGuitars.com, 3 January 2018.

Adrian Belew: Power Trios & Crimson Heads. Interview. Justin M, Smith. *All About Jazz*, 10 November 2008.

Caught by the Tail. Interview with Adrian Belew. Vintage Rock website, 29 January 2003.

Discipline internet newsletter No. 110, 8 October 1993.

Email from Fripp to Belew (September 2013), posted on social media, June 2017.

Ian McDonald comment on Ian McDonald Facebook Fan Page, 2017.

Ian McDonald Talks About His Foreigner Days. YouTube, 2006 (original source unknown). https://www.youtube.com/watch?app=desktop&v=UrazLRZ27n8.

Interview with Adrian Belew. George Khouroshvilli. *Music Box* (Russian Music Paper), 3 March 2000.

Interview with Adrian Belew. Mike Keneally. *Fender's Frontline*, 1994.

Interview with Adrian Belew. *Scene Magazine*, June 1995.

Interview with Bill Bruford. Scott K. Fish. *Modern Drummer*, July 1983.

Interview with Ian McDonald. *Big Bang Magazine*, 25 August 1999.

Interview with Greg Lake. Bob Harris Show. BBC Radio 2, 21 March 2018.

Interview with Mel Collins. Chris Groom. Elephant-Talk.com, 1997.

Interview with Michael Giles. Aymeric Leroy. Elephant-Talk.com, 1997.

Interview with Michael Giles. Elephant-Talk.com, April/May 1997.

Interview with Pat Mastelotto. *Music Radar*, 8 March 2017.

Interview with Richard Palmer-James in Calamity. Elephant-Talk.com, March 2000.

Interview with Robert Fripp. *Financial Times*, August 2012.

Interview with Robert Fripp. *Mojo Magazine*, May 1994.

Interview with Robert Fripp. Rob Hughes. *Daily Telegraph*, 31 October 2014.

Interview with Robert Fripp. *Rolling Stone Magazine*, 19 December 1974.

Interview with Sylvian & Fripp. Steve Holtje. *Creem Magazine*, September 1993.

Interview with Tony Levin. *Boston Herald*, 13 September 2019.

Interview with Toyah. Joel Krutt. WHUS Radio, Storrs, Connecticut, 1991.

Interview with Trey Gunn & Tony Levin. *Bassist Magazine*, April 1998.

Introduction to Summerfold Records. Interview with Bill Bruford. 2003.

King Crimson—Sheer Visceral Power. Anil Prasad. Inner Views website, April 2019.

Let It Rock. Interview with Ian Wallace. Dmitry M. Epstein. Dmme.net, April 2003.

Peter Sinfield interview with David Buckley, 17 June 2003.

Peter Sinfield quote. Ladiesofthelake.com (original source unknown).

Power to Believe review. Tom Johnson. *Something Else*, 4 March 2015.

Review of King Crimson Live in Chicago. John Kelman. *All About Jazz*, 12 October 2017.

Robert Fripp comment on Patricia Fripp's Facebook page, 4 December 2017.

Robert Fripp's Diary (23 & 24 April 1981). DGMlive.com.

Robert Fripp's Diary (28 April 1981). Elephant-Talk.com.

Robert Fripp's Diary (8 September 1999). DGMlive.com.

Stuff Happens & You Learn from It. Interview with John Wetton. Nick DeRiso. *Something Else*, 17 May 2012.

The Artist Shop/Talk City web chat with Ian McDonald, 3 May 1998.

The Outer Limits: Al Stewart. Loudersound.com, 2 July 2014.

Uncertain Times Tour, DGM Tour publicity. October 2017.

Without Friction You Don't Get Heat: Interview with Fripp, Sinfield et al. Uncut.co.uk, July 2012.

**Album Sleeve Notes (CD releases unless stated otherwise) / Vinyl messages**

40th anniversary edition notes by Sid Smith, *In the Court of the Crimson King*. King Crimson. 2009.

*A Blessing of Tears*. Robert Fripp. 1995.

*A Temple in the Clouds*. Fayman & Fripp. 2000.

*Absent Lovers*. King Crimson, 1998.

*At the End of Time: Churchscapes*. Robert Fripp. 2006.

*Beat*. King Crimson. 1982.

*Breathless*. Camel. 1992 (re-issue).

*Discipline*. King Crimson. 1981 (vinyl).

*Discipline*. King Crimson. 2009.

*Epitaph* (Volumes 1 & 2). King Crimson, 1997.

*Exposure*. Robert Fripp. 2006 (remaster).

*Foreigner: The Definitive Collection*. Foreigner. 2006.

*Ladies of the Road*. King Crimson, 2002.

*Let the Power Fall*. Robert Fripp. 1981 (vinyl).

*Live at Hyde Park 1969*. King Crimson, 2002.

*McDonald & Giles*. McDonald & Giles. 2002 (re-release).

*Nerve Net*. Brian Eno. 1992 (cassette).

Notes by Bob Belden, *Inner Mounting Flame*. Mahavishnu Orchestra. 1998.

Notes by Jeremy Holiday and Dave Gallant, *Asia: The Definitive Collection*. Asia. 2006.

Notes by Jeremy Holiday, *Sacred Songs*. Daryl Hall. 1999 (re-release).

Notes by Malcolm McDonald, *Pictures at an Exhibition (Mussorgsky)*. Odense Symphony Orchestra. 2009.

Notes scratched into vinyl, *Exposure*. Robert Fripp. 1979 (vinyl).

Notes scratched into vinyl, *God Save the Queen / Under Heavy Manners*. Robert Fripp. 1980.

Notes scratched into vinyl, *League of Gentlemen*. League of Gentlemen. 1980.

*Radiophonics*. Robert Fripp. 1996.

*Sometimes God Smiles: The Young Persons Guide to Discipline, Volume 2*. Various artists including King Crimson, Adrian Belew, Mr McFall's Chamber, Bill Nelson. 1998.

*Space Groove*. ProjeKct Two. 1998.

*Starless & Bible Black*. King Crimson, 1974 (vinyl).

*Stillusion*. Peter Sinfield, 1993.

*The Bridge Between*. Robert Fripp String Quintet. 1994.

*The Brondesbury Tapes*. Giles, Giles & Fripp, 2001.

*The Cheerful Insanity of Giles, Giles & Fripp*. Giles, Giles & Fripp, 1968 (vinyl).

*The Deception of the Thrush: A Beginner's Guide to The ProjeKcts*. King Crimson. 1999.

*The Gates of Paradise*. Robert Fripp. 1998.

*The Lady or the Tiger*. Toyah & Fripp. 1986 (cassette).

*The Night Watch*. King Crimson, 1997.

*The Roches*. The Roches. 1979.

*Thrang Thrang Gozinbulx*. The League of Gentlemen. 1996.

**Websites**

Al.kirtley.co.uk

Bournemouth Echo (bournemouthecho.co.uk/news)

Charisma Record Co. (charismalabel.com)

David-cross.com

Discipline Global Mobile (dgmlive.com)

Elephant Talk (Elephant-Talk.com)

GiniWade.com

Gordon Haskell (gordonhaskell.com)

Greg Lake (greglake.com)

Ian McDonald Fanpage—Facebook (https://en-gb.facebook.com/groups/759151907494516/)

John Harvey: Intersections of sound, image, word and light—Staking the Lizard (http://intersections.johnharvey.org.uk/2013/06/12/staking-the-lizard-4/)

Judy Dyble (judydyble.com)

P. J. Crook (pjcrook.com)

Patricia Fripp (patriciafripp.com)

Robert Fripp (robertfripp.com)

ronanchrismurphy.com

Song Soup on Sea (Songsouponsea.com)

steveball.com

Stick Enterprises Inc. (stick.com)

Toyah.net (toyah.net)

Toyahwillcox.com

UKrockfestivals.com

Wikipedia—The Fourth Way (https://en.wikipedia.org/wiki/Fourth_Way)

**Radio / TV Programmes / other media**

*Behind the Music Remastered: Bad Company*. VH1, 2013.

Broadcasting House, edition featuring Toyah Willcox. BBC Radio Four, 4 March 2017.

Ghost Stories—edition including Toyah. BBC Radio 4 extra, 26 October 2019.

*Heroes 40th Anniversary*. Zinc Media Productions for BBC Radio 2, 2017.

Neil Armstrong. BBC TV broadcast of Apollo 11 moon landing, July 1969.

Personality Test. BBC Radio Four, December 2006.

RCA marketing slogan for Heroes. David Bowie. 1977.

Toyah interview on John Shuttleworth's Lounge Music. BBC Radio Four, 27 July 2014.

# Index